GW01045138

# THE ENGLISH IN BRAZIL

Aspects of British influence on the life,
landscape and culture of Brazil

GILBERTO FREYRE

Foreword by
Maria Lúcia G. Pallares-Burke

Afterword by
Evaldo Cabral de Mello

Translated from the 3rd Brazilian edition by
Christopher J. Tribe

Vignettes by Rosa Maria
With 16 plates

BOULEVARD

*The English in Brazil*



Rua Dois Irmãos, 320 Apipucos, Recife-Pernambuco-Brasil
Cep. 52071-440 www.fgf.org.br mail: fgf@fgf.org.br
Boulevard Books
71 Lytton Road
Oxford OX4 3NY, UK
Tel 01865 712931
info@babelguides.co.uk
babelguides.co.uk

The publisher acknowledges the financial support of the Embassy of Brazil in London

ISBN 978-1-899460-61-8
Boulevard Books are distributed in the UK & Europe by Gazelle Book Services Limited White Cross Mills High Town Lancaster. LA1 4XS.
Tel: +44(0)152468765 Fax: +44(0)152463232
email: sales@gazellebooks.co.uk
and available from Gardners

Cover Design João Guarantani
Cover Image "Harbour of Rio de Janeiro, with the Benedictine Monastery, part of the City and the Ship Duff" in James Wilson, *A Missionary Voyage to the Southern Pacific* London: T. Chapman, 1799. Courtesy of the British Library board.

Typeset by Studio Europa
Printed and bound by InType, Wimbledon, London

# CONTENTS



## THE ENGLISH IN BRAZIL

# FOREWORD

*Maria Lúcia G. Pallares-Burke*

British influence on Brazil during the nineteenth century was so prevalent that it gave rise to the complaint that the British presence was 'Londonizing our land'. For centuries the country had been isolated by the Portuguese crown in an effort to retain sole control of the colony's riches. Everything changed when the Portuguese court, following Napoleon's invasion of Portugal in November 1807, sailed to Brazil escorted by a British fleet. In January 1808, as soon as he arrived in Bahia on his way to Rio de Janeiro, the King, Dom João, opened the Brazilian ports to the 'friendly nations', and Britain soon became the chief beneficiary of this act, with Brazil as its greatest Latin American market.

In *The English in Brazil*, Gilberto Freyre studies what he calls the 'gentle, velvet revolution' produced by the multitude of British manufactures, ideas and habits which invaded the country, from trams, gas lamps, railways, sewers and glass windows, to beer, hats, bread, butter, afternoon tea, the use of knives and forks, the habit of shaving daily, and much more.

At first sight, *The English in Brazil* may seem to be little more than a varied, colourful and often confused description or mosaic of the traces that the British left behind. Yet this substantial, pioneering piece of research – valuable in itself, as it has been crafted by a master – is more important than might be supposed from its fragmentary nature and its modest subtitle: *Aspects of British influence on the life, landscape and culture of Brazil.*

Behind this immense inventory, *The English in Brazil* contains what might be termed a 'manifesto for an anthropological history' or, rather, a 'quasi-manifesto', since the lightness and informality characteristic of Freyre's discourse are clearly present here, far removed from the solemnity and academic rigour usually associated with manifestos. Starting from the premise that eminent personages and grandiose events only tell one side of history, Gilberto Freyre shows that to reveal the influences of one culture on another demands a study of more shadowy characters and 'significant details'. It is the mechanics, firemen, engineers, sailors, traders and other 'Cinderellas of history' who disclose the less grandiose but more humanly significant aspects of cultural influences.

Working along lines advocated decades later by historians such as Carlo Ginzburg and Natalie Davis, Freyre makes the point in this fine book that studying the apparently minor, irrelevant facts of daily life in the home, in workshops, on the railways and in newspaper advertisements can be an excellent way to access the more general aspects of a culture's past.

Like his earlier books, *The English in Brazil* is written in Freyre's extremely personal, unorthodox style – vivid, sensuous yet colloquial – which established the author as one of the masters of twentieth-century Portuguese prose.

## Author's note to the second Brazilian edition (extracts)

The books *Um engenheiro francês no Brasil* and *Ingleses no Brasil*, like the more recent *Nós e a Europa germânica* and *O brasileiro entre os outros hispanos*, and the older *O escravo nos anúncios de jornais brasileiros do século XIX*,[1] may represent new approaches, in any language, to the analysis and interpretation of foreign presences in the life and culture of a people – the Brazilian people in this case. Rather than looking at the grandiose, official or academic side of these presences, they offer a different outlook: that of less obvious, but in many ways more meaningful, influences than those hitherto formalized or glorified. Including humble ones. Modest ones. Influences ignored by more conventional historians and sociologists.

In this respect, I believe I have almost single-handedly brought about a change in outlook in the more systematic kinds of historical-social studies on the formation of societies such as Brazil's, a change that is by no means insignificant in its implications. I may also have contributed in some way to a quasi-revolution in the depth of such studies, whether essays or social history. That started with *The Masters and the Slaves*, with its major emphasis on an almost intimate history and its virtual disregard for a nation's official or public past.

When an analyst of less obvious pasts of a society like Brazil's, or of any other trans-European society, seeks to interpret or reinterpret such pasts and, to do so, pauses to examine the influences received not only from figures like Chateaubriand, Montesquieu, Rousseau, Adam Smith, Swift, Jefferson, Comte, Pasteur, Darwin, Goethe or Marx, but from almost unknown engineers; soon-forgotten doctors; novelists, essayists and poets scorned by their successors; consuls always secondary to ambassadors in their own times and afterwards; simple yet innovative joiners such as Berenger and Spieler in Brazil; hairdressers, tailors, mechanics, labourers, magicians, acrobats, photographers, stylists, cocottes, actresses and cooks, he discovers revolutionarily modest transmitters of values from an advanced culture to one still in formation, and people by no means insignificant in what they achieved. A revolution in historical-social outlook. As it was to devote attention as never before to black slaves, women, children, Amerindians, Jews and Arabs as active and even creative presences in the formation of a society and culture like those of Brazil. Even when dominated, oppressed or restrained by slave-holders, or by the so-called stronger sex, or by the race considered superior, or by the civilization and religion likewise held

[1]The titles translate as: *A French Engineer in Brazil*, *The English in Brazil*, *Germanic Europe and Us*, *The Brazilian among the Other Hispanics* and *The Slave in Brazilian Newspaper Advertisements of the Nineteenth Century* (Translator).

to be superior, those underdogs had a great and decisive influence on the formation of Brazil. Acknowledgment of their influence is now growing in Brazil and even becoming in some ways popular among Brazilians.

That has just been shown by the wonderful spectacle provided by the latest samba school parade in Rio de Janeiro, an event of some significance for its anthropological and sociological meaning: the expansion of everything that these huge parades of people have been expressing in the former capital of Brazil, using Carnival revelry as an excuse for their manifestations of eugenic and aesthetic interest, on one hand, and democratically social interest, on the other. They are now rapidly growing in prominence in Brazil as manifestations, not so much of a black African minority in the Brazilian population that has kept true to its Afro-Brazilian heritage, but of a whole, vast population that is increasingly brown – in various shades of brownness – and upfront about admitting to the African and Amerindian roots of its cultural Brazilianness, without adhering to any exclusive ethnic or racial dogma. Brazilianness as a mixed culture and a mixing of bloods, which an analyst of such processes would term metaracial, given the disdain found in both processes for strictly ethnic attachments.

Could the English – or the British – who for centuries have been so present in the development of Brazil, especially in technology, have been completely absent from those processes? The most penetrating study of their most intimate relations with Brazil ever since it was a kingdom with Portugal, when it already had a population to a great extent of mixed Amerindian and European or African blood, seems to suggest they were not. It seems to suggest a by no means rare blending of imperially British blood with native Brazilian blood. Witness the integration, in an already brown Brazil of Silvas and Alencares, of an Abbot, for instance, or a Cochrane or a Cox.

Moreover, the English – in the broadly Brazilian sense of the term – should also be remembered here as the paradoxical agents in Brazil of a process of ecological tropicalization, in that they were the prime movers for the adoption of white denim for men's clothing; the introducers of the Indian bungalow in Brazilian domestic architecture; the introducers of curry, also from India; and, to a great extent, pyjamas – which the English had also adopted from the Indian possessions they had held for some time – for the Brazilian middle classes. It was because it was worn by Englishmen in Manaus, Belém, Recife, Salvador and Rio de Janeiro that white denim, almost always in the form of dolmans[2] – and therefore without the anti-tropical tie, its abolition in the tropics perhaps being an

[2] Loose, lightweight tunic and trousers suitable for tropical climates (Translator).

Anglo-Orientalism – began to shine out in those cities from the end of the nineteenth century among solemnly dark frock coats, even more solemnly black dress coats and likewise gloomily dark overcoats, like the black alpaca ones and the grey frock coats pioneered by the semi-Anglicized Rui Barbosa, representing timid protests against heavy, black, woollen or worsted attire.

Nor is it inappropriate to mention those Englishmen who introduced into Brazil the principal sporting and recreational replacements for our colonial jousting tournaments: horse-racing, tennis, cycling and football itself, which here became fully naturalized as a game not for fair-haired European expatriates in the tropics but for local people: at first Anglicized Brazilians who were native-born but had something British about their bearing and appearance, such as the aristocratic Marcos Carneiro de Mendonça; later, people increasingly of varying shades of brown; with de-Anglicization culminating in the admirable Pelé, after shining with Leônidas.

What better example could there be of the extent to which two cultures as apparently irreconcilable as the British and the Brazilian can be reconciled and merge into new forms of expression than football as currently expressed by the so-called 'football dancers', the Brazilians? From being an Apollonian game, as it was at first here when Brazilians imitated English masters, it has become Dionysiac. It has become a veritable Afro-Brazilian dance, with footwork never imagined by its inventors. Has it stopped being British? Not in the slightest. Association football cannot be separated from its British origins to be considered a Brazilian or Afro-Brazilian invention. What it is, in its current, triumphant Brazilian expression, is an Anglo-Afro-Brazilian game.

What is the current status of Anglo-Brazilian relations? Cordial, without a doubt. But they could be closer than that.

The visit by Queen Elizabeth II to Brazil[3] seems to have demonstrated that Brazilian people in general, and not just some members of the élite in particular, feel a certain affection for anything English, that is to say British. Even for what is Britannically monarchic, as well as being democratic and even 'Labour'. Brazilians, like the English, also know how to appreciate contradictions. Balance and, even more than that, the interpenetration of opposites through what is known formally in English as 'compromise' and colloquially in the Portuguese of Brazil as *jeito*. In other words, a gentle ability to find peacefully intermediate solutions to difficult situations of maladjustment, disharmony and even conflict between extremes.

[3] In November 1968 (Translator).

They are two arts that resemble each other: neither Brazilians nor the English are much given to radicalism, extremism or absolutes. They have each in their own way become masters of the wisdom of finding third or alternative solutions to situations presented as polarized absolutes.

The leaders of the British empire did not perhaps apply their art of compromise as plastically and effectively in their dealings as Europeans with non-white non-Europeans, in the various parts of the world that were at some time under their dominion, as Brazilians have applied their almost instinctive transracism, their almost intuitive beyond-racism, their way of crossing boundaries of race, colour and class, to their now long-standing – since the sixteenth century – dealings with Amerindians, Africans, Jews and descendants of Amerindians, Africans, Asians and Jews. People who are increasingly just as Brazilian, despite not only ethnic but also religious differences, as those descending from Catholic Iberians. Just as integrated throughout Brazil within the same Brazilian transethnic and trans-Catholic complex.

There was a time when Brazil began to grow through a balance of antagonisms. Without resorting to any significant violence to reject the antagonisms in its ethnic and cultural formation, but instead balancing them. Harmonizing them by means of a number of compromises. A number of arts. A number of quasi-policies. Hence it was able to advance towards what many people saw as the surprising unity it would eventually achieve. Which it has now partly achieved in a manner that is perhaps unique.

It has achieved unity in part by gradually replacing that balance of antagonisms with what could perhaps, in a new and perhaps daring form of anthropo-sociological characterization, be called interpenetration of contraries. Or of opposites. Or of differences. An interpenetration that starts creating new forms of national expression and perhaps new ways of defining life and the human condition. Creating art, lore and relations from which any trace of exclusivity in race, class, region or faith has increasingly been disappearing.

Is it just rhetoric to consider that there is an undeniable trend in today's Brazil – through processes that sometimes seem to go beyond everything of value that the British people's art of compromise achieved for itself and its civilization, in particular, and for human well-being, in general – to become, in its own way and in circumstances very different from those that characterized British actions, a continuer of that people, which was for some time trans-European through its political and economic power? Some think not.

Clearly, there is no sign at all in Brazil's future that it may become politically or economically trans-Brazilian, even within very restricted limits, through deliberate or systematic effort. But it would be overmodest on our part to ignore the fact that Brazil is beginning in today's world, which is so split by hatred even between brother faiths, as in Ireland – and also split between apparent brothers in Belgium, Russia, Canada, the United States, Asia and Africa – to project an image of a vast nation united by the same language. By the same language and by the adherence to a number of cultural values common to its large population – over a hundred million: the most miscegenated on a large scale of all peoples anywhere in the world.

In this respect, Brazilians may well become the new British by triumphing in the art of combining opposites and getting them to interpenetrate. And, just as the British people have contributed in this area on such a vast political, economic and also cultural scale, such interpenetration may enable Brazilians, through the voice of their opulent literature which is becoming well known, and also through the sciences and innovating forms of knowledge, to contribute to opening up new outlooks on the human condition.

G. F.

Santo Antônio de Apipucos, 1976

# INTRODUCTION

For years now I have been thinking of writing something on the influence of the English in Brazil – English in the sense of British, of course – that would go beyond the simple, improvised pieces that have so far appeared on the subject. And for years I have been collecting material for such a study or essay.

I have now felt the urge to write it. The urge and, I must be frank and confess the rest, also the fear that some opportunist might snatch from my hand a subject I have been wooing for years: the study of the actions, adventures and even abuses of English people scattered around nineteenth-century Brazil as consuls, businessmen, technicians, mechanics or missionaries, or who had come here earlier as pirates or simply as travellers or adventurers.

On leafing through the documentation I had already gathered and the notes on interpretation that I had jotted down, I found that they were more copious than I had imagined. In fact, I was quite amazed at how much there was. I have therefore decided to publish this first volume on the subject straight away, with two others to follow: *Outros ingleses no Brasil* and *Ainda ingleses no Brasil.*[4]

In *Ingleses*[5] and particularly in a preparatory note to the study of British influence in Brazil through newspaper advertisements, published in issue 2 of the *Revista da Sociedade Brasileira de Cultura Inglesa*[6] of Rio de Janeiro, I had already touched on the subject. But now I am really venturing into it, examining it from the viewpoint that has been mine in other works or attempts to reconstruct and interpret the history and ethos

[4]These additional volumes were never in fact published (Translator).

[5] A collection of Freyre's newspaper articles on the British, published in 1942 (Translator).

[6] The Sociedade Brasileira de Cultura Inglesa ('Brazilian Society of English Culture') was founded in Rio de Janeiro in 1934 to teach English language and culture. Freyre's article 'Traços de influência sobre a vida brasileira na metade do século XIX, revelados pelo anúncio do jornal' appeared in the second issue of its magazine, in 1939 (Translator).

of the Brazilian. These are works carried out on new scaffolds, in addition to those generally used in historical or sociological reconstruction work, perhaps with new perspectives, and without the old hoardings customarily or traditionally erected in Brazil, behind which established historians from Varnhagen[7] to Pereira da Costa[8] have sought to conceal their best sources of information from novices.

My viewpoint in interpreting the history of Brazilians remains that of one who sees in them and their formation not merely a biological process – miscegenation – but, almost independent of that, the action, expansion and development of a social process: the interpenetration of cultures. This process has acted less in the sense of disintegrating or degrading any of the cultures present in our formation than in that of integrating them all into a new, hybrid society and culture: one that is multiple and rich, albeit motley, in its heritage, in its methods of development and in the values and styles of its moral, intellectual, aesthetic and material life.

The technique used in the essays that follow on the English in Brazil is that of someone who supplements his efforts at historical and sociological – or historico-sociological – reconstruction with an attempt at psychological interpretation, and who attempts both kinds of reconstruction and their interpretation while working in full view of the most curious readers and the most demanding critics, as regards sources and methods, and even welcoming their vigilant collaboration. There are, it bears repeating, no hoardings erected between the author and his most demanding or most critical readers. They too, readers and critics, can climb up onto the scaffolding retained by the author and check with their own eyes and feel with their own hands the evidence presented.

That is precisely why the author has here retained the ugly scaffolding that makes his earlier essays look unfinished or forever under construction or repair. This has irritated another group of readers or critics: those who regard an author's many citations of sources and the numerous bibliographical references on which he takes such pains, and which he uses as scaffolds to erect a building of more than one storey, as a mere show of erudition or display of knowledge.

I have been accused by more than one such critic or reader of citing my sources to excess. Perhaps they are right. Indeed, what is the point in citing them so much? But I am too old now to shake off the habit and the taste for doing so. I still think it is better to cite too much rather than too

[7] Francisco Adolfo de Varnhagen (1816-78) was a diplomat and historian whose works include the *História Geral do Brasil* (Translator).

[8] Francisco Augusto Pereira da Costa (1851-1923) was a prolific writer who focused mainly on the history of his native Pernambuco (Translator).

little – even when the sources are obscure and the references are to little-known authors: those little-known authors who really deserve to have a monument erected to them by the majority of celebrated writers, one of whom was that plagiarist of genius William Shakespeare. He never cited his sources, either.

The technique followed in the pages below is also that of the portrait in which the artist combines, or attempts to combine, the personal element with the social, the individual with the universal, the historical with that which transcends time, and even the scientific with the poetic. Baudelaire was one of those who noticed this potential of the portrait proper: its potential to be both history and poetry at the same time. The same may be said of the psycho-sociological portrait that is sketched of an individual or a family, a period or a people: this other kind of portrait can also become poetry and history, science and art, and even time and eternity, like the portrait of Christ sketched by the evangelists.

Raphael's portraits are said to be pure lyrical poetry, whereas those by Titian and El Greco contain in their poetry – intensely dramatic poetry in El Greco's case – elements of history. That is because Titian and El Greco sought to immerse their subjects in the atmosphere of the time.

It was not, according to one of the most insightful modern critics of painting, Professor Lionello Venturi, a solely visual immersion: it was also a moral immersion, based perhaps – adding to Professor Venturi's view – on consideration of the fact so strongly highlighted in literature by Proust and in historical or psychological sociology by the case-study method that man is never in a moral – or social – vacuum: man is always acting in relation to someone or something. In relation to a social and cultural complex. An overall situation made up of a thousand and one particular situations. Always, at every moment in his life. Hence, as Professor Venturi observes, Titian's portraits are neither 'ideal' nor 'abstract' but capture the living and the real, just as – one might add – El Greco's do: the real caught at extremely particular moments, which succeed in revealing the whole, or the principal part, of the sitter's character. This is the technique of fixing on the significant detail of which psychological novelists – particularly English novelists – are masters.

To return to Raphael, the kind of painter of the human character or personality who is most opposite to the Proustian and, in some way, to the psychological kind of painter that is El Greco, even more than Titian – Raphael portrayed man almost in a vacuum. He was so concerned with the poetic or aesthetic universality of his art that he was afraid of or unsure about descending from the generality of class or civilization represented by his sitter to personal or individual particularities. Titian and El Greco, in contrast, attained such generalities, and universality itself, by starting with the moment, the particular, the personal, the regional and the individual in the sitter. Hence the coincidence of the real with the artistic, the artistic with the scientific, and the historical with the poetic is more natural in Titian or El Greco than in Raphael. Such coincidences are characteristic of great or good portraits, whether in the fine arts or in the biographical or psychological literature, and even in that kind of sociological psychology, or psychological sociology, that uses portraits of people, isolated or in groups, as starting points for its generalizations about class or civilization. For its extending of the particular into the general and of the regional into the universal.

In this respect, it should be remembered that the trend among today's most progressive sociologists is what one of the Brazilians most in touch with the philosophy of the social sciences, Professor Mário Lins,[9] calls 'suppression of the divisions and dualistic postulates of the old systematics'. This suppression clears the way for a new solution to the ancient problem of the 'unique' and the 'general', which, within Aristotelian logic, excluded individual cases from the concept of laws, scientific laws. As Professor Mário Lins says, 'there were, at that time, two orders of facts in nature, one subject to laws and the other subject to 'chance', according to whether or not they displayed the *universal* characteristics of the class to which they belonged'. The new conceptual logic, however, tries to overcome that 'division in the unity of nature...' The universal and the particular are considered to be 'inseparable aspects of one and the same reality...', the future of sociology as a science therefore depending 'on how it develops the technique for overcoming' that division. This approach is similar to the one upheld above by the writer of this essay, on the pages where he sought to set out his sociological creed or orientation.

I believe one such technique for overcoming the division lies in the attempt to produce a sociological, or psycho-sociological, study of figures representative of a particular social space and time, figures who at the same time contain universal characteristics, so that the study of their actions and attitudes comes to resemble those studies that have been produced by great portrait painters such as Titian and, in literature, by great novelists or, rather, memorialists such as Proust. Here it may be suggested that art – when mainly objective – and science are also inseparable aspects of the same technique of man seeking to understand human nature. The search for this understanding has led scientists such as Professor Carr and artists like Proust to look for the primary *point d'appui* for generalizations (which

[9] Mário Lins produced several works on sociology and philosophy, principally in the 1940s and 50s, in which he sought to apply the rigorous approach of the physical sciences (Translator).

for the former are termed *scientific* and the for latter become *classical* after sometimes having been considered impressionist or *romantic*) in studies of facts considered, not in isolation, but in the entirety of their situations. Quantitatively and qualitatively at the same time. This is what the aforementioned Professor Mário Lins, in his admirable recent essay analysing the most modern theory on the restructuring of sociological systematics – *A transformação da lógica conceitual da sociologia* (Rio de Janeiro, 1947) – calls the 'field of action' of these facts. In this he agrees with the various forms of modern sociological and psycho-sociological situationism – including the Brazilian version described in another recent study – in which events are 'determined' – I would say conditioned – by the 'totality of their current situation'. In the same vein, Professor Lins highlights the observation made previously by Professor J. F. Brown, that 'concrete cases gain a fundamental new meaning in science'. Just as, it may be added, meaning is enriched in portraits like Titian's, in painting, or in memoirs or autobiographies like Proust's, in literature. Some critics, such as Stuart Hampshire, already accept the possibility that the novel may soon be superseded by the autobiography, not because the novel has worn itself out as a literary form, but because modern man has become too self-conscious to want to describe or interpret himself in any terms other than primarily objective ones. One might add to the English critic's remarks, in line with what appears to be his approach, that such description or interpretation will always be achieved by integrating the particular or the individual into the total situation, the environment and the atmosphere, without such integration implying the sacrifice of the personal to the social. It must simply be acknowledged that neither do personalities develop in a vacuum nor do events occur disconnected from the entirety of the situations to which they belong. The *social* and the *personal* interpenetrate, just as what are termed the *individual* and the *universal* interpenetrate, and as do the *historical* and the *sociological.*

In a recently published book, *The Use of Personal Documents in History, Anthropology and Sociology* (New York, 1945), a joint work by Louis Gottschalk, Clyde Kluckhohn and Robert Angell, these researchers point out that the methodical use of such personal documents in recent years seems, in social studies of a scientific nature, to be taking us away from the old antithesis of *idiographic* science versus *nomothetic* science. As the first author of that book highlights, history is becoming a dual study of man: as a participant in collective life and as an individual creator (p. 72). Kluckhohn adds that the analysis of personalities as participants in cultures reveals idiosyncratic and functional variations within a given society. These variations are generally obscured by the assumption that all individuals in a society predominantly conform to the styles of culture that, through the abstract construction of the anthropologist or sociologist studying it, are established as being absolute.

I believe that the facts gathered in the following pages from a vast amount of archive and library material – facts amassed from both official (especially consular) and personal documents, some public, some private (especially tradesmen's advertisements) – confirm Gottschalk's and Kluckhohn's suggestions, within the historical and psychological (and not merely sociological or anthropological) approach followed in the study and interpretation of these facts or of the material selected as being demonstrative or typical. The documents reveal English people whose personalities were conditioned by a shared social situation: that of being subjects of His or Her Britannic Majesty, that is, of a power that was clearly and sometimes arrogantly imperial in its dealings with Brazil during the nineteenth century. Principally in the early decades of the century. But they were also conditioned by particular social situations within the shared one, as engineers, technicians, consuls, businessmen, adventurers and missionaries. And furthermore, by idiosyncratic and functional variations within each person's particular situation, so that clear differences can be seen between Consul Parkinson's behaviour and Consul Cowper's, for example, which cannot always be accounted for by the external changes in social space and time, that is, by the depression that Great Britain's imperial power began to experience in Brazil after King João VI's return to Portugal.[10] Principally in Bahia and Pernambuco, which in those days seem to have been less pliant to the caprices of British imperialism than Rio de Janeiro.

Political imperialism, naval imperialism, commercial imperialism – it was almost total imperialism at first, in the days of Sir Sidney Smith and his all-powerful fleet.[11] In the days of Lord Strangford and the consul James Gambier. After the court returned to Portugal, it was mostly economic imperialism. Although absolute at first, that economic imperialism would itself reach the middle of the nineteenth century with very different attitudes towards Brazil from those it had held in the days of King João VI

[10] Dom João VI returned to Portugal in 1821, leaving his son, Pedro, as regent of Brazil. Brazil's status had officially changed in 1815 from colony to joint kingdom with Portugal (as the United Kingdom of Portugal, Brazil and Algarves); in 1822 it became an independent empire (under Dom Pedro I), and in 1889 a republic. There were three periods of regency in the nineteenth century: until 1816, when Dom João acted as regent for his mother, Queen Maria I, who was insane; in 1821-22, when Dom Pedro was regent of Brazil after his father's return to Portugal; and from 1831 to 1840, during the minority of Dom Pedro II (Translator).

[11] Sidney Smith, the commander of the British naval force, had threatened to bombard Lisbon and destroy the Portuguese fleet to prevent it falling into French hands, if the prince-regent (the future João VI) did not embark for Brazil. British ships then escorted the royal family to Rio de Janeiro (Translator).

and Dom Rodrigo de Sousa Coutinho, the Count of Linhares.[12]

*

It should be noted that while the material influence of the British in Brazil declined their influence in the intellectual field constantly increased. This influence grew to be considerable during the glory days of British imperialism, that is, when it exerted its greatest economic pressure on Brazilian life. At that time, people in Brazil were reading translations of *Robinson Crusoe*, Addison's *Spectator*, the Earl of Chesterfield's *Letters to His Son*, the novels of Walter Scott and Ann Radcliffe, essays by Pope and Bentham, poems by Milton and Byron, and Shakespeare. What was lacking was any noteworthy translation produced in Brazil or by a Brazilian of any of these earlier British writers: that was a fortune reserved for Victorians such as Elizabeth Barrett Browning. Some of the sonnets that Mrs Browning entitled *Sonnets from the Portuguese* can now be found in Portuguese, thanks to a Brazilian translator who is also one of the greatest poets in our language.[13]

Several Victorian and post-Victorian British novelists have been fortunate in finding Brazilian translators into Portuguese: Jane Austen and the Brontë sisters, for example, and even Samuel Butler are now within reach of the Brazilian reader in translations produced by some of the greatest novelists in our language. Rachel de Queiroz, Lúcia Miguel Pereira and Dinah Silveira de Queiroz are among the translators of good English novels into Portuguese, a task performed with a sensitivity of which only true writers – incapable of betraying their peers or their masters – are capable.

No one should be deceived about the growing influence of the English novel on the Brazilian, an influence that can be glimpsed even in those novelists of ours who are most attached to the land or their province, such as José Lins do Rego. Far from being the talented ignoramus that certain critics who are more emphatic in their generalizations try to make of him, he abandoned pamphlets for novels to a great extent under the spell of reading English-language authors translated into French and Spanish: Hardy, Dickens, the Brontës, Stevenson, Joyce, Wells, Lawrence, Conrad and, strange as it may seem, Pater. These were the great books he read in

[12] Rodrigo de Sousa Coutinho, Count of Linhares (1755-1812), a minister who accompanied the Portuguese court into exile in Brazil, was instrumental in establishing the early trade agreement with the British (Translator).

[13] Manuel Bandeira (1886-1968) (Translator).

his youth as a convert from journalism to literature, when he insisted that a friend who had arrived from Europe should give him his first lessons not only in English but in English literature. The lessons also included a kind of initiation into English novels and essays of which no translations yet existed in Brazil in French or Spanish, let alone in Portuguese: Strachey, Dorothy Richardson, Chesterton, George Moore, Samuel Butler, George Gissing, Meredith, Newman, Rebecca West, Virginia Woolf and Katherine Mansfield. English influences are even more apparent in Monteiro Lobato, Lúcia Miguel Pereira, Carolina Nabuco, Rachel de Queiroz, Dinah Silveira de Queiroz and Luís Jardim than in José Lins do Rego. They are also easy to glimpse in historians like Joaquim Nabuco and Oliveira Lima, in political writers like Oliveira Vianna, and even in painters like the semi-Lawrentian Cícero Dias. In literature or political journalism, 'Sr Dantas's Englishmen'[14] became famous and, even before the furore surrounding such anglophiles, an American observer, the Reverend Fletcher, wrote as follows about Brazilian political writers, on page 602 of the ninth edition of *Brazil and the Brazilians* (1879):

> Formerly their political theories were greatly influenced by French writers, but at the present time no foreigner so influences the minds of the younger and middle-aged Brazilian statesmen as John Stuart Mill. The keynote and, indeed, the burden of Sr. Zacarias' *Poder Moderador* is John Stuart Mill on *Liberty*.[15]

That is to say, such writers had formerly been greatly influenced by the French in their political theories, but the French influence had in this respect been superseded by the English, which, at the time when Fletcher visited Brazil, was represented by John Stuart Mill. In the *belles-lettres*, the superiority of French influence over any other was to survive in Brazil almost to the present day. And in the philosophy of law there has never been a movement of British inspiration among us similar to the Germanism kindled in Recife by Tobias Barreto,[16] whose 'Teuto-Sergipans' were, in this particular, analogous to 'Sr Dantas's Englishmen' in literature or political journalism.

[14] 'Sr Dantas's Englishmen' (*os ingleses do Sr. Dantas*) were writers and politicians who, in the late nineteenth century, used English pseudonyms to endorse the liberal policies of Senator Manuel Pinto de Sousa Dantas (1831-94), particularly with a view to securing the abolition of slavery. One of the most prominent of these 'Englishmen' was the statesman Ruy Barbosa (1849-1923) (Translator).

[15] James C. Fletcher and Daniel P. Kidder, *Brazil and the Brazilians, portrayed in historical and descriptive sketches*, 9th ed., Boston, 1879, p. 602. Quoted by Freyre in English (Translator).

[16] Tobias Barreto de Meneses (1839-89) was a philosopher, poet and political writer from Sergipe. Inspired by the writings of the German evolutionary scientist Ernst Haeckel, he immersed himself in German culture, which he promoted not least to counterbalance the predominant French cultural influence in Brazil (Translator).

*

A further word about the sociological symbolization of the historico-social material brought together in the following pages. I have sought to study British imperialism in Brazil – that is, the form established in space (Brazil) and time (the sixteenth to nineteenth centuries, especially the first half of the nineteenth century) by a process whereby one culture or economy (the Brazilian) was dominated by another (the British) – in the attitudes or actions not so much of statesmen or other public figures, who have already been studied by distinguished historians, but of pirates, technicians, adventurers, businessmen, missionaries, governesses, teachers and especially consuls. I have sought to study the reaction to that process as expressed through other processes – submission, accommodation, insubordination – in the attitudes or actions less of monarchs or ministers of state than of simple captains-general, priests, provincial presidents, land- and slave-owners, political writers, journalists, businessmen, *moleques*[17] or street urchins.

Two sociocultural systems faced each other within the space and the time studied: one system embodied by the British, the other by the Brazilians, or Luso-Brazilians. Nobody should be surprised to see the *moleque* included among the representatives of the Brazilian system: he was the caricaturist *par excellence* of the intruder; it was he who insulted him in the streets, reduced him to a Judas effigy for burning on Easter Saturday, and aped him in Carnival tricks, ridiculing him for the sake of the invaded culture. It was the *moleque* who spread pejorative names for the Briton in Brazil: *bode* (goat), *missa-seca* (dry-mass) or *bíblia* (bible) for Protestants, as well as *gringo*, *baeta* (baize), *bicho* (animal, insect), *beef* and *marinheiro* (sailor). However great the number of persons cited or referenced in the following pages, this abundance of personalization of historical-social material implies neither disdain for the apparently impersonal systems to which each individual or person belonged, nor a betrayal of the sociological approach by the biographical. Instead, it means that one approach does not exclude the other. What we seek to study in the relationships between people, or interpersonal relations, is not so different from what we seek to study in the clashes between antagonistic sociocultural systems – culture shocks – since the systems are made up of people, and these people are inseparable from the systems within which they are transformed from individuals into people.

[17] Derived from a Bantu word for 'boy', *moleque* originally referred to a slave child, but it has come to mean a mischievous youngster of any origin, or even a rogue, scoundrel or trickster (Translator).

The personal and the social – it bears repeating – neither repel nor exclude each other, but complement each other within the human. The biographical approach is not necessarily the enemy of the sociological one, just as in sociology the historical is not the mortal enemy of the formal. Within modern sociological situationism – to which Brazilian efforts have been contributing for years, through studies that have not always been properly understood by official or academic sociologists in this country or even in the United States – the biography of a French engineer like Vauthier,[18] for example, far from being a betrayal of sociology, lies fully within the purest sociological legality. The same will always be true of any biography in which the so-called individual, or a particular aspect of an 'individual's' action, is studied not in a vacuum but in relation to the totality of his situation. To the entirety of his sociocultural system. Or in light of the conflict between two or more systems in which the main study 'individual' participated all his life or at a decisive moment in his life. Such is the case of the biography of Newman, viewed as a psycho-sociological study (albeit not produced according to the rationale suggested here, although Strachey's brilliant pages sometimes equal or even surpass it) of the clash between the sociocultural system represented by Anglican Catholicism and that represented by Roman Catholicism. Another Englishman, Manning, adapted to it much more easily than Newman, showing how important differences in personality or temperament can be in such contacts between apparently impersonal systems or in such assimilations of personalities by cultures.

The presence of British culture in the development of Brazil, in the space, landscape and overall civilization of Brazil, is of the kind that cannot – or should not? – be ignored by a Brazilian interested in understanding and interpreting Brazil. In the form of pirates, adventurers and traders, the English, almost as much as the French, arrived early on the tropical American shores discovered by Portuguese and Spaniards. Outstripping their long-standing French rivals, English traders and technicians eventually achieved an economic preponderance in our country that, having been manifest in the days of João VI, first as regent and then as king – when that predominance acquired a not merely imperial but a frankly imperialist complexion – reached its peak from 1835 to 1912, only then to slowly decline, overcome by the expansion of the United States and undermined by that of Germany. That economic preponderance of the British was bound to overflow into other areas or spheres of influence, as it did. Possibly significant aspects and details of that set of influences – influences from all kinds of culture, both immaterial and material – are to be found in the following pages, the first in what may become a long

[18] The subject of Freyre's book *Um engenheiro francês no Brasil*, Rio de Janeiro, 1940.

study. These details will be reconstructed and interpreted according to the general theme announced above: that of the interpenetration of cultures.

Enormous as British influence was in Brazil, the technically and literarily superior culture did not act in an absolute or always sovereign fashion upon the inferior one. The contact of Britons with Brazilian society also resulted in Brazilian influences on the culture of the imperial people. These influences require more penetrating eyes to spot them in their pure state, since it is so easy to fall into the countless pitfalls of confusing Brazilian influence with that of the Portuguese or of other peoples and cultures of the Americas and tropics on British culture. Unmistakable expressions of Brazilian influence on Britons are rare. Oliveira Lima[19] came across one when he was a minister of Brazil in Tokyo. He was dining in one of the Japanese capital's large cosmopolitan hotels when he was surprised to see an English couple at a nearby table solemnly and Britannically savouring that most Brazilian of desserts: jam and cheese. He enquired as to who those Brazilianized Britons were and discovered that they had lived in Rio de Janeiro, and their palates had become so accustomed to that Brazilian combination – jam with cheese – that they could not go without it anywhere, not even in Tokyo. Not in China or in Tibet, not in the Congo or in the Philippines. After dinner, wherever they were, they would always have to find some jam and cheese to savour, now incorporated forever into their routine or their dining ritual. Every evening, wherever they were, they would have to find a jam and cheese dessert to savour, with the same liturgical rigour with which every morning, wherever they were, they would eat their classical breakfast and, every afternoon, they would drink their almost sacred tea adopted from the Orient by now remote ancestors. For the English are like that. They loathe making new friends abroad or acquiring a habit or even a word that is exotic. But once they have developed such a friendship or taken up a habit or adopted a word, it becomes as sacred and firm as their old friendships, habits and words. English dictionaries bear witness to that, since they are full of barbarisms acquired by the British from all parts of the world, from all languages and peoples, no matter how remote.

They are everywhere, those English! [wrote Eça de Queiroz[20] at the end of the last century. It really seemed to him as though the world was becoming melancholically and monotonously English.] Because, however unknown and unheard-of the village that one is entering may

[19] The historian, critic and diplomat Manuel de Oliveira Lima (1867-1928), a fellow Pernambucan and close associate of Gilberto Freyre, was Brazilian trade attaché in Japan in 1901-03. He published his impressions of the country in 1903 (Translator).

[20] José Maria Eça de Queiroz (1845-1900) was a Portuguese novelist, one of the great exponents of realism (Translator).

be, however lost in an obscure corner of the universe the stream along which one is walking may be, one will always find an Englishman or a trace of one!... Always an Englishman! Utterly English, just as when he left England, impermeable to other civilizations, passing through different religions, habits, arts and cuisines without changing one single iota, one single crease, one single line of his British prototype [...] wanting to find everywhere else what they left behind in Regent Street, and expecting *pale ale* and *roast beef*[21] in the deserts of Petraea; wearing black frock coats on a mountain top on a Sunday out of respect for the Protestant Church, and scandalized that the local people do not do the same; receiving their *Times* or *Standard* at the ends of the earth, and basing their opinion not on what they see or hear around them, but on the article written in London; their soul always facing backwards, towards *home*; abominating everything that is not English, and thinking that other races can only be happy if they have the institutions, the habits and the manners that make them, the English, happy on their northern island!

What Eça exaggerates here does indeed exist in the English. It principally characterizes the English of the Victorian era: the great era of British imperial supremacy. But Eça's brushstrokes are those of a caricature and never those of a fair or merely Greco-like portrait. The Englishman that he caricaturizes, always eating roast beef, always reading *The Times*, always a stranger to what is happening around him, always abominating what is not English, always impermeable to other civilizations and their religions, cuisines and arts – that Englishman has aspects that Eça de Queiroz has forgotten, which are traits as characteristic of the British character as are the ones that his caricature fixes and exaggerates. Contradictory and inconsistent, that Englishman impermeable to the exotic has, in the West, been one of the best interpreters and propagators of the exotic, the tropical and the oriental. And Brazil is among the exotic countries that have been most intelligently discovered and interpreted by Britons: by Mawe, Luccock, Koster, Maria Graham, Walsh, Bates, Wallace and Burton.

Whereas Darwin took pleasure only in the reefs and the trees here, but detested the men he met and the Recife he visited and shut himself off from any coexistence with the human nature of Brazil, for Burton, Koster and Walsh that was their speciality: that coexistence with the human nature of Brazil and its particularities. The discovery not of new species of fish or plants, but of new aspects of human nature.

Those Britons could not have come to understand the human nature of Brazil to the point where they could reveal it to the Brazilians themselves, in portraits that were less what might be called 'documentary'

[21] Words in italics were used by Eça in English (Translator).

than 'psychological', had they not approached the people, the common folk, the men, the houses, the kitchens, the churches, the plantations and the farms with the same thirst for knowledge and the same taste for seeing and understanding people – and not just for contemplating landscapes – with which Darwin approached the objects of his predilection, which nowhere consisted primarily of people but rather of irrational creatures, plants and minerals. The portraits of Brazil sketched by those Britons show that their authors are as good at that genre as other compatriots of theirs are at the genre of portraits proper: those 'true portraits' in the National Portrait Gallery, London, in which the likeness is not sacrificed to any purely aesthetic, decorative or literary artifice or caprice, and of which the *Shelley* by Miss Curran remains a significant example. In pictorial literature, the case of the full-length portrait of Dr Johnson patiently and scrupulously sketched out by Boswell. The case of the Victorians resurrected by Strachey with all their colours and movements of living men. And, among the portraits of entire nations, and not just of an individual or figures characteristic of a period, the case of the book that Rebecca West wrote a few years ago about Yugoslavia. In this portrait in book form – a vast portrait of an extensive family expanded into a nation – if there are any artifices they are of the kind that do not betray but instead accentuate reality, like El Greco's famous elongated forms. No Briton of the literary stature of Strachey or with the capacity for both artistic and psychological interpretation of Rebecca West – a novelist, and not only a novelist but a woman, which in English literature is almost always a guarantee of extraordinary insight and sensitivity – has yet written a book about Brazil that is a literary masterpiece. That is despite the fact that, in addition to Robert Southey's *History* and Burton's book about the interior of Brazil and Bates's about the Amazon, there are the *Brazilian Sketches* by Kipling and *A Brazilian Mystic: The Life and Miracles of Antônio Conselheiro* by R. B. Cunninghame Graham and, more recently, the one by Peter Fleming; and despite the fact that among the authors of British portraits of our people there are two Englishwomen, almost two novelists: one good, the other bad. The bad one was a certain Mrs Kindersley, who was here in the seventeenth century;[22] the good one – excellent, even, for her insight and objectivity – was Maria Graham, who visited Brazil in the early nineteenth century and portrayed it in pages that remain fresh today. Even though none have stood out for their literary excellence – apart, of course, from Southey with his classic history and Kipling with his *Sketches* – several Britons who have written books about Brazil, including the two Englishwomen, have contributed not only to the documentation of Brazilian society but also to its interpretation. Without those books, it would be difficult for us today to reconstruct certain less obvious aspects of our own formation

[22] A *lapsus* by Freyre; Jemima Kindersley in fact visited Brazil in 1764 (Translator).

or to understand certain less picturesque, yet significant, features of the moral physiognomy of our own forebears, which they saw, observed and portrayed at close quarters.

Nonetheless, not even those books – nearly all of which are mediocre from a literary point of view, albeit valuable when we view them in terms of the documentation they provide or the interpretation they sketch out of Brazilian people, things and events – not even those books are the principal concern of the pages that follow. Instead, they are concerned with the British influence in Brazil through less well-known and less illustrious agents: traders, engineers, technicians, adventurers, missionaries, doctors, translators, consuls, actors, magicians, auctioneers, mechanics, dentists, sailors, bank managers, managers of gas and sugar firms and factories, superintendents of telegraph and railway companies, engine drivers and firemen. The Cinderellas of history, considered in its less grandiose aspects and studied through people who, beside the cinders of the factories, foundries, workshops, warehouses, locomotives, steamships and machines, also helped different cultures to come together or to interpenetrate.

The same technique – as the reader who is not just now making my acquaintance but who knows me from earlier books must have noticed already – was adopted in *Um engenheiro francês no Brasil*, a little study that went unnoticed by Brazilian critics but, in countries where there is currently a greater concern with matters of technique in studies of the individual or of human societies, was treated extremely generously by expert or specialist critics. Some of those specialists discerned something both new and, at the same time, specifically sociological in that little study; one North American sociologist, Professor William Rex Crawford of the University of Pennsylvania, noted with surprise that the book *Um engenheiro francês no Brasil* had been received somewhat coldly by critics and the public in Brazil. Why should a historian-sociologist concern himself with a simple technician like Louis Vauthier, who had left just an indiscrete and sometimes crude diary about the four years of his stay in Brazil? A simple engineer who was still young and had not made a name for himself? Why not some already famous Frenchman who had been here – the poet Paul Claudel or the psychologist Dumas, Anatole France or Clemenceau, for example? Or Sarah Bernhardt? Or Mme Curie? Or Paul Adam?

For that specialist, however, the book (*Um engenheiro francês no Brasil*) can be considered 'a sociological case study',[23] within a new technique of sociological study, of course. Professor Arbousse-Bastide, the generous French patron of those pages, had discovered in them 'the merit' of having

[23] Quoted by Freyre in English (Translator).

highlighted the sociological interest 'of contacts of seemingly the most humble technicians' with Brazil; 'the merit' also of having pointed out that 'contacts of that kind played a considerable part in the relations of Brazil with France, which are generally considered in exclusively intellectual and artistic terms', at a time when 'the two aspects of cultural influence were closely linked'; and 'the humblest of French craftsmen always brought with his tools a certain outlook on life, indissolubly associated with the plying of his trade'.

The work commenced in those previous pages, on Frenchmen, blends into these pages on English people in Brazil. The same approach, the same method, the same somewhat novel technique of drawing a psychological portrait of a representative individual or a group of typical individuals against a sociological and historical background.

While those early pages – on Frenchmen – encountered little understanding in Brazil and aroused little interest among critics, who are almost always indifferent or cold to subjects that are not 'illustrious' – it even seemed to one of them that, in these days of expensive paper, writing a whole book on an obscure Frenchman like Vauthier was to waste candles on 'an unimportant corpse' – there were people abroad who did understand and appreciate them. That in itself is compensation, considerable compensation, for a Brazilian writer.

It is possible that these pages on Englishmen – almost all of the same kind as the Frenchmen evoked in the essay on Vauthier – will have the same fate. In recent years, however, militant criticism in Brazil – practised from a principally literary point of view by Sr Álvaro Lins and by critics even younger than that perceptive Pernambucan, such as the two admirable Wilsons, from Paraná and Rio Grande do Sul, or the now masterful Antonio Candido[24] of São Paulo and Octávio de Freitas Júnior of Recife – has been gaining in perspective (without, of course, sacrificing the *belles-lettres* approach for any intruder) what it may perhaps fortunately have lost in didactic emphasis or academic *hauteur*. Criticism specializing in sociology, anthropology and history is another kind that has recently been making headway in Brazil.

The younger militant critics as well as the more lucid among the older ones will understand that, even though an essay on Englishmen in Brazil may not occupy itself with figures of the eminence of Canning or Southey, Cochrane or Burton, but only with secondary, even obscure Englishmen, it can have some human and even literary interest, in addition to its

[24] Antonio Candido de Mello e Souza (b. 1918), a prominent Brazilian scholar and literary critic, was just beginning his career in the 1940s (Translator).

possible scientific or sociological value as a 'sociological case study'.[25] This is a speciality which today provides perhaps the most secure basis for the development of truly scientific sociology, which will, for a long time yet, be reserved less for works of doctrinal generalization than for those of analysis accompanied by interpretation and comparison.

The pages that follow were written with that aim, although they have not succeeded in extracting from this lush and almost virgin subject either the interest or the value referred to above. That is not through any fault of the subject, which is indeed extraordinarily rich, but due to the author's deficiencies. In any case, the path has now been cleared for other studies in the genre that may better combine art with science in this still new species of portraits, which have to be as psychologically accurate as they are sociologically and historically true.

They are portraits that others must sketch – some are doing so already – with more felicitous brushstrokes, of those Italians, Poles, Swedes, Spaniards, Chinese, Japanese, Jews, Syrians, Austrians, Russian Gypsies and Hungarians who have also been associated with Brazil's development, although to a lesser extent in space or time than the British and French. I do not mention the Dutch, because their influence on the formation of Brazilian culture and society is being studied down to its deepest roots by two of the most serious scholars that Brazil has today, both of whom were for some time my fellow researchers: José Antônio Gonsalves de Mello Neto[26] – whose essay *Tempo dos Flamengos* has just been published – and José Honório Rodrigues,[27] who specializes in researching the history of the sugar economy in Brazil, particularly during the time of the Dutch.

A work that is at once biographical and sociological about an 'English doctor' in nineteenth-century Brazil – Dr Abbott or Abbot – is being written by one of my oldest collaborators in researching the archives and manuscript sections of libraries in the north of the country: José Valadares.[28] Certain aspects of the cultural relations – culture in the sociological sense – of the United States with Brazil are at this moment occupying another

[25] Phrase used by Freyre in English (Translator).

[26] José Antônio Gonsalves de Mello (1916-2002), whose name is often written with 'Neto' ('Grandson') appended, was a Pernambucan historian who specialized in the history of north-eastern Brazil, particularly during the period of Dutch occupation. *Tempo dos Flamengos* was first published in 1947 (Translator).

[27] The historian José Honório Rodrigues (1913-87) published *Civilização Holandesa no Brasil* in 1940 (co-authored with Joaquim Ribeiro); his later work focused especially on Brazilian historiography (Translator).

[28] José Antônio do Prado Valadares (1917-59) was an historian whose main area of interest was art and museums in his native Bahia. His work on the Abbot collection, Bahia's first art gallery, was published in 1951 (Translator).

of my younger colleagues, Diogo de Mello Menezes,[29] who has already published a thought-provoking preliminary note on the subject in the *Revista do Brasil* (in its Octávio Tarqüínio de Sousa[30] phase). Several of the sociological aspects of the relations of German immigrants or their children with the environment and culture of Brazil have been studied for years by Professor Emílio Willems[31] of São Paulo, within a modern American approach.

I myself hope soon to add a few notes to what has recently been written about Germanism in Recife: the Germanism of Tobias Barreto and his disciples. These notes will not be about the Germanism with which that talented writer from Sergipe sought in a way to compensate for being a mulatto next to white men still impregnated with their purely European origin, such as Taunay, or merely home-grown white men, such as Zacarias[32] or the Viscount of Uruguai,[33] setting against these admirers of all things French his own intellectual or philosophical identification with white men even whiter than the French: the Germans. Instead, they will deal with the activities of German technicians who had been settling in the capital of Pernambuco since the early 1800s and who have left us drawings as interesting as those by L. Schlappriz, prints as excellent as those by the engraver Carls, and furniture such as that by the master craftsman Spieler, which today is the pride and joy of those who own it. At the same time, I shall seek to recall the tropical adventure of the Germans who settled in Cova da Onça or Catucá,[34] and, among other facts relating to the virtually unknown German venture in tropical Brazil at the beginning of the nineteenth century, the significant detail that the Brazilian historian Alfredo de Carvalho descended from one of those Germans. Having failed to prosper as an agricultural settlement, the Germans had a variety of fates. Some descended to charcoal making, humbly adopting rustic ways

[29] Diogo de Mello Menezes (b. 1910) served as his cousin Gilberto Freyre's research assistant and authored a biography of him in 1944 (Translator).

[30] Octávio Tarqüínio de Sousa (1889-1959) was a lawyer and historian, whose main works dealt with nineteenth-century Brazil, including a biography of Emperor Pedro I. He edited the periodical *Revista do Brasil* between 1938 and 1943, and also, from 1939, the book series *Coleção Documentos Brasileiros* (previously edited by Gilberto Freyre, and published in Rio de Janeiro by José Olympio), in which several of Freyre's own works were published, including the first edition of *Ingleses no Brasil* (vol. 58, 1948) (Translator).

[31] The anthropologist Emílio Willems (1905-97) emigrated from Germany in 1931 and settled in Brazil, where he introduced the subject to the University of São Paulo and trained a generation of Brazilian anthropologists and sociologists. He left Brazil for the United States in 1949 (Translator).

[32] Zacarias de Góis e Vasconcelos (1815-1877) was a prominent politician in the 1860s, who advocated reducing the Emperor's power (Translator).

[33] Paulino José Soares de Sousa (1807-1866) was a lawyer and politician who became minister of justice and minister of foreign affairs in the 1840s and 50s. He was made Viscount of Uruguai in 1854 (Translator).

[34] An area in the hinterland of Recife occupied by runaway slaves (Translator).

and blending into the rural populace of the region. Others came to cities such as Recife, married Brazilian wives and dissolved into the bourgeois population of the Empire. Some seem to have returned to Europe or gone to the south of Brazil, which was already settled by Germans. They deserve a study, to add not only to the pages that have already been published on intellectual Germanism in Brazil – the literary and juridical Germanism that was centred on Recife and had as its prime mover the extraordinary figure of Tobias Barreto – but to the sociological essays on the relations of German immigrants and their descendants with the Brazilian populations in the south of Brazil, published by Professor Emílio Willems, which have already been mentioned here. They are works that reveal an enlightened, honest researcher.

With such news – news about works that have appeared or are in preparation, on topics that are in some way related to the subjects of the following pages – I must conclude these words of introduction. But, since I mention 'news', I must be allowed to defend myself against the objections that may be made regarding the surplus of textual transcriptions in this and other works of mine by reminding the reader of that distinction once made by Mark Twain between 'news' and 'history'. History, he noted, took the vividness and surprise out of news, and so distorted events. An orthodox historian may hate to sacrifice the dignity of history – and, most of all, that of the historian who also has pretensions of being elegant and impeccable in his style – to excessive transcription of news items, including newspaper advertisements, just as they appeared in the periods that he is studying or seeking to reconstruct or evoke. News items that are sometimes poorly written, full of grammatical mistakes and inelegant expressions, veritable scribbles by nobodies: by the obscure, secondary, unpretentious, yet active, useful and productive people who scrawled them. But as I am neither an orthodox historian nor do I seek to be an impeccable stylist or elegant writer, I can take the liberty, or even the licence, of frequently transcribing not only news that has appeared in old newspapers, but also items communicated by one authority to another in official documents at the times when the events took place, sometimes secretly or confidentially. I preserve, therefore, all the vividness and surprise of this news and, as far as possible, avoid dissolving these qualities into a single, monotonous style dominated by the pretension that only the author of the book can write high prose. Let those who took part in the events speak for themselves with all the old vigour of their voices, and with all their grammatical mistakes and passions of the moment.

Even so – even if this kind of collaboration of the actors with the author is accepted – a writer of such a work as the one that follows – a writer who is not just a parasite on old papers as I am – can still show his creativity or originality in a number of areas. In the interpretation of those more significant facts that he selects (and selecting them is itself his own work) from the vast material gathered from libraries or copied from archives. In the reconstruction of environments that the documents do not reconstruct by themselves. In the resurrection of figures that do not rise alone from the archival grave. In the restoration of the shreds of life torn from a past that is apparently quite dead. This would almost be a task for one of the so-called realist novelists, whose reality was not just contemporary life but the reality experienced by our predecessors and kept, in scraps, in a variety of documents, through which the observer's vision and memory were prolonged in time, yet held in check by scrupulous respect for the facts.

*

My thanks to those who assisted me in the research necessary for an essay like this, which, rather than being an essay of interpretation or synthesis – I beg the enemies and critics of the attempts to interpret Brazilian history sketched out in these and others of my recent pages to forgive me for these audacious words – has had to be one of lengthy analysis and slow reconstruction. For it is only by studying many Britons from the past that one can form the images of a few of them: those who behaved most characteristically, as agents of British culture in the colony and then the Empire of Brazil.

Those who helped me in archival research were principally my friends José Antônio Gonsalves de Mello Neto, José Valadares and F. de Assis Barbosa. Also Arquimedes Mello Neto, Ivan Seixas and Diogo de Mello Menezes.

Particularly valuable was the collaboration of the director of the Sociedade Brasileira de Cultura Inglesa of Rio de Janeiro, Mr W. J. Craig, and through him that of Sir Henry Lynch, a member of the Board of that Society, a distinguished Englishman who has lived in Brazil for years. I am indebted to Sir Henry for Photostat copies of some of the rarities in the collection of books and old engravings that make up his Anglo-Braziliana – perhaps the best that has ever been gathered together either here or in England. To my friend Odilon Ribeiro Coutinho I am grateful for the copy of the portrait of Mrs Graham, which is another of the illustrations in this essay. And to the young and already notable painter Rosa Maria, for the drawings done specially for the vignettes on these pages, according to the author's suggestions.

I also owe thanks to my friend Aureliano Leite[35] who, both personally and through his two articles on the British in São Paulo, published in the *Jornal do Commercio* in Rio de Janeiro on 30 January and 30 April 1944, told me of several interesting facts regarding British influence in our country. In one of these articles this distinguished commentator found fault with me somewhat unjustly, finding it strange that I should consider Rio, Pernambuco and Bahia 'perhaps the points in our country that have been most marked by contact with the British people', and remarking, 'Haste remains the greatest enemy of perfection.' It was neither as a whim nor in haste that I arrived at that conclusion, but slowly and even objectively: it was by means of a map, published in this volume, on which I marked the points in Brazil that saw the first and most vigorous flowering of those British institutions and activities that may, without any controversy, be considered the most characteristic and expressive of British influence on our country, in the phase when that influence was at its most widespread, profound and apparent, that is, the half-century that followed the opening of Brazil's ports to foreign trade, particularly with Great Britain. No one will deny that those activities or institutions were: HBM consuls, the Judges Conservators of the English Nation, chaplains or chapels, cemeteries, hospitals, shops, factories, foundries, doctors, engineers, scientists, newspapers, schools, libraries, charities, clubs and sporting associations. It was in Rio, Bahia and Pernambuco that such institutions flourished most intensely and in the greatest numbers in those decisive times. English pirates did, of course, appear early on in São Paulo, as did British traders. But they also appeared early on in Pernambuco and Bahia. On the other hand, São Paulo never experienced the figure of the Judge Conservator of the English Nation. It never had an Anglican church until 1873. It never had a hospital for British seamen. Although Fleming, an Irishman, took part in the 1842 Revolution in the Paraíba valley,[36] as recalled by Sr Aureliano Leite, Bowen, an Englishman, had already taken part in the 1817 Revolution in Pernambuco. British influence in São Paulo intensified at the end of the reign of Dom Pedro II and the early years of the Republic, when it started to decline in most of Brazil, especially in those parts – Rio, Bahia and Pernambuco – where it had reached the point of being nothing less than imperial.

Santo Antônio de Apipucos, December 1947.

[35] Originally from Minas Gerais, the historian Aureliano Leite (1886-1976) settled in São Paulo and focused his work on the history of those two states (Translator).

[36] In São Paulo state (Translator).

# CHAPTER I

# ADVENTURE, TRADE AND TECHNOLOGY

> *Whereunto ech man paused to make answere: wherefore I delivered my opinion; which was, that we were forbidden to use violence to any nation for trade. Secondly, I considered that divers of our nation, worshipfull merchants, and now adventurers in this voyage had set out the Minion hither, and begun a trade, which with our forcible dealing might be spoiled, and our nation brought in hatred.*
> *Lastly, that with force we were not like to atteine so much commodity, as we were in possibility to have with courtesie.*[37]
>
> (The Voyage Intended Towards China, wherein M. Edward Fenton was Appointed Generall: Written by M. Luke Ward his Viceadmiral, and Captaine of the Edward Bonaventure, begun Anno Dom. 1582, in The Principal Navigations... by Richard Hakluyt.)

[37] Quoted by Freyre in English (Translator).

A kind of angel – not just a guardian angel, but a guiding angel, able to lead its protégé to enchanted treasures – seems at times to light the way not only of artists but also of scientists and historians enthusing over the study of some subject or problem that is more than usually difficult to elucidate or resolve. That, perhaps, is why the painter Pablo Picasso said, 'I do not seek: I find.'

I remember that in 1937 I was interested in the rather shadowy figure of the French engineer and socialist Vauthier – who built the Santa Isabel Theatre in Recife – when one fine day my friend Paulo Prado arrived back from Paris with a present for me, a manuscript: the intimate diary of Louis Léger Vauthier. The record of the French engineer's experiences in Brazil (1840-1846). It had come into his possession without any effort on his part, by sheer chance. He had not sought: he had found. As he glanced through the faded notebook of the Frenchman – 'a certain Vauthier' – Paulo Prado had thought the diary might interest me, as it dealt mainly with Pernambuco, socialism and foreigners in Brazil, subjects he knew were my predilection. That is how, at the beginning of my studies on a forgotten Frenchman called Vauthier, my literary guardian angel favoured me with a precious document, the kind I most desired. A personal diary. A notebook full of sometimes indiscreet notes. A piece of autobiography. The confessions of a sinner who was not always repentant for his sins.

I must declare at the outset, in this second introduction – longer than the first – to the studies that I plan to publish on English activities in Brazil, that I have not yet lost hope that something similar may happen to me with regard to some English engineers called De Mornay, pioneers of the railway from Recife to São Francisco. Around them, using the same technique of combining biographical study with sociological study that I used in the Vauthier case – the technique of combining the individual with the universal, the regional with the ecumenical, and the colonial with the metropolitan – I hope one day to try to reconstruct and interpret forgotten aspects of British influence in Brazil in the nineteenth century.

There must exist letters, remains of diaries or notes written by those De Mornays – who were in fact twins, according to information from Mansfield, and so alike 'that many people do not know them apart'[38] – or by other Englishmen like them. Something that might elucidate their participation in Brazilian life.

A year or two ago, I thought that my long-standing wish might be answered. I had been taken by a friend to have dinner with an English couple who had long been resident in Pernambuco when, during dessert, the good man told me that he would pass on to me a document of possible interest for my studies: notes – another handwritten notebook! – by a Great Western of Brazil engineer or employee, an Englishman, who had recorded a series of facts or events in Brazil at the end of the last century from the viewpoint of a British technician. The author of these notes is not one of the De Mornays, but it is enough that he is an English technician or engineer for me to venture to weave around his manuscript a study that I have been planning for years concerning forgotten aspects of British influence in Brazil. An effort of reconstruction and interpretation for which, in fact, I already have a large amount of untouched material that I have collected from archives in Rio de Janeiro, Bahia and Pernambuco with the help of José Antônio Gonsalves de Mello Neto, Diogo de Mello Menezes and Ivan Seixas here in Pernambuco, José Valadares in Bahia, and Francisco de Assis Barbosa and Arquimedes de Mello Neto in Rio.

I have already outlined some aspects of this influence in a preliminary note published in the *Revista da Sociedade Brasileira de Cultura Inglesa*, Rio de Janeiro: aspects gathered from a source almost as untouched as the diaries and unpublished letters of travellers or the reports or dispatches of consuls. I am referring to newspaper advertisements.

Several such advertisements allow us to observe one significant and as yet unstudied aspect of British influence in Brazil: the renewal introduced by manufacturers and importers of machinery and articles of iron and steel, and by technicians and engineers. The latter figures were admired and even hero-worshipped by those Brazilian children who, since the first half of the nineteenth century, had been more partial to the modern English than to the ancient Romans, and keener on technical and mechanical matters than on philosophy or law, theology or rhetoric. Boys whom the books

[38] Charles B. Mansfield, *Paraguay, Brazil and the Plate*, Cambridge, 1861, p. 43 (quoted in English – Translator).

by Samuel Smiles – a real mediocrity of the Victorian era – which were translated into Portuguese during the reign of Pedro II, only made more eager for a life of action and 'self-help' and for the marvels of technology or engineering.

It was precisely the figure of the British railway engineer somewhat romantically cast adrift in Brazil and struggling with those

> iron chimeras fed with fire[39]

(from a poem written by a certain Scottish novelist and poet, who came from an old family almost entirely composed of orthodox Presbyterian engineers who wanted him to be an orthodox Presbyterian engineer as well, and not a bohemian poet – Robert Louis Stevenson) that I had the joy of encountering one day on some of the pages of the study that Professor Estêvão Pinto has written about the Great Western of Brazil. It is a contribution to the study of that railway company's history and its relations with the economy of north-eastern Brazil.

Knowing of my long-standing interest in the subject, the author has been kind enough to allow me to peruse his very interesting work before delivering it to his publisher. I must congratulate Professor Estêvão Pinto on the capable way in which he has carried out the task entrusted to him by the engineer Manuel Leão, when he was superintendent of the Great Western; in writing a difficult commissioned work, he has successfully breathed human interest into his study. Had it been penned by someone else, this essay on the venerable British company – the oldest of its kind in Brazil – would perhaps have turned out to be a mass of boring dates and complicated names, dry facts and apologias about the railway capitalism of the English in Brazil. A drearily bureaucratic report. And not an attractive chapter in the social history of Brazil's North-East written from a sociological angle and, at the same time, with a sense of local colour, as well as vivacity and literary elegance.

While I welcome Professor Estêvão Pinto's as yet unpublished work, I cannot help considering him a trespasser on an academic estate that, deep down, I rather selfishly and ungenerously hoped would remain unexplored until I had carried out my long-cherished plan of writing a study both biographical and sociological – or psychological and historical, as in the art of the portrait alluded to in the first introduction – on British influence in Brazil, reconstructed and interpreted through some now half-forgotten or

[39] Quoted in English from the poem 'The Iron Steed' by Robert Louis Stevenson (1850-94), *Collected Poems*, London, 1950 (Translator).

unknown technician, engineer, businessman, missionary or adventurer; but whose notes or unpublished letters might reveal to us a figure characteristic or typical of his people and of the more or less imperial relationship that Great Britain maintained with the still semi-colonial Brazil of the nineteenth century. A Brazil in which the first modern foundries, the first submarine cable, the first railways, the first telegraphs, the first trams, the first modern sugar mills, the first gas lights, the first steamboats and the first sewerage systems were almost all the work of Englishmen. Almost all due to British technology or initiative. Just as the locomotive came to capture the imagination of children and the common people in Brazil more than any other kind of English machinery, it was mainly English railway engineers that came to embody the Brazilian mystique of viewing England as a country of modern magicians: engineers, technicians, mechanics, tamers of iron and steel, glass and copper. Magicians who were sometimes seen as evil sorcerers, and sometimes as good wizards, whose instruments made in England were also like magic wands capable of working technical wonders.

That is why a people like the Brazilians, who for some time had been detached from Europe – a continent more revolutionized by the new machines and the new, coal-fired production techniques – attached so much importance to the English engineer, the *mister*, the *godene* or *godeme* (from 'God damn'), the *bife* ('beef'), or the *gringo*; the railway, mining or telegraph company manager; the importer of machinery; the seaman from HBM Navy brig or frigate; the *bíblia* ('bible'), *bode* ('he-goat') or *missa-seca* ('dry-mass') for Protestants; the *baeta* ('baize') or the *bicho* ('animal', 'vermin'), whose toes had to be counted to make sure they did not belong to Satan in person. In the Brazilian theatre, the figure of the Englishman – especially that of the English engineer – first appeared in plays such as *O inglês maquinista* ('The English Engineer') by Martins Pena, and soon became one of the most common subjects of magazines, cartoons, street and café jokes, carnival costumes, folklore and risqué stories. In these the Englishman was seen as being undersexed or excessively cold towards women, who were always being abandoned in favour of sport and drink, machines and books. In that he was contrasted with the colonial nd semi-colonial Brazilian who, although generally puny and wan, made the exertions of Venus almost his sole recreation and, at the same time, the best way to assert his energy. The thousands of jokes of the kind where an Englishman is sexually outcompeted by a sallow little Brazilian gave the latter the chance, or at least the illusion, of getting his revenge for the imperial arrogance of Her Britannic Majesty's ministers, such as Mr Christie,[40] and for the equally imperial insolence of red-haired, red-

[40] Heavy-handed diplomacy by William Christie, the British minister in Rio, in 1862 led to a breach

faced sailors from British ships anchored in Brazilian ports; for bankers, missionaries and even scientists like Darwin who, indignant with Brazilian 'inferiorities' during the time of slavery, inveighed not always fairly against Brazilian customs or feelings, bruising or slashing them with the claws of enraged lions or bulldogs. Or who behaved in the eyes of local people with the disagreeable air of selfish masters not only of the most powerful ships, the most powerful boats and the most advanced technology or science in the world, but even of the very seas and all their fish, not least cod. This was poor people's food in Brazil, but the trade enriched many Englishmen, or many Brazilians and Portuguese who chartered English ships specially fitted out to transport the fetid dried fish. Some of these wealthy men were forever known as So-and-so *Bacalhau* – 'Codfish'.

All that has been written about the English in Brazilian popular poetry is a task worthy of a researcher who specializes in that kind of study. I do not remember where – perhaps it was in Sergipe – I heard an interesting muleteer's song in which the smell of alcohol was described as *catinga de inglês*, or 'stench of an Englishman'. In Rio de Janeiro, 'the Englishman of Leopoldina'[41] has featured in popular rhymes and carnival songs, while in the old days in Recife there was 'the Maxambomba Englishman' (referring to an urban railway line running from Recife to Caxangá, Várzea and Dois Irmãos), who for many years was a Mr Henry Fletcher. This Mr Fletcher was once seen to respond in true Brazilian style with a 'St Francis's salute'[42] when jeered by the *moleques* of the Praça da República – those defiant *moleques*, bitter enemies of the more red-haired and arrogant Europeans, whom Walsh saw in Rio de Janeiro during the reign of Dom Pedro I confronting with savage fury the German and Irish soldiers who were rebelling against the Imperial Government: 'The Moleques rushed on every foreigner they met in the neighborhood, with their knives, and butchered them with the most savage mutilation...' An Irish tailor, who had nothing to do with the revolt of his compatriot soldiers, was stabbed to death, says Walsh, by two *moleques* who left him 'with his bowels hanging out'.[43]

The Brazilian *moleque's* fury towards the British invader did not always go to such extremes. Sometimes it was confined to burning or ripping up an effigy of the red-haired enemy, seen as the heretic or Judas: a rite from the Inquisition that survived most crudely and picturesquely in the former Judas-burnings on Easter Saturdays in Brazil. That is what

in relations between the two countries for several years (Translator).

[41] Leopoldina is the name of a railway line originally linking the states of Minas Gerais and Rio de Janeiro, which was taken over by a British company in 1898 (Translator).

[42] The gesture made by St Francis in Caravaggio's *St Francis in Ecstasy* – the hand held out, palm upwards, fingers slightly curled and the tip of the thumb touching the fingers, considered vulgar in Brazil (Translator).

[43] Walsh, *Notices of Brazil in 1828 and 1829*, Boston, 1831, I, p. 165.

happened one Easter Saturday, or 'hang-Judas' day, in the time of Pedro II: Judas appeared in one of Rio de Janeiro's streets in the form of a horrible caricature of the then minister of Great Britain in Brazil. The interesting thing is that the *moleques* stoned, slashed and hanged him in effigy in reprisal for his 'opposition to the slave-trade'. That information is given by Thomas Ewbank in *Sketches of Life in Brazil.*[44]

Another Englishman, an important merchant in the days of Pedro I, was also targeted by the *moleques* of Rio de Janeiro, who mistreated him in effigy – him and his wife. One fine Easter Saturday morning saw his front door adorned with two Judas figures, one of which Walsh says was the exact resemblance – or caricature? – of the merchant; the other was of his wife. It was easy to see the likeness when the English lady appeared at the window. Walsh was told that the couple had incurred the wrath of the *moleques* because they had criticized the popish 'exhibition' that commemoration of 'Hallelujah Saturday' in Brazil represented to their Protestant eyes; and also because they had refused to contribute to the festivities, unlike all the other residents in their street, the Rua Direita.[45] Walsh adds that he watched the Judas-burning from a window in the Rua Direita, which was decorated along its length with several figures to be burnt, including one of Satan. Many rockets exploded in the air. The two Britons were also burnt in effigy. And Walsh tells us that their figures bore labels that were so coarse as to be 'intranslatable'. Humour typical of *moleques*, rascals and ruffians. That humour is also the source of nicknames or sobriquets that have been irreverently given to Englishmen or women living in Brazil, such as '*Iaiá Foguete*' ('Miss Rocket'), applied to an eminent lady who resided for a long time in Recife, where she died a few years ago at a ripe old age: she had the dress and manners of a Victorian lady who, in Brazil, had acquired the vivacity of the most spirited young women of the time of Pedro II.

Of great age, dating from the period when Brazilians first started objecting to the abuses of British imperialism in our country – and especially on our seas – is the piano carriers' song recently published[46] by Mr Silvino Lopes in one of the most interesting of his chronicles:

> We don't fish with nets any more
> We're not allowed to fish

[44] Thomas Ewbank, *Life in Brazil; or, The Land of the Cocoa and the Palm. With an Appendix, Containing Illustrations of Ancient South American Arts in Recently Discovered Implements and Products of Domestic Industry, and Works in Stone, Pottery, Gold, Silver, Bronze, etc.*, London, 1856, p. 236. (Ewbank actually used the word 'thrashed' instead of 'slashed', which is the translation of Freyre's '*rasgaram*' – Translator.)

[45] Walsh, *Notices of Brazil*, II, p. 218.

[46] *Diário da Noite* (Recife), 18 June 1947.

We've all heard the news here
The English have bought the sea.[47]

That gives a taste of the days when all the seas were English waters – as if stolen from the rule of Iemanjá[48] – and English sailors were ruffians who fell on Brazilian ports, chasing after black women with not so much as a by-your-leave, or drunkenly singing in the streets even on Sundays, to the scandal of those of their compatriots who were more angelic or intransigent in their Protestant observance of the Lord's Day. That did not stand in the way of the naive patriotism of some Brazilians, who wanted to confront Great Britain's then immense naval power with the two or three ships that Brazil had inherited on its independence. One such naive patriot told the Reverend Walsh one day, 'We must seize all your ships in our harbour, confiscate all your property...' All because of some sharp words that were known to have been exchanged between Pedro I and the minister of Great Britain in Rio, Mr Gordon, regarding a house in Botafogo: an entirely personal matter.[49]

The *mister*[50] or Englishman was clearly characterized as such in caricature and anecdote. He was as clearly characterized there and in the theatre – in the symbolic form of an ugly, arrogant individual, with projecting teeth, fair or almost white sideburns, a pipe hanging from the corner of his contemptuous mouth, check clothing and thick-soled ankle-boots – as was the *madama* or *francesa* (Frenchwoman), in the form of a blonde, sophisticatedly elegant and finely erotic woman, whose influence on Brazilian life in the last century likewise needs to be studied and interpreted. The colonial and semi-colonial Brazilian learnt a great deal from the *mister*. To his influence, in fact, may be attributed not only the introduction or popularization in Brazil of the white suit, tea, wheat bread, beer and later *whisky*, *gin* and *rum*, *beef*, or beef and potatoes, *rosbife* (roast beef), lamb chops, *pijama* (pyjamas), the cloth cap, the revolver, the sporting gun, *macadame* (macadam), the *water-closet*, the 'ball-game' (tennis) and other sports, living in the suburbs, the English saddle, the English piano (superseded by the German), the English clock (superseded by the Swiss), the rubber cape, English shoes and the *waterproof*; but also the beginnings of certain Protestant sects that today prosper in our country, and of modern teaching methods for children (with the addition

[47] Não se pesca mai de rede
não se pode mai pescá
qui já sube da nutiça
que os ingrês comprou o má.
[48] The Afro-Brazilian *orixá* (goddess) of the sea (Translator).
[49] Walsh, *Notices of Brazil*, II, p. 225.
[50] English words in italics here are used in Portuguese and quoted as such by Freyre (Translator).

of physical education to scholarly education); a taste for detective novels (especially Sherlock Holmes), *grogue* (grog), picnics, *clowns*, *habeas corpus*, the *jury*, *meetings*, scouting, the art of the *debate*, *humour*, *reides* (from 'raid', though in Brazil the expression acquired an arbitrarily new meaning[51]), English china, the *sandwiche*, the *lanche*,[52] *ponche* (punch), and the figure or manners of the *gentleman*. And, through English influence, Brazilians who were *snobs*, or simply elegant or *smarts* and *up-to-dates* – words that go into the plural in Brazilian manner because their incipient Brazilianization has reached the point of allowing such a liberty – developed a taste for the English way of walking, the English way of horse riding and the English way of being a *dandy*; for walks or promenades (which came to be known among us by the phoney English expression *footing*, perhaps invented by some João do Rio[53]); the English gentleman's habit of shaving every day; the English way of speaking softly and laughing silently; the English boys' school (like the one Mr John H. Freese ran in Nova Friburgo and the one that Mr Morethson and Mr Charles W. Armstrong founded in São Paulo); the *bufete* (buffet – sideboard, larder or small station restaurant) and later the *bar* (it should be noted in relation to *bufete* that the English word *buffet* also became common in Portuguese to mean a slap or punch; the word has both meanings and is of early French origin, but was probably introduced into Brazil by the English); the iced *drink* (which, for many years, the local gentry in minor ports such as Maceió used to drink aboard English ships); the *iate* (yacht) and the *clube* (club); English men's fashion, English wool or worsted, the English fashion for ties and socks, the dinner jacket (called a *smoking* here and in other Latin countries, but not in England), flannel trousers, *knicker-bockers*, the *redingote* (from *riding coat*) and the English hat (the round hat that replaced the three-cornered style here); five-o'clock teas, 'English sauce',[54] *soda water*, Eton collars for boys, pith helmets, mustard, English toilet soap, English biscuits, the English kind of port or sherry, and the English pipe; the English governess, 'English time' (meaning strictly precise time), the 'word of an Englishman' (meaning almost 'word of honour'), and the English *valet* of the kind immortalized by Eça de Queiroz; *breakfast*, the *garden-party*, the *bungalow*, the *cottage*, fruit salts, *whist* and *poker*, the English racehorse, the *turf*, and the Jockey or Derby Club races; the English hound or pedigree dog, especially the *buldogue*; Sandow exercises; *maple* (syrup); an English accent when speaking English and even Portuguese itself; sailing on English steamships, especially – starting in 1839 – the Royal Mail ships; English dairy or pedigree cattle

[51] A long journey on foot or by any means of transport (Translator).

[52] From 'lunch', meaning a snack (Translator).

[53] The pseudonym of the Rio de Janeiro journalist and playwright Paulo Barreto (1881-1921) (Translator).

[54] *molho inglês*, i.e. Worcestershire sauce (Translator).

(Durhams, Herefords and Polled Angus), which ennobled fields or pastures in southern Brazil and some cowsheds and meadows in the north; and the banker's cheque. As all these Anglicisms arrived, the language itself became anglicized, with the naturalization of verbs such as *chutar* and *driblar* (to shoot and to dribble, as in football), *blefar* (to bluff), *boicotar* (to boycott), *macadamizar* (to macadam), *boxear* (to box), *esbofetear* (to buffet), *brecar* (to brake), *liderar* (to lead), and *lanchar* (to lunch or snack), in addition to the words already mentioned and several others: *handicap*, *esporte* (sport), *match*, *futebol* (football), *gol* (goal), *golquipa* (goalkeeper), *beque* (back), *sportsman*, *refe* (referee), *time* (team), *off-side*, *craque* (crack, in the sense of a first-rate player), *turfe* (turf), *truque* (railway truck), *estoque* (stock), *pudim* (pudding), *uísque* (whisky), *recorde* (record, in the sense of record-breaking), *bill*, *pedigree*, *buldogue* (bulldog), *bifada* (a meal of beef steak), *coque* (coke), *bolina* (bowline), *crossima* (crossing, a railway term), *sulaque* (slide-valve), *catgute* (catgut), *pôquer* (poker), *iate* (yacht), *mister*, *miss*, *esnobe* (snob), *Júlio* or *jule* (joule), *gin*, *rum*, *tênis* (tennis), *set*, *pônei* (pony), *draga* (drag, dredge), *capimbó* (ceiling ball), *smart*, *drink*, *lanche* (lunch, snack), *warrantagem* (warranting[55]), *escuna* (schooner), *drawback*, *cheque*, *gaff-top*, *repórter*, *report*, *palhabote* (pilot boat), *nurse*, *barca-férri* (ferryboat), *revólver*, *knockout*, *round*, *standard*, *stand*, *cottage*, *waterproof*, *whist*, *rifle*, *alô* (hello, on the telephone), *hurrah*, *ring*, *scratch*, *bloco* (block), *lockout*, *slogan*, *slack* (slacks), *high-life*, and *best-seller*. And there are grounds for attributing an English origin to *cornimboque* (hornbox), *sinuca* (snooker) and *sucata* (succotash[56]).

That is without mentioning political writers, masters of parliamentarianism, philosophers and economists, poets like Byron and novelists like Walter Scott, by whom Brazil had been influenced to varying degrees ever since the earliest years of its independent life, either directly or through France or Portugal. An Englishman, Bowen, even took part in the republican revolution of 1817; he phlegmatically awaits a patient historian who will study him. Who he was is still a mystery, although the wise researcher Rodolfo Garcia once emphatically assured me, in the presence of Paulo Prado, that the mystery had been solved. But who has heard of the solution to the Bowen mystery? It is a name mentioned in passing by Professor Hill in his study of diplomatic relations between Brazil and the United States. For my part, the most I have succeeded in doing so far has been to discover the following sign of his passage through Pernambuco: his name appears among the subscribers to a charity fund for the officers and crew of a ship that caught fire here in 1816. Their names are listed in

[55] Provision of a negotiable receipt (warrant) for goods deposited in a warehouse (Translator).

[56] Succotash, originally a Native American bean and corn stew from New England, seems an unlikely source for *sucata*, which means 'scrap metal'. The *Dicionário Aurélio Eletrônico* (1998) suggests a more plausible Arabic origin for the word (Translator).

a now rare publication, the title of which means *Gratulatory Verses for the Beneficence in Favour of the Officials and Crew of the Ship Balsemão Burnt in Pernambuco on 2 January 1816, Offered, Dedicated and Consecrated by the Captain, Pilot and Surgeon of Said Ship,*[57] by Nuno Alvares Pereira Pato Moniz, Lisbon, 1816.

The list is interesting. It is headed by the illustrious name of a Brazilian merchant closely associated with England: Domingos José Martins. And he starts it with 300$,[58] which shows the size of his fortune in those days. Charles Bowen follows next with 100$. Then comes Antônio Gonçalves da Cruz with 51$200. Other English merchants' names follow: Thomas Stuart, with 50$; Samuel Acton, with 40$; George Thomas Mitchel, with 40$; Samuel Preston, with 25$; Wm. Pelly, with 20$; Robert Tod, with 12$; James Caksshot, with 12$800; Jorge Buchmore, with 6$400; and Samuel Pach, with 6$400. All of them English and all of them perhaps masons.

Recently, in the National Archive, which is directed these days by Mestre Vilhena de Morais – a conscientious man of learning who, instead of hindering, facilitates the work of younger scholars – my research associate José Antônio Gonsalves de Mello Neto came across a formal petition with the signature of Charles Bowen, showing that he was in Recife in 1809. Thus he was one of the first English merchants to establish himself in Brazil after the opening-up of the ports; and his political, revolutionary activity in Portugal's American colony – an uncommon attitude for a merchant – seems to suggest he was a freemason, perhaps under the protection of the Duke of Sussex. While Canning was called the 'godfather of Brazilian nationality' for having come out in favour of the independence of Portuguese America, it seems that the Grand Master of British Freemasonry also favoured the cause of his Brazilian brothers in his own way: that is, in the masonic way, which is to act quietly in the shadows. A quietness that seems all the greater when the mason is English, and not merely of half-English origin or upbringing, like the agitator Ratcliff.

Referring to the execution of Ratcliff, or Radcliffe, or even Racticliff – as his name also appears in Brazilian documents – Walsh writes: 'John William Radcliffe, born in Portugal, of English parents...'[59] Yet Mr Tobias

[57] *Versos Gratulatorios para a Beneficencia a Favor dos Officiaes e Campanha do Navio Balsemão Incendiado em Pernambuco no dia 2 de Janeiro de 1816, O. D. C. o Commandante, Piloto e Cirurgião do Mesmo Navio.*

[58] Three hundred mil-réis. A mil-réis (= 1,000 réis) was written 1$000 or simply 1$. Walsh says that in 1828 five réis were worth one English farthing (Walsh, *Notices of Brazil*, I, p. 250), the equivalent of 4$800 to one pound sterling (Translator).

[59] Walsh, *Notices of Brazil*, II, p. 224. The historian Octávio Tarqüínio de Sousa writes as follows on this subject, with his expert authority:

'Ultimately, who was this person? For the Barão do Rio Branco, a man of sober judgment, Ratcliff, who was "well known in Portugal as an agitator and revolutionary", was no more than an "unfortunate adventurer" who, on arriving in Pernambuco having been forced to leave his country, "soon adopted the cause of the separatist revolutionaries and prepared to fight for the dismemberment of Brazil." There we have the portrait of the man: a mere adventurer, an agitator and revolutionary, moved only by the aim of destroying Brazil. To leave no shadow of a doubt about his malevolence, Rio Branco claims, without giving any kind of evidence, that Ratcliff had aided and welcomed Portugal's recolonization policy, which had been espoused by the minister José da Silva Carvalho.

'When seen in his human proportions, John William or João Guilherme Ratcliff should not, perhaps, inspire the revulsion that our great diplomat and historiographer could barely disguise. A more objective appraisal might even find a few good qualities or virtues in him.

'Born in the city of Porto, in the Rua das Flores in the cathedral parish between 1776 and 1783, Ratcliff – blond, tall, stout, fair-skinned and red-faced, was the son of a Polish father (who owned a shop selling nautical and musical instruments) and a Portuguese mother. He visited several countries, learnt languages, read widely and, as a man of his time, was passionate about liberal ideas. When the constitutionalist revolution of 1820 broke out in Portugal, Ratcliff revelled in it together with the most extreme radicals. In the new regime he was chosen by the people to hold a number of positions, including justice of the peace, parish elector, chairman of the electoral committee, company commander in the National Guard, etc. Later he was appointed an official in the Department of Justice where, always an ardent liberal, he volunteered to draw up the decree banishing Queen Carlota Joaquina, after she refused to swear allegiance to the constitution.

'Inevitably, with the success of the absolutist reaction in Portugal in 1823, Ratcliff found himself pursued and only escaped from the hatred of his adversaries by fleeing the country. It appears that he first exiled himself in England, then the United States and finally Brazil, where he disembarked in Pernambuco just as the unrest caused there by the dissolution of the constituent assembly was reaching its revolutionary stage. What liberal of his stamp would waste such a great opportunity? A revolution against despotic power, a revolution to avenge the suppression of the people's elected assembly – what more could a man with Ratcliff's political ideas and fervent temperament need? In the repository of collective aspirations that he embodied, João Guilherme Ratcliff, like so many of his contemporaries, belonged more to his time than to any one particular country. He was certainly Portuguese and loved his country – there is no lack of evidence and emphatic declarations to that effect – but he was also liberal, republican, a freemason, ready to fight and give his life for the ideals that burned in him. That transnational or universal aspect of Ratcliff's actions, which scandalizes notable historiographers, marked the behaviour of many individuals from diverse countries at the time when liberalism started to prevail. There was an abundance of people like Ratcliff. Did many foreigners not take part in the French Revolution? That is the case, for example, of Thomas Paine, born and brought up in England, who arrived in North America at the age of thirty-seven and, ever committed to the Quixotic defence of trampled rights wherever he might be, wielded enormous influence in the process of America's political emancipation through his *Common Sense* and other writings. After returning to Europe in 1787, he soon became involved in the French Revolution, true to his principle that "my country is the world, and my religion is to do good". Many foreigners – English, French and especially Portuguese – took part in the struggles for Brazil's independence. They were led to do so by the most varied of motives. Many of them were defending a social status that they had already won; there were idealists; there was a good proportion of adventurers. Yet a distinction needs to be made. Cochrane was an adventurer in both the good and the bad sense: running risks, serving, and at the same time fighting for material gain and anxious for glory and wealth. A spirit of adventure inspired all those foreign fighters who defended the new fatherland that was created here – people like Labatut, Taylor, Jewett, Welch, Beaurepaire and Nicol. Ratcliff was undeniably an adventurer, but in the best sense of the word: self-denying and capable of making the greatest sacrifices for his ideas, and of dying for them.' ('Ordem e Aventura', *Correio da Manhã*, Rio

Monteiro claims in his history of Pedro I's reign (*História do Império – O Primeiro Reinado*, Rio de Janeiro, 1839, I, p. 247) that he was the son of a Pole. Should that be accepted uncritically? Might the agitator have been born in Portugal of an English mother and a Polish father? Or 'of English parents'?

It is worth noting that, when Félix Ferreira deals with the execution of 'Ratclicff' in Rio in his work *A Santa Casa de Misericórdia Fluminense* (Rio de Janeiro, 1894-1898), he says the same as Walsh about the agitator: 'He was born in Lisbon, but of English origin ...' And in *Biographias de Alguns Poetas e Homens Illustres da Provincia de Pernambuco* (Recife, 1856), Antônio Joaquim de Mello wrote that, once the foreign agitator had resigned himself 'to the shameful penalty that his tormentors would inflict on him', he wrote his now famous sonnet 'in his exquisite English calligraphy'.

On page 308 of his essay, based on documents from the Santa Casa archives, Félix Ferreira also notes that:

> Ratcliff was a mason, and it was due to the protection of Freemasonry that he escaped from the clutches of the Lisbon police and took refuge in Pernambuco, just as before him, thanks to the same protection, Hyppolito José da Costa Pereira had succeeded in escaping from the dark prisons of the Inquisition and taken shelter in London, where he founded and edited the *Correio Braziliense*.

Masonry at the time seems to have been largely English in its political orientation and anglophile in its activities in Brazil, and it may have done its best to protect Ratcliff in view of his 'English origin', just as in the case of Hipólito da Costa it made every effort to help the journalist in London, apparently not only on account of his liberal views in politics but also because he was married to an Englishwoman.

In any case, it seems that Ratcliff had had an English education, because his handwriting style was English. And perhaps other links tied him to the masonic, English liberalism of the time, although his violent, impetuous way of being a liberal and his impulsive, tragic personality were more Latin or even Polish than British; and he mistrusted his own masonic brothers, like his companion in political agitation and subversion against the Brazilian Empire, the 'Maltese adventurer' Metrowich, as Tobias Monteiro states on page 248 of the above-mentioned work on the reign of Pedro I.

---

de Janeiro, 6 July 1947.)

It is also a fact that Brazilian journalism began in London with the *Correio Braziliense*, founded there in 1808 by Hipólito José da Costa, a Brazilian married to an Englishwoman and protected by the Duke of Sussex and British Freemasonry. Newspaper advertisements reveal considerable English influence on the beginnings of the typographical art among us, an aspect of the history of newspapers and books in Brazil that, perhaps, was not given the emphasis it deserves by Mr Carlos Rizzini in his recent, well-documented study of the subject, a veritable Brazilian masterpiece of research and erudition.[60]

We should not forget that in Pernambuco an Englishman, F. Pinthis, was 'the printer who taught Pernambucans how to put the letters together and compose the columns of a newspaper', a fact that is generally forgotten. On 28 September 1856, the writer of the 'A Carteira' column in the *Diário de Pernambuco* paid tribute to Pinthis with those words, and emphasized that

> F. Pinthis should be regarded as the first of Pernambuco's teachers, and his name should be known and revered by all our compositors.

Another English pioneer in the technical modernization of Brazil was D. W. Bowman, 'for many years established among us as an engineer and mechanic', according to the *Diário de Pernambuco* for 7 July 1856. It was this Bowman – another forgotten name – who

> made some of our capitalists see the benefits that would accrue from the construction of a railway that would start at Ponte da Boa Vista and pass through Mondego, Estancia, Capunga and Torre, passing close to Magdalena, Ponte de Uchôa, Poço da Panella, Caldeireiro, Monteiro and Apipucos, to terminate at Caxangá.

A dream that came true. That was one of the first urban railways

[60] Carlos Rizzini, *O Livro, o Jornal e a Tipografia no Brasil, 1500-1822 – Com um Breve Estudo Geral sobre a Informação – Meios de Comunicação, Correio, Catequese, Ensino, Sociedades Literárias, Maçonaria, etc.*, Rio de Janeiro, undated. See also the equally well-documented study by Professor Hélio Vianna, *Contribuição à História da Imprensa Brasileira (1812-1869)*, Rio de Janeiro, 1945, which refers to an 'unfindable' *Litterary* [*sic*] *Intelligencer* of 1830 as the 'second English periodical printed in Brazil' (p. 71). The first appears to have been the *Rio Herald*. In the work cited above, Mr Carlos Rizzini mentions that 'Silva Serpa, the Bahian typographer, advertised for work in the *Gazeta do Rio de Janeiro*, promising fast delivery, agreeable prices and good English lettering' (p. 322). He also notes that the Pernambucan revolutionaries of 1817 set up a printing shop owned by a Ricardo Rodrigues Catanho, thanks to the skills of 'two friars, an Englishman and a French sailor' (p. 324), information that he drew from Tollenare.

built in South America: the Brazilian Street Railway, which was opened in Pernambuco in 1866, eight years after the opening of the Recife and São Francisco Railway Company's line from Recife to Cabo. The Brazilian Street Railway replaced a horse-drawn coach service, which itself was an English initiative in Pernambuco. From 1842 onwards, newspapers in Recife had carried advertisements by the Englishman Thomas Sayle for his 'new, splendid and decorated Omnibus with famous horses and well-known coachmen...'

The many Britons who took part in our military and naval wars of independence and our political revolutions, whom Viscount Taunay recalls in emotional terms in his book on foreigners who have been of service to Brazil (*Estrangeiros ilustres e prestimosos ao Brasil*, Rio de Janeiro, 1896, re-edited in 1932 by the historian Affonso de E. Taunay) – Cochrane, James Norton (who lost an arm here), Taylor, Grenfell, Parker, Craig, Rose, Clare, Wilson, Sheperd ('died in combat on 7 March 1827'), Cowen, Hayden, Broom, Crosbie, McErving, Eyre, Steel, Thompson and several others – should not make us forget the even greater number of those who engaged in other wars and revolutions among us: the wars against routine, ignorance and disease, for example; and the vast technical revolution that allowed us to abandon slave labour for freedom, replace monoculture with a diversified economy, and move from human and animal power to mechanized transport. These Britons, who renovated Brazilian life, included organizers of omnibus companies such as Sayle, and railway dreamers; explorers of the wilderness like J. H. Elliot and Palm, who ventured through a large part of Paraná; doctors; educators and English language teachers such as Father Tilbury, Freese the elder, James Maze, Thomas Gossling and John Joyce, who was Evaristo da Veiga's teacher in 1818, as the historian Octávio Tarqüínio de Sousa reminds us; engineers like a certain Ginty, who built the gasworks in Rio de Janeiro and the 'new' Tijuca road, and Isaac Denning, who drilled artesian wells in Ceará in 1837; Thomas Grimm, who taught landscape painting at the Academy of Fine Arts; naturalists like Gardner, Wallace and Bates; merchants like Mawe and Koster; foundry mechanics; miners; missionaries; governesses; pioneers of the country's industrialization like the organizers of The Central Sugar Factories of Brazil; and master compositors of newspapers and books. In 1826 the *Typographia Nacional* in Paraíba do Norte began to print the *Gazeta* mentioned by the Paraíban historian Irineu Pinto on page 96 of volume II of his *Datas e notas para a história da Paraíba* (Paraíba, 1916), and the person who printed it was the Englishman Waller S. Boardman. It came out on Saturdays in quarto format – more like a book than a newspaper – at the price of eighty réis a copy and, significantly, its motto was words by Bentham in French: '*Sans publicité, point de bien durable*' etc.[61]

[61] 'Without publicity, no good is permanent.' Jeremy Bentham, *Essay on Political Tactics*, London,

On the subject of books, it should be noted that in Brazil in the first half of the nineteenth century English bindings were famed for being the best in the world. On 15 December 1841, the *Diário de Pernambuco* printed an article on Father Francisco Coelho de Lemos, the most notable of the master bookbinders in Recife at that time, who had been established in the Rua da Florentina since 1835 with a workshop:

> adorned with substantial presses and beating stones, a large assortment of gilding irons, embossed boards and facets, beautiful marbled endpapers and excellent leather skins for binding.

The author of the article wrote that the priest's bindings:

> in consistency and elasticity rival English bindings, which in our opinion are now the best ...

Father Lemos had mastered the 'chemical processes to make the leather impermeable and have a permanent shine', which were the secret of those good British bindings – both full and Bradel bindings. Through the influence of English techniques, Father Lemos had become a renovator of the art of bookbinding in Brazil. It appears, in fact, that the English discovered how to improve the leather for binding books through the chemistry used for improving the leather for horses' saddles and for riders' shoes and boots. But that is no reason for us to detract from the contribution made by British minds to the development of more intellectual arts than horsemanship.

In the Brazilian Parliament during the Empire, the English were the most imitated speakers right from the earliest debates and speeches. They were imitated in their manner of speaking, their gestures and even their style of shaving: English sideburns were worn by several members, including Paranhos the elder.[62] And the Byzantine argument between José de Alencar[63] and Zacarias on the pronunciation of 'Pall Mall' became legendary. Speeches gradually went from just being peppered with quotations from Latin to overflowing with quotations from English authors and characteristically English technical expressions: Adam Smith, budget, deficit, bill, *warrantagem* (warranting), funding loan, Ricardo, Bagehot, John Stuart Mill, bond, and drawback. 'Drawback' is a word that appears

1791 (Translator).

[62] José Maria da Silva Paranhos the elder, Viscount of Rio Branco (1819-1880), was a modernizing statesman, at the height of his powers in the 1870s (Translator).

[63] José de Alencar (1829-1877) was a romantic novelist and politician (Translator).

in José Ferreira Borges's treatise on economics, published in 1844.[64]

In the Academies of Law in Olinda and São Paulo, future scholars spent long years learning their best political economy from English books that they read in the original or in translation. One of these books was by Bentham, another by Mill. Cairu[65] mainly devoured the ideas of British economists and fought against Gallomania by countering it with English authors, principles and examples. He was almost an Anglomaniac. Álvares de Azevedo[66] found his inspiration in Byron. Machado de Assis[67] assimilated British models of humour and style to such an extent that satirists started calling him the 'English mulatto'. Sílvio Romero[68] learnt much from Spencer, and Euclides da Cunha[69] something from Carlyle. Spencer gained disciples in Brazil. Mill, in fact, had already done so, as had Adam Smith and Darwin. One of Darwin's Brazilian disciples was Arthur Vianna de Lima, whose work in French, *Exposé sommaire des théories transformistes*, was reviewed at length in as important an English newspaper as *The Morning Post.*

In a library that he visited in São João in the Province of Minas Gerais in 1829, run by 'a mulatto padre' who was also the editor of the *Astro de Minas* newspaper, Walsh was surprised to find a number of English books: the *Revolutionary Plutarch*, Smith's *Wealth of Nations*, Pinkerton's *Geography, Paradise Lost, Sentimental Journey* and *Trials for Adultery*, and among the newspapers *The Times* and *The Chronicle*. Walsh found there were three people in the town who spoke English, while a larger number could read it.[70]

English was decidedly conquering the very redoubt of Latin in Brazil: Minas Gerais in the early nineteenth century was famed for its Latinist priests and judges. This conquest was a result of the opening-up of the ports, the establishment of English businessmen in Brazil and the importing of English books, which had hitherto been banned by the Inquisition or by less liberal priests.

According to Walsh, despite the poor education the Brazilian clergy

[64] *Principios de Syntelogia: Compreendendo em Geral a Theoria do Tributo e em Particular Observações sobre Administração e Despezas de Portugal, em Grande Parte Aplicáveis ao Brasil*, Lisbon, 1844.

[65] José da Silva Lisboa, first Baron and Viscount of Cairu (1756-1835), was a politician loyal first to D. João VI and subsequently to D. Pedro I (Translator).

[66] Manuel Antônio Álvares de Azevedo (1831-1852), a romantic poet and essayist (Translator).

[67] Joaquim Maria Machado de Assis (1839-1908) was one of Brazil's most famous writers, who wrote his best-known works during his realist phase (Translator).

[68] Sílvio Vasconcelos da Silveira Ramos Romero (1851-1914), a poet and philosopher (Translator).

[69] Euclides Rodrigues da Cunha (1866-1909), a republican writer best known for his study of the Canudos rebellion, *Os Sertões* (1902), translated as *Rebellion in the Backlands* (Translator).

[70] Walsh, *Notices of Brazil*, II, p. 84.

received in the seminaries, they had already 'felt the effects' of – that is to say, had been raised up both morally and intellectually by – the 'intercourse with strangers' that occurred after the opening-up of the ports. Principally by intercourse with English authors, he meant to say. So much so, that he highlights the fact that a translation of Paley's *Moral Philosophy* was at that time widely read by Brazilian priests and seminarists and found in libraries, as were Blair's *Sermons*. Walsh states that the florid style of these was 'accommodated to their taste in pulpit oratory'.[71] Therefore they were often preached in churches in a style of Portuguese that must not have sounded like a translation from English. That suggests that the English technique of church oratory, in the form of translations of Blair, merely fanned the flames of the rococo style of eloquence that was current in Brazil and Portugal, rather than curbing its excesses, as it did in the case of parliamentary or political eloquence. Since the earliest decades of parliamentary life in Brazil, political oratory had lost some of the worst, most exaggerated forms of rhetoric taught in the old church-run schools under the influence of the British technique of speaking or debating, which, while still retaining its share of bombastic sonority, was already developing – or contracting – in the direction of clarity, concision and sobriety. Certain members of the Brazilian Parliament, such as the Viscount of Rio Branco, became noted for these qualities, since they were more influenced by the British way of making parliamentary speeches, debates and repartee than by the Portuguese or even the French.

That influence seems to have been exerted primarily through a severely technical book, *Tactica das Assambleas Legislativas*, a work first extracted from Jeremy Bentham's manuscripts into French by Étienne Dumont of Geneva; the Portuguese translation was published in 1832 by Pinheiro, Faria & Comp., of Rua do Amparo, 22, in Olinda. In the early decades of Brazilian independence, this obviously anglophile publishing house made Olinda a source for the dissemination of British culture in Brazil. In addition to translations of Bentham, other works published there in Portuguese were Mill's *Principles of Political Economy* ('translation from the French compared with the English original by Dr Pedro Autran da Matta e Albuquerque and the then Academy members Álvaro and SérgioTeixeira e Macedo')[72] and even Ann Radcliffe's *The Cavern of Death*.[73] Ann Radcliffe, who wrote mystery novels, was perhaps the first English woman novelist to be read in Portuguese in Brazil.

[71] *Ibid.*, I, p. 204.

[72] Alfredo de Carvalho, *Anais da Imprensa Periódica Pernambucana de 1821-1908, Dados Históricos e Bibliográficos*, Recife, 1908, p. 44.

[73] This is apparently a misattribution. *The Cavern of Death* was a very popular Gothic novel published anonymously in London in 1794 (Translator).

When Thomas Lindley was in Brazil in the early years of the nineteenth century, he came across a Portuguese translation of *Robinson Crusoe* in Bahia.[74] This was perhaps the first English novel read in Portuguese in Brazil, and it was not long before Walter Scott became the most widely read novelist, and the most beloved. That may be due to the fact that he was a novelist of the old Scottish castle way of life, to which the Brazilian way of life was somewhat similar with its almost feudal plantation mansions. On visiting a Brazilian family in a distant part of Minas Gerais, Gardner came across copies of *Ivanhoe* and *Guy Mannering* in Portuguese translation. The two novels were being read by a young woman whom the English botanist described as a person of 'excellent learning': she even composed verse fluently. Who could that young woman have been in Minas Gerais in 1836, so well read, so gifted with poetic talent and such a great admirer of Walter Scott?

In the library of a scholarly friar in Bahia, in the early days of the nineteenth century, that prying Englishman Lindley came across not only astronomical instruments, which he immediately identified as English, but Smith's *Wealth of Nations*, Robertson's *America* and the works of Paine. Inflammatory material. English books were also found a few years later in the library of Dr Sabino – Locke, Newton, Pope, *Outlines of Midwifery*, *The Lancet*[75] –although the most widely read foreign literature at the time in both Bahia and Rio de Janeiro was French, and the best-known and most admired French author was Voltaire. Indeed, the Englishwoman Maria Graham wrote from Bahia in 1821 that many of those given to reading political works were disciples of Voltaire, whom they also followed in his 'indecency' with regard to religion: 'hence to sober people who have seen through the European revolutions, their discourses are sometimes disgusting.'[76]

On Rio de Janeiro in the same period, there is an account by another English observer, Mathison, who remarks that little was read in Brazil at that time, either in the interior or even in the towns. The most widely read books were French. English books were read almost solely by English residents in Brazil, of whom there were many in 1821 or, rather, a 'very considerable' number. In Rio de Janeiro, the British colony included

[74] Thomas Lindley, *Narrative of a Voyage to Brazil Terminating in the Seizure of a British Vessel and the Imprisonment of the Author and the Ship's Crew by the Portuguese, with General Sketches of the Country, its Natural Productions, Colonial Inhabitants and a Description of the City and Provinces of St. Salvadore and Porto Seguro to which are Added a Correct Table of the Latitude and Longitude of the Ports on the Coast of Brazil, Table of Exchange, etc.*, London, 1805, p. 108.

[75] Luís Viana Filho, *A Sabinada*, Rio de Janeiro, 1938, p. 146.

[76] Maria Graham, *Journal of a Voyage to Brazil, and Residence There, During Part of the Years 1821, 1822, 1823*, London, 1824, p. 147.

'respectable merchants, besides tradesmen, artisans, and others'.[77] Owners of counting houses in the Rua Direita, Rua da Alfândega and Rua dos Pescadores, as well as blacksmiths, shoemakers, tailors and shopkeepers. To these he might have added a few adventurers, although some spirit of adventure was present in all of them – in some more than others: even men of fortune or capital – 'respectable merchants' and not just 'tradesmen' – were taking a risk by coming to live with their families in the cities or wildernesses of a country so different from England as Brazil in the days of the colony or of Dom João VI.

Those differences gradually faded, not only as Britons came to live in the country, but also as Brazilians read English books in translation or imported British-made articles for domestic, personal or daily use. Such articles are the kind that most rapidly modify the culture of a people – culture in the sociological sense: cutlery, chinaware, foodstuffs, furniture, fabrics, ready-made clothing, hats, footwear, saddles and carriages. Not forgetting glass and iron which, when used in domestic architecture, diminished the use of the country's fine timbers; and machines, the influence of which on the poor, mixed-blood segment of the free colonial population (who, through using these machines and mastering their technical mysteries, found ways to raise themselves up socially and culturally) will be examined on other pages. Here I shall confine myself to noting that the influence of English machines on the Brazilian colonial population was the influence of a mystique and not merely a concrete or material influence.

*Gulliver's Travels*, *Robinson Crusoe* and *Treasure Island*, and not just Walter Scott's novels, have been read and re-read in Portuguese, if not in English, by many a Brazilian child and convalescent; and also by many a healthy adult equally familiar with the novels of Dickens and, in our days, with those of the Brontë sisters, Jane Austen, Conrad, Kipling, Wells and Conan Doyle, and the comedies and fantasies of Wilde, if not in the original then in Portuguese translations. As for poets and essayists, not every English writer – not even Shakespeare or Milton – has had the luck that has befallen Elizabeth Barrett Browning in recent years: to have found a translator for some of her sonnets who has a poetic talent equal to hers. Or the American educator Calkins, whose *Manual of Elementary Instruction* was translated from English into excellent Portuguese by Counsellor Ruy Barbosa, who was also the author of an essay on Swift, the famous *Cartas de Inglaterra* ('Letters from England') and an essay on the 'Torrens Law', which is a truly masterful interpretation of the spirit of British common law.[78] With regard to Spencer, his fellow-countryman James Bryce was

[77] Gilbert Farquhar Mathison, *Narrative of a Visit to Brazil, Chile, Peru and the Sandwich Islands During the Years 1821 and 1822*, London, 1825, p. 128 (phrase quoted in English – Translator).

[78] *Governo Provisório dos Estados Unidos do Brasil. Anexos ao Relatório do Ministro da Fazenda. Anexo*

surprised at the evolutionist philosopher's 'popularity' – among scholars and well-educated people, of course – not just in Brazil but throughout South America. That led him to ponder the fact that Spencer's books were more highly regarded by South Americans and Russians than by the English and North Americans.[79]

Mauá, Paranhos the elder, Carvalho Moreira, Sousa Correia, Joaquim Nabuco, Ruy Barbosa, Oliveira Lima, Eduardo Prado, Afrânio de Melo Franco and Régis de Oliveira II were elegantly anglophile in their methods of making or writing history. Indeed, in matters of history, the Brazilians owe much to an Englishman – Robert Southey – for his pioneering work, which has become a classic and has, to some degree, been completed by the work of another Englishman – Armitage's *The History of Brazil, from the Period of the Arrival of the Braganza Family in 1808, to the Abdication of Don Pedro the First in 1831*. 'João Armitage' is how his name appears in the Brazilian edition of his book, published in Rio de Janeiro in 1837 and 'translated from the English by a Brazilian'. On p. vii, Armitage writes:

> Perhaps there is no country with which the relations of Great Britain are so extensive, and yet of which she at the same time knows so little as the Empire of Brazil.

We should not forget the nineteenth-century Brazilians who were educated at British universities, schools or seminaries: doctors like Eustáquio Gomes or Rodrigo Soares Cid de Bivar, who, according to J. F. Velho Sobrinho in his *Dicionário Biobibliográfico Brasileiro* (Rio de Janeiro, 1922), was the first doctor in Brazil to use 'chloroform in natural childbirth', a technique he had learnt at the University of Aberdeen; clerics like Bishop Cardoso Ayres; engineers, technicians and merchants. Nor that Brazil in the last century was full of children named after illustrious Britons that the people here admired: Addison, Cromwell, Milton, Newton, Wellington, William, Walter (after Walter Scott), Gladstone, Spencer, Carlyle, Southey, Shakespeare, Earle Hamilton, Jack, Harvey, Herbert, Watson, Halley, Nelson, Lucy, Elizabeth, Victoria, and Mary – often Brazilianized as Maryzinha. Nor that the pseudonyms adopted by our political writers in abolitionist and liberal newspapers at the end of the

*B: A Execução da Lei Torrens na Capital Federal. Informação ao Chefe do Governo Provisório*, Rio de Janeiro, 1891. In this work, Barbosa, an eminent jurist, states that 'no people clings to the severity of ancient judicial practices more than the English'. Nonetheless, even in England, 'immemorial law' could not withstand the 'thrust of common sense' represented by laws like Torrens, which also represented 'today's industrial civilization'. It was as a result of 'the impacts of the simplifying reforms inherent' in this industrial civilization that the 'scaffolding of the old Roman formalism' was gradually collapsing (p. 20).

[79] James Bryce, *South America, Observations and Impressions*, London, 1913, p. 581.

last century were mainly the names of Englishmen and Americans noted for their liberal ideas. Nor that the Brazilian navy – still peppered with names of English origin even today – grew and developed by following English examples, Taylor being one of the Englishmen who most helped to improve naval technology in Brazil.

It would also be unfair to forget that, alongside all the exploitation of our gold by British imperialism, it was British technicians who were first responsible for raising the value of our red topaz, chrysolite and the blue variety of topaz known as Brazilian sapphire on the gemstone market. Clado Ribeiro de Lessa highlights this in the fascinating introduction he wrote to the Portuguese translation of John Mawe's book, *Travels in the Interior of Brazil, Particularly in the Gold and Diamond Districts of that Country* (London, 1812). He also points out the importance to Brazilians of another book by Mawe, a treatise on diamonds and precious stones, notable as a 'scientific, commercial and gemmological study of our precious stones'.[80]

Another fact to remember is that it was an English merchant living in Rio in the first half of the nineteenth century – a certain William Harrison – who helped to make Brazilian orchids known in Europe: his brother Richard's house in Liverpool became a 'Mecca to which orchid lovers paid annual pilgrimages'. The English doctor John Pechey had done the same for Brazilian ipecacuanha in the seventeenth century: he was one of those who had propagated it in Europe. Pechey even published a study on the Brazilian drug: *Observations Made upon the Brasilian Root Called Ipecacoanha* (1682).[81]

In 1830 Lindley praised the Brazil nut in his *Natural System of Botany*, and back in 1764, when Commodore Byron was in Rio de Janeiro, the English started to value the yellow wood from Brazil that they called 'fustick-wood'.[82] They later became great enthusiasts for our jacaranda, which they used for making luxury English piano cases: the famous English pianos of the nineteenth century. And more than one Englishman living in Brazil had furniture made here, including Mr Leveson-Gower, secretary to the British legation in Rio in 1882.[83]

[80] John Mawe, *A Treatise on Diamonds and Precious Stones, Including their History, Natural and Commercial, to which is Added some Account of the Best Methods of Cutting and Polishing them* (London, 1813). See Clado Ribeiro de Lessa's introduction to *Viagens ao Interior do Brasil... por John Mawe*, translation by Solena Benevides Viana, Rio de Janeiro, 1944, p. 8.

[81] Lilian Elwyn Elliott, *Brazil Today and Tomorrow*, New York, 1917, p. 312.

[82] *Viagem Feita à Roda do Mundo pelo Comandante Byron*, translated by Jacintho Alves Branco Moniz Barreto, Bahia, 1836, p. 21. (Translation of *A Voyage Round the World in His Majesty's Ship the Dolphin, Commanded by the Honourable Commodore Byron [...] By an Officer on Board the said Ship*, Dublin, 1767. 'Fustic' a yellow dyewood, is mentioned on p. 25 – Translator.)

[83] Ulick Ralph Burke, *Business and Pleasure in Brazil*, London, 1884, p. 53.

In a work in preparation about Rio de Janeiro, the writer Gastão Cruls, author of *Hiléia Amazônica* and a researcher always on the lookout for facts of botanical interest that concern the history of Brazilian culture, points out – as Von Martius did before him, similarly basing himself on the narrative of James Cook's travels, published in London in 1781 under the title *Collection of Voyages Round the World, Performed by Royal Authority* (with maps and engravings)[84] – that when Sir Joseph Banks, Captain Cook's companion on his voyage of circumnavigation, was exploring the island of Rosa[85] he 'had the pleasure of discovering the beautiful *Moraea Northiana* (Iridaceae) which was soon a focus of admiration in the gardens of Europe'. That was still in the eighteenth century. It should be noted that Cook's own report on his voyage, entitled *A Voyage towards the South Pole and round the World*, published in London in 1777, mentions Capevi or Copaíba balsam, which according to Elliott appeared in English gardens in 1774.[86]

In the early nineteenth century, a large number of tropical plants were collected from the interior of Brazil, classified with the greatest care and sent to the collections in Kew and Glasgow by the botanist George Gardner, superintendent of the Royal Botanical Gardens in Ceylon. He discovered one of those plants high up in the Serra dos Órgãos, at an elevation of about 4,500 feet; he named it *Cereus Russellianus* in honour of the late Duke of Bedford, and he was delighted to see it later in English hothouses.

Gardner's book, *Travels in the Interior of Brazil, Principally Through the Northern Provinces and the Gold and Diamond Districts During the Years 1836-1841* (London, 1846), is one of the most interesting ever written in English about not only the plants but the animals, people and customs of Brazil. Gardner is one of those who best represent British technology or science when it is moved by that age-old spirit of adventure that sometimes leads the people of Albion into almost quixotic activities or attitudes. So

[84] George William Anderson (editor), *A New, Authentic and Complete Collection of Voyages round the World, undertaken and performed by Royal Authority. Containing an authentic, entertaining, full, and complete history of Capt. Cook's first, second, third and last voyages*, London, 1784-1786. This is a compilation of the accounts of James Cook's three voyages, on the last of which he was killed in Hawaii. Banks had sailed with Cook on the first voyage (Translator).

[85] *Sic*, for Rasa, a small island at the mouth of Rio de Janeiro harbour (Translator).

[86] Elliott, *Brazil Today and Tomorrow*, p. 313. Freyre has misread Elliott here, and confuses two captains who had similar names and wrote books with somewhat similar titles: Captain James Cook (whose surname Freyre spells with a final 'e'), author of *A voyage towards the South Pole and round the world: performed in His Majesty's ships the* Resolution *and* Adventure, *in the years 1772, 1773, 1774 and 1775* (London, 1777) (the account of his second voyage); and the writer whom Elliott actually mentions in this connection: Captain Edward Cooke, author of *Voyage to the South Sea, and Round the World, perform'd in the years 1708, 1709, 1710, and 1711, by the ships Duke and Dutchess of Bristol* (London, 1712) (Translator).

quixotic in the case of this absent-minded Briton that one day he arrived in Arraial de Cocais, in Minas Gerais, having almost completely run out of money. He therefore decided to turn to the English manager of one of the British mining companies operating there, a Mr Goodair. He asked him for twenty-five pounds. There ensued a clash between technology and capital, between scientific adventure and commercial routine, between the Don Quixote of Science and the Sancho Panza of Money: contradictory aspects of the British character as much as of the Spanish. Mr Goodair refused to help his fellow-countryman. He advised him to seek the help of the company doctor: he was a Scotsman like Gardner – a somewhat ironic statement, given the Scots' reputation for miserliness – and might feel inclined to help him. After saying that, he walked out without even bidding the botanist good day. Gardner admits that his personal appearance – deeply sunburnt, wearing the same clothes in which he had set out from Rio de Janeiro, and his body suffering from the fatigue and privations of his long travels – had perhaps contributed to making a poor impression on Mr Goodair. In any case, this clash between two Britons in a remote town in the middle of Brazil during the first half of the last century is significant.[87]

In 1845, Mr Bridges – another Briton, like Gardner, who was keener on adventure than routine – was exploring a tributary of the Mamoré, when he reached the shores of a lake hidden away in the middle of the Amazon forest and came across a colony of Nymphaeaceae water-lilies floating on its waters. He was dazzled. So much so that he was about to dive into the waters of the wonderful lake. He was saved from this Byronic impulse by the common sense of the Indians with him, who just in time pointed out the wild alligators lazing near the seductive plants. The romantic Englishman then rushed back to the town of Santa Ana and found a canoe there to take him to the tropical marvel.

Mr Bridges later left for England taking the seeds of the Amazonian plant with him in damp mud. Two of them germinated in the aquarium in the hothouse at Kew. One was then sent to the large hothouses at Chatsworth, where the temperature was raised specially to receive such a noble guest. The Amazonian plant developed rapidly there, and grew so large that a child could stand on one of its leaves. What could be more charming than a little blonde, pink-cheeked English girl standing on the leaf of an Amazonian plant?

The first bud of the plant cultivated in England opened at the beginning of November 1849. The open flower was offered to Queen

87 George Gardner, *Travels in the Interior of Brazil, Principally Through the Northern Provinces and the Gold and Diamond Districts During the Years 1836-1841*, London, 1846, p. 487.

Victoria by the man who designed the Crystal Palace, Sir Joseph Paxton. Lindley had already given the name *Victoria Regia* to the plant from Brazil, which the Indians called *Uapé Japona*. That is how the story is told by Fletcher and Kidder in their *Brazil and the Brazilians*.[88]

When Loudon, the author of *Hortus Britannicus* (1830), wrote in his *Encyclopaedia of Gardening* (1835) that some of the most beautiful flowers in British gardens originated from South America, there were not yet any *Victoria Regia* in England. And George Gardner the Scottish botanist had not yet travelled through Brazil on the memorable journey mentioned above.

The London Royal Horticultural Society, however, had had collectors of rare plants in Brazil since 1830. Moreover, more than one British merchant who had settled in Brazil after the opening-up of the ports spent his spare time in the surroundings of the cities collecting plants, which gardeners sought to acclimatize in English gardens.

Despite Hooker's statement, quoted by the geographer Mrs Elliott, that for more than half a century England was 'the grave of tropical orchids', by 1850 the cultivation of orchids in that country had turned into a splendid victory for British gardening.[89] That victory had been helped not only by more or less romantic naturalists but also by English merchants who had settled in Brazil: apparently prosaic, middle-class men like Mr Harrison.

The begonia is another plant that British gardens owe to Brazil, or to tropical America – since the flora is not always confined or characterized by political frontiers – just like 'hundreds of other beautiful plants'.[90] Beautiful and delicious plants. The latter include pineapples (*Ananas sativa*). Which shows that the English in Brazil almost always tried to combine the useful with the agreeable. Gold digging combined with caring for simply beautiful plants.

Several of the initiatives involving British capital or labour in Brazil became famous: mining companies in Minas Gerais, such as Gongo Soco; shoes made by Clarke, and fabrics made by Coats in São Paulo and Carioca in Rio; the Harrington & Starr and the Bowmann foundries in Recife (where the De Mornays' tradition is also kept up); the old firms of Stevenson's and Duder's in Bahia, specializing in the cacao and whale-oil trades; Boxwell's in Pernambuco, specializing in cotton; Clark's in Piauí and Maranhão, specializing in carnauba wax with the drive of a far-sighted pioneer; and Wilson's and Cory's with their coal depots, shipyards

[88] Fletcher and Kidder, *Brazil and the Brazilians*, pp. 570-572.

[89] Elliott, *Brazil Today and Tomorrow*, p. 310. The British botanist Joseph Hooker (1817-1911) was the director of the Royal Botanic Gardens, Kew, and a great friend of Charles Darwin (Translator).

[90] Phrase quoted in English (Translator).

and lighters famed throughout Brazil; the British Bank, the London and Brazilian Bank, the River Plate Bank, the Hotel Bennett, Mrs Brack's *Casa Ingleza* in Recife, Proudfoot & Co. of Rio Grande do Sul, and the *Casa Ingleza* of Ceará, founded by William Wara, an Irishman who had arrived in that part of Brazil in 1811. According to the historian Raimundo Girão, in his excellent *História Econômica do Ceará* (Fortaleza, 1947), this last establishment was renowned in the commerce of Ceará for its service and its longevity (p. 236), continuing the tradition of the schooner *The Mayflower*, which, in days long gone, brought calico, china, silk stockings and fine cotton cloth from Liverpool to the people of Ceará (p. 215). And it should not go unrecorded that it was an Englishman linked to a shipping company, Mr John Gordon, who discovered that the beaches of southern Bahia and Espírito Santo were full of monazite sands. Mr Gordon soon started sending large quantities of these sands to England as ships' ballast; the Brazilian authorities, however, did not immediately realize the value of the sands, which appeared to be like any others, except shinier. Their value was eventually discovered and duties were imposed on such ballast material; 2,114 tons of it were exported in 1908, to Brazil's profit. At the end of the 1914-18 war, British investments in Brazil were calculated to be worth £300 million;[91] numerous English firms were established here; many English ships were plying between Brazil and other countries; and a considerable number of English articles were consumed by Brazilians, especially the middle classes.

Such British influence on Brazil's economy and culture went back a long way. One of its earliest economic manifestations must have been the trade in dried cod ('poore John') – Newfoundland cod – an old connecting rod between the English and Portuguese that continued to tie the Portuguese in Brazil to the English, the Brazilians to the British. Another connecting rod was the two Methuen Treaties, under which Portugal was reduced to a virtual British colony.

The exploitation of Brazil's gold by the English is yet another old aspect of British relations with the Brazilian sub-colonial economy. These relations were for a long time indirect – through Portugal – and became direct only after the Imperial Brazilian Mining Association was set up in 1825. By that time the British merchant colony in Rio de Janeiro was a power that, without any exaggeration, may be described as imperial: apart from economic privileges, it even came to have its own judge in the new capital of Brazil, as it had in the former one, Bahia. From up in their country houses, usually situated on hills and surrounded by groves of trees,

[91] Elliott, *Brazil Today and Tomorrow*, p. 291. On this subject, see also the book by William Scully, who was the director of the *Anglo-Brazilian Times*: *Brazil, Its Provinces and Chief Cities; the Manners & Customs of the People; Agricultural, Commercial, and Other Statistics*, etc., London, 1866.

the more opulent of those merchants gradually exerted a renovating and even revolutionary influence on the semi-colonial culture of Brazil.

One of them, Mr Duval, once held a dinner for Brazilians from Rio with the aim, quite scandalous at the time, of introducing mutton to our gentlefolk's tables.[92] Gentlefolk who, owing to some strange religious prejudice, had until then never dared to touch mutton: it was 'the meat of the Lamb of God'. A daring Englishman was thus responsible for starting a real revolution on the country's tables, which, also due to English or British influence, were enriched with the habit of consuming wheat bread, ale and porter, and tea. Even champagne,[93] it seems, was introduced into certain regions of Brazil not by the Portuguese or the French, but by the English. There is some reason for ordinary people to call it '*bebida de lorde*' – 'the drink of lords', *lorde* and *lordeza* (lordship) now being words as Portuguese as their synonyms *fidalgo* and *fidalguia*. Except that a *lorde* is always a rich *fidalgo*.

The organization of a cavalry corps in Dom Pedro I's army was due to another Englishman, Colonel Bacon. British influence on the organization of Brazil's land forces, however, cannot be compared to the influence of English adventurers or experts on the organization of our navy. One need only mention Grenfell, the Earl of Dundonald, or Taylor, referred to above. As technical experts they were powerful agents of British penetration in Brazil, which was still virtually isolated from northern Europe. Even so, when Commodore Byron was in Brazil in the late eighteenth century, after observing how slow the work in the Rio de Janeiro dockyard was, 'from their making use of small narrow tools', he found something surprising: the stern-piece, which was made from a whole cedar tree. Byron also noted that, although an English caulker could do more in one day than his local counterpart could do in three, on the other hand the workers in the Brazilian dockyard performed their work more thoroughly, which enabled Portuguese ships made in Brazil to withstand very long voyages.[94]

English seamen did not always disembark in Brazil as mere observers, as Commodore Byron did. There is much to relate about the exploits of British officers and men in the ports of Brazil of old. It is a subject that would demand an essay of its own. More conspicuous than mere merchants or technicians, British sea dogs were always inclined to treat

[92] Walsh, *Notices of Brazil*, II, p. 88: 'He procured some sheep, fattened them well, invited the people to dine with him, and placed before them mutton cooked after the English fashion; he induced them with some difficulty to taste it.'

[93] *Ibid.*, II, p. 88.

[94] Byron, *Viagem Feita à Roda do Mundo*, p. 19. (*A Voyage Round the World*, p. 17. These observations were in fact made by the anonymous author of the book, who describes himself merely as 'an Officer' on Byron's ship, and not explicitly by Byron himself – Translator.)

Brazil as a country that ought to belong more to them than to the Brazilians or Portuguese. An English sailor is credited with the feat of having climbed the Sugar Loaf mountain one day in the early nineteenth century and planted a Union Jack on its summit; the Brazilian authorities had considerable trouble in removing it.[95] Other English seamen did the same on the Brazilian island of Trindade, perhaps less as a prank than in earnest. The first English sailors to explore the island were the crew of the *Agamemnon*, also in the early nineteenth century. Even so, they came across some American Robinson Crusoes already there.[96]

Ever since the seventeenth century – since the treaty of 1661, or in fact that of 1654 – the government of Portugal (which was so jealous of the gold and precious stones of Minas Gerais that it had decided to turn Brazil into a kind of new China closed to foreigners) had granted the English the right to keep four British families in each commercially important city in Brazil: Pernambuco, Bahia and Rio de Janeiro. Throughout that period, these families enjoyed the protection of their Commissioners of Trade and Plantations, who, as good commissioners, always staunchly upheld the right – apparently not always exercised – to have four families residing in each of the three most important cities in colonial Brazil. After the arrival of Dom João VI in Brazil, these English families were favoured with privileges that no other nation enjoyed. One such privilege was that only 15% duty was paid on British-made merchandise, as calculated by His Britannic Majesty's consuls, whereas the rate payable on other foreigners' products was 24%, the value of their merchandise being fixed by the Portuguese authorities according to their invoices. It was almost as if a British flag were flying over Brazil's customs houses, through the efforts not of arrogant sea dogs but of the wily foxes of British imperial diplomacy, who did their work on land but were always ready to call on the dogs at sea. The fact is, however, that after a period of almost scandalous economic and even political privileges, the British started offering easy credit to their Brazilian clients and investing capital in our country to a degree that the French, who had long been their main rivals, never attained. The English would only be exceeded in this lavish confidence in their South American clients by the Germans, and then only in the twentieth century.

In acting in this way, the English, like the Germans after them, were of course only serving their own interests. That is precisely the point made by a work on trade and navigation published in French by M. F. J. de Santa-Anna Nery in 1889; as if to spur on French capitalists, who were being excessively cautious in their relationship with Brazil, it transcribes

[95] W. H. Koebel, *British Exploits in South America. A History of British Activities in Exploration, Military Adventure, Diplomacy, Science, and Trade, in Latin America*, New York, 1917, p. 372.
[96] *Ibid.*, p. 293.

the following statement from the *Fortnightly Review*:

> From Brazil's railways alone, over the last thirty years English capitalists have made the enormous sum of 135 million francs, yielding six to seven per cent interest.[97]

There is no doubt that Brazil owes a considerable part of its economic progress and cultural development to this 'colonizing capital'; but there is equally no doubt that some of the railway companies in Brazil gave the British enormous profits. Scully, an Englishman, was not entirely right when he grumbled about British railway companies in Brazil from a commercial viewpoint, in his book published in 1866, although he considered them necessary for the European colonization of this country; and he wanted to see his countrymen taking part in that colonization:

> Industrious farmers, and persons who will turn their attention to agriculture or grazing...[98]

In an essay on the economic position of the British in nineteenth-century Brazil – a work as notable for its lucidity as for its assured scholarship – Professor Manchester points out that, despite the Prince Regent's decree favouring or encouraging British immigration to Brazil (which for more than a century, that is to say since 1661, had been limited to those families who were, so to speak, strategically located from an economic point of view: four of them in Pernambuco, four in Bahia and four in Rio de Janeiro), such immigration had always been low in numbers of people, although significant in technical and economic impact. Among those few immigrants were mechanics, bankers, merchants, doctors, technicians and engineers,[99] but not many farmers. Even though he lived in Brazil for many years, Scully never had the pleasure of seeing them settle the fertile lands of the south in as large numbers as the Germans, who are more inclined than the English to face the adventures of establishing farms in foreign lands.

They were mainly merchants and engineers, as Professor Manchester might have added, in view of the importance of the engineer in the days of the carboniferous[100] civilization that had come into the world with

[97] *Le Brésil en 1889*, Paris 1889, p. 461 (quotation translated directly from Santa-Anna Nery's French rather than from Freyre's Portuguese version – Translator).

[98] Scully, *Brazil, Its Provinces and Chief Cities...*, p. 398 (quoted by Freyre in English – Translator).

[99] Alan K. Manchester, *British Preëminence in Brazil, Its Rise and Decline. A Study in European Expansion*, Chapel Hill, 1933, p. 75.

[100] The word is used in this sense of 'coal-based' by Lewis Mumford in *Technics and Civilization* (New York, 1934): 'Carboniferous capitalism' is a section heading in his chapter IV, 'The

the Industrial Revolution and was centred on Great Britain. It must be emphasized again that, among the engineers, it was railway engineers that were to play a particularly notable role from the middle to the end of the nineteenth century, given Brazil's size and its growing importance as both producer and importer as a result of the development of rail transport. In the early decades of the nineteenth century, a large proportion of the articles imported from Great Britain were consumed in Rio, Bahia and Pernambuco – including hats, footwear, china, glass, cheese, butter, mirrors, hams, various types of cloth, iron, steel and drugs. By the end of the century, however, the Brazilian market had expanded, due in large part to the development of rail transport. Railways also helped in the export of Brazilian goods to Europe. Gold, diamonds, precious stones, sugar, cotton, hides, tobacco, eau-de-vie and Brazil-wood itself were at first the main Brazilian products imported by the British; subsequently, rubber and coffee were to become more important.

With the claws of a lion, British trade soon controlled almost the entire Brazilian market, leaving mere scraps for the French and the United States. Professors Manchester and Rippy have explored the subject in well-documented works, and it has also been examined from the French standpoint by Say[101] and Jay, the latter in the introduction he added to Koster's book, which he translated from English into French in 1818, adding discerning notes and comments. In this introduction Jay wrote:

> The apparent abolition of the colonial system was therefore merely a change of metropolis; and Brazil stopped depending on Portugal to become a colony of Great Britain.[102]

In an admirable page of synthesis, Professor Rippy highlights the rapid development of Britain's trade with independent Brazil – independent from Portugal, that is – to a great extent attributing it to the skilful efforts of British 'diplomacy'. One might add that this 'diplomacy' should include the work of consuls, which was less obvious than that of the ministers to the Court in Rio de Janeiro, but longer-lasting or more constant. From £20,000 in 1825, British trade with Brazil rose to almost £30,000 in 1830. By 1829 English bankers already had £6,000 invested in Brazilian

Paleotechnic Phase' (Translator).

[101] Horace Say, *Histoire des Relations Commerciales entre la France et le Brésil*, Paris, 1839.

[102] *Voyages dans la Partie Septentionale de Brésil depuis 1809 presqu'en 1815... par Henri Koster, traduits de l'Anglais par M. A. Jay*, Paris, 1816, I, p. xl. (Freyre quotes the sentence in French – Translator.) Koster's work is something of an apologia, as it seeks to highlight the advantages Brazil gained from the trade with Great Britain, which British diplomacy had succeeded in basing on a reciprocity that was more apparent than real. On this subject, see also the equally apologetic pages written by Silva Romero, an anglophile.

government bonds, and English money put into mining was yielding good profits for the English.[103]

Like Rippy, Professor Manchester notes that Brazil's relations with Great Britain came almost to resemble those of a colony with its mother country. Indeed, Liverpool began to absorb a large part of the cotton from Bahia and Ceará, and Great Britain as a whole took three quarters of the cotton exported by Pernambuco and half of its sugar, while the articles carried by English ships from Pará to Europe included cacau, coffee, rubber, timber and sarsaparilla.[104] Although other factors also affected the rate and volume of such exports, including, for instance, the development of beet sugar and improvements in cane sugar production outside Brazil, several of these products became more profitable to export once the railways, almost all built by British technicians or with British capital, provided the main sugar-, coffee-, cotton- and hide-producing areas with easier access to the major Brazilian ports than the means of transport used in colonial times: barges, ox-carts and mule trains.

In 1835 – the year when the Limpo de Abreu Law was passed, authorizing the government to grant favours to one or more companies that would construct railways from the capital of the Empire to the provinces of Minas Gerais, Rio Grande do Sul and Bahia – the goods sent from Great Britain to Brazil were worth a little over two and a half million pounds sterling. In 1854-55 – with the first trains running on the Mauá Railway from Rio to Fragoso on 30 April 1854, after the first locomotive to run in Brazil had been blessed by Canon Chaves – their value had doubled. In 1863-64 the goods were worth forty-one per cent more than in 1854-55, and in 1873-74 fifteen per cent more than in the previous decade. Although Professor Manchester does not claim that the correlation between this economic phenomenon and the development of rail transport in Brazil is as important as it is considered to be here, he not only highlights those successive rises in the value of British exports to Brazil from 1835 to 1874, but he also points out that between 1835 and 1912 the British managed to increase their sales in this part of the Americas by 600 per cent. The American scholar confines himself to noting the important role played by the British in developing rail transport in Brazil; and he transcribes the estimate given by the consul-general Mr Rhind in his report for 1901 that British capital invested in our country amounted

[103] J. Fred Rippy, *Rivalry of the United States and Great Britain over Latin America (1808-1830)*, Baltimore, London, Oxford, 1929, p. 130. On this subject see also C. K. Webster, *Britain and the Independence of Latin America, 1812-1830*, London, New York, Toronto, 1938. This is a two-volume selection of documents from the Foreign Office archives.

[104] Manchester, *British Preëminence in Brazil*, p. 32. See also Alberto Randolpho Paiva, *Legislação Ferro-Viária Federal do Brasil (1828-1871)*, Rio de Janeiro, 1922, 13 vols.

to approximately thirty million pounds by that date.[105]

To Professor Manchester it seems that Pernambuco, just as much as Rio and, later, São Paulo, was a 'centre of special English interest' in Brazil, in terms of the British capital invested in this part of Brazil in both railways and other major improvements. The number and importance of British firms operating in Recife in the mid-nineteenth century point to the truth of that generalization. In fact, Recife became one of the major centres of radiation of British influence in Brazil in the early part of that century on account of the large community of English businessmen who settled there after the ports were opened up, some of them with their families. Henry Koster states the importance of this colony of English merchants in almost autobiographical terms, as he was one of the Englishmen who settled in Pernambuco as part merchant and part farmer: he owned the Amparo sugar plantation. He describes it so vividly that we can watch as their influence on the landscape, life and culture of the region expanded during a period that was, so to speak, decisive. He witnessed changes in domestic architecture and, for example, saw the dark, heavy lattice screens disappear from many houses, to be replaced with glass windows and iron balconies,[106] although he tells us nothing about the source of this glass and iron, which were among the most characteristically British articles. He mentions three families from England living in Recife who would go out to walk every afternoon 'for amusement', and their habit was soon imitated by many of the local families.[107] He remarked on the replacement of silks and satins – probably from the Orient – for dresses worn on high days and holidays with white and coloured cotton fabrics: articles made in England. And the replacement of cocked hats with round hats. And he did not fail to notice the sometimes ridiculous appearance of orientally fat local ladies – whose size would better be suited by Oriental fashions in dress, it may be noted in passing as a brief comment on the Englishman's observations – when they sought to imitate European, or English,[108] fashions designed for more slender women than those of Brazil. Designed for women who were already creatures of the new industrial civilization of northern Europe, which was less strict than the feudal civilization in separating or distinguishing a woman's figure from a man's.

Much of that 'special interest' should be attributed to the fact that the British had viewed Recife as an economically strategic point for their commercial operations in Brazil ever since the sixteenth century. Strategic in that it was the ecological centre of an entire economic region in which

[105] Manchester, *British Preëminence in Brazil*, p. 324.

[106] Henry Koster, *Travels in Brazil*, London, 1816, p. 188.

[107] Ibid.

[108] Ibid., p. 189.

all roads led to that regional metropolis, closer to Europe and Africa than any capital of Brazil, and favoured by the winds as a port for sailing ships. Hence the considerable number of British firms that had long been established in the capital of Pernambuco or, rather, the capital of the North-East – the region that was to be dominated by the Great Western of Brazil. The *Almanak de Pernambuco para o Anno de 1845* introduces us to their names, which were not always spelt correctly: Charles Roope & Co. (in Rua do Trapiche), Deane Youle & Co. (Rua do Torres), Fox Brothers (Rua da Conceição), F. Robilliard (Rua do Trapiche), G. Kenworthy & Co. (Rua da Cruz), João Stewart (Rua do Trapiche), Johnstone, Pater & Co. (Rua da Madre de Deos), James Crabtree & Co. (Rua da Cruz), Mc Calmont & Co. (Praça do Corpo Santo), Russell Mellors & Co. (Rua da Cadeia), Wm. E. Smith (Rua do Trapiche), Latham & Hibbert (Rua do Trapiche), I. Ridgnay & Co. (Rua da Cruz), Adamson Howie & Co. (Rua do Trapiche), Henry Gibson (Rua da Conceição), Ricardo Royle & Co. (Rua do Trapiche), Diogo Cockshott & Co. (Rua do Trapiche), Johnston & Vash (Rua da Senzala Velha), Roope Brooking (Rua da Moeda), and Guilherme Collins Cox. Alongside these twenty major English businesses, established mainly in the Rua do Trapiche and the Rua da Cruz, there were just nine Portuguese, eight French, seven German, three American, two Dutch and two Swiss, while even Brazilian businesses numbered no more than twenty-seven. A truly meaningful list.

Any shipping line calling at Recife on its voyages between Rio and Great Britain would place that imperial group of merchants residing in the metropolis, if not of the whole North of Brazil, then of almost all the North – the North of sugar and cotton, at least – in contact with the capital of the Brazilian Empire: Rio de Janeiro. At that time, Rio de Janeiro was still the economic metropolis of the South, until Santos became the coffee port and the gateway through which the produce of much of the country's southern economy would pass.

In those days of Rio's economic and not merely scenic and political splendour, a list taken from the *Almanak dos Commerciantes* by the historian Octávio Tarqüínio de Sousa, a copy of which he has kindly passed on to me, tells us of the number of British merchants there towards theend of Pedro I's reign and the prestige they enjoyed compared with local merchants and those from other countries. In terms of imperial might, their numbers and prestige remained almost unchanged from the days of Dom João VI until the middle of the century, although it bears repeating that from 1840 onwards, with the development of coffee in the São Paulo area, São Paulo and Santos lured or enticed British technicians and merchants who had a keener nose for opportunity. The Rua Direita in Rio, however, remained the centre of English imperial domination in Brazil, as that and the adjacent streets – Alfândega, Pescadores, Rosário, Quitanda and Viola – were the location of the major stores or trading houses of such important businessmen as Alexandre Gilgillan, MacGrowther, Boog, Pearson & Co., Bourdon and Fry, Brown and Douglas, David Stephenson, Diogo Birkhead, Diogo Hartley, Brown Watson & Co., Guilherme Scott, Henrique Miller, Heyworth Brothers & Co., Guilherme Platt, Holland, Dale, March, Sealy, Walker & Co., Plowes, Roseal & Co., Bates, Rostrom, Brink & Co., Hudson, Warre & Co., Carlos Baker, Thomas Russel, Carlos Cannell, Jorge João Dodsworth, and George March, to mention only a few.

Of all these Englishmen who had set up business in Rio soon after the ports had been opened up to foreign trade, none stood out so much for their opulent lifestyle as George March. In *O Rio de Janeiro como é (1824-1826)*, on page 26 of the Portuguese translation of this work published in Rio in 1943, C. Schlichthorst describes March's *quinta* or country-house as one of the principal residences in the district of Botafogo, rivalling that of the Russian vice-consul, the palace of the Duke of Lafões and the house in Moorish style of Antônio Pereira – all houses that caught the eye for the 'beauty of their gardens' and their 'architectural and ornamental richness according to each owner's national taste'.[109] A sign that it was less a *quinta* in the usual sense than a residence to the British taste adapted to the tropics. So much so that there, as in the houses of the consul, Mr Chamberlain, the consul's wife, Lady Amherst, and the rich English businessmen, Johnson Clark and T. Hardy, the furniture was in the 'styles of Adams, Chippendale, Hepplewhite, Sheraton and Queen Anne', according to information obtained by the eminent architect Adolfo Morales de los Rios Filho for his book *O Rio de Janeiro imperial* (p. 303). Incidentally, Professor Morales de los Rios Filho spells March's name as Marck on more than one occasion.

Yet it was not only in Botafogo that March left the mark of his English taste on the landscaping and layout of his house. He also did so in Teresópolis. He had built a country house there prior to 1821, having acquired a land grant measuring no less than four square leagues in the Organ Mountains.[110] That information is given by Mr Armando Vieira in his book *Teresópolis* (1938), where on page 10 he claims that the life of Teresópolis as a summer resort began with March, who spread the habit of spending the summer in the mountains to other foreigners and to

[109] *Rio de Janeiro wie es ist: Beiträge zur Tages- und Sittengeschichte der Hauptstadt von Brasilien*, Hanover, 1829, p. 287 (Translator).

[110] The Serra dos Órgãos, a range rising to over 2000 m that runs approximately east-west some 50 km north of Rio de Janeiro. Four square leagues in Brazil was about 174 km$^2$ or 67 square miles (Translator).

Brazilians. A not insignificant revolution in the habits or lifestyles of Rio's nobler inhabitants. That revolution was brought about by the example set by this Englishman, who, there as in Botafogo, changed the Brazilian landscape by adding British elements to it or softening it to accord better with British taste. What March established on his land in Teresópolis was in fact a model farm producing a variety of crops and livestock. After building the farm headquarters high up at the Campo das Éguas, he added fields of cereals and potatoes at Quebra-Frascos – the potatoes were highly prized in Rio and were perhaps the first to be cultivated in Brazil, according to Vieira – while he kept his foals and yearling cattle at Imbuí, today called Posse, 'a name that applies to the whole broad valley of that stream'. Vieira assures us that the Englishman made lawns in all parts of his farm and tended them with great care and affection. Through the labour of his African slaves, March placed such a British stamp on the landscape of his Teresópolis estate that even today, more than a century after he had his summer residence up in those mountains, tracts of land are still said to be covered in 'Bermuda grass'.

In an interesting recent article, 'Aspectos Serranos', which appeared in the *Jornal do Commercio*, Rio de Janeiro, on 16 April 1944, Mr Virgílio Corrêa Filho stresses the importance of March's farm in the founding of Teresópolis:

> The nucleus of human settlement first emerged from the original farm headquarters, a short distance from the pass now known as Alto do Soberbo...

It seems possible that March not only brought Brazilians themselves to the as yet unappreciated heights of Teresópolis, by passing on to the people of Rio the salutary habit of spending the hottest months in those mountains now famed for the mildness of their climate and the beauty of their scenery, but also inspired people elsewhere who were seeking to tame tropical nature in accordance with European styles. In that respect, Mariano Procópio[111] was perhaps a follower of March. When the English consul, Burton, visited Juiz de Fora in 1868, he discovered in that Brazilian's already well-established property that 'our fastidious English taste could find no fault in house or grounds, except that they were a little fantastic', since 'the contrast with Nature was somewhat too violent – an Italian villa-garden in a virgin forest'. The Italian villa-garden lay next to Chinese bridges. But the grass on which Burton stretched out to eat

[111] Mariano Procópio Ferreira Lage (1821-1872), a politician and engineer who built the first macadamized highway in Latin America between Petrópolis and Juiz de Fora, opened in 1861 (Translator).

oranges may have been English, and there were Wellingtonias in the park. It is worth reading the entire description that Burton gives of Mariano Procópio's strange property in *Explorations of the Highlands of the Brazil* (London, 1869), I, pp. 51-53.

In Bahia, Maria Graham's notes for 1821 reveal how important the colony of English merchants was in relation to Bahian society and economy at that time, a situation that appears to have persisted almost unchanged throughout the first half of the nineteenth century. The English merchants established there dismayed Maria Graham with their solely commercial or material concerns:

> ... whose thoughts are engrossed by sugars and cottons, to the utter exclusion of all public matters that do not bear directly on their private trade; and of all matters of general science or information.[112]

They did not know the names of the plants that grew beside the doors to their homes. They were not acquainted with the country ten miles outside Salvador. The men gambled as much as the Portuguese. The ladies danced and loved music. They lived well – good drink, good food and good delicacies – although Mrs Graham did not think the food these English people gave their slaves to be the best. They were not, in their countrywoman's opinion, people 'of the first order'.[113] But there was an Anglican chaplain and a hospital for English sailors there, and a dispatch addressed to the British consul in Salvador from the president of the province in 1831 reveals that the English in Bahia during the first half of the nineteenth century indulged not only in gambling, good food and merry dancing, but also in the theatre. And they would soon provide the School of Medicine established there with two extraordinary practitioners: Dr Abbott or Abbot and Dr Paterson. So they were not so strictly concerned with their trade as they appeared to be to Mrs Graham, although she must have had her reasons for retaining a better impression of the English people she met in Pernambuco.

Among the important English businessmen in Recife in 1845 were the De Mornays: the two engineers who first thought of planning a railway for the North-East similar to the one Thomas Cochrane had been dreaming of for the Rio de Janeiro-São Paulo-Minas Gerais triangle since 1840. What is more, the De Mornays' dream seems to have been for a railway to link the centre of 'special interest' to the British imperial economy – Pernambuco – with the capital of the Brazilian empire, where

[112] Maria Graham, *Journal of a Voyage to Brazil*, p. 148 (quoted by Freyre in English – Translator).
[113] *Ibid.*, p. 148.

British interests had grown even more substantial since the days of Dom João VI. As Mansfield states:

> ... the De Mornays are getting up a project for a railway to Rio de Janeiro ...[114]

When they did not achieve that, one of the De Mornays, at least, contented himself with associating his name and brains with the lesser but nonetheless grandiose scheme of a railway from Santos to São Paulo, an idea thought up by the head of a trading firm in Santos. The initial technical studies for this 'grandiose project' were the work of 'the English engineer Mornay',[115] whose activities had begun in Pernambuco, as we have seen, where they roused the enthusiasm of Mansfield, a quasi-socialist.

Mansfield was an enthusiast for the socialism of Charles Kingsley but at the same time an apologist for British or at least Anglo-American expansion into Portuguese America, since he confessed with romantic candour – a confession that irritated Burton, his compatriot – that he was 'continually thinking, what would not be made of this place in the hands of Englishmen' or Anglo-Saxons,[116] since he was convinced that Brazil was going to be 'the garden of the world' and the gardeners would be Anglo-Saxons, either 'Englishers or Yankees', doubtless in conjunction with blacks. In Pernambuco, Mansfield himself associated not only with the De Mornays but also with those British merchants who were then so important and living in such numbers in Recife. He tells us of the McCalmonts' counting-house on the shore of the harbour – a harbour marked out by reefs and full of ships, most of them English.[117] He notes how ignorant the English living in Pernambuco were of the region and its products; they could tell him nothing, for example, about palms and their varieties. Referring more specifically to the English residents of Recife, he records that it was said that more than 300 English people were living there at that time – out of a total population of 70,000, a third of which were slaves. He says they then had a church and maintained a clergyman.[118] He finds it lamentable that they live in the city 'with such necessities as England yields'.[119] He points out that it would be better to have just one well-organized British merchant house than the twenty that existed, each of them selling the same goods as their neighbours or competitors. He was

[114] Mansfield, *Paraguay, Brazil and the Plate*, p. 41 (quoted by Freyre in English – Translator).

[115] Adolpho A. Pinto, *História da Viação Pública de São Paulo*, São Paulo, 1903, p. 26.

[116] Mansfield, *Paraguay, Brazil and the Plate*, p. 72.

[117] *Ibid.*, p. 34.

[118] *Ibid.*, p. 74.

[119] *Ibid.*, p. 75 (quoted in English – Translator).

sad to see English merchants – 'real gentlemen, well-educated, fine-hearted men' – lounging among their crates of goods and fancying themselves 'of use' and 'of superior dignity' to other traders.[120]

As a half-socialist or, at least, co-operativist, Mansfield felt that what Brazil – including the British colony in Recife – needed was 'association', which in his view was even more necessary in the tropics than in temperate climes.[121] He even says that when Britain had a socialist government it would set about promoting home industry by using capital raised by direct taxation to develop those enterprises that were most favoured by nature and most needed by the people. Yet they should not, he cautions, spend money on iron factories in Brazil; it would take at least a century before Brazil could become a metallurgical country. In his view our country should be principally agricultural, producing food and exporting it to the whole world instead of importing even manioc. And the development of agriculture should be done with free labour and Anglo-Saxon capital.[122]

Mansfield – who was to die soon after his trip to South America, still young and already one of the most notable chemists of the new generation – then astutely asks: 'How is it that English money is not invested in the improvement of this land, where, without the necessity of naturalization, any foreigner can purchase the soil?' There was, of course, the difficulty of labour. Meat-eating white men (Mansfield was a vegetarian) proved incapable of working the fields in Brazil; and black men worked unwillingly and without any interest at all – which the Englishman found perfectly natural: 'and they are quite right, poor fellows!'[123] Mansfield must have concluded that in the predominantly feudal economic system in Brazil black people had no kind of incentive for agricultural work; they merely worked for parasitic, albeit often benignly paternal, masters. Even so, Mansfield – an Englishman educated in Cambridge, incidentally – observed that he had found surprising dignity in the appearance and bearing of slaves in Brazil; he wished he could see the cheerfulness he had found in these slaves among the poor people of England. Because the English, according to him, were slaveholders just as much as the Brazilians. For Mansfield the half-socialist, where there is competition, that is to say economic competition, there is always some form of slavery; that was the case of his England – the England of the early decades of the Victorian era; the England of the first big factories and the horrors of the exploitation of the poor by the rich described so acutely by Dickens; an England ironically characterized by

[120] *Ibid.*, p. 76.

[121] *Ibid.*, p. 75.

[122] *Ibid.*, pp. 70-71.

[123] *Ibid.*, p. 71 (quoted in English – Translator).

Mansfield as having 'highly cultivated followers of Christ for lords...'[124]

The Anglo-Saxons that he dreamt of seeing spread throughout Brazil, not as merchants, who were strictly individualistic and competitive – like the score of them he had come across in Recife in the mid-nineteenth century – but as arable and livestock farmers able to associate together and with the black people, about whom he once again enthuses, regretting that he had not been able to fraternize with them in Bahia, would be examples of the advantages of 'association' or co-operation among men. They would – if we can perhaps interpret Mansfield's forthrightness in this way – usher in an era of co-operative or fraternal imperialism of the kind that Whitman later dreamt of for Anglo-Americans.

Of the voices of English technicians who ventured to remark on the social situation in nineteenth-century Brazil – voices which have come down to us through diaries or travel writings – none is as modern or up to date as that of Charles Mansfield the chemist, the Cambridge MA. He was perhaps somewhat romantic, an admirer of Charles Kingsley. But man does not live on realism alone; he also lives on romanticism. The danger lies in living on only one or the other of these 'isms', each of which is just as incomplete or insufficient for life or art as the other; each of which needs the other to become complete and fertile.

The agents of British penetration in Brazil during its most active phase, that is, from 1808 to 1914, were individuals as varied in kind as the Reverend Tilbury – English teacher to Pedro I, who must have been a terrible student (it seems in fact that he learnt more English from his groom, who was British, than from the reverend, since the groom taught him a good many curses and swear words in English, as another Briton, the Reverend Walsh, discovered) – and Bates, the naturalist. They all played their part in this penetration, each one in his own way and for his own reasons. Purely for the sake of methodological convenience, it is reasonable to reduce that variety to technicians and adventurers, engineers and merchants. Missionaries, pure scientists, governesses, artists, acrobats, and rich noblemen who only came to Brazil to visit the tropical forests and hunt jaguars, do not sit easily in this squared-off simplification hostile to the rounded edges of those vocations that are more complex or delicate than purely technical or commercial activities are. Or than the adventures of the coarsest pirates – Englishmen like Knivet, Barroway or Barwell (who spent the rest of his life in our country, where his name was naturalized as Baruel), James Lancaster, Edward Fenton or Thomas Cavendish, whose sailors pillaged the town of Santos back in 1591. Or the misadventures of more Conradian treasure-seekers such as Knight, or the Stammers

[124] *Ibid.*, p. 30 (footnote) (quoted in English – Translator).

brothers, Englishmen who lived in the quiet little town of Lorena in São Paulo state and suddenly set off for the island of Trindade in 1896, in search of treasure hidden there by the English pirate Zulmiro.[125] Perhaps it was the effect of some dream or a ghostly apparition: one of those dreams or apparitions that are so common among the English.

Some of the railway engineers themselves were more than just engineers, just as some of the British consuls, ministers, merchants and vicars were more than just consuls or merchants or vicars. Burton, for instance – Sir Richard Burton – is remembered less for the official papers that he signed as Her Majesty's consul in Santos than for the book he wrote on Brazil, or for the books he translated from Portuguese into English, sometimes in conjunction with his wife, a staunchly orthodox Catholic. When in 1836 John Armitage published his *History of Brazil from 1808 to 1831* – a continuation of Southey's work – he had been a merchant in Rio de Janeiro for many years. The Reverend R. Walsh, having been chaplain to the British colony in Rio in the early years of the nineteenth century, left us a fascinating book on our country. Similarly, Luccock and Koster were merchants who wrote books.

As regards J. J. Aubertin, who disembarked in our country as a railway engineer in 1860, less is known about what he did in Brazil as a technician in his field than as a scholar fascinated by the genius and poetic work of Camões. The first book he read on arriving in Brazil was *Os Lusíadas*. He was so impressed with the poem that he decided to translate it into English. He worked on the translation for seventeen years. His work was published in London in 1877 and was received by critics with high praise for his literary talent as a translator.[126]

There were, however, Britons who came to Brazil merely out of literary interest in the exotic aspects of our countryside or our lives. Kipling was one of them. Another was Cunninghame Graham, the author of *A Brazilian Mystic*, a biography of Antônio Conselheiro.[127]

Let us not forget, either, that virtual British institution that English doctors became in nineteenth-century Brazil: Dr Dickson, Dr Coates and Dr Cochrane in Rio; Dr Paterson and Dr Abbott or Abbot in Bahia; Dr Loudon and Dr Mayer in Pernambuco; Dr Hall and Dr Arbuckie in Maranhão; and Dr Morson in Minas Gerais. Doctors from the time of the

[125] Aureliano Leite, *História da Civilização Paulista*, São Paulo, 1946, p. 152.

[126] William C. Atkinson, *British Contributions to Portuguese and Brazilian Studies*, London, 1945, p. 21. (Burton also published his own translation of the *Lusiads* in 1880 – Translator.)

[127] Antônio Vicente Mendes Maciel (1830-1897), better known as Antônio Conselheiro ('the Counsellor'), was the messianic leader of a near-communist community at Canudos, Bahia, which was savagely destroyed by the government in 1897 (Translator).

medical supremacy of Edinburgh and Aberdeen. Doctors from the time of the supremacy of calomel treatment. Doctors from the time when the remedies that most cured people included – as they still do – English milk of magnesia for digestive upsets, fruit salts for excesses of eating and especially drinking, and pastilles for the coughs of preachers and parliamentarians. These doctors have also phlegmatically waited for a biographer who is also a historian of British influence in Brazil. I trust my friend José Valadares will not take too long to publish his essay on Dr Abbott.

The most romantically adventurous Englishmen to have been in Brazil deserve a separate study. They were pirates, such as those of the early days of the colony – fierce men like Lancaster, who made Portuguese in sixteenth-century Pernambuco pull carts full of sugar along the rough roads of the time,[128] but who, in contrast, is thought to have been the first European to use lime juice against scurvy. Or eighteenth-century adventurers like a certain son of an illustrious English family who, to avoid dishonouring his father's name, adopted the pseudonym James George Semple Lisle. Under this name, before coming to Brazil, he had been in France during the Terror, as well as in Russia, Germany and Denmark, always getting into debt, seducing women and fighting duels.[129] In Brazil he very much admired the Brazilians' sense of cleanliness and hygiene, especially in Rio Grande do Sul; once, naked but for a pair of slippers, he ran through the streets of Salvador chasing a certain Bahian tailor who had incurred his displeasure, perhaps less for botching his work than for tactlessly trying to collect what he was owed.

Not to be forgotten are those adventurers – the word is not used here in a pejorative sense – of a modern kind, such as Savage Landor, Colonel Fawcett, Peter Fleming and the afore-mentioned E. F. Knight – the almost Conradian character who went searching for old treasure on the island of Trindade (an island that for some time was highly coveted by British imperialists) and whose book on his travels and excavations revealed a man disappointed not only with the barren island but also with republican Brazil.

And there were the Englishmen on board the sixteenth-century

[128] 'The Prosperous Voyage of Master James Lancaster to the Towne of Fernambuck in Brazil, 1594', in *The Principal Navigations Voyages, Traffiques & Discoveries of the English Nation made by Sea or Overland to the Remote and Farthest Distant Quarters of the Earth at any Time within the Compass of these 1600 Years, By Richard Hakluyt*, London, 1927, vol. 8, p. 26.

[129] *The Life of Major J. G. Semple Lisle; Containing a Faithful Narrative of his Alternate Vicissitudes of Splendor and Misfortune. Written by Himself*, London, 1799. On this subject see the study by Alfredo de Carvalho, 'Tribulações de um Degradado Inglês no Brasil', *O Estado de São Paulo*, 29 September 1908, reprinted in the posthumous publication edited by the Governor Estácio de Albuquerque Coimbra, *Aventuras e Aventureiros no Brasil*, Rio de Janeiro, 1929.

(1530) ship commanded by William Hawkins, who left their compatriot Martin Cockeran behind in Brazil and took a genuine Indian chief back to England, where he died; there were the Englishmen from Southampton, one of whom was Robert Reniger, who in 1540 were already trading with Brazil in their own manner and in the manner of the time; there was Pudsey, who was trading with Bahia in 1542; the Englishmen of the *Minion* who were invited by Whithal or Whithall to come to Santos to negotiate with sugar-rich Brazilians;[130] Abraham Cooke's Englishmen, who already in the sixteenth century were engaged in trafficking black slaves from Bahia to Santa Fé; Withrington's Englishmen, who did not sack Bahia in 1586 only because they feared that the Jesuits and their Indians would resist; James Purcell's Englishmen, who tried to settle in the Amazon in 1626 and were expelled from there by the governor of Maranhão's troops; the Englishmen following Roger Fry or Roger Frere – another one who tried to conquer the Amazon in the seventeenth century, apparently with some method and good resources because, soon after he had died fighting the Portuguese, a ship arrived in that part of Brazil bringing 500 English settlers, some of whom were imprisoned.[131] These adventurers were coming to colonize the Amazon.

But of all aspects of the *misters'* influence in Brazil, perhaps the area most deserving of study is the work of civil engineers. That means both railway engineers like Wells or Dent and port engineers like Sir John Hawkshaw, for example, or Charles Neat, who directed the work to modernize the Rio de Janeiro docks, which was described by Borja Castro in an interesting illustrated quarto volume published in the capital of the Empire in 1877. Or indeed sanitary engineers, like Douglas Fox or Oswald Brown. There were also foundry or factory technicians and actual manufacturers or importers of machinery, half technicians and half merchants. It is almost impossible for a Brazilian to hear about machines, engines, tools, railways, tugs, dredges, submarine cables, telegraphs, iron and steel ware, mechanical toys, sprung chairs, chinaware, bicycles, skates, sanitary ware, warships, steamships, launches, or gas or coal-burning stoves without thinking of the English. The English are associated like

[130] See 'The First Voyage of M. William Hawkins of Plimmouth, Father unto Sir John Hawkins, to Brazil Anno 1530'; 'The Second Voyage of M. William Hawkins to Brazil, 1532'; 'The Voyage of M. Robert Reniger and M. Tho. Borey to Brazil in the Yere 1540'; 'The Voyage of Pudsey to Baya in Brazil 1542'; 'A Letter Written to M. Richard Staper by John Whithal from Santos in Brazil, the 26 of June 1578'; 'A Letter of the Adventures for Brazil sent to John Whithal dwelling at Santos, by the Minion of London, dated the 24 of October 1580'; 'The Voyage of M. Stephan Hare in the Minion of London to Brazil anno 1580'; all in Hakluyt, *The Principal Navigations*, vol. 8, pp. 13-25.

[131] Michael G. Mulhall, *The English in South America*, Buenos Aires, London, 1878, chapter 2. See also 'The Voyage of M. Edward Fenton and M. Luke Ward his Viceadmirall etc.'; 'The Voyage of M. Robert Withrington, etc.'; and 'A Discourse of the West Indies and the South Sea written by Lopez Vaz, etc.', in Hakluyt, *The Principal Navigations*.

no other people with the beginnings of the modernization of material living conditions in Brazil: the conditions of production, housing, transport, recreation, communication, lighting, food and relaxation in our country. Only in recent times have they been equalled and, in some areas, outdone by the Germans and above all by the Americans, the makers of machines and engines now famous around the world and sought after by almost everyone. In the case of railways, the Americans have succeeded in developing their industry to such an extent in the last fifty to seventy years that the name of one American locomotive manufacturer – Baldwin – has, more than that of any Englishman, become an everyday word in Brazilian Portuguese to mean not only any large locomotive but indeed any particularly powerful machine or even man: 'That's a *balduína*' or 'He's a *balduíno*.' There are some people in Brazil called 'Balduíno' – José Balduíno, Antônio Balduíno, João Balduíno – named after the American locomotive that inspired one of the most passionate cults or crazes among ordinary people in the areas first served by that imposing engine.

A similar fate befell the English railway term 'sleeper', which became naturalized as *sulipa*, as mentioned in the recent work on the Great Western of Brazil by Professor Estêvão Pinto, who, however, has overlooked the importance of the word *balduína*, which from being a railway term became a household word. The word *sulipa* also crossed over from railways into the erotic or phallic vocabulary in Brazil, although this significant fact is not recorded by Professor Estêvão Pinto in his interesting study, in which he also fails to mention other anglicisms of rail or road transport origin, such as *breque* ('break', a type of carriage, or 'brake'), *macadame*, *bonde* ('tram'[132]), *tílburi* (from the inventor's name), *cróssima* (from 'crossing', referring to the frog), *sulaque* ('slide-valve'), *troli* ('trolley'), *tênder*, *vagão* ('wagon') and *loré* ('lorry'), *vitória* ('victoria', Queen Victoria's favourite kind of carriage), *cab* and *faeton*. Nor should we forget *Lloyd*, which crossed over from England's maritime and trading vocabulary to Brazil's, together with *paquete* ('packet-boat'), *brigue* ('brig'), *escuna* ('schooner'), *cúter* ('cutter'), *iate* ('yacht'), *destróier*, *chalupa* (from the Dutch *sloep*, apparently through the English 'sloop'), *deque* ('deck'), *scout*, *wharf*, *coque* ('coke'), *estoque* ('stock'), *warrantagem* ('warranting'), *iarde* ('yard'), *doca* ('dock'), *grumete* (from 'grummet', a cabin boy) and *grumetagem* (all a ship's cabin boys), and *bolina* ('bowline'). Nor *publicau*, an anglicism derived from 'public house' which for a long time meant a hostel or bunk-house in Rio de Janeiro, which was much visited by British sailors and ruffians. Incidentally, one such Englishman, a certain Thomas Barret – a criminal on his way to Australia – is credited with the first crime of counterfeiting

[132] The word appears to be derived either from the financial bonds issued by an early tram company, or from the name of a person or company who introduced this form of transport (Translator).

uncovered by the police in Brazil. That was in 1787.[133]

I trust Professor Estêvão Pinto will allow me to mention this and other so-called sins of omission that in my view he has committed in his Great Western study, which is to be published soon. Such defects, however, will not make his work less interesting to the more acute reader or the more understanding critic. On the contrary: a Wildean might perhaps arrive at the paradox that perfect or complete works are the most insipid kind in the world, since they hardly allow the reader or critic any chance to collaborate with the author. When they are good – that is to say well organized, well written and well documented – defective works may be considered more interesting than complete ones, on account of the collaboration that they demand or elicit from those readers or critics who only really enjoy reading a book when they are invited to collaborate with the author, by filling out his ideas or details at some points, or enlivening his information or moderating the force of his generalizations at others.

Professor Estêvão Pinto's main sin in his new work is not immoderate generalization but these sometimes serious omissions; he fails to mention one feature of the Brazilian railway complex – the dust-coat – which for a long time I assumed was of British or Indo-British origin. That is, until I discovered that both Hastings Charles Dent, an English engineer who specialized in building railways, who was here in 1885, and other foreign observers were surprised to come across that picturesque and useful habit in Brazil. Dent suffered greatly from all the dust on a train journey from Rio to Queluz. He found himself covered in veritable clouds of it. That was when he noticed that stylish Brazilians protected themselves from the dust of the tropics by travelling in dust-coats.

Dr. Rebouças[134] is with us [he wrote in one of his letters to England, in which he refers to this notable Brazilian mulatto, a fellow-engineer]; he and all the Brazilians travel in long white cotton coats down to their ankles, or else white ponchos, to keep off the dust.[135]Andrews too remarked on the Brazilian habit of wearing dust-coats:

> It is the fashion among Brazilian male passengers to wear brown or white linen over-coats to keep off the dust...[136]

[133] Mello Barreto Filho and Hermeto Lima, *História da Polícia no Rio de Janeiro*, Rio de Janeiro, undated, I, p. 130.

[134] André Pinto Rebouças (1838-1898) was an engineer, politician and abolitionist of Afro-Brazilian descent (Translator).

[135] Hastings Charles Dent, *A Year in Brazil*, London, 1886, p. 25 (quoted in English – Translator).

[136] C. C. Andrews, *Brazil, its Conditions and Prospects*, New York, 1887, p. 135 (quoted in English – Translator).

He had already observed that in Brazil the sleepers were laid on more or less sandy soil; none of the Brazilian railways had been built on rocky ground, which would be the only way to avoid all that dust.

Not all dust-coats were simple cotton or even linen tunics or overcoats. There were even silk dust-coats, fit for princes. Just forty years ago,[137] someone who boarded a first-class carriage on the Recife-São Francisco Railway – a line that Burke, who knew a lot about railways, did not hesitate to call 'a very good line'[138] in a letter he sent from Recife in 1882 – would still have found among the dark-haired gentlefolk one or two fair-haired people, like some Wanderley or Acióli Lins[139] truer to their Nordic origins, preparing for their train journey from Cinco Pontas as if it were a Muslim ceremony, dressed almost liturgically in white: wearing immaculate white or pale-coloured dust-coats. They were the most opulent or distinguished travellers on that line. Plantation owners, vicars, magistrates, doctors, lawyers and politicians who were also landowners and had been slave owners as well. The aristocracy from Cabo, Escada, Serinhaém, Rio Formoso, Palmares and Água Preta. In Rio, the Imperial capital, dust-coats were worn at that time even on longer tram journeys; and Ramalho Ortigão even spotted the *corps diplomatique* – the foreign ministers and *attachés* residing in Rio – going to greet the emperor on a reception day, not each buried in his own private carriage, but all on the tram 'to avoid the bumpy roads', wearing bowler hats and 'sealed up from top to toe in whitish dust-coats'. Unfortunately, he does not tell us what those dust-coats were made of; he just says that the top hats and swords of the dust-coat-clad ministers followed behind in their carriages.[140]

Since he had only visited the south of Brazil, Dent never encountered those genteel travellers on the Great Western in southern Pernambuco wearing linen and silk dust-coats, which, however, did not prevent the greedier of their wearers from stocking up at the stations, and even making a mess of themselves, with mangaba fruit (the famous Prazeres mangabas) cashew apples, conserves, sugar flowers, sugar twists, fish, biscuits and crabs. Dent gave in to the temptation of protecting himself from the dust with what he calls 'a white cotton overcoat'. In a letter dated 20 July 1885 he tells his family and friends that he had acquired a dust-coat for his journeys. The English engineer also adopted Brazilian ways by purchasing a blue

[137] At the beginning of the twentieth century (Translator).

[138] Burke, *Business and Pleasure in Brazil*, p. 119 (quoted in English – Translator).

[139] Names of upper-class families in Pernambuco, Wanderley being of Dutch and Acióli of Florentine origin (Translator).

[140] Ramalho Ortigão, 'O Quadro Social da Revolução Brasileira', *Revista de Portugal*, Porto, 1890, II, p. 98.

poncho lined with scarlet with a black collar, in southern Brazilian style, to keep out the morning and evening cold on his longer railway journeys.[141] Incidentally, before Dent another Englishman, the aforementioned Burke, who had seen half the world and was particularly familiar with British railway projects and companies abroad, was travelling by train from Rio to Barra do Piraí in 1882 when, enchanted with the novelty of the spectacle, he observed that all the Brazilian first-class passengers were

> wearing long white coats or cloaks, looking like a company of priests or acolytes. But it seems this over-garment is de rigueur...[142]

Also by Burke is a page of almost lyrical enthusiasm for the typically British but entirely timber-built house belonging to Mr Hunt, an English engineer and superintendent of the Minas and Rio Railway, where he (Burke) stayed in Cruzeiro. Hunt's house reminded him not only of the Hotel Badrut in Saint Moritz, but also of the little Indian bungalows of Mofussil,[143] from which the architect had perhaps taken his inspiration. The well-travelled Burke rather arrogantly calls his compatriot's bungalow 'an oasis of cleanliness and civilization and comfort in the midst of – the contrary',[144] and points out the whiteness of the linen tablecloths and sheets, the crystal and glassware, the furniture, the good food and the English newspapers and magazines as veritable delights for a civilized person's palate and eyes. An overstatement, perhaps, by a Fradique-like[145] Englishman who, isolated in the almost archaically pastoral and rustically feudal Brazil of Emperor Pedro II, felt nostalgic for the characteristically English comforts and refinements of the British upper-middle class or aristocracy of the latter half of the nineteenth century. There is no doubt, however, that English railway engineers and technicians like Mr Hunt, together with other Englishmen and women – merchants, bank managers, industrialists, teachers, governesses – in Brazil in the later part of the last century and the beginning of this, acted not just as experts in their individual specialities but as agents or transmitters of the values – and not merely propagators of the inconveniences – of Victorian British civilization, which was superior to any other in Europe or the Americas in the technical aspects of and middle-class attention to housing, leisure and food.

[141] Dent, *A Year in Brazil*, p. 43.

[142] Burke, *Business and Pleasure in Brazil*, p. 76 (quoted in English – Translator).

[143] Freyre seems to have understood this word to mean a specific place, whereas it denotes any rural or up-country area, as correctly used by Burke: 'an Indian Mofussil station' (Translator).

[144] Burke, *Business and Pleasure in Brazil*, p. 77.

[145] A reference to the fictional poet and traveller Fradique Mendes, introduced by Eça de Queirós and Ramalho Ortigão in the novel *O Mistério da Estrada de Sintra* (1870) and developed by Eça in *Correspondência de Fradique Mendes* (1900).

On one of his journeys through the interior of that still rustic Brazil, Dent watched as the locomotive stopped near Carandaí and was surrounded by a crowd of people who only wanted to wash their hands, face or feet with water from the engine. This water was eagerly collected by others in pots and pans for cooking.[146] Scenes like this must have been repeated with Great Western trains wherever they stopped in the more arid parts of the North-East. Scenes like this and scenes like another that Dent recorded as well: cattle often strayed onto the line, holding up the trains. Another clash between carboniferous civilization and the patriarchally agrarian or pastoral civilization of tropical and semi-tropical America.

In the history of the Great Western, as in that of other railways built in Brazil by Britons through areas that were still sparsely populated or inhabited by a rustic population, more than one English engineer must have found himself in the situation Mr Dent experienced in Minas Gerais: that of being seen by the people of the interior as a curiosity, a strange being, a heretic who might even have duck's feet, in short an 'Englishman'. Frederick James Stevenson – the Englishman who gave Thomas Edison his first job on a railway when the great inventor was still a young lad: selling newspapers on the Grand Trunk Railway – was known as '*O Inglez*', 'the Englishman', when he was in the hinterland of Alagoas in 1867; one day, while going up the River Panema, he heard the crew of his boat remark 'Holy Mary! What devils these English heretics are!'[147]

In Barra de Panema Stevenson found a young lad who offered himself as a guide to '*O Inglez*' in those lands. Like the grown men of those parts, the youth wore a long dagger at his waist. 'What is the dagger for?' asked the British engineer. The lad replied that it was for killing anyone who insulted him. At that, Thomas Edison's patron could not help giving the rustic boy a lesson in British ethics:

> In England we do not kill people who affront us, but only knock them down with our fists.[148]

That was perhaps the first boxing lesson ever given by a British railway engineer to a Brazilian adolescent armed with a knife. In Minas Gerais, Dent found himself in the situation of being considered not only an '*Inglez*' but particularly a '*Senhor Doutor*' or '*Doutor Inglez*', because of the Brazilian tendency to use 'Doctor' for anyone well educated or with a degree, rather than just for medical doctors, dentists and veterinary

[146] Dent, *A Year in Brazil*, p. 43 (page number corrected – Translator).

[147] Frederick James Stevenson, *A Traveller of the Sixties*, London, 1929, p. 78.

[148] *Ibid.*, p. 79.

practitioners, as in Europe (except in Germany). In England, it is also used for theologians – Reverend Doctors – and the rare doctors *honoris causa* of the intellectual nobility of the kingdom or empire. For Hastings Charles Dent, who was trained in civil engineering at the Crystal Palace School and, like any good Anglican and Englishman, dabbled in natural history and theology, it was a surprise and a gift for his British sense of humour to be called '*Senhor Doutor*' by the people of Minas Gerais (Dent was in Brazil working for the Minas Central Railway). He became known in those parts as the '*Senhor Doutor*' or the '*Doutor Inglez*'.[149]

Unaccustomed to this Brazilian usage, Dent must at times have feared being called out to care for a smallpox victim or attend a woman in labour or extract a rustic's tooth or treat a cow's maggot-infested wound. A request that might perhaps have been made more imperative by the gleam of a dagger or knife. To comply as far as possible with the medical implications that the title of 'doctor' had to his English ears, he appears to have digested a copy of Chernoviz's *Dicionário de Medicina Popular*;[150] from its pages he learnt how to treat his own body, at least, as the work of building the railway kept subjecting him to some of the country's pests: chiggers, ticks and even botfly larvae. What he was very careful to guard against was smallpox, very common in Brazil at that time, and yellow fever, the bane of foreigners, particularly the British engineers or technicians who were forced to travel through the interior much more than the merchants installed in their residences in the healthier surroundings of Rio de Janeiro, Recife or Bahia.

Two other British railway engineers were in Brazil before Dent and Stevenson, and were known here as either '*doutores*' or '*misters*' depending on how they appeared to Brazilian eyes, since they did not wear graduation rings.[151] In their books, these two distinguished engineers left a record of their adventures as Englishmen and technicians in Brazil, a country which at that time, in the remote areas through which they journeyed, knew little about Englishmen or locomotives. The only machines they knew of were the old presses for making sugar or rustic mills for crushing manioc.

Few books on Brazil are as interesting as the one we owe to Thomas P. Bigg-Wither, an English engineer who specialized in building railways and who also enthusiastically advocated the settlement of Paraná by English farmers. The book is entitled *Pioneering in South Brazil* (London, 1878); in it the author reveals himself to be a typically English engineer, representative not only of his country but also of his time and his profession – imperial

[149] Dent, *A Year in Brazil*, p. 79.

[150] 'Dictionary of Popular Medicine', Paris, 1878 (Translator).

[151] It was, and often still is, the custom in Brazil for graduates to wear a ring identifying their profession (Translator).

England in the best days of Queen Victoria. The Great Britain of Robert Louis Stevenson. The spirit of adventure that was then beginning to inspire the youth of England was leading young men not only into adventures of piracy, or near piracy, on distant seas, as in the days of Queen Elizabeth and Sir Walter Raleigh, but into equally romantic, albeit less theatrical and more bourgeois adventures in new or underdeveloped countries that needed Great Britain's technology and capital and, according to some Englishmen, its bibles and missionaries as well.

James Wells, an engineer of Bigg-Wither's generation, confessed that when he found himself on his way into the interior of Brazil he felt as if transported to heaven. That had been his dream since boyhood: to force his way through the forests of a tropical country. He blamed Defoe and his *Robinson Crusoe*, Captain Mayne Reid and other writers of adventure stories for sending so many young Englishmen out on travels in the tropics; for encouraging so many to set out on adventures throughout the world; and for inspiring the expansion of the British Empire itself.[152] Consequently, the mystique of British expansion must have had deep literary and not just economic roots. He stated at the outset that from a young age he had been one of those Englishmen whom fate had decreed should leave his homeland in quest partly of adventure and partly of better opportunities 'than the crowded ranks of home seemed to offer.' Brazil had attracted him 'with the glamour of romantic imaginings of its wondrous tropical life...'[153]

This English engineer came to Brazil in the flower of his youth, full of dreams that were more down to earth than rose-tinted, more about adventure and technology than trade or material profit. He came not to the Brazil of Petrópolis, where refined and delicate foreigners at that time escaped from the sun, the heat, malaria and snakes, as if inside a vast English bell-glass. But to the Brazil of yellow fever, plebeian food cooked with masses of grease, onion and garlic, difficult journeys through marshlands, and cachaça instead of port wine. The Brazil of poor and even destitute rustics ('If London has her scenes of awful misery, so have the backwoods of Brazil,' wrote Wells[154]) for whom any Englishman was as rich as a Rothschild, even the young engineer with fair sideburns who arrived in their midst. He too must be rich. The rustics could not understand that this young engineer had come to face all kinds of perils in the interior

[152] James W. Wells, *Exploring and Travelling Three Thousand Miles through Brazil from Rio de Janeiro to Maranhão, with an appendix containing statistics and observations on climate, railways, central sugar factories, mining, commerce, and finance; the past, present, and future, and physical geography of Brazil.* 2nd ed., London, 1887, I. p. 41.

[153] *Ibid.*, p. vii (quoted in English – Translator).

[154] *Ibid.*, p. 402 (quoted in English – Translator).

not merely for the sake of adventure but also to make some money, and to use that money hard-earned in the tropics to establish a comfortably middle-class home in England. Despite their reputation for being rich, English engineers were received by almost everyone in Brazil with the best Christian hospitality. It was rare to find one exploited by self-seeking backwoodsmen or rustics.

Wells came to our country in the third quarter of the nineteenth century, at the very time the first railways were being built. His book rivals Bigg-Wither's and outdoes Dent's in its acute observation and rich information about Brazil in the time of Pedro II. In the time of the second emperor's maturity and not just his old age.

James W. Wells was the full name of that romantic Englishman who, at the same time, was terribly practical in his technical speciality: his hands were those of a workman and not just of a graduate in mathematics. From the notes he took in Brazil, he wrote a book in two volumes – like Bigg-Wither's – *Three Thousand Miles through Brazil from Rio de Janeiro to Maranhão*, which was only published in London many years after his stay in the Brazilian Empire, which he first visited from 1868 to 1873. In fact, he had begun writing the book in Olinda and finished it in Kent.

Wells remarks that in Brazil he, like any engineer or bachelor of law – such as Dent, as we have seen – was often called '*doutor*'. Doctors were so classified not so much for the universities they had attended but for their appearance or behaviour. They formed a caste who lost their privileges if they stooped to manual work like any labourer or ordinary man. As a civil engineer, Wells was often called '*doutor*', '*senhor doutor*' or 'the doctor'. On other occasions, he would suddenly lose the title or caste and be simply '*senhor*' or 'Mr Wells'. While he was working on the building of the D. Pedro II Railway, for example, he one day took off his jacket and rolled up his sleeves so he could more easily teach a group of workers how to make bricks; he noticed that to his assistants, newly graduated Brazilian engineers, he had immediately stopped being a '*doutor*'. He had become '*Senhor* Wells'. They could not understand how a '*doutor*' could roll up his sleeves, get his hands dirty with clay and mix with workers as if he were one of them.[155]

Wells also philosophically lists the various names by which he was known during his stay in Brazil: *estrangeiro, homem de fora, pagão, doutor, branco, inglês, bixo.*[156] He was generally addressed as '*doutor*' in the

[155] *Ibid.*, II, p. 45.
[156] *Ibid.*, II, p. 97. Wells himself translates these terms in a footnote as '"Foreigner," "a man from beyond their district," "pagan," "doctor," "white," "Englishman," "*bixo*." This latter means any living thing.' (Translator).

backlands and, like Dent after him, he sometimes had to act the doctor; in the backlands of Brazil in those days anyone who was a '*doutor*' ought to know how to treat the sick. Wells decided to approach less serious cases of disease with Cockle's pills.[157]

One of Wells's most interesting accounts concerns English railway workers – ordinary labourers – whom he eventually avoided and only wanted to hire Brazilians. Simple Brazilian backwoodsmen and rustics. He had been less than happy with a certain Mr Joe Mortimer, whom he had employed; he was an Englishman who claimed to be a former seaman. While searching for diamonds, this former seaman had ended up in Diamantina – a town with a name that seemed to attract all kinds of adventurers to its streets. Not having found his fortune in Diamantina, he had decided to offer his services to Wells the engineer, his fellow-countryman, who at the time was near the mouth of the Buriti Comprido. Wells put him in a group of his workers building huts for a camp. They gave the new English worker an axe, but he was fat and slow and proved useless and clumsy at manual work. Not only that: he was the butt of jokes and banter among the backwoodsmen. So the engineer decided to make his compatriot the camp cook. But Joe proved incompetent at that as well. One day, one of the *caboclos*[158] came to tell Wells that the beans were all burnt while Joe was so fast asleep beside the food that no one was able to wake him. He was drunk. He only got to his feet when his boss kicked and slapped him. He was doused with buckets of water. Wells dismissed him, hurt by the exhibition his fellow-countryman had made to the backwoodsmen. After recounting the case of Joe, he generalizes that his many years' experience of the 'lower class of Englishman in Brazil' had convinced him of the 'utter unworthiness' of such people in a tropical environment. They did not work. They would not work. Although they were well treated by Brazilian workers, they assumed superior, arrogant airs, squandered their high wages and became not only inveterate drunkards but workers that no employer could trust. There were exceptions, but he, Wells, had resolved not to hire English workers for engineering works in Brazil if he could possibly do without them.[159]

Burton had already discussed the subject. It was a matter of some importance in those days, since there were numerous British workers in Brazil in the middle of the nineteenth century: some had been brought to our country to work in building the railways; others had come earlier and worked as miners in the old British mining companies; yet others

[157] *Ibid.*, II, p. 104.

[158] A *caboclo* strictly speaking is a person of mixed indigenous and European ancestry, but the word sometimes refers to any rustic (Translator).

[159] *Ibid.*, I, p. 279.

worked in British foundries or workshops, like the one that had existed in Pernambuco since the beginning of the century. Burton, an upper middle-class Englishman, had contact in Brazil with some such countrymen of his, who were common labourers and manual workers. He concluded that in Brazil, as in the United States, European proletarians seemed to delight in asserting their 'independence', surpassing themselves in 'insolence', which he describes as 'unnecessary'. He was therefore scandalized by a former English seaman in Brazil who addressed him unceremoniously as 'Burton' the very first time they met.[160]

The 'insolence' or 'arrogance' of these white workers and their tendency to treat their middle-class compatriots as their equals and not their superiors can be explained. It was due to the feeling of superiority they acquired in a new physical and social environment. Any technical skill more advanced than that of simple backwoodsmen was, in such an environment, a form of superiority of the neo-European over nature. The mere fact of being a white man, and especially a fair-haired Englishman, a subject of the most powerful monarch in the world, made him feel he belonged to an aristocracy or a superior caste. This caste might have numerous subdivisions. But they were all one with respect to the black proletarian population of a poor country like Brazil, particularly the vast mass of slaves, with whom European – mainly English or French – mechanics and workers made a point of not being confused in the eyes of their middle-class compatriots. Hence the emphatic gestures and insolent attitudes in asserting their 'independence' – behaviour that was observed in English workers in Brazil by both Burton the consul and Wells the engineer, neither of whom, however, understood the reasons for such gestures and attitudes. This is a subject that I hope to discuss more thoroughly in another study: in notes to the new edition of an old essay that I am expanding and updating for publication in the near future. And also in one of the chapters of a new essay, soon to be published as well, on the social formation of Brazil, regarded principally as a patriarchal, slave-owning society, both at its height and in the process of disintegration. Here I shall confine myself to merely conjuring up the figure of ordinary English workers in Brazil in its first decades as a nation: railway workers, miners or clerks, not always properly understood by those middle-class Britons who settled in our country as merchants or industrialists or lived here as engineers or consuls during that time. Because those ordinary workers were not men of no importance in our life, but bearers of British culture, particularly technical culture, who made their contribution to the

[160] Richard F. Burton, *Explorations of the Highlands of the Brazil, with a full Account of the Gold and Diamond Mines, Also Canoeing down 1500 Miles of the great River São Francisco from Sabará to the Sea*, London, 1869, I, p. 263.

flourishing of English capital in Brazil and the material development of our country. Several of them had families here. They dissolved into the Brazilian population here. They rose in society here and changed their status.

Some English companies in Brazil during the Empire, such as the Morro Velho Company, afforded their workers who came out from England due protection and paid for their passage back to Europe in the event of illness. Others, however, abandoned them after dismissing them for whatever reason. The result was what Burton himself regarded as 'degradation': English workers wandering the streets in rags and barefoot, degraded because they had been arbitrarily dismissed from their employment. Some minor company official or workshop foreman had thrown them out. Hence Burton's suggestion that even those English workers who had been dismissed for ill conduct should have the right to return to England at the expense of the company that had brought them out. Such an obligation would, in Burton's view, make companies more circumspect in hiring workers.[161]

Burton found that the conditions for British workers to make a living at Morro Velho were almost ideal. They worked hard, outdone only by those who worked in England itself. Their drunkenness was mitigated, if not cured, by the opportunities that working at Morro Velho opened up so they could prosper, save money and go to England with their savings.[162] Consul Burton provides us with some interesting information on this subject – interesting both for the history of the English in Brazil and for the history of employment and workers' protection in our country. In this respect it seems that the way English capitalists dealt with their own people abroad was sometimes more advanced than the measures that applied within England.

Even so, there were English workers who ran away so as not to fulfil their contracts with their English employers established in Brazil. At a time when the law tended to protect the interests of the employer rather than the rights of free workers, such fugitives soon became cases for the police. That was what happened to Thomas Spink, who had been hired at Harrington & Starr's Ironworks at Boa Vista, Recife, but disappeared in 1830. A dispatch from HBM Consul in Pernambuco, dated 24 November 1830, now in the manuscript collection of the state's public library, casts some light on the affair, but only from the employers' viewpoint. In the dispatch, the consul informed the provincial president that he had received a complaint from Harrington & Starr against Thomas Spink, who had

[161] *Ibid.*, I, p. 264.
[162] *Ibid.*, I, p. 266.

been engaged by the ironworks – where many technicians and workers at that time had been brought under contract from England – 'under the regulations, for 3 years, as an ironworker'. He had abandoned his job, however, and taken money belonging to Sarah Johnson, with whom he was living. So it was likely he intended to leave Brazil. In the same dispatch, therefore, the consul asked the president of the province to order the arrest of the fugitive and sent His Excellency a description of the accused for police purposes. Unfortunately neither I nor my fellow researchers have been able to find this description in the Pernambuco archives. A pity, because what must have been a detailed description of this English fugitive would be valuable material for an anthropological characterization of a poorly studied type of Englishman living in Brazil: an Englishman who had come to our country as a worker, initially – in the first few decades following the opening-up of Brazilian ports to foreigners – for the mining companies in Minas Gerais and the Harrington & Starr Ironworks in Pernambuco, and later for building the first railways during the second half of the nineteenth century. On the case of Harrington & Starr versus Thomas or Thomaz Spink, the above-mentioned manuscript collection yielded only one other dispatch from HBM Consul in Pernambuco to the president of the province, in which the consul informed the Brazilian authorities that Spink was in Paraíba and that Messrs Harrington & Starr had asked him to petition the president to have him arrested and brought 'to this City and held in a secure place'.[163] It should be noted in passing that the Harrington & Starr Ironworks is one of those English institutions in Brazil in the first half of the nineteenth century that deserve special study, such was the influence they exerted in Brazil through both their technical innovations and the number of English technicians and workers that they brought to this country.

The situation of young men from Great Britain who came to Brazil to work as lowly clerks or assistants in British warehouses, merchant houses and trading companies seems to have remained deplorable for a long time. Poor and from modest middle-class backgrounds – *petit bourgeoisie*, that is – many of these fair-haired young men found themselves forced to live a life that resembled less an English romantic novel than a Russian one, sometimes ending in suicide. Deprived of contact with the families of important Englishmen – *grande bourgeoisie* – established in Brazil, and little access to Brazilian middle-class family life, they fell victim not only to the old Moorish habit of Brazilian patriarchal society, whereby families were closed to visits from young bachelors, unless very highly recommended, and to what a long-term English resident in Rio de Janeiro calls 'that

[163] Letter of 25 November 1830. Pernambuco State Library, manuscript collection.

snobbishness of English intercourse nowhere greater than in Brazil...'[164]

They were therefore left with no other kind of life than something close to what that same Englishman calls 'immorality and dissipation': in other words, nights with prostitutes, alcohol in excess and debauchery. The result was that some caught syphilis; having caught it, the weaker ones committed suicide, such was the deep-rooted English horror of syphilis. Others became maladjusted or neurotic for the rest of their lives. Far from being a great adventure to be remembered in their old age, their time in Brazil was a hellish experience for them. That was less due to Brazil, however, than to the rich Englishmen themselves, who were terribly snobbish towards their compatriots of modest or what they considered 'inferior' origins.

Of great interest not only for the history of the English railway companies in Brazil but also for the history of labour itself in this country are advertisements by English engineers or contractors for Brazilian workers. Such advertisements are valuable research material, the importance of which appears to have been missed by Professor Pinto. In one of them, dated 1 January 1859 and published in the *Diário de Pernambuco* newspaper, John Bayliss, agent for the contractor George Furness, offered a reward of 10:000$[165] to anyone who could supply him with 2,000 workers, required by the engineer in charge of the work of building the railway from Recife to São Francisco. But there were conditions attached: the deadline was by 20 February; 200 of the workers had to be 'mechanics or other skilled tradesmen'; ordinary workmen would be paid at a rate of 1$280 per day, while mechanics and others would receive 2$ to 4$ per day 'according to merit'.

From the same period is an advertisement published in the *Diário de Pernambuco* and signed by W. M. Peniston at 'the Chief Engineer's Office, Villa do Cabo, on 22 January 1859', in which the English Company (Recife-São Francisco Railway) says it wishes to 'make a contract to scrape, clean and paint the iron bridges of Afogados, Motocolombó, Jaboatão and Pirapama' in the then province of Pernambuco. To that end it wished to 'deal with any person who will contract to supply at least ten yokes of oxen and twenty horses to haul timber from the company's forests in Utinga de Baixo to the workshops in Barbalho.' It also wished to 'engage the services of two engineer's assistants and four surveyors who understand either English or French to receive their instructions in those languages.' Additionally, it needed 'bricklayers, stone cutters, carpenters and painters'. And the following note of cordiality or, at least, courtesy of the English

[164] Scully, *Brazil, Its Provinces and Chief Cities*, p. 7 (quoted in English – Translator).

[165] Ten *contos de réis*, or ten thousand *mil-réis*, a substantial sum at that time (Translator).

towards the region's plantation owners should not go unrecorded:

> Should any plantation owner in the vicinity of Villa do Cabo wish to make use of the company's sawmill in exchange for the service of oxen, he may so do by coming to an understanding to that end with the undersigned.

Here was the Industrial Revolution on good terms with the Feudal Reaction, in a truly remarkable exchange of favours or services between the English Company's modern sawmill and the old-fashioned oxen of patriarchal plantations.

It appears that not all of the terms and conditions agreed between the Brazilian Government and the English regarding the railway construction works were strictly observed. While the building of these railways and the employment provided on the lines already built, in their machine-shops and on their engines and trains, greatly raised the value of the free worker in Brazil, it is equally true that slave labour continued to be used. Had Professor Pinto delved deeper into this by no means insignificant aspect of a typical English railway company in Brazil, such as the Recife-São Francisco (later taken over by the Great Western of Brazil), he would have come across newspaper advertisements from the early years of the building of that line such as the following, placed in the *Diário de Pernambuco* of 6 July 1857:

> Any person who has slaves and wishes to hire them out to work on the railway at a rate of one mil-réis per day, or even free men who wish to be hired, should go to Rua Estreita do Rosário No 25, second floor.

The 'even free men who wish to be hired' is a moving sign of how arduous such slave work really was. The conclusion has to be that railway construction in mid-nineteenth-century Brazil made martyrs not only of fair-skinned Nordic men – the Englishmen who perished here from tropical diseases – but also of black- and brown-skinned people, not forgetting the Portuguese, large numbers of whom were used for the same gruelling work in Rio de Janeiro.

In another railway advertisement in the *Diário de Pernambuco* of 22 December 1858, John Bayliss asks anyone who has claims to make against George Furness, the contractor – including the slave-owners, of course – to put them in writing to him, Bayliss, 'so that they may be examined' and, if found correct, paid. All within 'seven days'. Bayliss was the agent for a contractor who must have taken pride in maintaining the prestige of 'an Englishman's word' and 'English punctuality'; there also seems to be no doubt that such English railway contractors helped to raise wages and improve working conditions for Brazilian workers from the mid-nineteenth century onwards. For mechanics, at least.

Furthermore, Professor Pinto should not have overlooked the significant remarks made by a Brazilian engineer, the editor of the *Revista de Estradas de Ferro*,[166] when abolition was adopted in 1888. In the *Imprensa Fluminense* of 21 May that year, Engineer Francisco Picanço stated that the railway was 'the material force that played the greatest part in the disappearance of slavery in Brazil.' By penetrating into the hinterland, it had provided agriculture with the 'means to prosper, replacing the nefarious institution of bondage with free labour.' It was not all that, for sure, but it was important.

During the construction of railways in Brazil, a large number of Englishmen fell victim to yellow fever and cholera. It should also be noted that the first accident on the D. Pedro II Railway, in 1859, caused the death not only of a Brazilian – the inspector-general of traffic – but by his side an Englishman – Isaac Howard, a contractor who built housing for railway workers.[167] That railway had been opened in 1858, and the name that had stood out on the locomotive at the centre of the festivities had been that of its maker, William Fairbairn, an Englishman: William Fairbairn & Son, 1853, Manchester. On the day after the opening, which had been on 29 March 1858, the *Jornal do Commercio* ran the news that the engine had devoured space, racing across the fields through frightened livestock. People then congratulated the British who had made that wonder possible.[168] The name of an English-educated Brazilian – Irineu Evangelista de Sousa, later the Baron of Mauá[169] – should not, however, be forgotten in any history written about the beginnings of the railways in Brazil. Neither Mauá nor the names of the De Mornay brothers or the romantic Dr Cochrane.

In the history of the Great Western, Professor Estêvão Pinto discovered among the names of victims of yellow fever and other diseases, such as 'Borthwick and his assistant Incken' (here we carefully follow the author's

[166] 'The Railways Magazine' (Translator).

[167] Barreto Filho and Lima, *História da Polícia* ..., II, p. 195.

[168] *Jornal do Commercio*, 30 March 1858. See also Koebel, *British Exploits in South America*.

[169] Irineu Evangelista de Sousa, Baron and Viscount of Mauá (1813-1889), was an industrialist and entrepreneur who in 1854 built the first railway in Brazil, between Porto de Mauá and Fragoso in the then province of Rio de Janeiro (Translator).

spelling of those names full of 'k's and 'w's[170]), that of a young poet who had died in Pernambuco of yellow fever: Stewart Lockyer, the author, according to Professor Pinto, of *St Bartholomew's Day and Other Poems* (1856) and *Earl Godwin's Feast and Other Poems* (1857). Why did the author of the work on the Great Western not delve deeper in his research on such an interesting figure of a poet adrift among engineers? In view of his literary talent, Lockyer may have written interesting letters to his family or friends about what he saw and experienced in Brazil.

In any case, it is clear that British 'colonizing capital' in this part of the Americas had at its service splendid examples of young men imbued with the spirit not just of adventure but of heroism. They came here for a bitter struggle with the age-old horrors of this tropical part of the world: malaria, yellow fever, cholera, snakes, wild animals, savage Indians, mosquitoes and the sharp knives of *moleques* or *capoeiras*[171], who were often fired up with nativism or 'Romanism' against the fair-haired foreign heretics – the English. I must say, in passing, that I hope on another occasion to publish an interesting document from an almost unexplored archive regarding the English dread of the knives carried by *capoeiras* and yokels.

Many Englishmen – not only engineers but scientists or naturalists – were also to be seen on expeditions through the interior of Brazil, forced to replace their whisky with cachaça, their lamb chops and bread with jerked beef and manioc meal, their port with *vin ordinaire*, their tea and biscuits with salt cod (which Dent found so revolting) accompanied by water from an earthenware jug or pitcher, their roast beef with *feijoada*[172] (which Dent found equally disgusting at first sight, although his palate eventually adapted to this most Brazilian of flavours), and their plum pudding with guava conserve. The early English travellers through the interior of Brazil, such as Mawe, had to guard against highway robbers, and they must have been just as horrified as he and Luccock were at the filthy kitchens of some colonial houses, even opulent ones. In compensation, however, there were gardens around many of the houses and villas of those times, with jasmine, carnations, roses and *Palma Christi* to perfume the air, making them a delight for Britons avid for tropical sensations.

Quite a number of Englishmen building railways in the Brazilian hinterland or studying the soils, people, fauna or flora of Portuguese America became so familiar with the culinary habits of the rural people that they became fans of the most regional delicacies, even when cooked in dirty, greasy earthenware pots by a black or Indian woman. Dent himself

[170] Letters foreign to the Portuguese alphabet in Freyre's time (Translator).

[171] People who perform *capoeira*, a formerly outlawed blend of dance and martial art which is now accepted and regulated as a sport (Translator).

[172] A stew of beans (usually black) and dried, salted meat, sometimes with vegetables (Translator).

admits to enjoying roasted flying-ants.[173] And armadillo and paca[174] meat. He also seems to have adapted to local orange gin and black tobacco. When Stevenson, the engineer, was in the Amazon region he tried not only *açaí* but also parrot with *cará*;[175] he enjoyed both the gruel and the meat, which reminded him of chicken. At the beginning of the century another Englishman, Waterton, a naturalist, had tried monkey with cayenne pepper, which he thought tasted like kid or he-goat.[176]

Stevenson, in the meantime, was once furious with his 'companion' on his journey through the hinterland of Alagoas – where he went as far as Paulo Afonso – when he discovered that the joker had strained the breakfast coffee through the sack used for soiled linen, which was also used for carrying the *mister's* boots and hammock – the coffee must have been very tasty.[177] On the subject of servants, early in 1847 HBM Consul in Pernambuco paid dear for the luxury of having an English cook, who of course was superior in cleanliness to local black cooks or Indian 'companions'. One Sunday night in January that year, the consul's chef – a 'John somebody' according to the article in the *Diário de Pernambuco* for 26 January 1847 – disappeared, taking with him three linen jackets, twelve Henry Low shirts, a morocco leather box from Russia containing seven razors and a silver teaspoon. The chef was a lean man, five feet six inches tall, with sparse hair and a dark beard, and about forty years old. He had already jumped ship from an English brig, the *Prompt*. He may be seen as an example of the Brazilian saying 'white in colour and black in deed', which is completed by 'black in colour and white in deed', sometimes said in the form 'dirty in colour and clean in deed'.

In his travels through the interior of Brazil, Dent the engineer could no longer bear sleeping on the ground and in 1885, like Stevenson in 1867, took to sleeping in a hammock like any backwoodsman. Dent's hammock was made of buriti palm fibre. Stevenson, true to the English custom of a daily bath, found himself one day forced to bathe in very Brazilian fashion in a stream in which some half-wild cattle of the region were cooling themselves; he and his 'companion' had to carefully shoo them out of the water[178] for fear of being chased naked through the fields by some bull that was less friendly to intruders. Wells had to watch out for piranhas in case his bath were to cost him painful or even fatal bodily

[173] Dent, *A Year in Brazil*, p. 93.

[174] A dog-sized rodent related to the guinea-pig (Translator).

[175] Stevenson, *A Traveller of the Sixties*, p. 23. (*Açaí* is the fruit of a palm; *cará* is a kind of yam – Translator.)

[176] Charles Waterton, *Wanderings in South America*, London, 1812, p. 276.

[177] Stevenson, *A Traveller of the Sixties*, p. 86.

[178] *Ibid.*, p. 86.

injury.[179]

These adaptations by Englishmen or Britons to the customs of backwoodsmen or rustics must have been common to a large number of the great many engineers that railway construction scattered over this part of South America. Some later travelled from here to that paradise for British capitalism, particularly railway companies, which in the late nineteenth century was to become the Argentine Republic. There, according to a now famous book by Raul Scalabrini Ortiz, British railway capital merely capitalized on 'the product of Argentine labour and wealth' in favour of London financiers.[180] An exaggeration, perhaps, by an Argentine nativist committed to rejecting so-called 'colonizing capitalism' in all its aspects. No one can deny, however, that such capitalism sometimes wrought piranha-like devastation in parts of the world that took no precautions against its greed for excessive profit.

Stevenson travelled round half the world: he did not stop in either Brazil or Argentina. He was still young when he was in Brazil, and was the butt of jokes by the more yokelish natives of the interior of Alagoas because of his 'yellow moustache',[181] which was uncommon in some stretches of the so-called forest zone of the North-East that had been less populated by Cristóvão Lins and Gaspar van der Lei.[182] But Stevenson only died at the age of ninety, after many travels, adventures and experiences in foreign lands. Perhaps no adventure had so greatly touched his feelings – feelings that the British, highly sentimental people who just pretend to be unmoved, are just as bashful in hiding from strangers as the Portuguese are unabashed in displaying everything that goes on in their enormous hearts to all and sundry – as the surprise he had in Penedo: one day he found himself resting – stretched out Brazilian fashion in a hammock – on board a certain little steamer named the *Jaquitaia*, belonging to the Bahia Steam Navigation Company, which turned out to be none other than the *Dumbarton Castle*, on which as a schoolboy he had often sailed down the Clyde between Glasgow and Greenock. Now (1867) it was a new steamship on the São Francisco and regarded with great curiosity by the

[179] Wells, *Exploring and Travelling Three Thousand Miles ...*, II, p. 271. Wells describes these 'small but ferocious fish' as follows: 'The face is quite that of a pug dog, and the mouth is armed with a most formidable array of keen-edged, sharp-pointed, serrated teeth, so sharp that one of the fish, flapping about the deck, easily bit in two a stick that I inserted in its mouth.' (Quoted in English – Translator.)

[180] Raul Scalabrini Ortiz, *Historia de los Ferrocarriles Argentinos*, Buenos Aires, 1940, p. 17.

[181] Stevenson, *A Traveller of the Sixties*, p. 86

[182] Cristóvão Lins, of German and Portuguese descent, was one of the first Europeans to settle Alagoas in the 16th century; Gaspar van der Lei, a Dutch nobleman, founded the Wanderley family in Pernambuco (Translator).

local country folk, who called it *O Bicho*[183] and only ventured onto its decks when encouraged by the officers, and then only after crossing themselves first.[184] It is interesting to note that Captain Richard Burton, who was then HBM Consul in Santos, was travelling in the São Francisco region at the same time as Stevenson. And in Rio, the capital of the Brazilian Empire, before Stevenson embarked for Montevideo, he met the famous traveller, a kind of spiritual grandfather for Lawrence of Arabia, or *das Arábias*,[185] as a comedian who likes facile puns might say. One night while at dinner with his countryman the engineer, Burton praised the black servants that he and Lady Burton had in Santos. They may well have been *malês*[186] with Arab blood, for that Englishman, who was so keen on Muslims, to praise them so. But they had all taken to stealing his shirts and cigars after Lady Burton had decided to convert them to Catholicism.[187] A jest that Stevenson noted was not to Lady Burton's liking.

Several English engineers like Bigg-Wither, Wells and Dent returned to the comfort of their British homes, taking with them parrots or monkeys, collections of butterflies and beetles, tins of quince and guava conserve, jaguar and alligator skins, and sometimes even live coatis. Before they left they would auction off their furniture, jacaranda, porcelain, chinaware, silver, crystal, engravings and kitchenware: the famous 'English auctions' that served to educate many a Brazilian in matters of domestic comfort, although the more astute Englishmen took with them to England the items of jacaranda, gold or silver that they had acquired here, or furniture they had had made in Brazil from good local hardwoods.

So serious were some of these auctions that they were announced in Latin:

> *Splendida ornamenta auctionari* [sic], *vehicula nova Londimi* [sic] *facta sunt* [sic], *vasa, crystallina vera, argenta legis, lychins* [sic*]* *majestatis patroli* [sic] *Londins* [sic] *et altera.*

This auction took place in Rio in 1858. The Englishman was Mr Campbell Scarlett, Her Majesty's Minister. The auctioneer, Manuel de Oliveira e Sá.[188] Auctions held by Britons in Brazil will be dealt with in greater detail in the chapter of this book in which the English residing in our country during the first half of the nineteenth century are seen

[183] Stevenson offers the translation 'grub or vermin' (Translator).

[184] Stevenson, *A Traveller of the Sixties*, p. 93.

[185] Literally 'of the Arabias', meaning 'shrewd' (Translator).

[186] Muslim slaves from West Africa or their descendants (Translator).

[187] Stevenson, *A Traveller of the Sixties*, p. 95.

[188] Escragnolle Dória, *Cousas do Passado*, Rio, 1909, p. 135.

through newspaper advertisements. Indeed, some of the most prominent auctioneers in Rio de Janeiro in the first half of that century were Englishmen, like Dodsworth, the founder of the eminent Brazilian family of that name. During the Empire, both Rio and Recife had English hotels, English shops, English clubs and ship chandlers, some of which still exist, such as Papai Ayres's establishment in Recife, which is today owned by one of his sons. A huge, ruddy man like his English father, the Brazilian Ayres is proof that tropical Brazil is not entirely hostile to Englishmen: it allows them to keep their giant stature and baby-like complexion into old age.

There were some Englishmen – engineers, merchants, missionaries and doctors – who stayed here for good. When they died, they were buried in an English cemetery, almost always after a ceremony presided over by an English vicar or pastor in an Anglican or Protestant chapel. Several of them had families here, like Dodsworth, Thom, Grey, Street, Boxwell, Studart, Cox, Ayres, Taylor, Lynch, Brotherhood, Ellis, Comber, Clark, Cochrane the elder (father-in-law to José de Alencar), Gibson, Thompson, Hime, Whatley, Dale, Rudge, MacDowell, Smith, Maxwell, Ashworth, Drummond, Fox, Baruel (from Barwell or Borroway), Robson, Scott, Martin, Thomas, Nelson, Miller, Muir, Brown, Daunt, Stammers, Bentley, Brack, Rulle, Dulley, Fogg, White, Rickett, Purcell, Chance, Williams, Fellows, Snell, Fell, Hardman, Lorimer, Abbot, Turton, Connoly, O'Connell, Belford (Bedford), Rawlinson, Watts, Fleming, Caroll, Dabney, Pollock, Murray, Simonsen, Russell, O'Grady, Tate, Cirne, Clarkson, Watson, Asquith, Newlands, Campbell, Richmond, Stuart, Duncan, Kelly, Mortimer, Heilbuth, Revert and Dayrell. Some children or descendants of English parents became Brazilianized straight away. Others remained 'freshwater Englishmen' for a generation or so, keeping the island's habits, speaking Portuguese badly or with an accent, and exaggerating the reserve, coolness and silence of the English.

Some married rich local girls here, following the example set in the sixteenth century by John Whithall, or Whithal, whose name was in fact Brazilianized to *Leitoan* or Leitão when he became the son-in-law of Giuseppe Doria, an eminent and wealthy man of Santos. Or they left offspring here that were not strictly Arian. Or their unions were not always constituted legally or with the blessing of the Church. Some mulatto or half-Indian women are still famous today for the luxury of the lodgings they had when young and kept in Rio, Recife or Salvador by English merchants, engineers or managers of powerful banks: gentlemen who preferred brown or even black local women over blondes. Other Englishmen who left Brazilian descendants, such as the Count of Leopoldina, became known for their horses, zebras and magnificent carriages; or for their strange houses isolated on hilltops, beside the sea, on river banks or near the forest. Unmistakable Englishmen's houses surrounded by trees and a certain air of mystery, some of them feeling as if haunted or plucked out of a detective story – all of us Brazilians of the generation brought up on Sherlock Holmes imagine that such a detective has always existed inside every thin, silent Englishman.

Since I have mentioned the mystery surrounding certain old houses belonging to English people in Brazil, let us not forget the Brazilians around whom there are legends, or perhaps true stories, of mysterious, remote, rich or noble British forebears from whom they have been separated by circumstances. That would appear to be the case of the Brazilian Cochranes. And in São Gonçalo, in the middle of Minas Gerais, Burke met a 'Sr. Drummond Mendoza' [*sic*], who was said to be

> heir-at-law of the Scotch Earl of Drummond attainted in some rebellion and entitled through this distant descent to untold millions lying in the Bank of England.[189]

Back in 1618, there was a poor English farmer who had been living in Brazil for forty years; he was married to a Portuguese woman and had a great many descendants. He was

> Thomas babintão ingres [Thomas Babington, English, as recorded in the] List of all Foreigners living in the Captaincies of Rio Grande, Parahyba, Tamaracá & Pernambuco and Bahia who shall not be held in suspicion.

That is recorded in the seventeenth-century codex recently acquired by the Documentation Department of the Brazilian Ministry of Foreign Relations.

There were also Englishmen who came to Brazil in search of a dry climate where they could recover their health, ravaged as they were by the damp, cold and fog of those islands that are sometimes so cruel to their most eminent children. Cruel almost all year round, though less in April and May, months so feted by poets and so beloved by British consumptives. One Englishman brought to Brazil by disease was Henry Koster. In the early nineteenth century he came to settle in Pernambuco, where, like the English who had settled around Campos and had helped to improve sugar-cane production and the sugar industry there, he became the owner of two plantations: Jaguaribe, four leagues from Recife, and Amparo, on

[189] Burke, *Business and Pleasure in Brazil*, p. 88 (quoted in English – Translator).

the island of Itamaracá. In the leisure time of a convalescent who was never fully cured of his disease but just succeeded in prolonging his life in the Brazilian sunshine, Koster wrote about the North-East of this country in a brilliant book so full of human sympathy – praised by Southey himself in the *Quarterly Review* – that this good, brotherly figure of an Englishman will never be forgotten by our people. In the history of Brazilian-British relations, people like Koster have always turned up to count against the Christies of this world. In Koster's case, even the awkwardness of his English name was lost when pronounced by the simpler people who knew him, and he became known as Henrique Costa.

Some Englishmen who settled in Brazil abjured Protestantism and became solemnly Catholic, Apostolic and Roman (in an earlier work I published a document on four such converts in the eighteenth century, and I shall return to them again soon, in the second volume of this series of studies on the English in Brazil). They were a kind of minor compensation for the anti-papal or anti-Roman missionaries, who were initially jeered at as 'goats' and received with a hail of stones by more ignorant people in the towns and countryside, but who eventually organized sects, distributed bibles, founded schools and converted Roman Catholics to Evangelism with sermons given in quaintly broken Portuguese. One aspect of the legend that has grown up in Brazil around the English is that they are all totally incapable of learning to speak Portuguese correctly, even after living in Brazil for a long time. The Englishman who appears in the interesting novel *Os Irmãos Marçal* by Olívio Montenegro is quite characteristic in this respect; his ridiculous mistakes in Portuguese are the stuff of legend or stereotype, with '*mim*' ('me') instead of '*eu*' ('I') and the verb always in the third person singular. On the other hand, another Brazilian writer, Alencar Araripe Júnior, turned Miss Kate, an Englishwoman, into a charming character in his novel. And few people have yet to know the Portuguese language better than Captain Richard Burton, the author of one of the best English books on Brazil: a book in the same category as those by Mawe, Luccock, Koster, Maria Graham, Walsh, Gardner, Bates, Wallace, Bigg-Wither, Wells and Peter Fleming. And let us not forget the case already mentioned here of Aubertin, an Englishman who came to Brazil as a railway technician and made himself famous for his translation of Camões, which he managed to produce during his time off from the hard work of dealing with locomotives, train timetables, line extensions, and clashes between feudal Brazil and the new transport technology represented by the English locomotive.

In the study that Professor Estêvão Pinto has just written on the Great Western, I find no reference to the clashes that must have occurred, sometimes violently, in such a particularly feudal region of Brazil as the sugar-cane-producing North-East, between the more conservative landowners with their exaggerated sense of private property and the English engineers who first invaded their lands with the somewhat irreverent novelty of the railways. Well, the new machines only showed respect for one lord: the Crucified Lord on Good Friday, when locomotives whistled softly as if hoarse, by order of Protestant engineers who did not want to offend the state religion. Mr Júlio Bello – who wrote *Memórias de um Senhor de Engenho*[190] – mentions the irritation felt by the more feudal plantation owners at the lack of respect shown by the first locomotives that passed in front of their big houses whistling, roaring and filling the air with black smoke. Not only that – we might add to Júlio Bello's account – but they also frightened the cattle and thrilled the little *moleques*: those good little *moleques* throughout Brazil, in cities and on sugar plantations, in suburban back yards and at the gates of patriarchal country houses, who were just as excited by the trains as children of wealthy families, for whom the toy train became one of their favourite toys. Even now that the aeroplane is king, many boys still prefer playing at trains, chanting nonsense rhymes to the rhythm of the engine:

Café com pão
Bolacha não.

or

*Vou danado pra Catende*
*Com vontade de chegar.*[191]

More enlightened landowners, on the other hand, must have acted in precisely the opposite way to those conservatives: they must have tried to attract the English engineers surveying the route for the railways onto their properties – their farms or plantations – so that these could be served by stations or halts, even at the cost of an unexpected bend or two in the line under construction. Wells noticed that the railway line that had been built in the Paraíba valley – an area owned by a few important barons and viscounts – had to cross the river five times between Piraí and Porto Novo do Cunha by means of long and expensive bridges, in order to serve the interests of some baron on one side and then a viscount on the other.[192] These feudal barons were progressive in their feudalism, that is to say

[190] 'Memoirs of a sugar-plantation owner' (Translator).

[191] These rhymes literally mean 'Coffee with bread / Biscuits no' and 'I'm storming off to Catende / longing to arrive' (Translator).

[192] Wells, *Exploring and travelling three thousand miles*, I, p. 44.

they were capable of adapting to new circumstances of life, the better to safeguard their personal interests.

In Minas Gerais, the railway engineer Dent met one such feudal lord in the person of Colonel João Luís de Oliveira Campos, the owner of the Fazenda da Mata. A tall, stout man with a long white beard, the owner of extensive lands and many slaves in good Brazilian patriarchal style. 'Patriarchal' was the word that Dent himself thought best described the lifestyle of this farmer and his people.[193] Campos only failed to embody his vision of a Brazilian Abraham in that he wore 'a pair of spectacles and a large Inverness cloak'.[194]

After a *Mineiro* dinner of pork, the conversation between the colonel and the engineer naturally turned to the building of the railway. The patriarch in spectacles then showed the English 'doctor' a sketch map that he had drawn of his estate and neighbouring lands, on which he had plotted the route that the new railway should take: 'through a good deal of his property, and near the fazendas of many of his friends.'[195] The good patriarch did not wear spectacles in vain.

Other patriarchs in the region with whom Dent had to deal, however, appeared to suffer from a lack of spectacles: Major João Ferreira of the Fazenda do Curtume, for example, whose men, in a naive act of sabotage, even destroyed a rough bridge the English engineer had built;[196] and Padre Pinto, who was also a farmer. Dent writes in *A Year in Brazil* that this priest had 'the most violent antipathy to the railway',[197] leaving the engineer in a difficult position, since the railway being constructed was to pass within twenty feet of the curmudgeon's house. The priest was terribly ugly, his left side paralysed and his face always contorted with the pain in his back and stomach, which afflicted him in his old age as a breeder of pigs rather than a shepherd of souls. A surly, archaic old man. A kind of Don Quixote wanting to stop the railway, ranting against the triumphant locomotive from on high in his big house and threatening the engineers with the stick he used for beating slaves. In his view, if the railway crossed his land it would destroy his pig breeding. When the Englishman promised to try to alter the position of the line, the old landowner and pig breeder was so moved by the powerful invader's generosity that he wept. He wept and presented him with 'two bottles of vinho virgem'.[198]

[193] Dent, *A Year in Brazil*, p. 57.
[194] *Ibid.*, p. 57 (quoted in English – Translator).
[195] *Ibid.*, p. 57 (quoted in English – Translator).
[196] *Ibid.*, p. 81.
[197] *Ibid.*, p. 135 (quoted in English – Translator).
[198] *Ibid.*, p. 168 ('virgin wine', i.e. must, or unfermented grape juice – Translator).

The Ferreiras at Fazenda do Curtume were not so extreme in their aversion to the railway, although the major enjoyed greater prestige than Padre Pinto and could cause the English technicians greater difficulties. As it happened, however, while Dent was still working on the railway's alignment across the major's land, the old patriarch died. The engineer then received a letter from the family addressed to 'Ilmo. Sr. Dr.[199] Hastings Charles Dent', informing him of the death of the head of the family; the letter was written in violet ink and sealed with a violet wafer, according to the Brazilian custom of the time.[200] It was somewhat ironic – one of those ironies of fate – that the change-bringing technician attended the burial of the conservative patriarch. Dent saw the deceased: he was dressed in a black habit, white cloak, white stockings and black shoes, and the old land- and slave-owner's head lay on a pillow covered with local lacework.[201] Three priests took part in the long burial ceremony: Dent writes that in the middle of the service all three scandalously took snuff. A band played. Much weeping from the widow, the good Dona Gertrudes, and the children. And many people, because the major had been held in truly great esteem. The house at Curtume filled with guests, some of them fine-looking old gentlemen, who at first ignored the foreigner. But when the major's sons introduced Dent to them as the 'Doctor' the old gentlemen gradually approached the important Englishman. One of them asked him whether one could go by land from Minas to England. Dent made the most of the opportunity to promote the railway and told them that, once it was built, they could reach Rio de Janeiro in a day. They all thought that was mere fancy.[202]

It was evident in 1885 that agrarian or pastoral feudalism in Brazil – in a large part of Brazil – was already beginning irremediably to fall apart, so that its representatives had to be content with tiny victories for their formerly vast power over the new means of transport. Such was Padre Pinto's victory in getting Dent to promise him a small change in alignment. Or Major Ferreira's in ordering his men to tear down a bridge erected by the engineers, who were invading land that he felt was as much a part of his own flesh as his family, his slaves and his house.

The new form of transport seemed to precede changes in production techniques, but in fact it accompanied them. It soon changed the rural landscape to such an extent that, in Pernambuco and other sugar-producing states in the North-East, the irreverent tracks of the Great Western of Brazil

[199] *Ilustríssimo Senhor Doutor* ('Most Illustrious Sir, Doctor ...'), a standard, formal form of address, still in use today (Translator).

[200] Dent, *A Year in Brazil*, p. 101.

[201] *Ibid.*, p. 103.

[202] *Ibid.*, p. 105.

created new facets not only of particular economic relations, but of social relations in general among the region's people, who until then had been served only by ox-carts, barges, hammocks, litters, horses and mule trains. It also changed the physical form and structure of the landscape itself. One need only mention the forests felled to produce sleepers and fuel for the engines, and even to build wagons, carriages and stations. Only in recent years has the Great Western been careful to reafforest areas devastated to feed the greedy mouths of its engines: a long-standing sin of the old English company to which Professor Estêvão Pinto discreetly turns a blind eye, deviating from his duty as a historian.

Another mark made by the railways on the Brazilian landscape, apart from the tracks – shining brightly in the tropical sun – was the bridges, especially the iron ones, and viaducts. The tunnels should not be forgotten either. In some parts of Brazil railway building was noted for major victories of technology over nature. We need only think of the Santos–São Paulo line – the work of an English engineer and one of the technical wonders of Brazil.

Yet another mark made by the railway complex on the Brazilian landscape was the station. Not just the often pretentious metropolitan terminus or main station. But also the little station almost lost in the woods, in the fields, on plantation or farm lands, or near up-country towns.

While travelling by train through Minas Gerais in 1883, Andrews noticed the station architecture: concrete buildings with tiled roofs and white walls with a red strip. Sítio station, at the foot of the Mantiqueira mountains, particularly attracted his attention since it had a flower garden next to it in the style of railway stations in certain northern European ountries.[203]

Andrews, the U.S. consul, made other observations during his train journey through rural Brazil: the company employees did not wear uniforms, but were inconspicuously dressed like any ordinary person; he saw no special carriages for ladies; he noticed no discrimination against passengers on account of colour; he found no carriages or compartments for smokers: smoking was allowed anywhere on the train; he observed that the closets were of the American type or system;[204] passenger trains travelled at a speed of twenty to thirty miles per hour.[205] When going by rail from Santos to São Paulo, this traveller came across a telegraph office, a bar and water closets at the station at the foot of the mountains.[206]

[203] Andrews, *Brazil, its Conditions and Prospects*, p. 135.

[204] *Ibid.*, p. 135.

[205] *Ibid.*, p. 107.

[206] *Ibid.*, p. 140.

Such country railway stations were evidently little centres of European or American civilization within the still archaically agrarian and pastoral Brazil of the time of Pedro II.

It is important to note that some English railway engineers, who built several of these lines and stations, got to know Brazil very well through their detailed research and practical observations on certain parts of the country. They corrected generalizations made by men who were more eminent but less accurate in their knowledge of our country. Buckle, for example. From the heights of his armchair science, this eminent Englishman pronounced the whole of Brazil to be covered with 'a vegetation of incredible profusion'[207] which, instead of stimulating, only repressed or weakened man's ambition. This generalization caused a stir in Brazil, and for many Europeans it fixed their idea or image of Brazil as an exuberantly tropical country from north to south.

When Thomas Hardy, the great novelist, decided to extend the action of one of his novels and the suffering of one of its characters to our country, of all of Brazil he chose Paraná, a mostly gentle land where nature is almost entirely in balance, to represent that kind of America most hostile to the civilized European, as suggested by Buckle's eloquent generalization.[208] Simple technicians like Walter J. Hammond and Bigg-Wither were just as English as Buckle and Hardy but, unlike these men of genius, were prosaically meticulous in their personal knowledge of the lands across which railway tracks were to be laid, and were therefore able to make important corrections to such generalizations. That shows how difficult it is to separate disinterested science from self-interested technology, or pure science from applied science. They almost always complement each other.

Bigg-Wither left us a detailed portrait of Paraná, seen and studied through the eyes of an Englishman from the carboniferous age. A portrait that does not seem to justify Hardy's choice of that province in southern Brazil as a backdrop for his fictional character's sufferings – although from the engineer's description Paraná is no piece of a lost Paradise in Brazil. In a much-read report written during the Empire, based on his knowledge of Brazil as a railway technician, Hammond greatly discredited the idea of the 'surpassing fertility' of our country, judged not merely from one or two islands of fertile soil – like much of Paraná – but as a whole; and not from the viewpoint of electrification technology, but from that of coal burning. A country full of sterile land, in some parts poor grasslands, in others

[207] Henry Thomas Buckle, *History of Civilization in England*, Vol. 1, London, 1857, New York 1864, p. 74 (quoted by Freyre in English) (Translator).

[208] In this respect, see Gilberto Freyre, 'O Brasil num romance de Thomas Hardy', in *Ingleses*, Rio de Janeiro, 1942.

sandy plains – that is the real Brazil discovered by railway surveyors in the second half of the nineteenth century. A country that lacked Argentina's fertile prairies and therefore could not be considered an immediate source of 'railway prosperity',[209] as Argentina could. A country of few navigable rivers and countless waterfalls to hinder navigation on them. A country only suitable for tropical agriculture and rich only in minerals that were difficult to extract. A country corrupted by plantation monoculture or by what Scully, in a book published in 1866, termed the legacy of the old colonial regime of 'large grants of land' or *sesmarias*.[210]

Hence the high cost to Brazil of almost all its railways. Hence the high cost to Brazilians of the interest – seven per cent interest guaranteed on the capital outlay – paid on the bonds issued by several of the English companies that brought the novelty of railways to the country, with coal and rails imported from England, much of the timber for wagons imported from India, and many of the locomotives from the United States. Hence the high transport costs that have always afflicted small producers in Brazil. As in Mexico,[211] the producers who benefited from the railways in Brazil were almost exclusively the sugar and coffee monoculture landowners who knew how to use the new means of transport to their advantage, by making the new lines make unexpected detours that were inexplicable from a public interest viewpoint, though not from the viewpoint of their plantations or large private estates.

[209] Andrews, *Brazil, its Conditions and Prospects*, p. 97 (page reference corrected; quoted in English – Translator).

[210] Scully, *Brazil, Its Provinces and Chief Cities...*, p. 126. Scully appears to have exaggerated the Brazilian conditions of physical space and social space – as modern sociological language would say – that hindered the spread of railways in Brazil, making them 'unprofitable speculations, both for the companies which have made them and for the Government which guarantees their dividends.' After describing 'the nature of the country', which in the mountains fringing the high plateau of the interior presented 'engineering difficulties of the highest order', he refers in caustic terms to the English railway technicians in Brazil: 'Add to this, that, supported by English capitalists, planned by extravagant engineers, and superintended by extravagant *employés* at extravagant salaries, they have been constructed with costly stations, and with grades, tunnels, curves, and ways suited, no doubt, to the great speed and traffic of an English railway, but utterly incommensurate with the circumstances of a new and undeveloped country' (p. 125) (quoted in English – Translator).

[211] On this subject, see Bernard Moses, *The Railway Revolution in Mexico*, Berkeley, 1895. For the purposes of sociological generalization, the information given in this book, as well as the two-volume *Historia de los Medios de Comunicación y Transportes en la República Argentina* by Ramón J. Carcano, published in Buenos Aires in 1893, and the study by Federico Costa y Laurent, *Reseña Histórica de los Ferrocarriles del Perú* (Lima, 1908), could be compared with information on the railways built in Brazil by the English or with primarily English capital provided by William Hadfield in his *Brazil, the River Plate and the Falkland Islands* (London, 1854), Cyro D. Ribeiro, *Estudo Descritivo das Estradas de Ferro do Brasil* (Rio de Janeiro, 1886), Francisco Pereira Passos, *As Estradas de Ferro do Brasil* (Rio de Janeiro, 1880) and Adolpho Augusto Pinto, *História da Viação Pública de São Paulo* (São Paulo, 1903). For an overview of the subject, see the excellent study by J. Fred Rippy, *Latin America and the Industrial Age*, New York, 1944.

As an antidote to the poisoning of our more gullible folk by myths or legends making out that Brazil was a second paradise on earth, it would not be a bad idea always to add a chapter on railway history to all general histories of the country. A chapter on railway history written as objectively as possible and not according to the preconceived notion that all the economic ills of Brazil may be ascribed to the greed of so-called 'colonizing capital', largely represented by transport companies.

The idea of some dreamers in the middle of the last century that the only thing Brazil needed was railways for the Empire to become awash with gold was tempered by the British railway builders themselves. It was not quite like that, although there were exceptions; that is to say, there were areas of Brazil that were as capable as Argentina of becoming an immediate source of 'railway prosperity'. Rio Grande do Sul, for example. Some people soon saw how the Brazilian treasury would benefit from a railway in that region:

> The sum expended annually on the interest on capital [wrote Francisco Cunha, a republican from Rio Grande do Sul in the time of the Empire, who enthusiastically supported the idea of a railway in his state] is most likely to be recouped through the increase in tax revenue, which today is lost on a large scale due to cross-border smuggling. In addition, it will be possible to make good use of a large volume of beef products that today is wasted for want of affordable transport.[212]

Railways alone could not work miracles in a country like Brazil, which was much less fertile than it was imagined to be by patriots whose dreams were more rose-tinted than bathed in the cold light of day. Even so, the railways did bring more modern living conditions to many parts of the country and, although at first they served the interests of slave-based monoculture, they subsequently paved the way to democratic polyculture and the expansion to rural areas of comforts and conveniences hitherto restricted to major cities or to the mansions of rich gentlemen who had travelled to the capital or around Europe. They spread certain aspects of material progress which either travelled by train or followed the railway lines to reach the backlands. They also spread nuisances. But then, who today believes in absolute Progress, apart from some mystic of Historical Materialism, with a capital H and a capital M?

On one of the more insightful pages of the work he has just written about the Great Western, Professor Estêvão Pinto makes the following

[212] Francisco Cunha, 'Via Férrea do Rio Grande', *Reminiscências*, Rio de Janeiro, 1914, p. 647.

remark about the route covered by the first line in the North-East – a route laid out with brilliant foresight by the French engineer L. L. Vauthier, which later, after becoming the Recife–São Francisco Railway, came to form one of the main lines of The Great Western of Brazil Railway Company Limited:

> while on one hand it ruined villages, towns or cities in the areas alongside the old coastal roads, on the other it brought prosperity and progress to those that it reached.

That was the case of Cabo, Escada, Ribeirão and Palmares, among the towns that reaped the benefit. And among the rural properties, there was Muribeca, Santo Inácio, Mercês, Timbó-açu, Mameluco, Freixeiras, Bosque, Cabeça de Negro, etc. Professor Estêvão Pinto, in this case quoting Mr Mário Lacerda, another enlightened researcher of Pernambuco's history and economic geography, says that Una (today Palmares)

> in the mid-nineteenth century was a mere village that depended for its livelihood on the Trombeta sugar plantation. The village started growing around the railway station erected on the banks of the River Una until it became larger than Água Preta, the chief town of the municipality and district.

In the meantime, villages and properties avoided by the railway gradually declined. Their decline was a gift to Pernambucan reactionaries in the mould of Padre Pinto. They were keen to be left alone in peace with their children or nephews, their pigs or cattle, their black women and their forests, and the trains would not annoy them or diminish their patriarchal prestige or disturb their endogamy. Conversely, however, in Pernambuco and throughout the North-East there were gentlemen who, like the old patriarch in spectacles that Dent the engineer met, could clearly see from the terraces of their mansions, like the one at Goicana, or from the verandas of their town houses, such as those in Rio Formoso, that if the trains abandoned them their plantations or towns would be virtually left to the nettles. The railways represented an inescapable future of economic interdependence in particular, and human or social interdependence in general.

Whether in the North-East or in other areas or regions of Brazil, railways did not always meet the greatest needs of the regional populations. After travelling by train from Camocim to Sobral in 1884, Antônio Bezerra came to the conclusion that that line ran through a 'rocky, sterile area

[...] to the detriment of the fertile municipalities surrounding the Serra Grande, the advantages of which are only contested by those who do not know them.' Those remarks are made in his *Notas de viagem ao norte do Ceará* (2nd ed., Lisbon, 1915, p. 307). In his view, the route had not been laid out in the public interest, but to satisfy 'the vanity of aggrandizing one of the poorest places in the province'. Overall, however, the routes chosen for the Great Western lines seem to benefit the general needs of the region rather than places favoured by transiently powerful politicians.

It is also noteworthy that railway construction and operation in Brazil had an effect on working conditions, in that it made them more democratic and more equitable, on one hand, and more efficient or more productive, on the other. It played a part in breaking down the feudal conditions of slave-based manual and agricultural work, which had been predominant in this country until then. It helped to bring about social legislation which, if it was not exactly democratically socialist, at least protected the human dignity of workers in offices, in machine-shops and even in the field. Indeed, as Professor Estêvão Pinto points out, in the 1852 Act, expanding on the 1831 Act proposed by Diogo Antônio Feijó, under which Brazil guaranteed English investment in railway creation and development, the Brazilian Government banned companies set up for that purpose from owning slaves. It thereby encouraged the employment of free workers who, 'if Brazilian nationals, would be exempted from military service and, if foreigners, would enjoy all the benefits granted to useful and industrious settlers'.

This act was to be followed by others that promoted the hiring of workers by railway companies, particularly to work in their offices and machine-shops. One that stands out is the Elói Chaves Act (1923), which established pension and benefit funds in these companies for their workers. It was passed at the same time as the Conselho Nacional do Trabalho, the National Labour Council, was set up in Brazil. Employees of the Central do Brasil railway company were perhaps the first workers in this country to be targeted by modern social protection measures, some of which were insistently called for in the Republican Constituent Assembly by a pioneer who is somewhat overlooked today, the naval officer José Augusto Vinhas, and others were put into practice by Demétrio Ribeiro as Minister for Agriculture. Those initiatives to protect railway workers were later reinforced by more recent legislation introduced since 1930, which, however, does not get the honours for first setting foot in that already trodden America. The politicians who triumphed in 1930 had the merit of seeing Lindolfo Collor, with his Germanic capacity for work and French love of synthesis, as the ideal man to systematize all the scattered and vague aspects of an area that had previously been addressed by men of the Empire and, especially, politicians of the First Republic, who had added new laws, some of which were unsuited to the milieu or conditions of Brazil. It was those laws, systematized and expanded by Collor, to which the Getúlio Vargas presidency and then dictatorship – which provided a former official of the British consulate and embassy in Brazil with the subject for a very interesting book: His Majesty the President213 – owe their popularity, lately in decline.[214]

The fact is, however, that even prior to this social legislation in Brazil some railway companies here took great care of their mechanics. That was due to their English superintendents. In 1883 Andrews, the American consul, visited the workshops of the Santos and São Paulo Railroad Company in the city of São Paulo and was struck by the welfare provisions for the mechanics and other employees of the company's workshops and offices: he had never seen anything like it! There was a library, a reading room and a billiard room for employees. Good books. English magazines and newspapers. He was told by the manager, Mr Barker, that skilled mechanics came from England on contract at a salary of 180 mil-réis per month, rising to 190 a month after three years in Brazil, from which nothing was deducted for sickness or holidays. Brazilian carpenters were paid about five mil-réis per day, labourers about 1,500 réis, and apprentices about 500 réis to begin with. They worked fifty-two hours a week, and this English company already operated a kind of 'English week'[215] in 1883.

Andrews was also surprised to discover in the company's machine-shops – which pioneered modern social welfare for urban workers in Brazil – that the carriages were not made of native types of wood but of teak, that the English imported from India. A strong, handsome Indian wood. Even so, the English company's workshops in São Paulo used a large amount of

[213] Ernest Hambloch, *His Majesty the President: A Study of Constitutional Brazil*, London, 1935 (Translator).

[214] In a brief but well-documented study of the subject, Heitor Beltrão has shown that 'the laws that really benefit workers and employees' in Brazil predate the so-called *Estado Forte* ['Strong State' – Translator] dictatorship and even the Vargas Presidency; they include Act No 3,724 of 15 January 1919 on accidents in the workplace; Decree No 5,109 of 20 December 1926 extending the railway workers' pension fund scheme to river and maritime navigation companies and those operating ports belonging to the Union, states and municipalities or in private ownership; Decree No 4682 of 24 June 1923 creating a pensions and benefit fund in every railway company in the country, not only for salaried workers but also for any kind of worker hired on a daily basis; the Municipal Decree of 21 December 1911 setting the maximum opening hours for shops at 12 hours per day with mandatory closure on Sundays and bank holidays; and the Holidays Act No 4,932 of 1925 (*Trabalhadores, alerta!*, Rio de Janeiro, 1945, pp. 3-4).

[215] *Semana inglesa*, a five-and-a-half-day working week, with Sunday and half of Saturday off (Translator).

local timber, which the experienced Mr Barker found to be very good.[216]

Protection for railway employees did not seem to be so necessary for office workers in Brazil during the last century as for those employed in the machine-shops or in the field, although it was the tradition in English companies to take office work more seriously than in the Central do Brasil company, which for many years was a paradise or heaven for parasites. When Burke was in our country (1882) he met an English engineer from the Minas and Rio Railway, a Mr Bennaton – who, incidentally, was married to a Brazilian – who told him of the experience he had had when he was appointed to a senior management position in that company: several Brazilians of his acquaintance had immediately asked him for jobs for their sons or protégés. The Englishman did in fact give some of those young men a job. But they did not last long as company employees because, unlike the engineers in government-owned companies, Mr Bennaton demanded that the politicians' protégés and his friends' sons worked as hard as the rest. For that he gained the reputation of being a very 'impertinent' Englishman.[217]

Everything suggests that the Great Western had more than one Mr Bennaton in its history. Otherwise it would not have managed to survive the party strife during the Empire or the disputes between political factions or sub-factions during the Republic over office jobs for sons and godsons who were unwilling to work or accept the routine. It would have become another Central do Brasil. The latter company entered the twentieth century with seven employees – most of them clerks – per kilometre of operational line, whereas the Leopoldina Railway functioned better than the Central with barely more than one man per kilometre of line, and the Great Western with just two.[218]

The managements of British railway companies must have expended considerable energy to achieve efficiency and regularity in the work done in the field and in machine-shops, using free workers in a country that was still dominated or marked by slavery and which remains disorganized in its attitude to manual labour even today. As Koebel aptly remarks, the British railway engineer in South America had to adapt to labour situations specific to each of the various areas of the continent; in the field, he had to deal with indigenous, mestizo, black or white labourers, depending on the location, and had to use all his 'powers of leadership and diplomacy'[219] with them – and, I might add, with the office staff.

[216] Andrews, *Brazil, Its Conditions and Prospects*, p. 146.

[217] Burke, *Business and Pleasure in Brazil*, p. 94. (Burke, in fact, uses the expression in Portuguese: 'muito impertinente' – Translator).

[218] Paul Walle, *Au Brésil*, Paris, undated, p. 85.

[219] Koebel, *British Exploits in South America*, p. 159 (quoted in English – Translator).

One aspect seems to have been almost entirely neglected by the English railway builders in Brazil: the moral and religious welfare of ordinary workers. Including English workers. When the Reverend Fletcher was in Rio in 1855, a ship's engineer from Manchester told the American pastor that in the district of Saúde at that time there were many English workers who were not given any moral or intellectual guidance at all. Several were sliding towards ignorance and cachaça drinking. The following year a thousand English and Irish workers were due to arrive for the D. Pedro II Railway. The Reverend Fletcher succeeded in interesting English and American merchants in the fate of these English-speaking railway workers, for whom a school was founded: the Saúde School.[220]

In his study on the Great Western, the manuscript of which I have just read, Professor Estêvão Pinto refers to several aspects of the history of labour in Brazil associated with the history of the establishment and spread of railways in our country, especially in the North-East. But only in passing. Without putting the spotlight on the Brazilian navvies, train crews or mechanics, without whom any English engineer or railway entrepreneur here would have become a mere ghost, acting in a vacuum.

I have already highlighted what James Wells, one of the most eminent railway engineers to spend a long time in Brazil during the reign of Pedro II, had to say on this subject. And the American geologist John Casper Branner left another valuable appraisal of the Brazilian railway worker. In an article he wrote shortly before he died – which I had asked him to write for a student magazine, El Estudiante, which I was editing at the time (1921) in New York together with a Chilean colleague – he says that he was travelling by train through the interior of Brazil when the locomotive broke down. He was then able to watch the skill of the local engine driver, a barefoot mestizo – like the sallow Brazilian in the joke, I imagine – who, with the assuredness of a fair-haired expert, a blond mechanic or an Englishman born amidst engines and fed on the best and most succulent of beef steaks, fixed the engine and set the train swiftly and triumphantly on its way again.

Railway companies in Brazil owe a great deal to their firemen and engine drivers, their brakes-men and machine-shop workers, their navvies and guards – most of whom were mestizos. The same perhaps should not be said of their conductors in general; while some of them were good, honest, exemplary employees, that was not true of others. In any case, Professor Estêvão Pinto's study would have been enriched by a chapter on the relations between bosses and workers, and between the English and the Brazilians, in the history of an old company as characteristically

[220] Fletcher and Kidder, *Brazil and the Brazilians*, p. 318.

English in its virtues and faults as the Great Western. A chapter examining the reasons for some apparently 'anti-English' but actually 'anti-capitalist' strikes or workers' movements that might be considered typical.

Professor Estêvão Pinto's study would also gain from the inclusion of another chapter of sociological interest discussing the impact of the train, the railway, the Great Western, the English engineer and the railway network, not only on the region's folklore, but on its literature and art as well. The novelists José Lins do Rego and Jorge de Lima, the poet Ascenço Ferreira, the painter Cícero Dias and the columnist Mario Sette – to name but a few – all dealt with the railway in general, and the Great Western in particular, in their novels, poems, columns and paintings. And that impact is also found in the region's jokes and caricatures.

If all these suggested additions were accepted, however, Professor Estêvão Pinto's study would perhaps grow too large for the kind of work that he was asked to write by his superior, the engineer Manuel Leão. Commissioned works always have their strict limits and inflexible obligations. In ridding himself as far as possible of these limits and obligations, the learned professor from the Escola Normal in Recife has in fact succeeded in sketching out a profile of an English railway company in Brazil that is one of the best historical and geographical studies of transport that exists in this country; it provides a number of suggestions or useful pieces of information for anyone interested in studying British influence in Brazil, including the influence of British capitalism and British railway technology.

The fact is that, in this work that I have mentioned so often, Professor Pinto has succeeded in going beyond what is promised in the title and subtitle: to contribute to the study of the history of the Great Western and the relations of this characteristically British railway company with the economy of the Brazilian North-East. He does not confine himself to suggesting relations with the economy: he goes on to consider other aspects of the company's relations with the life of the region. The professor's study sometimes extends to the entire social landscape of the region, seen in its most characteristic aspects. That is why I have felt it necessary, in this kind of general introduction to a long series of studies on British influence in Brazil, to lay such emphasis on an as yet unpublished work that the author has allowed me to read, because I realize that those studies – some already written, others barely begun – hinge on what English capital and technology, spirit of adventure and organizing spirit, science and trade have achieved in Brazil.

Of these activities, or this assemblage or complex of activities, none expressed the British genius or character better than railways. None – not even trade or mining companies or consular work or religious activity – brought more characteristically English brains to Brazil than the number that forged links with the country by surveying, constructing, commercially operating or managing railways. Pure science certainly brought English people of great intelligence or even genius to our country, Darwin, Wallace and Bates among them. Men of great intellectual value or professionalism were here on diplomatic and consular service, such as Lord Strangford, Burton and Casement. The navy, sanitary engineering, dock and bridge construction, telephone and telegraph systems, city gas and water mains, banks, tramways and factories all brought English technicians of similar value to Brazil. But none of these activities, I repeat, so constantly brought to this country such a large group of characteristically British intellects, some specializing in the technical aspects of line layout and construction, others in the commercial aspects, others in the science or art of managing such complex businesses. Almost all of them were touched by that spirit of adventure – scientific, commercial or personal adventure – that Wells the engineer admitted was responsible for bringing him to Brazil.

Unless we understand how strongly the English character has, for centuries, been influenced by the spirit of adventure, which complements rather than dispels the British taste for stability, order and man's technical dominion over nature, we can only superficially grasp the as yet little-studied and little-known history of British expansion in Brazil. Expansion of capital and technology, trade and industry, culture and religion. An expansion that found its most characteristic affirmation in our tropical lands – on the surface, at least – in the building of railways.

Today it can be seen that this form of English expansion in Brazil, like almost all the others, resulted in little direct material benefit to the majority of the country's population, which tolerated or received it almost passively; the only ones to benefit directly were the imperial capitalists in London. It is also accurate to say, however, that the expansion of the railways in the United States, which were mostly funded by domestic capital, benefited just a small number of adventurers directly, and the American public only indirectly. Professor Bernard Moses therefore prophesied that in Mexico – where the railways were built mainly with United States capital and engineering, just as Brazil's were built mainly with British capital and engineering – the rich would perhaps become even richer with the progress brought by the railways; the majority of the population, however, would only benefit from them if other factors came into play. A pessimist might have made the same prophesy about Brazil back in the days when Thomas Cochrane and Charles Pentland signed the first railway construction contract with the Brazilian Government. This English innovation was of direct advantage almost solely to Brazilian landowners on one hand, and British capitalists and their managers or superintendents, who were paid in gold, on the other. Nevertheless, as has already been pointed out in this chapter, the English railways in Brazil soon began to provide the Brazilian workforce, and not just the English, with benefits that only recently have been extended to other fields of mechanical and manual activity. And the railways in Brazil also dealt a powerful blow to slave labour itself – in fact, that was in the interests of British capitalism or imperialism, since that kind of labour no longer existed in Britain's own colonies. Only those landowners who were able to adapt to free – or apparently free – labour truly profited from the English innovation.

The same had happened with the slave trade: that too was repressed by the expansion of British industry in Brazil, damaging the Brazilian economy at the time, certainly, but benefiting the workforce, most of whom were slaves. British repression of the trade in Africans merely helped to bring about the abolition of slavery in Brazil and an improvement in the status of workers.

It should be noted in this respect that the English demand in the 1810 treaty for chaplains on board the ships transporting or trafficking slaves from Africa to Brazil seems to have been one of those characteristically British cases of interference in Portuguese or Brazilian affairs that, even though insincere or hypocritical in their ostensive philanthropy, did in fact improve the conditions under which Africans were traded. In a recent book, Mr Luís Viana Filho recalls the traffickers' outrage at such a demand:

> They complained that the business could not bear the cost of the Church representative, who in 1799 earned 450$ per voyage. He was, moreover, an inconvenient sailing companion, who was not always willing to acquiesce to the traffickers' countless tricks to defraud the exchequer.[221]

The constant outcry by less enlightened capitalists against employment protection laws.

That demand, issued if not inspired by the British, who at the time were more concerned about working conditions and worker protection in other countries than at home, deserves consideration by any historian who decides to trace the history of employment and the protection of labour, slave and free, in Brazil. The Portuguese crown did bring in laws and measures in this respect – not least regarding the conditions under

[221] Luís Viana Filho, *O Negro na Bahia*, Rio de Janeiro, 1946, p. 36.

which Africans were transported to our country – which are worthy of the Christian spirit of the Portuguese monarchy. We must not forget, however, that, although on one hand the English acknowledged, on the basis of official enquiries and individual statements, that slaves' working conditions on Brazilian plantations were less harsh than on British ones, on the other hand they did more than anyone else to ensure that the conditions under which slaves were transported to Brazil were improved.

Those Africans were almost always the victims of traders who, rather than being well-established in life, like the majority of cane planters ennobled as sugar barons, were seeking a quick and easy fortune without worrying about how they came by it. Society and the Church in Brazil only began to despise such traffickers in the second half of the nineteenth century, as a result of European pressure or influence, especially from Britain. During the eighteenth and early nineteenth centuries, in fact, slave traders were to some extent respected in Brazil: in Bahia they formed 'a class as respectable as any other, including eminent figures from the colony's economic and financial world', as Mr Luís Viana Filho points out. He is perhaps exaggerating in saying 'as any other' but, in any case, much of his somewhat emphatic generalization can be supported by the fact that traffickers in Bahia even had a brotherhood or a 'kind of association with Saint Joseph as its patron saint': Saint Joseph was expected to 'watch over the vessels that sailed in search of Africans to be enslaved and converted to Christianity through baptism'.[222]

When Fletcher visited Bahia in the middle of the nineteenth century, he noted that the ideas associated with the slave trade in his days contrasted with 'the semblance of philanthropy' under which it had formerly been conducted.[223] It seems, however, that the kind of men who devoted themselves to the trade and continued to make a fortune from it once opposition to trafficking had grown, not only in England but throughout the more advanced Christian nations of Europe, were – like Brazilian cross-border smugglers in more recent times – always motivated by a spirit of adventure and a craving for a quick profit, and were tolerated rather than admired by the country's more morally upright and solid members of society. The latter people would use slaves on their land and in their homes without feeling any scruples in using or exploiting their fellow human beings: on the contrary, they felt that they were protecting or improving the pagans that they converted. What they found repugnant, however, was the idea of getting rich from that crude, sordid kind of trade. In fact, to their patriarchal or feudal minds, it was repugnant to get rich by trading in anything but the produce of their farms, mills, slave quarters or corrals.

[222] *Ibid.*, p. 30.

[223] Fletcher and Kidder, *Brazil and the Brazilians*, p. 483.

So it is hard for people in Brazil – a feudally agrarian, or agrarianly and pastorally patriarchal country – to accept that traders of any kind, except those dealing in sugar, could be 'as respectable' a class as land- and slave-owners.

Of all the major kinds of trader, slave traffickers were the least able to aspire to equal status with landowners. Except when the landowners themselves – as appears to have been the case with Breves senior in Rio de Janeiro and certain members of the Rego Barros and Cavalcanti families in Pernambuco – joined the trade, taking on the work of a less prestigious class than their own. Less prestigious, perhaps, but more likely to provide an individual or family with quick and easy wealth.

In other cases, marriage or other family connections must have given traders in slaves, cloth, cod or cutlery a route into the rural aristocracy. Oral tradition tells us of more than one example of such social elevation.

Koebel, the English historian, correctly distinguishes slave-owning Brazilians, who were known for their benevolence towards their slaves, from those 'whose livelihood depended directly on the traffic in the bodies of the Africans'. Based on information from Walsh, he points out that a great many of the slave traders in Rio de Janeiro were gypsies. And he does not understand how anyone could have remained in such an evil trade after the eighteenth century unless they had dispositions like those of 'the hyena and the carrion crow'.[224]

Those who made their fortunes from the slave trade before it was considered evil by austere England were thus excluded from the category of 'hyenas' or 'carrion crows' or 'vultures'. In the early decades of the nineteenth century, several respectable Brazilians seem to have continued to trade in slaves as a sideline. But by the middle of the century the moral and social status of this kind of trader had changed in Brazil. None of them could even aspire to being made a baron: Dom Pedro II made a point of refusing to give noble titles to traders whose hands were soiled by the degrading trade. Ewbank, who was in this country at the time, writes of the huge fortune that Fonseca (Pinto de Fonseca) had amassed by trafficking in Africans; but he hints that his 'splendid dwelling' in Rio de Janeiro, located in the commercial Rua da Quitanda next to his store, was merely the showy town house of a *nouveau-riche*.[225]

Following the arrival of Dom João VI in Brazil, the presence of a considerable number of British merchants who imported fabrics, iron,

[224] Koebel, *British Exploits in South America*, p. 336 (both quotations transcribed by Freyre in English – Translator).

[225] Ernesto Mattoso, *Cousas de meu tempo (Reminiscências)*, Bordeaux, 1916, p. 60. Thomas Ewbank, *Life in Brazil*, p. 86.

glass, tea, and machines and tools that could do the work of slaves – merchants who were regarded as superior beings because they were British and reputed to be rich – helped to raise the status here of mechanics, workers able to deal with machines, just as it also enhanced the standing of merchants themselves. Or at least of wholesale merchants, who owned warehouses filling formerly high-class town houses; who had more imposing carriages and horses than those belonging to noblemen and high-court judges; whose clothes were sometimes finer than those of the local grandees; and who lived in castle-like suburban residences that dominated hills and provided names for places or streets: 'the Englishman's hill', 'the Englishman's villa', 'the Englishman's house', 'the Englishman's street or alley'. The area on the slopes of Corcovado mountain in Rio de Janeiro where the merchant and banker William Young had his residence in the early nineteenth century did in fact become known as '*Morro do Inglês*' – the Englishman's hill.[226] There is, however, disagreement over the origin of this name between historians like Tobias Monteiro and chroniclers of the city like Mr Morales de los Rios Filho: the latter considers the '*Morro do Inglês*' to be the hill in Cosme Velho that 'had belonged to the Englishman George Britain'.[227] Perhaps there were several 'Englishman's hills' in Rio de Janeiro.[228] In São Paulo as well, John Rademaker, an Englishman who died in 1824, prompted the name of 'Englishman's hill' or 'Englishmen's hill' for a hill in the city, according to the historian Aureliano Leite in his interesting notes, 'Ingleses no Estado de São Paulo' published in the *Jornal do Commercio* on 30 January 1944. And there is an 'Englishman's sandbank' (*Banco do Inglês*) in Recife harbour.

The presence or action or influence of the English in Brazil was to a great extent responsible not only for the above-mentioned advancements in Brazilian life – the rise in status of labour, of mechanics and of merchants – but also for other less material and more spiritual improvements, if these qualities can in fact be clearly separated from each other. There are aspects of religion or Christian practice that became better appreciated after the contact between Brazilian Catholicism and British Protestantism. The cult of Mary appears to have gained strength here, as in other Catholic countries, after this contact, in opposition to the exclusive cult of Christ

[226] Tobias Monteiro, *História do Império. A elaboração da Independência*, Rio de Janeiro, 1927, p. 241.
[227] Adolfo Morales de los Rios Filho, *O Rio de Janeiro imperial*, Rio de Janeiro, 1946, p. 187. He also points out that Rua Taylor was laid out in the Chácara da Lapa, belonging to Commodore John Taylor (p. 189), and that the rear of the Pedra da Gávea [a mountain in Rio – Translator], which has 'the rough outline of a human face looking up, with a beard and hooked nose', was called by the English 'Lord Hood's face' or 'Lord Hood's nose'. He gathered this information from Walsh and Gardner (p. 182).
[228] Since the district of Cosme Velho also lies at the foot of Corcovado, it is possible that both authors are referring to the same hill, where more than one Englishman lived (Translator).

emphasized by the Protestants. And the same may perhaps be said of the cult of the saints. The development or preservation of these two cults in Brazil may perhaps have been a means by which orthodox Catholics in a land economically invaded by the English could withstand the invaders' influence and differentiate themselves from them, at least insofar as religion was concerned. In their representations against the establishment of English traders in Brazil in 1808, the merchants of Bahia termed their religion 'this most solid base of Empires!' And Brazilians' pure religion should not be tainted in any way whatsoever.

Even in this area, however, there would eventually be considerable English influence in Brazil, not so much through the limited interpenetration between Catholic and Protestant practices, but through spiritualism. Through English ghosts – for even they carried or propagated British culture to Popish lands.

There are, in fact, English ghosts that have been part of Brazilian culture since the time of the Empire, having been brought here by English devotees of spiritualism or through the books of English scientists, who since the middle of the nineteenth century have been more committed than anyone else to conducting research as scientifically as possible into phenomena that the French term metapsychical. Katie, the ghost with fair, almost blonde hair whom Sir William Crookes one day picked up in his arms as if he were carrying a young woman or lifting a lady, as he wrote with all his common-sense as a chemist and an Englishman in one of his more sensational statements on such phenomena,[229] is perhaps the most beloved by Brazilians of all English ghosts. That is not in the least surprising. Because Katie is a kind of reincarnation in spiritualist literature of a heroine in an English novel. The ghost of an attractive young woman, a fair lady, 'the pale madonna of my dreams';[230] and not some repulsive soul of the dead, or much less a monstrous headless mule. A ghost worthy of the best of British civilization in the Victorian age. Worthy of the best of Christian civilization in Britain.

[229] William Crookes, *Researches into the Phenomena of Spiritualism*, London, 1878. It seems that there are more 'haunted houses' in Brazil today than in Great Britain: 150, according to Ingram in his *The Haunted Houses and Family Traditions of Great Britain*. Which means that Europe should bow to Brazil. In any case, it would be interesting to compare the behaviour of ghosts in British manor houses and castles with that of ghosts in old Brazilian mansions and town houses, to see whether there are differences as well as similarities. In Recife, the ghost of a British sailor is said to have been seen more than once climbing up and down the mast of an old English ship lying in the grounds of an old house that once belonged to an Englishman. And there are vague reports of fishermen seeing phantom ships that might be English, and of Englishmen and Brazilians seeing the ghosts of English sailors or pirates pointing to buried treasure on desert islands or beaches.

[230] A reference to 'Ó pálida madona dos meus sonhos', the first line of the poem *Pensamento de Amor* (1865) by Antônio Frederico de Castro Alves (1847-71) (Translator).

What English spiritualism did with ghosts – even Katie, almost always the terror of the living – in the days of our grandparents, British scouting has done in our own or our parents' days with children and adolescents. In Brazil, as in other countries, they have gone from being the bane of adults to acquiring new dignity under the English name of 'boy-scouts'. As if they were Robinson Crusoe's nephews capable of being shipwrecked on any desert island without starving to death or perishing through ignorance of nature or the principles of mechanics.

That did not happen with the suffragettes. The English suffragette movement was poorly received in Brazil. Few Brazilian women adopted the crude methods of those bony, ugly Englishwomen to win political rights. One or two freaks here started following the British example and dressing more like men than women. But none of them smashed shop windows or threw stones at policemen just for the pleasure of asserting their equality with the coarsest of men.

There was however an Englishwoman in Brazil back in the eighteenth century who even then showed some similarity with today's suffragettes, so outspoken and even insolent was she in her attitudes all that time ago. Her name was Mrs Kindersley, and she was in Bahia in 1764. She bears the distinction, as pointed out by the historian Affonso de E. Taunay, of being the first woman writer to have dealt with Brazil.[231]

She found the city of São Salvador, or Salvador, disappointing, with filthy streets and dirty houses 'without the ornament of paint'. Watched the whole time by the authorities, she interpreted such excessive care for her person as being 'to prevent my going to the nunneries ... or becoming acquainted with any of their women', for fear that she might corrupt them.

She learnt that there was an Englishwoman residing in Bahia, the wife of a Portuguese merchant. But when the merchant's wife asked the authorities for permission to give lodging to her fellow-countrywoman, the governor replied that 'two English women in one house was too much'![232]

This eighteenth-century Englishwoman complained almost like a suffragette about the priests in Salvador, who were 'abominably insolent and oppressive' towards the people, and claimed with obvious exaggeration that they were always dispatching people 'accused of spiritual crimes' to

[231] Affonso de E. Taunay, 'Na Bahia Colonial', *Revista do Instituto Histórico e Geográfico Brasileiro*, t. 90, vol. 144, p. 386.

[232] *Ibid.*, p. 387. (Mrs [Jemima] Kindersley, *Letters from the Island of Teneriffe, Brazil, the Cape of Good Hope, and the East Indies*, London, 1777, p. 26. Freyre must have been unable to find a copy of her book himself, since he quotes her opinions from Taunay's version in Portuguese. The quotations here are in Mrs Kindersley's own words – Translator.)

the Inquisition in Lisbon.[233] She ridiculed the military officers in Bahia. She spoke ill of the Portuguese Government, which did not educate the Brazilian people but instead restricted the entry of books into Brazil. Books and foreigners. The result was the situation of women in Bahia: totally uncultured, poorly dressed and kept under strict watch, since 'their male relatives do not place any confidence in their virtue'. After relating what she had seen in Brazil in a series of letters that were often interesting and in some parts quite accurate, she ethnocentrically addressed her countrymen in England:

> May you enjoy long life, in that country, where men profess less zeal, and practise more virtue.[234]

Ethnocentrism of the crudest and most simplistic kind. For not all Christian virtues were practised by the English and disregarded by Brazilians at that time. Or today, for that matter. The history of relations between the two peoples, each with its own way of being Christian, shows that some virtues have flourished better among the English and others among the Brazilians. The same could be said of faults. The interpenetration of the two cultures has allowed the technically richer to enrich the other with a variety of values, while the poorer has not failed to provide the richer with new perspectives on life, nature and humankind. And even new techniques and new areas of adventure for the soul or the personality, and not merely for the senses.

That accounts for the fact that when an Englishman of the stature of Burton departed from Brazil he wrote as follows not only of his fellow-countryman but of any foreigner who could only speak ill of Brazilians and their institutions:

> ... whenever I hear a foreigner complain that he has failed in the Brazil, and rail against the people and their institutions, it is proof positive to me that the country has every right to complain of him – in fact that he is a "ne'er do weel," [*sic*] that he drinks, or he is an idler; he is incorrigibly dishonest; or finally, to be charitable, that he is an impossible man.[235]

[233] *Ibid.*, p. 388 (Kindersley, p. 31 – Translator).
[234] *Ibid.*, p. 390 (Kindersley, p. 52 – Translator).
[235] Burton, *Explorations of the Highlands of the Brazil*, I, p. 263 (quoted by Freyre in English – Translator).

# CHAPTER II

# THE ENGLISH IN BRAZILIAN NEWSPAPER ADVERTISEMENTS DURING THE FIRST HALF OF THE NINETEENTH CENTURY

*The 'Journal do Commercio,' like the 'Diario,' is printed on wretched paper, and the typography so bad that it is hardly legible, though it is in more demand than any other. It is almost entirely filled with editals and advertisements; every publication containing from 80 to 100.*[236]

(*R. Walsh,* Notices of Brazil in 1828 and 1829, *Boston, 1831, I, p. 238.*)

*... the anodyne Gazeta do Rio de Janeiro [...]*

(*Oliveira Lima,* Dom João VI no Brasil, *2nd ed. Rio de Janeiro, 1945, I, p. 103.*)

[236] Quoted by Freyre in English. 'Editals' (an Anglicized plural of the Portuguese *edital*) are official notices (Translator).

The almanacs and commercial registers of Rio de Janeiro, Bahia and Recife in the first half of the nineteenth century are full of English names. People established in the most important cities on the Brazilian coast with stores selling fabrics, ironware, paint, crockery, and cutlery, as well as foundries, workshops, auction houses, offices, hotels and ship-chandleries. There were also a few doctors and English language teachers. And several engineers, technicians, governesses, dancers and magicians.

Chronicles of greater distinction than almanacs and commercial registers tell us of English naturalists like Darwin or English clergymen like Walsh who visited Brazil in those days or lived here. Others refer to diplomats who worked here and were involved in international intrigues or plots. Yet where but in advertisements published in newspapers during the colony and early Empire would English dancers spring out before our surprised eyes, such as those who – according to an advertisement in the *Idade d'Ouro do Brazil* – performed in the Bullring of the city of Salvador da Bahia de Todos os Santos on 4 October 1818, and characteristically sent up into the air 'a machine with one man balancing head-down on top and two others beneath' – a show in the purest English palaeotechnic taste – ending, however, in Spanish style with castanets and, especially, in Portuguese style with 'an admirable firework: the Royal Arms and the distich *Viva D. João VI*'? Or magicians such as Sutton, who in the *Diário de Pernambuco* of 19 May 1846 announced his next performance in the *Teatro Público*, with the 'passing of the sun-hat, in a different manner from the way he presented it last night', and also promised to make 'the delicious and enchanting slimming coffee, both with milk and without', which he would give to the spectators to drink; to work 'with the Chinese magic rings' for the first time; to cut off 'the nose of any spectator who might wish to submit to this operation'; and to use, also for the first time, 'a magnetic-galvanic machine with which he will galvanize any of the audience who so agrees'? Or shadowy English figures like Mr Brown who, in an announcement in the *Jornal do Commercio* of Rio de Janeiro on 9 January 1828, confessed to being 'infinitely grateful to the respected audience' for the 'proof of munificence received on the day of his benefit performance [...] fearing that the result of his efforts as a theatre artist that day was not equal to the desire to please that drives him at all times [...] since he found himself highly disturbed on that day of his benefit, and that agitation had a great influence on his physical strength', preventing him from 'executing with due precision some of the exercises announced'? Hence his 'sincere confession of his poor performance that day'. It is for such revelations made in newspaper advertisements – the voices of people confessing sins, like Mr Brown, and not just showing off their virtues or announcing the quality of their wares and goods for sale – that I do not tire of leafing through collections of old newspapers full of 'advertisements' and 'announcements' and 'private notices'. And I have always found useful material for the study of Brazilian society in the paid sections of these newspapers, not only when interested mainly in 'African slaves', but also with regard to English gentlemen and engineers, or French artists and technicians.[237]

As I am naturally a grumbler, I regret that these collections – like, incidentally, the manuscripts in several Brazilian archives that I know – are so poorly conserved or are treated as so unimportant that, as far as I know, not a single archive in the country, nor any of our public libraries, has yet seen fit to cover such valuable documents with protective tissue paper. As a result, many rare newspapers over a century old are crumbling with age or rotting away in damp corners of provincial libraries and archives and even in the capital of the Republic, when it would be so easy to protect them all and keep them for the eyes of future generations – who may be more wisely curious about the past than we are – simply by covering them in Japanese tissue, as is done in archives and libraries in other countries.

The fact is that the advertisements in these old newspapers – so deprecated by historians in the past that even Oliveira Lima, an enlightened

[237] A reference to previous works by the author: 'O escravo nos anúncios de jornais do tempo do Império' ('The slave in newspaper advertisements in the time of the Empire' – a lecture read at the Sociedade Felipe d'Oliveira in Rio de Janeiro in 1934 and published in that society's *Boletim* for that year), which a specialist in questions of historical sociology, Professor Richard Pattee, generously considered unique in its field for its innovative method of analysing anthropological or historico-sociological material; and *Um ingenheiro francês no Brasil* ('A French engineer in Brazil' – Rio, 1940). The advertisements studied, the most typical or characteristic of which are highlighted here, have been collected mainly from the *Gazeta do Rio de Janeiro* and the *Idade d'Ouro do Brazil* – since these were the first newspapers published in Brazil, the former in Rio de Janeiro and the latter in Bahia – and the *Diário de Pernambuco* (Recife) and *Jornal do Commercio* (Rio de Janeiro), since they are the oldest still in circulation in this country, the former founded in 1825 and the latter in 1827.

master of his profession, disdainfully called the *Gazeta do Rio de Janeiro* 'anodyne' – provide us with information on the most profoundly human side of Brazil's past, which it would be pointless to expect more distinguished sources to reveal. It is not only the picturesque, the dramatic or the unique that bursts out of the advertisements: there is also the common, the oft-repeated and what in certain sciences is called the *demonstrative*, in contrast to what is considered *atypical* – extremes which, by the way, do not repel each other, as used to be supposed, but extend alongside each other. Advertisements are therefore valuable material for social studies in general and for sociological, anthropological or historico-social studies in particular. They even serve as 'clinical material' for the past, as has been demonstrated by one of my young research associates, Luís Robalinho Cavalcanti, a medical doctor, in an interesting study of the disease ainhum; and as I myself suggested back in 1934, in a note on the presence of rickets in Brazil, which until then had been emphatically denied by specialists and under-specialists. My suggestion was confirmed by another eminent doctor, Dr Rui Coutinho, another former research associate of mine, based on the evidence of numerous advertisements offering black slaves for sale in Brazilian newspapers during the time of slavery, which I had used to outline that somewhat revolutionary suggestion.

I also remember that I had recourse to those same advertisements to outline another equally daring suggestion, which would have stood on shaky ground had there not been ample confirmatory material: that among fugitive slaves – who were sometimes described by their disappointed masters in amazingly detailed anthropological portraits, albeit in simple, everyday language – the slender, long-limbed type was predominant over the stocky type; that suggests a broader interpretation of the question, which is that the stockier type adapted better than the opposite kind to the routine of agricultural or domestic work conditioned by the patriarchal system of slavery, whereas the slender ones were led by temperament or constitution more to a life of adventure and variety in their activities and occupations, a life of initiative, rebellion and even treachery towards white people or their masters. Like Shakespeare's Caesar, who preferred to surround himself with fat men and avoided lean ones, Brazilian slave-owners should have kept fat slaves rather than lean ones around them. During the time of slavery in Brazil, prudent or wise masters should have avoided buying the tall, lean-bodied black men that the newspaper advertisements and news items parade before our eyes all too often. No cautious man in those days should have given up his fat, round, merry cook – the traditional type in Brazil – for the Englishman who had jumped ship from the brig called the *Prompt*, whom a British consul in Brazil, perhaps poorly read in Shakespeare, ill-advisedly took into service in his house or kitchen – a 'lean-bodied' Englishman with 'sparse, black hair and beard with a few white hairs'[238] – only to have the displeasure of seeing the ingrate run away from his house too. And he did not run away like any 'fugitive black man', just in search of his freedom, but he took with him three linen jackets, twelve Henry Low shirts, six pairs of trousers and a little morocco box from Russia containing seven razors together with an ivory-and-silver handle, plus two razors from China with black handles, a silver waistcoat buckle, a silver teaspoon and several other items of clothing belonging to his countryman and protector. This 'fugitive Englishman', whose white skin contrasted with the black, brown and yellow of most of the black and mulatto fugitives in the missing persons advertisements that filled Brazilian newspapers in the first half of the nineteenth century, was called John – 'John something' – and, like most black and mulatto fugitives, was not only angular but, for Brazil, tall: 'height five feet six inches'.

Newspaper advertisements are sometimes irritatingly mysterious: they reveal only certain aspects of people or events, leaving the more curious reader with an irresistible desire to know the whole story. A desire that almost always comes to nothing. Because many things about the past that are reflected in advertisements leave no sign of life in any other kind of document. For example, whose son was the little twelve-year-old pageboy who, on 12 March 1833, ran away from the house of a certain Mr Antônio José Moreira Pinto 'at Ave Maria time':[239] 'quite fair, aged about twelve, blue eyes, blond hair, wearing a black woollen serge jacket, trousers of thick blue cloth, a shirt with an embroidered front and no waistcoat'?[240] Or the mulatto woman named Dina, 'of normal height and a freckled face', who spoke 'Portuguese and English', 'rather curly hair, aged about twenty-five', who ran away from a house in Rio de Janeiro in 1809, according to an advertisement in the *Gazeta*?[241] Or the slave boy with 'straight, rather fair hair and blue eyes' – almost like an English boy – who on 15 December 1835 disappeared from his master's house in Pernambuco?[242] Was he running from an English master like the one in Tijuca who, as Walsh discovered, used to sell the children he had by slave women, even when they turned out to be as fair as Angles and not just angels?[243] In Pernambuco, during the same period as when the fair-haired slave boy ran away, 'a slave called José Creoulo with his left hand cut off at the wrist' fled from the house of an Englishman, Mr Davis. This slave, however,

[238] *Diário de Pernambuco*, 26 January 1847.

[239] At dusk (Translator).

[240] *Jornal do Commercio*, 14 March 1833.

[241] *Gazeta do Rio de Janeiro*, 25 February 1809.

[242] *Diário de Pernambuco*, 21 February 1835.

[243] Walsh, *Notices of Brazil*, II, pp. 194-195 (Translator).

was dark, an adult and a ruffian. He was excessively fond of alcohol, but we do not know whether he acquired the vice from his master, Mr Davis, nor even whether his master was one of those Englishmen who drank and were famous in the stories of the time. Perhaps, on the contrary, he was a teetotaller and a vegetarian, a virtual ascetic with a loathing of roast beef and beer, like Mansfield, the socialist chemist, who was in Recife and Rio precisely in the mid-nineteenth century and whose angelic habits astounded Brazilians accustomed to the other kind of Briton.

Furthermore, how can we not be extremely grateful to the only source of information able, for example, with utter indiscretion and well-documented frankness, to tell us which of the elegant inhabitants of Recife in the mid-nineteenth century failed to settle their clothing bills with their fashionable or high-class tailors, who at that time worked almost exclusively with English fabrics? That is what we are told in an advertisement in the *Diário de Pernambuco* of 1 September 1850 with regard to a certain tailor established at Rua Nova, No 18, in the city of Recife. Some of his debtors were such noble or respectable persons of the time that even at a distance of almost a hundred years the researcher hesitates to name them: Dr Lourenço Avelino de Albuquerque Mello, Lieutenant Rego Barros, Firmino de Paula Albuquerque Maranhão, Father Calixto Correia da Nóbrega, Father Pedro Barbosa Freire and Dr Policarpo Sezario (*sic*) de Barros. Did they die without paying for their morning coats, frock coats and cassocks made of good English fabric? May God hold them all in His Glory and pardon them their debts to the tailor. Them and the seminarian – 'a Seminarian by the name of L. G. B.' – who also failed to pay for the fabrics he bought in the Rua Direita do Comércio in the city of Salvador in 1848, according to a 'personal notice' published in *A Marmota* on 7 July 1849.

Advertisements in Brazilian newspapers during the first half of the nineteenth century make it clear – and in this are backed up by other documents – that English merchants then owned the best fabric stores in the main cities in the colony and later the Empire, although they did not usually stoop to practising the tailor's art as the French did, who competed in this trade and also as cooks and confectioners with certain 'mulattoes' or 'well-spoken *crioulos*',[244] who also appear in newspaper advertisements. One such was the *crioulo* from Angola by the name of José, 'well-spoken, normal height, somewhat lighter-skinned, thin, long face, small eyes, mouth and nose [...] wearing an English check shirt, white trousers', portrayed in an advertisement in the *Gazeta* on 28 September 1816. The English preferred to be the great importers and wholesalers of fabrics to

[244] In Brazil, *crioulo* usually refers to a person of African origin born in Brazil, but the meaning is somewhat fluid and can include any dark-skinned person (as here) or, indeed, a white person born in the Americas (Translator).

be made into clothes for fine gentlemen, who were not always scrupulous about paying their bills. Few of them worked as tailors here, although the Rio de Janeiro that Maria Graham saw in 1821 had more English tailors than French. I have not found any trace of those English masters of the scissors in newspaper advertisements. They make no appearance, either to advertise their skills or to collect debts from remiss lords.

There are numerous English advertisements for fabrics from 1808 onwards. Wool, linen and cotton fabrics, such as those advertised for sale by auction in the *Gazeta do Rio de Janeiro* of 1 September 1810 by the English auctioneer 'Diogo'[245] Birnie; cloth of colours more in fashion at the beginning of the age of coal – dark ones – such as those mentioned in an advertisement in the *Gazeta*, again in 1810, by a certain Turner, Taylor & Co. of Rua dos Pescadores, No 11; black and coloured cloth: royal blue, bottle green, purple, wine-coloured or mixed; and just one or two pieces of scarlet to console colonial customers still attached to eighteenth-century romanticism – the century of light, bright colours in Europe and America. Especially in Brazil, which was then less closed to Asian than to European influence, and which brought plenty of cloth and chinaware in orientally bright colours from Asia. Incidentally, there is a hint of mystery in the Turner, Taylor & Co. advertisement: they wanted to find out who had bought, or the whereabouts of, the fabrics in the colours and amounts that they mentioned which had been released from the customs house in Rio de Janeiro by William ('Guilherme') Berley. Who might have misappropriated them?

Fabrics are perhaps the articles most often associated with the names of Englishmen in Brazilian newspaper advertisements towards the end of the colony and in the early years of the Empire. Auctions of nankeen and calico. Now and then 'a ready-made outfit from England' appears in a newspaper advertisement, as in the *Diário de Pernambuco* of 23 July 1829. As I mentioned above, what I have not been able to find through newspaper advertisements is an English tailor in Rio, Recife or Bahia in the first half of the nineteenth century, alongside the various French tailors. Incidentally, starting in the time of the Kingdom, some local merchants began to harm the English trade in fabrics and chinaware by importing fine cloth and even gilded tea services from France. One of them was José Francisco Lopes, who placed an advertisement in the *Idade d'Ouro do Brazil* on 3 July 1818.

In the *Gazeta do Rio de Janeiro* of 1 September 1810 James ('Diogo') Birnie advertises 'several Woollen, Linen and Cotton fabrics', as well as

[245] Portuguese form of 'James'; it was common practice to translate foreigners' first names (Translator).

'Canvases, copper sheets, lead' and other English goods. The advertisers almost always have the names of these goods printed with a capital letter, perhaps to distinguish them from goods from countries other than great England. The French might manufacture fabrics and send them to Brazil. The advertisements made sure that English products could be distinguished from French ones. English fabrics were spelt with a capital letter.

It is from that time that English fabrics and even ready-made English outfits begin to be promoted in Brazilian newspaper advertisements as fabrics and outfits truly worthy of well-bred or well-to-do people. English fabrics started to compete with fabrics from Asia, which – it bears repeating – had sent so much to Brazil during colonial times. Not only via Portugal but also directly, on ships that got round the prohibition of trading with Brazilian ports, which was in force for many years, by pretending that they needed to put in. During such stops they illicitly distributed chinaware and fabrics and other fine oriental goods to the local people. Such chinaware and fabrics often appear in auctions during the early decades of the nineteenth century, including auctions held by English auctioneers. Such auctioneers became a Brazilian institution in those days: the English auctioneer. Later the institution would change to being an 'Englishman's auction'.

Mr J. J. Dodsworth is the English auctioneer figure who most stands out in Rio de Janeiro in the first half of the nineteenth century, and the most sought-after item in his auctions was undoubtedly wool from England. And also baize, fleece, flannel, nankeen, calico, American cotton itself, denim, blue cloth, striped cloth, handkerchiefs, stockings, suede gloves, shirt buttons, wire for wiring ladies' hats, perfumes, tins of shaving soap, sewing boxes, fine beaver hatboxes and cavalry shakos. It is not uncommon in newspaper advertisements to find French articles being sold by Englishmen, the reason being the exceptional terms obtained by British trade from the Portuguese Government in Brazil.

Another English auctioneer from the same city and the same period emerges from newspaper advertisements: Mr Charles ('Carlos') Cannell, who also specialized in fabrics and cloth: madras cotton, muslin, calico, flannel, fustian, 'three-cornered cambric handkerchiefs', blue nankeen, broad woollen shoe laces, striped cotton boot laces, embroidered serge, fine cotton stockings, black cloth and denim. It would seem, however, that the first large auctions of English fabrics in Rio de Janeiro were held in the very year when the prince arrived in Brazil by Turner, Taylor and Company and T. W. Stanfeld. who displayed the brands of baize for sale in their advertisements: $\frac{J}{C}$, ◇S◇ and other almost masonic symbols. Their advertisement in the *Gazeta* for 26 October 1808 should be seen.

Another pioneer must be mentioned: James ('Diogo') Birnie. He too appears in 1808, in the *Gazeta* for 10 November of that year so long ago, with an advertisement for a public auction to be held at 9 a.m. on the tenth of that month at Rua da Alfândega, No 10, of the fabrics and other commercial articles of a certain Nathaniel Silkerk, which were to be 'sold without restrictions' since their owner intended 'to leave for his land at the first opportunity'. The auction consisted of '1 Collection of Fabrics', 'Porcelain and Glass', '1 assortment of Spectacles', 'Boots' and 'Ladies' Cloaks, etc., etc.' And there was a further pioneer called 'Diogo': Mr James ('Diogo') Gill. In the *Gazeta* of 9 November 1808, he too announced an auction, to be held on the eleventh at 10 a.m., of fabrics that had come from Liverpool on the *Paris*: baize and fleece. It should be noted in passing that, as the English sold and advertised baize so much, they seem to have become known in Brazil as *baetas*: 'baizes'.

The *Paris* must have sailed from Liverpool overflowing with English fabrics, as they were also received by Valentim Chaplin & Company: 'Baizes, Fleeces, Worsteds and Calicoes [...] brought from Liverpool aboard the Ship *Paris*, Captain Boswell, and on the Brigantine *Elizabeth*, Captain Appleton, from London', says an advertisement in the *Gazeta* on 26 November in the memorable year of 1808. The *Paris* also seems to have brought the 'Blue Cloth' announced by Barker and Marcher on 16 November 1808 and, perhaps, the 'superfine cloth and Butter' advertised by Robert ('Roberto') Kirwan and Company in the *Gazeta* on 30 November that year.

On 15 December 1808, just before Christmas, Nathaniel Lucas was advertising merchandise received from England in the *Gazeta*. And, like Birnie, with symbols that look masonic but are merely part of the commercial or customs ritual, if not also for typographic effect, the better to attract the public's attention:

| | | | |
|---|---|---|---|
| S + & Ca.<br>NL | 10 Bales of<br>White Paper<br>1 d.º of Superfine<br>Cloth | } | Shipped from<br>Liverpool on the<br>*Santo Antonio.* |

The following year, Dyson Brothers and Finnie, an Irishman, received a large shipment of English fabrics that they advertised for auction in the *Gazeta* of 26 July: cotton, coloured and scarlet fleeces, coloured narrow and broad baizes, ordinary and extrafine blue cloths. The English did not always force their blues *en masse* on the Brazilians, but sometimes alternated importing sober colours with bright ones that were more to the taste of Portuguese-American people.

On 8 November 1827, Mr Cannell appears in the *Jornal do Commercio* with an advertisement for 'a large assortment of Woollen, Linen, Cotton and Silk Fabrics'. On 9 November in the same year, Mr Dodsworth announces some novelties: 'plush caps', 'English pound threads', 'fine embroidered cloths', 'artillery shakos', 'checks', 'fustians, ribbons and silks'. And in the *Jornal do Commercio* of 26 October, the same Mr Dodsworth advertises not only 'a large quantity of fabrics, namely embroidered cloths, madras cottons, fine striped cloth, [...] blue nankeen, denim, fustian, fine black cloth, plain and embroidered satin, taffeta and embroidered serge', but also 'black and white English silk stockings, shawls, Scottish silk handkerchiefs, voile headscarves, two boxes of fine hats and select cravats', and also 'percussion shotguns and pistols'. Mr Dodsworth was a veritable Father Christmas for rich *Cariocas*[246] in the early days of the Empire. But he was by no means the only one. Nor was he the first Englishman established in Rio to auction such seductively new goods from Europe.

By 1815 the English stores in Rua Direita or Rua da Alfândega, like William ('Guilherme') Young's, had become places that fascinated not only adults but also children with the novelties they received from England, and via England from nearly every country in the world, even Macao and India. And there were not just cloths, fabrics and woollens. There were mirrors and panels, 'Veneers of elegant taste to adorn drawing-rooms', like those advertised on 6 September 1815 by the store at Rua da Alfândega, No 5, which also imported 'gilded and enamelled porcelain' from Macao, '*English* crystal and chinaware' (the italics are in the advertisement) and 'all kinds of trinkets for children'. We must imagine that the horrible term 'trinkets' covered toys – including mechanical toys – for boys, who until then played mainly with paper caravels and puppets perhaps made of cardboard. Unfortunately the advertisement does not tell us what kind of new toys the English had brought to Brazil. A rather more recent advertiser does us that favour: in the *Diário de Pernambuco* of 29 December 1846 – just before the New Year – he tells us he has received from Europe 'a large assortment of toys that attest to the progress and perfection of the work of the best manufacturers in Europe', including dolls that moved their eyes and had natural-looking hair, shotguns, cribs, toy furniture and dolls, among which was 'a John Bull'.

In 1830 there were already merchants in Brazil specializing not only in fine fabrics but also cravats, gloves, stockings and even, as mentioned above, 'ready-made outfits' from England.

[246] Inhabitants of Rio de Janeiro (Translator)

On 6 January an advertisement appeared in the *Jornal do Commercio* reporting the arrival from England of

> an assortment of varnished gentlemen's shoes, black Scottish stockings, ladies' riding hats, and English cloth jackets, coloured worsted trousers, also English, and other fabrics, all modern and in the best taste [...]

A merchant specializing in English goods, mainly for men, but also for ladies who rode. Jackets and, no doubt, riding coats were sold there for men and ladies, especially those who rode sitting astride like men, who were dubbed '*jerônimas*' in São Paulo.

In addition, more and more 'ready-made' outfits were imported from England. On 12 January 1831, Madame Valais & Comp., established at Rua do Ouvidor, No 90, 'near the amortization house', informed the 'respected public' through the *Jornal do Commercio* that she had just received from England

> a rich assortment of coats of all colours, civilian and military frock-coats, trousers of blue and brown cloth, ditto of fancy worsted, and fabrics suitable for summer, very fine silk waistcoats and more ordinary ditto, ditto of fancy fustian and ditto of flannel for men, silk stockings of all qualities, kid gloves in the latest fashion, colourful cloths and fabrics of superior quality for customers to have their garments made however they wish.

The expression 'coats of all colours' should be interpreted as advertising overstatement or rhetoric. For in 1831 English fashion in men's coats restricted the colours for these garments to blue, brown, grey and dark purple. Having studied English exports to Brazil in 1816 and the years directly afterwards, Professor Manchester states that plenty of 'fine cloth' came here and, 'particularly blue or black, sold quickly'.[247]

John ('João') Donnelly was an important merchant of English fabrics in Brazil during the first half of the nineteenth century. He appears in the *Diário de Pernambuco* of 28 November 1836, where he says that he

> has the honour of announcing to his Friends and to the public in general that he has just arrived from London with a large, select assortment of fabrics which, for their quality and good taste, invite

[247] Alan K. Manchester, *British Preëminence in Brazil, Its Rise and Decline. A Study in European Expansion*. Chapel Hill, 1933, p. 96.

> the attention of his customers and which consist of the following – Cloth from the principal Factories of England in all colours and qualities, worsteds, shawls and quilted material, plain and patterned velvet; silk cravats in exquisite taste and new styles; silk for waistcoats and a large assortment of ready-made outfits in the latest London fashion, which has never been surpassed in quality and elegance.

If Donnelly's advertisement lacks English sobriety in its purest form, it is perhaps because there was something of the Celt in this specialist in goods as characteristically English as men's wear. The fact is that Donnelly closes his advertisement with the same un-English exuberance, assuring

> his friends and customers that thanks to their favours he will never deviate from the system that he has always followed of selling his fabrics at the least possible profit: at Rua da Cadeia do Recife, No 37.

In the early nineteenth century, with transport from Europe to Brazil still difficult and subject to the caprices of the seas and winds (which, when very rough, could spoil the sailing-ships' cargoes), fabrics sometimes arrived damaged and cloth buyers ran the risk of making terrible mistakes and incurring huge losses at auctions. But not at those held by Freeze and Blanckenganger who, in an advertisement in the *Gazeta do Rio de Janeiro* on 18 January 1809, declared that 'the Fabrics presented at their auctions will always be faultless'. There were, however, auctions of goods – of English origin or transported in English ships – that were definitely damaged. Acknowledged to be damaged. Not just fabrics but foodstuffs, which, as we shall see later, made up a large proportion of English trade with Brazil. In an advertisement in the *Gazeta do Rio de Janeiro* on 6 November 1811, the 'Purser of the English Squadron' himself informed anyone interested that on 12 November he would 'put up for auction in the Warehouses on the Ilha das Cobras Pier the following spoilt provisions: Flour, 896 Barrels and 134 hogsheads; Barley ditto, 72 Barrels 19 hogsheads; Rice, 3 Hogsheads and 1 Barrel'. Auctions were always held in the morning: at nine, ten or half past ten. Or at noon sharp. At precise times, but not all at the same time. Not always or only at ten o'clock, as claimed by the English historian Koebel and recently by Mr Morales de los Rios Filho in his picturesque evocation of imperial Rio de Janeiro, with an emphasis that not only requires but demands correction.

In these advertisements for auctions, an 'Englishman's word' was used as the equivalent of 'word of honour', alongside 'English time'; these two expressions – which Koebel points out as being widespread in South America[248] – were characteristic of the gentlemanliness and exactness shown in business by the Englishmen who were setting themselves up here as merchants. The gentlemanliness and exactness with which the English marked their presence in a country where meetings would be vaguely arranged for 'between eight and nine o'clock', for example, and not even then were they always kept. They might well be put off until tomorrow or the day after.

Anyone who wanted to buy 'spoilt provisions' should buy them from the English at auctions held at nine, ten, eleven or twelve in the morning – times when there was plenty of light. The English did not refrain from selling them because they were spoilt and might harm people's health. They just announced that they were spoilt. 'An Englishman's word' in business.

With the confidence they inspired in Brazilians as sound, reliable businessmen, it was natural that before long the English would distinguish themselves in this country as insurance agents. That is precisely what happened, and it is worth noting that Robert Stevens's *Essay on Average*, published in London in 1816, was soon translated into Portuguese – by Antônio Julião da Costa – and published here in 1824. By then the work by Woolrych, *A Practical Treatise of the Commercial and Mercantile Law of England*, was known in Brazil. Silva Lisboa was a great disseminator of English works on economics and commercial law in this country. And, on 24 May 1809, the following memorable announcement in our mercantile or commercial history appeared in the *Gazeta do Rio de Janeiro*:

> William ('Guilherme') Harrison and Daniel Huntly, Merchants established in this City, make it known to the Merchants of this Place that they have been appointed agents for a large number of the most respectable insurers of Lloyd's Insurance House in the City of London to attend to and take note of any average, loss or damage that may result in loss to said insured parties.

It was Lloyd's in Brazil.

English insurance companies were to develop large businesses in Brazil. But these companies provided more characteristically bourgeois forms of insurance: against water, fire or theft. The Royal Insurance Company became famous. So did the Alliance, founded in London in 1828 and specializing in insurance for 'masonry buildings with tiled roofs'. These

[248] W. H. Koebel, *British Exploits in South America. A History of British Activities in Exploration, Military Adventure, Diplomacy, Science, and Trade, in Latin America*, New York, 1917, p. 529.

were the main kinds of insurance that the English promoted in Brazil. And not so much insurance for working people against old age, invalidity, sickness, accidents or industrial diseases.

A number of advertisements in the early years of the nineteenth century give the feeling that not only Lloyd's but His Britannic Majesty's Government itself was protecting the commercial activities of British subjects in Portuguese America. Thus the figure of the English Judge-Conservator himself looms out of the text of a notice published in the *Gazeta* on 21 August 1811:

> The administrators of the bankrupt House of Rutherford Manson & Co., of this city, make it known both to the Creditors and to the Debtors thereof that pursuant to Edictal Letters of this English Judge-Conservatorship they are summoned to put in an appearance in Court within the peremptory period of 3 months from the date of 1st August in order to legalize their credits and settle their Debts; those who fail to do so shall be excluded from any benefit or right in the Distribution of the property of said bankrupts and any payment made after the act of bankruptcy by any of the debtors or persons other than the Administrators of said firm shall be deemed null and void.

The same protection, albeit less direct, may be felt in a certain 'private notice' in the *Jornal do Commercio* of Rio de Janeiro fifteen years later, on 11 October 1827, when Brazil was independent of Portugal and the old Methuen Treaty:

> The undersigned Commissioners appointed by the Court of King's Bench of England for the examination of certain witnesses which is to take place in this capital city in a suit pending in that Court between Francisco Correa Garcia against Jaimes Fenning wish to know whether the following persons are still in this Capital or in ts district or in the Province – Teofilo Soares da Cunha Serpa – Custodio da Costa Berlão, or Bertão – Manoel Antunes – Manoel José Sequeira – José Gomes – and Rita Aurelia (black) – all said persons save the first having been occupied in the year 1820 in selling or peddling fabrics in the streets. Should any one or more of them still be here, the aforementioned Commissioners hope that they will be prepared to declare their address through this or any other broadsheet, if they do not wish to do so at the house of either of said Commissioners, that is to say at Rua da Ajuda, No 100,

> or at Rua dos Pescadores, No 50, and they are advised that if it is necessary for one or more of the aforesaid persons to be examined before the Commission each of them shall be compensated for the inconvenience and trouble they may be caused by this Act. Rio de Janeiro, 10 October 1827 – *Diogo Soares da Silva de Bivar – Carlos Raynsford.*

Advertisements or announcements actually written in English are not uncommon, and they are not always free of editing errors and dreadfully misspelt proper names. The *Jornal do Commercio* of 28 November 1827 ran the following advertisement for a public auction 'for account of the British Gouvernment [*sic*]:

> Sale of 380 Casks or thereabouts of English Bread On Thursday next the 29 Inst. will be sold by public Auction for account of the British Gouvernment at n. 187 rua Direita at 11 o'clock in the forenoon a quantity of English Biscuit of good quality as well as 160 bags of inferior quality. – The Bread in Casks is well worth the attention of ship Chandlers &c. It will be put in lots each not less than 20 casks as will suit the purchasers. Samples may be had on application at the Store N. 187 rua Direita.[249]

Or this one in the same newspaper on 26 November 1827:

> The Ship Chandlery & Grocery Business under the firm of C Harvey & C.º N. 148 rua Direita, will, on and after the first day of December next be conducted under the name of Thomas S. Martin who will pay & receive all outstanding accounts of the said firm.[250]

Rua Direita in Rio de Janeiro keeps appearing in English advertisements during the early years of the nineteenth century. It could be said to be the English commercial street *par excellence* in Rio de Janeiro at that time. But it was not just Rua Direita: all the streets around the customs house, starting with Rua da Alfândega[251] itself, were full, if not of English-owned stores, then of shops whose wares were almost entirely English: glass, iron, fabrics, china, paint, paper, beer and cutlery. The advertisements in the *Gazeta do Rio de Janeiro* in the last years of the colonial era and the first of the Empire show that quite clearly. In fact, this predominance of English

[249] Quoted in English (Translator).
[250] Quoted in English (Translator).
[251] 'Customs House Street' (Translator).

goods in the Rua da Alfândega and adjacent streets had been growing ever since the end of the eighteenth century, when Lord Macartney's embassy passed through Rio on its way to China.[252] Staunton, a member of Macartney's entourage, thought at that time that certain streets in Rio de Janeiro offered buyers almost as many English goods as certain streets in Manchester. A Rio merchant of the time even told the Englishmen that Brazil, like Portugal's other prosperous colonies and Portugal itself, were flourishing almost entirely for the benefit of England[253] – which, in fact, received the best Brazilian gold and, through Portugal, sent us prime necessities.

It is interesting to point out that this eighteenth-century English diplomat, who was on his way to the Far East as minister plenipotentiary of his country to the emperor of China and secretary to the special embassy under Lord Macartney, found Rio de Janeiro at the end of that century to be a prosperous city; its inhabitants satisfied with their lives; its houses mostly large and well-built of local stone or granite and suited to the climate; the shops and stores full of goods[254] (and apparently full of customers as well, although there were not yet any newspaper advertisements – which, incidentally, were introduced mainly by English merchants); a number of public and private buildings under construction; and workmen always busy. Although some streets were narrow, that was not an inconvenience in a climate like Brazil's: the excessive heat meant that people always sought the shade, and shade was never lacking in the narrow streets. He admired the aqueduct: proof that the Portuguese who built it knew the laws of hydrostatics. The fountains were always guarded by soldiers whose duty it was to oversee the distribution of their good water.[255]

He noticed the bookshops: just books of medicine and divinity. Neither the English novels nor the essayists had appeared there yet. Neither Walter Scott nor Pope, who were to be so prominent in newspaper advertisements in later years. Very few inhabitants knew any other language than Portuguese, which prevented them from being corrupted by the writings of modern philosophers. Or – I would add to the solemn Englishman's observations – distracted from their devotions and duties by

[252] Sir George Staunton, *An Authentic Account of an Embassy from the King of Great Britain to the Emperor of China*, London, 1797. The French edition of this work is more complete and has many interesting notes by the translator: *Voyage dans l'interieur de la Chine, et en Tartarie, fait dans les années 1792, 1793 et 1794, par Lord Macartney, Ambassadeur du Roi d'Angleterre auprès de l'Empereur de la Chine; Redigé sur les Papiers de Lord Macartney, sur ceux du Commodore Erasme Gower, et des autres Personnes attachées à l'Ambassade, par Sir George Staunton... Traduit de l'anglais, avec des notes, par J. Castéra*, 2nd ed., Paris, 1799.

[253] *Ibid.*, I, p. 206 (in the French edition; I, p. 79 in the English – Translator).

[254] *Ibid.*, I, p. 206 (I, p. 79 in the English edition – Translator).

[255] *Ibid.*, I, p. 205 (I, p. 79 in the English edition – Translator).

novels like Swift's or Ann Radcliffe's.

Much devotion in the churches and streets. Sexual irregularities. Opera, plays, masquerades. Notable disproportion between the numbers of whites and blacks.[256]

Although there were not yet any newspapers to publish charts of Brazil's imports and exports, like the *Gazeta do Rio de Janeiro* in its heyday, the diplomat discovered that the country's production was growing so large that the balance of trade was beginning to tip in its favour. And there were Brazilians who were already thinking about independence: either as the seat of the Lusitanian empire of Brazil, or Brazil unencumbered by the distant, exploitative metropolis. The people in the colony appeared to have a great interest in the French Revolution.[257] Enlightened Brazilians, that is, who cannot have been very numerous at that time.

Pombal,[258] the Englishman tells us, had wanted to transfer the seat of the Empire from Portugal to Brazil. That had even been considered before his time, when the Spanish invaded Portuguese territory, but King João IV had not had the 'wise courage' – as Staunton's French translator terms it in a footnote – to put such an audacious idea into practice. The result was a Brazil over-exploited by the mother country, whose agents in Rio de Janeiro levied twelve per cent on the value of the merchandise that Lisbon and Porto sent to them, according to information gathered by the members of the Macartney embassy. Whatever the political fate of Rio de Janeiro or Brazil, however, those perspicacious travellers saw that nature had made this country 'a land always worthy of attention'.[259] Principally, one might add, of British attention. British travellers at the end of the eighteenth century – repeating Whithal's enthusiasm back in the sixteenth for possible English trade with Brazil – used to sing the praises of the Brazilian market to their country's manufacturers, industrialists and businessmen: 'a land worthy of attention'. Worthy of attention for being rich in gold, diamonds and timber. And worthy of attention for not having glass in its houses, for few houses having cutlery, for not yet having light carriages, for kitchenware being poor, household containers being scarce, tradesmen's tools being deficient and the outside of houses needing paint.

[256] *Ibid.*, I, pp. 212, 227 (I, pp. 81, 82, 87 in the English edition – Translator).

[257] *Ibid.*, I, p. 239 (I, p. 91 in the English edition – Translator).

[258] Sebastião José de Carvalho e Melo, 1st Marquis of Pombal (1699-1782), was the Portuguese prime minister from 1750 to 1777 (Translator).

[259] Staunton, *Voyage dans l'interieur de la Chine*, I, p. 247. Freyre here repeats a slight mistranslation in the French edition. In the original English-language edition, Staunton refers only to the Rio landscape, not to the whole country in economic terms: 'Whatever may be the political fate of Rio de Janeiro, its natural appearance must always attract notice. [...] Its harbour, mountains, woods and rocks [...]' (Staunton, *An Authentic Account*, I, p. 94) (Translator).

All of that drew the attention of British observers such as Dampier, Rogers, Byron, Staunton, Lindley, Luccock, Cooke and Mrs Kindersley, who were here in the seventeenth, eighteenth and early nineteenth centuries.

The English diplomats who disembarked in Brazil in 1792 *en route* to China and who, like good diplomats, were also good spies, that is to say individuals anywhere in the service of their government and people, glimpsed in Rio de Janeiro the capital of another China, almost as unknown to Europe as the one in the Orient, where English glass, ironware, cutlery and paint might be profitably consumed. A land pleasing to the taste of the then Don Juan of markets which was British imperialism: it was virgin, plump and ready for penetration by the trade of His Britannic Majesty's subjects. Excited by such information as that gathered in the late eighteenth century by these enthusiasts for Brazil, Great Britain could not wait to establish herself in this better China: a China to be conquered for English goods more by means of newspaper advertisements than by the pure use of naval force or military might. Those prosperous Rio de Janeiro businessmen whom the Englishmen in Lord Macartney's embassy met would soon be hurt, if not wiped out, by competition from the many British merchants who, once Brazil's ports were opened to foreign trade, would establish themselves in Rio de Janeiro, Bahia, Pernambuco and Maranhão almost as if this were a conquered land, and advertise their wares, superior to those of other nations, in newspapers. The first Brazilian newspapers mainly served the Portuguese and Brazilians as a means to express their political hatreds or interests, but they were soon used by the British for their own ends: for commercial announcements and advertisements. And the importance of these advertisements as a revolutionary factor in Brazilian life and culture can hardly be exaggerated. They were veritable trumpets of Jericho, to the sound of which walls began to tumble and rivals fade away. In this respect, the *Gazeta do Rio de Janeiro* with all its advertisements for English goods was by no means the 'anodyne' rag of Oliveira Lima's remark but, on the contrary, a revolutionary newspaper or publication.

It would not be long before Brazilians' resentment or hatred towards the Portuguese – so clearly noticed by the English members of the Macartney embassy during the few days they spent in Rio de Janeiro in 1792 – spilled over into resentment or even hatred towards the English, although such hatred did not always extend to the British goods advertised in newspapers and hung at the doors of the new stores and shops as irresistible bait. The fact is that some of the British merchants who gradually established themselves in Rio de Janeiro, Bahia and Pernambuco after the transfer of the Court from Lisbon to Brazil – an old idea of far-sighted but over-cautious statesmen, which an indecisive man, the future King João VI, had the 'wise courage' to put into practice in 1808 – started behaving as if they were lieutenants or sergeants in a conquered land, not merely appropriating privileges hitherto exclusively or sovereignly enjoyed by local or Portuguese merchants, but expanding them under the imperial protection of His Britannic Majesty's Government.

'The hatred of the natives of Brazil towards England is more violent than I can describe', the minister of Great Britain in Rio, Viscount Strangford, told his country's foreign minister, Viscount Castlereagh, in a dispatch of 20 February 1814. He continues:

> It pervades every class of persons in this country, except perhaps the planters in the neighbourhood of the Northern ports, whose interests have certainly been benefited by the direct trade with England. The inhabitants of Bahia and of those parts where the Slave Trade forms the principal branch of commerce are driven to desperation by the measures which have been adopted by His Majesty's navy for the suppression of that traffic, and which have occasioned the ruin of many of the chief houses engaged in it. The merchants of Rio de Janeiro in like manner have suffered severely from the opening of a free trade between this country and Europe, by losing that exclusive monopoly of imports and exports which they formerly possessed, a circumstance which they do not fail to charge upon England, and which, united to the irritation of their feelings produced by the long detention of many of their ships at the time of the Prince's departure for Brazil, have generated in them an almost irreconcilable animosity against the British name and nation.[260]

The lords and lordlings in the prince's retinue were not the only ones to expel the former occupants or real owners from the best houses in the city. Some of the English merchants who arrived in Rio at the same time did almost that: they too gradually took over some of the best trading sites, to the detriment of Brazilian merchants, who were not only disfavoured by the 'free trade' that suddenly took away their long-standing monopoly, but also disoriented by that overwhelming invasion of English importers of European goods, whose advertisements in the *Gazeta do Rio de Janeiro* began to sound like a death-knell to local merchants. Mawe, who was in Brazil during the first feverish days of the English Revolution – the revolution brought about in the Rio de Janeiro market by English merchants – criticizes his countrymen for the 'excessive commercial speculations' to

[260] C. K. Webster, *Britain and the Independence of Latin America, 1812-1830. Select Documents from the Foreign Office Archives*, London, New York, Toronto, 1938, I, p. 171.

which they had so suddenly devoted themselves.[261]

Luccock, however, comments on the fact that soon after the prince had arrived in Rio he forbade Brazilians in that city – individuals or families – to occupy two or more houses; he points out that the ban extended to shops and warehouses, and it was not done to benefit needy persons who had come from Portugal or Europe, but 'commercial adventurers from every region'. Luccock adds that the English refused to take advantage of this, as such a brutal act seemed unfair to them, but preferred to pay 'liberal rents' for the houses and buildings from which the legitimate proprietors had been evicted.[262] In any case, however, Brazilians were expelled for the benefit of invaders; and one can only imagine the amount of gold amassed by the middlemen in all these removals into and out of houses and warehouses, in a period notorious for rackets and corruption among the men surrounding the prince.

To what can we attribute this greed in the commercial conquest of Rio de Janeiro, which so damaged the reputation of the British in Brazil? It was what Mawe called the 'incredible competition' among the British merchants themselves. In other words, the capitalist system in its raw, individualist form. As a result of such senseless competition among the British merchants, within days of the prince regent's arrival the Rio de Janeiro market was flooded with British goods: far more than could be consumed. We have seen that rents had soared for the buildings where part of this excess British stock was kept, with the result that the invaders paid dear to install themselves in houses vacated by Brazilians, several of whom moved out to their houses in the country, half humiliated and half indignant, even though they were earning high rents from this almost military occupation of their premises, buildings and city residences. Another part of the excess stock was left to rot on the beaches near the customs house, exposed to the sun and rain. Much of it was looted.

Some of the invaders had, in fact, succeeded in moving into commercially well-located premises, although at high rents, and thus had won the first battle with the former merchants: the English occupation of the best commercial area in the city, with the expulsion of the Brazilians from their best redoubts. The invaders were now installed in the best commercial buildings in town. An ecological revolution, brought about by the English invasion of the best commercial area in the city.

The privileges granted them by the 1810 treaty soon gave them enough to make a profit from their imports of British or exotic goods into Brazil,

[261] John Mawe, *Travels in the Interior of Brazil*, 2nd ed., London, 1821, p. 453.
[262] John Luccock, *Notes on Rio de Janeiro and the Southern Parts of Brazil... 1808 to 1818*, London, 1820, p. 100.

even if they did have to pay exorbitant rents to the Brazilian store owners. Ultimately, the ones who ended up paying for those exorbitances were the Brazilians themselves, who bought tempting British goods no longer from local merchants who received them via Portugal – as in Staunton's day – but from British merchants, who received large and highly varied direct shipments of manufactured goods from their own country and of products from other lands.

A book of impressions of Brazil written in the early nineteenth century by the English clergyman Robert Walsh, which has already been mentioned more than once in these notes, contains a detailed description of the streets of Rio de Janeiro in the early years of the Empire and helps us to understand better what the newspaper advertisements say about the location of British trade in the capital of Brazil. The streets, squares and alleys of the capital, together with their traditional names, their lengths and widths – Walsh deals with all of this in his account.

If we project onto his description, or onto a map of the city in those days, the newspaper advertisements for houses, stores and offices owned or rented by English merchants, we can attempt to make an ecological reconstruction of the old commercial heart of Rio de Janeiro and see which of those streets were dominated or preferred by British trade. This was the main, substantial trade in basics. The trade in 'prime necessities', as Commander Laplace noted, two or three years after Walsh:

> These merchants do not sell the most sumptuous products invented for the luxury of capital cities, as ours do; instead they use the same method here that they employ in Peru and Chile: they provide the people with all their prime necessities.[263]

The streets where the main English merchants installed themselves were – as has been pointed out already – the ones closest to the customs house and, in general, the less narrow ones. Such less narrow streets would have been preferred by the British invaders since they would have made it easier to come and go with wide bolts of fabric and the heavy goods that were so characteristic of British trade: iron, copper, machines, Baltic pine, and crates of window glass. Since French trade did not have the same space requirements as the English, it needed no more than the orientally narrow streets, which also became the capital's most elegant thoroughfares with their shops full of fancy goods, luxury items and women's fashions. One of

263 C. Laplace, *Voyage Autour du Monde par les Mers de l'Inde et de Chine exécuté sur la Corvette de l'État la Favorite pendant les Années 1830, 1831 et 1832*, Paris, 1835, IV, p. 8 (quoted in French – Translator).

them, the Rua do Ouvidor, where the rare English merchants established among the French give the impression of people sinning against nature: men who were untrue to their commercial sex, and effeminate or womanish. One such was Samuel Noel, a merchant who an advertisement in the *Jornal do Commercio* of 3 October 1827 tells us was installed at Rua do Ouvidor, No 88, with anchors, iron stoves for ships and bronze beds. Although the advertisement says the bronze beds were 'very elegant', the impression we get of this English ironmonger is one of an exile or renegade from the Rua da Alfândega, a hippopotamus or lion lost among gazelles. Whereas the Mr Harris who in 1818 had a shop in the Rua do Ouvidor with the 'latest fashions', together with 'a large number of hairpieces and hair ornaments for ladies, beautiful feathers, and roses with natural moss', as described in an advertisement in the *Gazeta* on 24 March that year, makes us think of an Englishman who preferred the company of the French to that of his somewhat unrefined compatriots in the Rua Direita or Rua da Alfândega.

The Rua do Ouvidor – a cramped yet charming street – was unsuitable for most traders in heavy goods like iron and copper ware, or wholesale fabrics and china, as has been pointed out already. In this respect, it is interesting to come across newspaper advertisements both seeking and offering suitable premises for English merchants in Brazil. Typical of the 'premises wanted' type of advertisement is one placed by 'An English Merchant' in the *Gazeta do Rio de Janeiro* of 12 September 1812, in which he says he needs

> a house with a good, large, light warehouse, from the Rua da Quitanda downwards, at a rent of 500 to 600$ per year.

A typical 'to let' advertisement is the one by José Saporiti – a rich Recife merchant in the first half of the nineteenth century – in the *Diário de Pernambuco* of 14 May 1846:

> Warehouse to let at an attractive price at house No 18, Rua da Cruz, Recife, stretching from one street to the next, all paved in stone, suitable for English fabrics or ironware, since it is not damp, or to store any other merchandise, since it is in a good location...

In Rio as in Recife, that is where the British wholesaler established in this country in the second half of the nineteenth century would set up his business: in a good location – in the best locations, in fact, for which they paid high rents; in large and preferably light buildings; in premises suitable for fabrics, ironware, glass, china and cutlery. That does not mean that there were no Englishmen selling English butter, but they nearly always traded in it alongside characteristically English products: goods of iron, steel, copper or bronze, glass, tea, beer, clocks, munitions, nails, whetstones, scythes, tinplate, paints, paper, gin, bricks, sunhats, coal, saddles, harnesses, baize, wool, salt cod, furniture, pianos and even dye for beards or sideburns. Articles, I repeat, that were more masculine in nature – and almost always in size and weight as well – than feminine.

As for the tendency for English warehouses to cluster around the customs house, it seems that it was also due to the density, weight, solidity and masculinity – as we might say – of the most characteristic merchandise of that trade, which was less inclined to spread to more distant streets than trade in lighter goods. What happened in Rio also happened in Recife and Salvador: after the opening of the ports in 1808, English merchants more than any others put down roots close to the customs houses, with their ship chandlers, warehouses and depots for heavy merchandise. Close not only to the customs houses but also to His Majesty's consulates – which were always located near the sea and the waves ruled over by Britannia. Newspaper advertisements help to document that fact by giving clear, precise locations of stores and business houses. In Recife, the English set up their stores in town houses in the Rua da Cruz and Rua do Bom Jesus and in Lingueta; in Salvador, at the Portas da Ribeira, where in 1817 William Murray was selling 18, 12, 9, 4 and 3-calibre iron mortars 'with their accessories and suitable balls', according to an advertisement in the *Idade d'Ouro do Brazil* of 30 December that year; in Rio de Janeiro, in the Rua da Alfândega, Rua Direita and Rua dos Pescadores. Always close to the sea and the customs houses.

Examination of the newspaper advertisements on which this study is based does not support the claim made by Mr Adolfo Morales de los Rios Filho that English merchants – 'the English', as the eminent architect says in a recent study of the architectural and social history of Rio de Janeiro – were expelled from the Rua do Ouvidor by the French: 'the French soon conquered the Rua do Ouvidor, expelling the English led by the irritated shoemaker Mr William.'[264]

It is not that there were no Englishmen in the Rua do Ouvidor. We have already seen there were. The zoning of types of trade in Rio de Janeiro did not become so strict after the arrival of European merchants that the Rua Direita was just for the English and the Rua do Ouvidor was just for the French. However, perhaps not all but at least the majority and the cream of those British merchants who established themselves in Rio after 1808 had their own ecological focus of activity: as clearly shown by

[264] Adolfo Morales de los Rios Filho, *O Rio de Janeiro imperial*, Rio de Janeiro, 1946, p. 240.

newspaper advertisements, it was not the Rua do Ouvidor but the area including the Rua Direita, Rua da Alfândega and Rua dos Pescadores.

Mathison, who was here in 1821, points out that 'during the last few years' over thirty English business houses associated with trading houses in England had been established in Rio de Janeiro, and such English houses were becoming more and more numerous every year. They were still not as numerous as the French in Rio de Janeiro, however, who were said to number more than a thousand. Almost all the English houses supplied 'goods of more solid manufacture'; they were wholesalers who extended their trade throughout the interior of the country.[265] A truly imperial trade, we might add to Mathison's account. The French traders' operations, on the other hand, with two exceptions, were confined to the cities. They were retailers, sellers of fancy goods, gems, 'jewellery and all sorts of novelties'.[266] Their shops and boutiques were ornamental and made the streets cheerful. Principally – one might add to Mathison's remarks – the Rua do Ouvidor; with its tradition of having been an elegant street, it quickly became the favourite of the French, who were less opulent than the English, for their more feminine than masculine, more retail than wholesale kind of trade. There is nothing to show that the French had had to expel 'the English'. At most, a few English were displaced. On this point, newspaper advertisements for French shops are also excellent illustrative material, since they very clearly show that French merchants established themselves preferably in the Rua do Ouvidor and the Rua do Ourives. On his arrival in Rio in 1828, Walsh found them there selling curtains, mirrors, ornamental clocks and vases, and they had about 140 shops or workshops where they carried out 'all manner of trades [...], characteristic of the nation', including bakers, gilders of metals, clock-makers and confectioners, while some thirty others had fashion houses or were jewellers, and twenty or more traded in all kinds of French novelties.[267] The French were also the only booksellers in Rio de Janeiro. Their bookshops – or one of them, at least – supplied books not only to Europeans and Christians, but also Bahian Africans and Muslims – the most literate non-whites in Brazil – as the Comte de Gobineau found to his surprise when he was in Rio. This French commentator, and not any newspaper advertisement, is the source of the information that a French bookshop established in the Brazilian capital was selling the Koran and Arabic grammars at very high prices ('*fort cher*')[268] to those Africans with a thirst for knowledge, perhaps unbeknown

[265] Mathison, *Narrative of a Visit to Brazil*, pp. 128-9.

[266] Quoted in French (Translator).

[267] Walsh, *Notices of Brazil*, I, p. 257.

[268] Letter to the French Foreign Minister from the Comte de Gobineau, Minister in Brazil, dated September 1869, quoted in 'Revue de l'Académie des Sciences Morales et Politiques, année 1870', *Journal des Economistes*, Paris, ser. 3, year 7, vol. 27, 1872, p. 101.

to the police. Further evidence of the way in which the East resisted the West in the battle fought between them in Brazil after the reopening of the ports to international trade. And the invaders' main control towers in that battle were in the large houses in the Rua Direita and the Rua da Alfândega, and not so much in the old houses in the Rua do Ouvidor occupied by the French.

A few more words on the Rua do Ouvidor in contrast to Alfândega, Direita and Pescadores. Referring to Rio de Janeiro in the early decades of the nineteenth century, the historian Noronha Santos says that the Rua do Ouvidor – the 'street of the French' – did not have 'sumptuous buildings' at that time but rather 'many old, dilapidated buildings' such as those in the 'area between the site of the former market and the Rua do Carmo'; they were so old and dilapidated that they were occupied by 'stables for animals' and coach-houses for carriages like the one belonging to the Frenchman Jean Guebel.[269] Everything suggests that it was through the efforts and skills of small French traders that prestige was restored to this street: decrepit yet well suited to their elegant trade in fancy goods because of its location and spatial characteristics.

Such a narrow, decaying street would not attract English merchants – veritable noblemen of the wholesale trade – to install their imperial merchandise there. The streets that tempted the English, I repeat, were the broader, more respectable ones that were more strategic from a wholesale viewpoint. The ones with more expensive premises in more sought-after locations, from which they gradually displaced the former residents, as we have seen, although in Rio and Salvador the odd English invader must have come across resistance like that which the 'fat-bellied Portuguese' and the 'thin-faced foreigner' found in Recife in 1835:

> the former encouraging and the latter proposing to purchase certain premises from a Brazilian just because they agree that Brazilians should not own anything good,

which led the owner of the premises coveted by the two foreigners to announce in the *Diário de Pernambuco* of 10 September that year that, instead of the premises, and for 60 réis instead of 60,000 cruzados,[270] he would offer them some 'fine *quiri* trees'.[271]

According to Noronha Santos in the work mentioned above, in 1808 dilapidated two-storey houses in the Rua do Ouvidor were bought 'for

[269] Noronha Santos, *Meios de Transporte no Rio de Janeiro*, 1934, p. 39.
[270] Cruzado: a coin worth 480 réis.
[271] A tropical hardwood also known as *freijó* (Translator).

600$, 700$ and $800'; in 1815 'Joaquim José da Cruz Secco purchased a small one-storey house in that street for 200$ from Joaquim José da Costa Franco and his wife'; and 'by 1850 the number of commercial houses located in the Rua do Ouvidor was no more than a hundred': 100 shops, with the odd misplaced warehouse among them. Mr Noronha Santos also points out in relation to the Rua do Ouvidor that

> a large part of its properties had a lower letting value than the houses in the Rua dos Ourives, Rua da Quitanda and Rua Direita, [...] where the large import-export trade predominated.[272]

These and the Rua da Alfândega, Rua dos Pescadores, Rua do Sabão and Rua da Viola were the streets where the most important English merchants mainly had their premises. One or two may have reconciled themselves to staying among the shopkeepers of the Rua do Ouvidor. In this respect, I reiterate that newspaper advertisements, which specify the street and house number of the premises in which the English merchants who had arrived in Rio after the opening of the ports set themselves up, are the most precise and detailed form of documentation, such that other sources should fall silent before them.

In his recent work, Professor Adolfo Morales de los Rios Filho claims that it was French merchants, with their

> fabric and fashion shops, hairdressers, florists and tobacconists, [who] introduced *vitrines* (large, glazed display cabinets), replacing the old habit of displaying fabrics and other merchandise on cords stretched across the fronts and in the doorways of trading houses.[273]

To refer not just to Rio de Janeiro but to Brazil as a whole, it would be fair to say that display cabinets were introduced not only by the French but by the English as well, in their shops and taverns, albeit in smaller numbers than in the French shops and boutiques. As we know, the French soon dominated the elegant trade in fancy goods, leaving the wholesale trade – the big and ugly, which had less need for display cabinets or glass cases – to the English.

It should be pointed out, however, that by the time Pedro II's reign began the luxury of vitrines was no longer limited to the elegant fashion and fancy goods trade, dominated by the French in both Rio and Recife; in Recife they were also found in taverns and grocers' shops, sometimes

[272] Noronha Santos, *Meios de Transporte no Rio de Janeiro*, I, p. 39.

[273] Morales de los Rios Filho, *O Rio de Janeiro imperial*, p. 240.

English-owned, which were full of fine goods and expensive preserves brought over from London. That is suggested by an advertisement in the *Diário de Pernambuco* of 28 May 1841 for

> a shop cabinet, partly glazed, with hinged doors, likewise glazed, suitable for a fabric shop or any other business.

Another advertisement in the *Diário* on 1 April 1842 states:

> For sale. Some cases from a grocer's shop, new, with 6 panes of glass in front, and all highly suitable for displaying wares.

Showing that in Recife at that time there were vitrines not only in fancy goods shops but in taverns, grocer's shops and fabric shops. On 10 October 1843 the *Diário* announced:

> Two glass cases for sale, suitable for displaying goods in taverns.

Such 'glass cases' seem to have been used in 'Augusto Corbett's house' in Rua da Cadeia, Recife, to display the 'Port wines, Sherry and Champagne' (particular favourites of the English living in Brazil) that he took great care to advertise to the *sportsmen*[274] of Recife. This Corbett, by the way, would occasionally go to the extreme of addressing those *sportsmen* in English:

> A few cannisters containing one pound each of Mes. John Stan & Sons fine glass London Gin powder may still be had on application to A. S. Corbett.275

The 'new store' in the Rua do Trapiche, Recife, at that time sold

> London cheeses, English hams, preserves, mustard, and large and small tins of peas, meat and salmon from England, black tea and Lisson, likewise English, hair brooms for sweeping the house and Dr Maurison's pills;276 [and also] very old bottled Port wine at 480 réis a bottle, dry Madeira at 800 réis [...] very fresh English biscuits at 200 réis [...] pale and dark beers at 440 réis a bottle.277

[274] Word used in English (Translator).

[275] *Diário de Pernambuco*, 26 September 1843 (quoted in English – Translator).

[276] *Diário de Pernambuco*, 20 August 1844.

[277] *Diário de Pernambuco*, 16 July 1845.

And it is not absurd to imagine that such fine goods would have been exhibited in those 'glass cases suitable for displaying goods in taverns'.

Still in Recife, which was as Anglicized as Rio and perhaps more so than Bahia in the first half of the nineteenth century, some English merchants – McCalmont & Co. – were selling 'the notorious C C brand champagne' in their 'house'[278] – which perhaps also had 'glass cases suitable for displays'. And an English ironmonger's shop – at Rua do Queimado, No 31 – was at that time, strange as it may seem, selling 'water to dye the hair and sideburns'.[279] Whether this item was English, French, German or local in origin, it would certainly not have been displayed in any cabinet but sold discreetly to gentlemen who had gone there to purchase scissors, screws, penknives or nails from London.

Ever since the early years of Brazil's independence, the main centre from which English influence over Brazilians' eating habits was disseminated in Recife was a tavern, probably fitted out with glass cases for displaying samples, which sold 'English Mustard, London Hams and Cheeses', alongside 'writing inks of all qualities recently arrived from London' and 'canaries in cages', the latter goods clearly being intended for Englishmen passing through the port or city. This establishment selling English goods was in 'Forte do Mato below the English Hostel', according to an advertisement in the *Diário de Pernambuco* of 27 November 1829; and the English Hostel in Forte do Mato was for many years a meeting place for Englishmen passing through the capital of Pernambuco. Something like Jolly Heath's boarding house in Rio de Janeiro. Or its successor, Johnson's Hotel, an English hotel outcompeted or superseded by the Hotel dos Estrangeiros, which was run more along French lines than English.[280]

In Rio de Janeiro, the French fancy goods and fashion shops may perhaps have been the only ones to have vitrines during the first half of the nineteenth century; in Recife, however, newspaper advertisements show that even taverns were beginning to use such 'glass cases' to display fine drinks and foodstuffs imported from England. Ewbank almost confirms what Professor Morales de los Rios Filho says when he writes in 1846 from Rio de Janeiro that

> probably not more than a dozen fancy stores can be found with glass windows. There are a few in Ouvidor (the Broadway of Rio), but in some of them the glass frames are removed at night, like the goods behind them.[281]

[278] *Diário de Pernambuco*, 11 October 1845.

[279] *Diário de Pernambuco*, 3 August 1844.

[280] Koebel, *British Exploits in South America*, pp. 372-3.

[281] Ewbank, *Life in Brazil*, p. 86, quoted in English (Translator).

But if we are to refer to Brazil as a whole, we have to consider the fact that newspaper advertisements in Recife in the same period mention the use of 'glass cases' for displays in taverns or food stores, a trade dominated at the time by the English and Portuguese. The main grocery stores belonged to English importers like McCalmont & Co.

We have already seen some typical advertisements that reflect the way in which British authority somewhat imperially asserted itself over commercial and civil life in Brazil in the early nineteenth century by having special judges or magistrates. In addition, newspaper advertisements never let us forget that, towards the end of the Kingdom and in the early years of the Empire, His Majesty's consuls in Brazil were prominent figures in the commercial life of the cities. While Laplace, the French commander mentioned previously, was circumnavigating the world in 1830-32, he quite rightly noted that in Brazil as well as in Chile and Peru it was the English who supplied the prime necessities for these peoples newly liberated from the political guardianship of Spain and Portugal, thus keeping them under a form of economic domination which for some time, in Brazil at least, exerted considerable political influence. Advertisements in colonial gazettes provide evidence for Brazil's status of being less a colony of Portugal than of England, which was undoubtedly the case during its transition from colony to politically independent Empire. A status from which it would not free itself overnight just by declaring political independence.

The highly privileged position that England had won for its products in Brazilian markets, while Brazil was still a colony, could not fail to give English influence in Portuguese America the aquiline profile of imperial influence. Oliveira Lima has rightly pointed out that the privileges Great Britain enjoyed in Brazil at that time recalled the European powers' imperial advantages in countries of the Far East:[282] their zones of influence, as today the republics of Central America are dominated by the United States, and the Slavic nations by Soviet Russia.

One fact is enough to characterize Brazil's quasi-colonial status in relation to Great Britain throughout much of the first half of the nineteenth century: even after Brazil had declared its independence, promulgated a criminal code and instituted its own judicial system, the British Government still obstinately refused to accept the judges appointed under the Imperial constitution as being sufficient, but retained its extra-special 'judges conservators' here: an extraterritorial privilege that would only disappear entirely in 1844.[283] It was under the shadow of such privileges

[282] Oliveira Lima, *O império brasileiro, 1822-1889*, São Paulo, 1927, p. 208.

[283] Manchester, *British Preëminence in Brazil*, p. 287. See also Dunshee de Abranches, *A expansão*

that the Brazilian economy had become imperially dominated by the British economy, to the extent that in 1812 Brazil consumed twenty-five per cent more English goods than the whole of Asia and more than four fifths of the total absorbed by South America.[284]

Since His Majesty's consuls themselves calculated the duty to be paid on English merchandise in Brazil, whereas for other foreign imports only the Portuguese authorities could set the invoice value of the merchandise, they gained demigod-like prestige in Brazilian territory. And it is with a rather demigod-like air that some consuls emerge from advertisements and announcements in gazettes during the Regency or Kingdom period, presiding over auctions, calling meetings and, in short, displaying an entirely special kind of authority. Similarly, some of them address the Brazilian authorities during the early years of the Empire in an overbearing tone – rather like the captain of a brig – in their letters, dispatches and communications. These will be examined and to some extent interpreted, in another chapter, as expressions of a form of imperialism that, after being almost omnipotent, came to endure competition from France and the United States and eventually mellowed under the influence of this competition, to the decided benefit of weaker nations at the time, such as Brazil. While the iron pots were clashing, the clay ones were hardening.

The special authority of HBM consuls in Brazil, however, was less visible in official papers than in gazette announcements or advertisements. The exceptional status enjoyed by English consuls in our country – not to mention the special judges – could not fail either to irritate the other foreigners or, once Brazil's independence had been declared, to touch the most exalted patriots on their sorest spot: that Brazil should be politically independent of any European control. That is precisely what happened, hence the unpopularity of the English in certain sections of the Brazilian population in the first half of the nineteenth century, particularly among people more influenced by the French, who at the time were actively spreading anti-British propaganda. That propaganda was an expression of intense commercial rivalry: the French against the almost absolute lords of the Brazilian or South American markets.

Despite their unpopularity, due to the political significance that their commercial dominance in Brazil had for a while, the English were more successful than other foreigners because of their business methods and procedures. Advertisements placed in Brazilian newspapers during the first half of the 19th century by English merchants, doctors and engineers reveal

*econômica e o comércio exterior do Brasil*, Rio de Janeiro, 1915, p. 70.

[284] *Exportation from Great Britain by Countries, 1822*, (*apud* Manchester, *British Preëminence in Brazil*, p. 97).

the superior methods through which they generally became respected, even though they were less liked than other foreigners. They may have been 'beefs', 'baizes', 'gringos', 'new sects', 'goats' (perhaps because they almost always wore sideburns) and 'old soaks' but, as merchants and professionals, they were almost always trustworthy and very few of them were swindlers or phoneys in the style of the French and Italians or, particularly, the French, German and Polish Jews, large numbers of whom were in Brazil at that time. The first half of the nineteenth century was a time when Brazilian cities were full of European conmen, charlatans and blackmailers, from the most refined types to the crudest. Some called themselves doctors; others pretended to be engineers. Some ventured to travel round the interior with boxes or chests of ladies' clothes – dresses that had gone out of fashion but which they presented to the country women as the latest styles from Paris. All of them scandalously exploited the ingenuousness of Brazilians, especially young ladies on sugar plantations and the more remote coffee estates. These young ladies were like sleeping beauties in the woods: they had slept through the long period – the eighteenth century – when Brazilians living in the interior, and even those on the coast, had been segregated from Europe. They were therefore easily swindled by pedlars with European merchandise, which were all new to people who had been used to goods from the Orient.

The honest and efficient methods of British merchants in Brazil during the first half of the nineteenth century (their honesty and efficiency were relative, since some of those Englishmen were accused of charging exorbitant prices for some of their goods or, like George Gibson, a money changer and broker in Recife, of having 'sent lots of people to Rata'[285]) are unlikely to be confirmed solely on the basis of advertisements, 'miscellaneous announcements' or 'private notices' in newspapers, which in this case would be somewhat suspect documents. It is actually nineteenth-century French travellers – the most impartial and objective of them – who acknowledge the superiority of the English over the French in commercial techniques and even ethics. They contrast the English methods with the French. D'Assier remarks that in Brazil the expression 'French business' had come to mean something like 'Punic business'.[286] The fact is that it is unusual to find an advertisement by a foreign merchant in a Brazilian newspaper in the first half of the nineteenth century like the one placed

[285] *Diário de Pernambuco*, 29 July 1843. (Rata island was used as a prison in the 19th century – Translator.)

[286] Adolphe d'Assier, *Le Brésil Contemporain, Races – Moeurs – Institutions – Paysage*, Paris, 1867. On p. 257 d'Assier writes: 'Today the term "French business" has become a saying in Brazil to mean any shady or underhand deal. The Brazilians say *negocio afrancesado*, just as the Romans used to say *fides punica*.' The contrast between the expressions 'French business' and 'an Englishman's word' shows that English trade was ethically superior in patriarchal Brazil.

by Charles Cannell in the *Jornal do Commercio* of Rio de Janeiro on 6 October 1827, informing the public of an auction of 'various fabrics with certain defects' or biscuits of 'inferior quality'. That was at a time when any European product, even if it was outmoded or worn, was advertised by its importers as perfect and new and was sold to less cautious Brazilians at many times, I would not say its worth, but its fair price.

That the efficiency of the business methods of the first English merchants to set themselves up in Brazil was only relative is an established fact. The agents of the large London firms that decided to open branches in Brazil (since it should be noted that 113 London merchants joined an association founded in that city in June 1808, on the basis of an invitation published in the newspapers by the Portuguese minister, the aim of which was to promote trade between Great Britain and Brazil, and also that the standing committee appointed to run the organization – the Association of English Merchants Trading to Brazil – included important businessmen and even Members of Parliament)[287] arrived here with delusions of grandeur. Professor Manchester records that they rented warehouses for fantastic sums, set aside the mornings for the pleasures of riding, spent the afternoons at their country seats, and at night went to parties or social gatherings. They did not serve behind the counter – a job considered inferior in Brazil. Almost all of them therefore sold their merchandise at auction, at ruinous prices; the ones who really profited were the retailers, whether English or not. The situation only returned to normal in 1816, after a number of bankruptcies and failures of English merchants, many of whom caused 'the judges conservators and the Brazilian authorities' not a little trouble.[288]

Hence the many auctions by English merchants advertised in the *Gazeta do Rio de Janeiro* between 1809 and 1816: they were held by merchants who did not stoop to selling their merchandise across the counter. They were auctions held by Englishmen tarnished by the Brazilian environment, which was still unfavourable to any kind of trade other than that of sugar wholesalers. The environment of a country that was more agrarian and pastoral than industrial and commercial.

The main interest for us in these newspaper advertisements by British merchants and technicians established in Brazil in the first half of the nineteenth century, as well as in the publicity or plain news items about merchandise imported from England, and in the announcements of auctions held by Englishmen, or by other Europeans or Brazilians who imported new English products, lies in the influence of British intellectual

[287] Manchester, *British Preëminence in Brazil*, p. 76.

[288] *Ibid.*, p. 96.

and material culture, industry, technology and fashions on Brazilian life at that time. The sole purpose of this study is to search for and to try to interpret such influences.

When D. João VI arrived in Bahia in 1808, Brazil, it should be remembered, was going through a period of almost complete segregation from Europe. Its intercourse with foreign countries was virtually confined to its relations with its mother country, Portugal, the slave markets of Africa and those parts of Asia that were in closest contact with Portugal or from where a ship occasionally put in at a Brazilian port on some pretext or other and 'just happened' to be full of attractive eastern merchandise that found eager buyers here. It seems the so-called 'black market' is nothing new in Brazil, although those clandestine imports of Chinese and Indian goods could perhaps more appropriately be termed a 'yellow market'. Sometimes the ships putting in at Brazilian ports were English, despite the ban; and according to Lindley even friars then indulged in contraband. Walsh reports that before 1808 no foreign ships were seen in Rio de Janeiro harbour, apart from those that were allowed in 'to refit or repair damages', which then with that excuse 'contrived to carry on some contraband trade'.[289]

While Lindley was in Bahia, he made the same observation: no foreign ships were admitted save as an exception: to repair damage, to take on water or provisions, or when in danger of shipwreck. These were easy excuses to make when ships from India or England wanted to put in, and to do so they relied on the goodwill or personal interest of the port and customs authorities or even the captain-general. In fact, contrary to the 'apparent rigour' of the ban, Lindley, referring to the eighteenth century, informs us that when such ships put in – generally for between four and twenty days – 'considerable contraband trade' was carried on, which often involved the very officials appointed to prevent it. Around the turn of the century, however, there had been a reaction against these abuses by the metropolis.[290] Nevertheless, some contraband continued to take place. Lindsey himself attended a dinner at a monastery, which he says was 'excellent' and accompanied by 'French wines of the finest quality', together with 'London ale and porter'. Importing English beer into eighteenth-century Brazil was strictly forbidden; hence it was considered the greatest luxury. The Englishman learnt that the superior of the monastery contacted every foreign ship that put in at Salvador harbour in order to smuggle in

[289] Walsh, *Notices of Brazil...*, I, p. 100 (quotations in English – Translator).

[290] Thomas Lindley, *Narrative of a Voyage to Brasil; Terminating in the Seizure of a British Vessel ... by the Portuguese. With General Sketches of the Country ... and a Description of the City and Provinces of St. Salvadore and Porto Seguro. To which are added, a Correct Table of the Latitude and Longitude of the Ports on the Coast of Brasil ...*, London, 1805, p. xix.

his drinks.[291] While the crooked or the wily could get hold of the best European or oriental goods in this way, ordinary people who could not resort to such methods were brought the leftovers from Lisbon's markets and sour or rancid Irish butter on the regular, legitimate and apparently honest ships that sailed from Lisbon.[292]

Lindley's comments – the philosophy he extracted from his observations in Bahia – are highly in favour of what he calls 'free exertions' in commerce and wholly against state restrictions on trade or industry. All the many 'prohibitions' in Brazil encouraged smuggling.

> [...] for men in all countries are too ready to engage in what is forbidden, losing sight of the risk, in the [...] prospect of superior profits.[293]

A similar remark to Lindley's in Bahia was made a few years later by Mathison with regard to Minas Gerais: there, due to the excessive demands made by the authorities and the way in which these demands were imposed on the people, smuggling was 'systematically pursued on a large scale'. Furthermore, 'the regular course of trade was very much impeded' and, instead, 'an undue advantage [was] given to the smuggler over the fair and honorable trader.'[294]

The fact that, once the ports had been opened up to international trade, Brazilians were initially granted the 'exclusive privilege' of importing goods from the Orient – a monopoly that lasted until 1827 – would seem to indicate that the country had a taste for such goods, which had formerly been obtained either through the metropolis or when ships from India put in for repairs or to take on water. Walsh says that while he was residing in Rio de Janeiro there were 'five East Indiamen trading from the harbour of Rio'.[295] That is how the trade between Brazil and India had been regulated, but in the end it would not withstand the imposition of British trade.

Brazil's relations with the Orient and Africa, whether irregular or through the metropolis, had led to the predominance of styles and fashions of Asian or African origin, rather than European, in various walks of life: the litter as a means of transport; tableware, dishes, jugs or jars from China, India or Japan; the mantilla or hood worn by upper-class ladies,

[291] *Ibid.*, p. 257.

[292] *Ibid.*, p. 268.

[293] *Ibid.*, p. 263 (quoted in English – Translator).

[294] Mathison, *Narrative of a Visit to Brazil*, p. 135.

[295] Walsh, *Notices of Brazil*, I, p. 248. Freyre mistranslates Walsh's 'East Indiamen' (i.e. ships used in the East Indian trade) as '*indianos*' ('Indians') (Translator).

and the turban worn by mulatto women and more elegant black women; Indian-style furniture in some of the more noble households; rings set with oriental precious stones shown off by the wealthy; walking canes from India; domestic architecture, full of oriental influences; fireworks from the East for church festivities, at which wax from Africa was also used; public and domestic sanitation more in line with oriental traditions than with the innovations of middle-class Europe; and magistrates' gowns imported from the Orient, together with the finest ladies' dresses, as shown by an advertisement in the *Gazeta do Rio de Janeiro* for 11 April 1821. That environment was dominated by oriental colours and forms, which the English trade came to Europeanize or re-Europeanize. I know of no more expressive or revealing documentation on this Europeanization or re-Europeanization process than the announcements by British merchants and engineers and the advertisements for English goods that were printed in the gazettes of the last few years of the Kingdom in Brazil and the early years of Empire. Advertisements for oriental goods only gradually disappeared; so strong was the taste for them in Brazil that some shrewder English merchants started importing them and selling them alongside European industrial products in general and English ones in particular. And English people who settled in Rio began to live in houses with considerable architectural influence from the East: to Europeans already familiar with China, some of them must have looked, from afar, like pagodas. The latticed windows, which were so suddenly and violently stripped from the best houses in Brazil's main cities, were not, after all, the only oriental feature in Brazilian domestic architecture and decoration. There were also the wall tiles, the china lions or dragons beside the gates, the concave roof tiles, the squat roofs, the mats and the bedspreads.

In the early nineteenth century, the English certainly discovered the best and healthiest places to live in Rio de Janeiro, Bahia and Pernambuco. But they dared not challenge all the Oriental or Moorish features they found in the layout or design of old Brazilian houses.

What did change in Brazil under the influence of British habits of comfort and domestic hygiene was mainly the ecology of middle-class houses. Instead of town houses built one next to the other, the English preferred isolated residences: in woodland, as in Tijuca (Rio) or Vitória (Bahia); next to rivers, as in Apipucos, Monteiro, and Poço da Panela (Pernambuco); or beside the sea, as in Botafogo (Rio) and Olinda (Pernambuco). Isolated old mansions, former country villas and even the big houses on plantations, with pagoda-like wings and porches for preparing manioc meal or sheltering horses, were adapted by them to their tastes and incorporated as far as possible into the urban space of the capital cities. British taste was very different from Luso-Brazilian with regard to a bourgeois place of residence. The fashion among the Portuguese and their Brazilian descendants was for city dwellers to live in town houses built next to one another, with no trees and, for a long time, with no glass windows – just cane or wooden lattices in oriental style – and with sleeping alcoves in the middle of the house. The wealthy would just go and 'spend the holidays' at their country seats in the outskirts of the cities. The British made these outskirts places to live, and not merely to spend high days and holidays. Maria Graham tells us that, in 1821, her fellow-countrymen in Recife lived in their country houses, or at least slept there, while they kept their 'counting-houses' – their business premises – in the cities, near the harbour,[296] although one or two may have lived in these business houses.

This was without doubt one of the most significant revolutions that the British caused or implemented in the still colonial and somewhat Moorish or, rather, Oriental habits of Brazil: the gradual displacement of the more noble residences of city dwellers from central town houses out to the suburbs, which then became fashionable, while it grew unfashionable for a refined, wealthy man to live in the commercial heart of the city. For the English example was imitated by Brazilians and Portuguese; newspaper advertisements at the time show how country houses rose in value as places to live, and not just to spend leisure time. This topic will be considered and examined in more detail in another essay.

In his album of *Views and Costumes of the City and Neighbourhood of Rio de Janeiro, 1819-1820* – which has recently been published in a Brazilian edition, with a Portuguese translation by Mr Rubens Borba de Moraes, the current director of the National Library, together with the original English text[297] – Lieutenant Chamberlain witnessed this revolution in Brazilian habits caused by the presence of the English in the main coastal cities. In his album he presents us with both the old and the new types of house.

Taking almost as much painstaking care as a miniaturist, Lieutenant Chamberlain reproduces both private houses and public buildings, as well as characteristic figures and types of the still colonial society that he found in the city of São Sebastião do Rio de Janeiro. He depicts 'the House, with the King's Arms over the door' which 'was for some years the

[296] Graham, *Journal of a Voyage to Brazil*, p. 98.

[297] *Vistas e costumes da cidade e arredores do Rio de Janeiro em 1819-1820; segundo desenhos feitos pelo t.te Chamberlain, da Artilharia Real durante os anos de 1819 a 1820, com descrições. Tradução e prefácio de Rubens Borba de Moraes. Em suplemento texto do original inglês*, Rio de Janeiro, 1943. (Original title: *Views and costumes of the city and neighbourhood of Rio de Janeiro, Brazil, from drawings taken by Lieutenant Chamberlain, Royal Artillery, during the years 1819 and 1820: with descriptive explanations*, London, 1822. Lieutenant Henry Chamberlain was the eldest son of Sir Henry Chamberlain, British consul-general and *chargé d'affaires* in Rio de Janeiro from 1815 to 1829 – Translator.)

residence of the British Mission'.[298] And also the house in Mata Cavalos that belonged to one of the judges who 'formerly held office of British Judge Conservator'.[299] And the house occupied by His Majesty's Envoy Extraordinary and Minister Plenipotentiary, Lord Viscount Strangford.[300] And on page 99 of his album there is this perceptive remark:

> The generality of Houses, more particularly those in the Outskirts of the City, are of one Story with Doors and Windows of Lattice Work, called Rotolas, very convenient for the admission of Air and Dust, and for intercepting a great proportion of the Rays of Light, which tends unquestionably to keep the apartments cool, whilst the Inhabitants can see all that is passing in the street – no small gratification to Brazilians.[301]

He also praises the Brazilian house on the estate of Bragança, 'granted to Sir Sidney Smith by the King of Portugal' in 1808, particularly its 'spacious Verandah'.[302] With the same objectivity, he points out that the builders of most well-to-do houses in Rio de Janeiro will not or cannot build them away from the streets or roads. 'Like their Progenitors from Portugal', he says, the Brazilians liked to 'build their Country Houses close to the Roadside, for the purpose of enjoying what is called the "Passagem"; that is, of seeing People pass.'[303]

The British rejected this habit of most wealthy Brazilians and built their houses in the same manner in which a certain Brazilian praised by Chamberlain himself had built his country house: 'surrounded by the beauties of this charming Country', where the owner could 'enjoy at his ease retirement, and the refreshing Breezes from the Sea.'[304]

It should be noted, however, that the first British merchants to become established in Brazil after the opening of the ports took up residence, like the more important local merchants, on the upper floors of the same town houses occupied by their stores. These town houses were the springboards from which they leapt out to the forested city suburbs that they could see from the hilltops. They went to these suburban forests not so much to build new homes there, but rather to adapt to their own taste the old country houses built by the Portuguese or Brazilians, in many of which

[298] Chamberlain, *Vistas e costumes*, p. 201.

[299] *Ibid.*, p. 200.

[300] *Ibid.*, p. 203.

[301] *Ibid.*, p. 213-214.

[302] *Ibid.*, p. 218-219.

[303] *Ibid.*, p. 222.

[304] *Ibid.*, p. 222.

(even if large and imposing from the outside) the interior seemed to suffer from 'a total absence or disregard of that attention to neatness and comfort which characterizes an English town', as Walsh observed.[305] The English added to those houses at least two British institutions that were eventually incorporated into the domestic architecture of Brazil: the hall and the WC, both English terms now having entered our architects' vocabulary as if they were native words. Therefore, Schlichthorst, a German official who lived here from 1824 to 1826 and wrote a book on the capital of Brazil entitled *Rio de Janeiro wie es ist*, does not seem to be entirely right when, in a passage recently highlighted by an eminent Brazilian architect working on the historical reconstruction of the city, he accused the English of not knowing how to appreciate the virtues of the kind of dwelling house they found in Brazil: a kind of house that was extensively praised by the German in that it had 'an entirely different use from houses in northern Europe', and had to 'protect from the burning rays of the sun and at the same time let in the cool night air'.[306] Schlichthorst unfairly turned against the English living in Brazil at the time, adding:

> All genuinely Brazilian houses correspond more or less to those twin purposes, whereas the national vanity of the English erects buildings that would suit London admirably but not the almost uninhabitable tropics.[307]

There are, however, plenty of advertisements for English auctions that suggest the opposite: Britons living in houses that they may have adapted to their taste or their notions of domestic comfort, but without disfiguring the best traditions of Brazilian architecture.

It is not the old houses built or rebuilt here by Englishmen that most strike us as having features of dwellings more suited to the poles than the tropics – unless we rebel against the innovations of the hall and WC. That is, instead, the sin of mansions erected in our cities not so much by Europeans but by *nouveau riche* Brazilians after visiting northern Europe. It is true that an English broker in Recife is believed to have had a house built in a pretentiously Gothic style in one of the oldest suburbs of the Pernambucan capital, among robustly tropical jackfruit and mango trees. But such cases appear to have been rare, whereas it was common for the English to adapt to their English taste traditional old country houses built by Portuguese or Brazilians with a Moorish or Oriental feel: houses with a veranda or porch, wings, patios, a belvedere, and water nearby. In 1821

[305] Walsh, *Notices of Brazil*, I, p. 33.

[306] Morales de los Rios Filho, *O Rio de Janeiro imperial*, p. 127.

[307] *Ibid.*, p. 128.

Maria Graham visited a country house belonging to an Englishman, Mr S., near Recife, which she compared with an oriental bungalow. A house of one storey surrounded by a veranda and standing amidst fruit trees, roses and pastures.[308] Houses of this type were very much in evidence in newspaper advertisements at this time – apparently to attract the attention precisely of those Englishmen who had just arrived in Brazil and could not bear living upstairs in urban houses.

What must it have been like inside an English merchant's house – one of the many who lived for years in town houses in commercial streets? That is what the Reverend Walsh tells us after visiting one of his countrymen who lived in the Rua dos Pescadores – Mr Price, 'an intelligent English merchant to whom I had letters', according to the Anglican clergyman. Walsh, who was very concerned in Rio to study the streets, lanes, alleys, squares and also the buildings, considers Mr Price's house to be typical or 'representative of all the houses of the British merchants',[309] referring of course to their town houses and not their country houses in the suburbs and even beyond, in the midst of the tropical forest or clinging to hillsides, like the one in Botafogo in which Charles Darwin stayed a few years later.

Walsh tells us that the ground floor of Mr Price's house was the store or large shop, filled with all kinds of goods. A stone staircase led up from this floor to what the Englishman calls the second floor, but we would call the first. Here there was a large room, half of which was used as an office while the other half was full of harnesses, saddles, hats and other articles of English manufacture.

Mr Price's quarters in a Rio de Janeiro town house were little different from those that a wealthy foreigner or a more Europeanized Brazilian aristocrat in Recife – for it was common at that time for a Brazilian family to have two residences: one in the country and a town house in the city – had in the residences and town houses that Maria Graham had seen in Pernambuco: that still colonial Pernambuco, which the eminent lady visited and observed with eyes like those of a good English novelist, such is her ability to point out significant details. There she saw houses in which the stores occupied the ground floor, where the family's slaves also lived; on the second floor was the office; on the third the living quarters, with the kitchen at the top of the building.[310] The same in Bahia. Except that the well-to-do houses she visited in Salvador seemed 'disgustingly dirty' to her, and had 'narrow and dark' staircases. Inside, nobody used the bowls, mugs

[308] Graham, *Journal of a Voyage to Brazil*, p. 129.

[309] Walsh, *Notices of Brazil*, I, pp. 85-86 (quotations in English – Translator).

[310] Graham, *Journal of a Voyage to Brazil*, p. 103.

and gourds that Luccock must only have seen in the houses of the less wealthy. At a time (1821) when little light was cast on Brazilian interiors by advertisements and news of private furniture and chinaware auctions – advertisements that were still over-reticent – what Maria Graham saw in the middle-class or well-to-do houses of Salvador or among the gowned aristocracy was chandeliers and mirrors, prints and pictures, and 'a good deal of handsome china', as in the house of a judge who was not especially rich.[311] Or pretty porcelain from France and India in the house of a naval captain, where the lady of the house was also neatly dressed in French style.[312]

In Recife, Maria Graham had noticed from the interior of the first house she had visited that there was little difference between a Brazilian drawing-room and a British one. Almost the same furniture. The same piano, which in the Brazilian house in Recife was a Broadwood.

The dining-rooms were different. The floor of the Brazilian one was covered with oilcloth, and the walls were hung with English prints and Chinese paintings, arranged without distinction of subject or consideration of size. In a corner of the room was a huge table with a glass oratory, in which there was an entire crib decorated with flowers and shells, gold and silver; on either side of the crib was a saint: Saint Anthony and Saint Christopher. The rest of the furniture consisted of ordinary chairs and tables and a kind of buffet or sideboard. Nine birdcages hung from the roof, some containing canaries. Larger cages in a side room held parrots and parakeets.[313]

Hardly had Mrs Graham sat down in the dining-room of the Pernambucan house when she was offered biscuits, cake, wine and liqueurs, as well as glasses of water kept cool in earthenware pots and jars made in Bahia. She noticed that the air and manners of the Brazilians in the house she was visiting were neither English nor French and yet were those of well-bred people. The men, however, wore calico or cotton jackets at home instead of worsted coats and did not wear cravats, although in the street they dressed in English style.[314]

In Madame do Rio Seco's house in Rio de Janeiro, Mrs Graham noted that there was a greater display of 'china and French clocks' than would occur to an Englishwoman, although that luxury went well with all the gilt and silks of the drawing-rooms.[315] When visiting the Baronesa de Campos,

[311] *Ibid.*, p. 135.
[312] *Ibid.*, p. 135.
[313] *Ibid.*, p. 127.
[314] *Ibid.*, p. 128.
[315] *Ibid.*, p. 226.

she saw bedrooms and dressing-rooms 'elegantly fitted up with English and French furniture'. She was told that the interiors of Rio de Janeiro houses were then (in 1822) very different from what they had been twenty years previously, that is to say more European than before.[316] Perhaps they had formerly been more oriental in some cases, and more rustic in others.

Let us return, however, to the town house where Mr Price lived, the Englishman whom the Reverend Walsh visited in Rio de Janeiro in 1828. At Mr Price's invitation, Walsh went to have dinner with the merchant, his countryman. Dinner at two o'clock in the afternoon, which he unfortunately does not describe. It was probably lamb and peas, brightened up with a bottle or two of English ale. Walsh describes only the ground and first floors of the building in which Mr Price lived – the two commercial or public floors – but leaves us no information on the interior, the larder, the decoration or the furniture of the third, which was where that English family had their home. An excess of British discretion.

Although the auction advertisements of the time are reticent in their descriptions of house interiors of Brazilians and Britons residing in Brazil, they do allow us to make up for the shortcomings or deficiencies of the account given by Walsh, who must deliberately, with the refined modesty cultivated by true gentlemen – those with a British upbringing – have avoided making any reference to the furniture, crockery or cutlery in his fellow-countryman's house. The fact is that Mr Price's house was probably nothing out of the ordinary. In the merchant's private office, perhaps a 'writing desk with its pigeonholes, as well as two drawers and two secret compartments for money and jewels, an antique but excellent in taste, richness and security' – an ideal desk for a merchant or an Englishman fond of security, method, privacy and secrecy, which exactly one year before Walsh arrived in Rio de Janeiro was for sale at an affordable price at Rua do Valongo, No 46. The drawing-room may have been lit by a new chandelier and its floor covered with a good carpet; the chairs may have been English, like the sideboard in the dining-room, the dining-table and the round tea-table that Mr Price would have bought from his countrymen Bourdon & Fry in the Rua Direita, who were always receiving new items from London, 'assortments of household goods', tea-, card- and sewing-tables, dressers, sideboards and 'chairs of various patterns'.[317] The crystal, glass, china, cutlery, iron beds and silverware must have been English, like the clock, and like the oilcloth on the bedroom floors, since this was an article that several merchants in the Rua Direita acquired from England; and it is not unlikely that Mrs Price played the piano and had one that had also been brought from England. The kitchen utensils would also have been

[316] *Ibid.*, p. 272.

[317] *Gazeta do Rio de Janeiro*, 31 January 1818.

English. The ledgers in which the business accounts were kept would have been English, like the writing paper – perhaps bought at Rua do Sabão, No 14, in a shop there that retailed English goods of that kind, according to an advertisement in the *Gazeta do Rio de Janeiro* of 26 July 1818. The gummed paper, quills and pencils would have been English, like those sold at Rua do Ouvidor, No 138, which were advertised in the *Jornal do Commercio* on 30 December 1828 alongside 'stamps [...] both black and red'. The remedies would have been English: soda powder, Siedlitz powder, Cheltenham salts, as were for sale at Rua dos Pescadores, No 56, according to an advertisement in the *Jornal do Commercio* on 11 January 1829. Since Mr Price was an intelligent man, as the Reverend Walsh points out without elaborating further, we can only speculate on which books he would have had at home. He may not have had any, but used the Subscription Library that already existed in those days among the English in Rio de Janeiro, according to information or a 'private notice' in a newspaper of the time. On 4 February 1830 the *Jornal do Commercio* tells us, in English, in its paid section, of a 'Meeting of the British Subscription Library' to be held on the following Friday, to which it sternly adds:

> All subscriptions must be paid before that day or the usual fine will be incurred.[318]

There was not just a subscription library, but in the early years of the Empire in Rio de Janeiro there was also a weekly English-language publication entitled the *Rio Herald*. It first appeared on 8 March 1828, when it pointed out that

> the benefits which have resulted to Europe and the United States from the diffusion of political and useful information by means of Public Journals are obvious...[319]

That must also have applied to Brazil, where 'knowledge of the English language' was spreading. The *Rio Herald* came out on Saturdays. It did not survive long, however.

Such institutions appear to show that the many English merchants established in Rio de Janeiro in those days were not all like those that Maria Graham had come across in Bahia in 1821: people that this English observer described as absorbed solely in business and the pleasures of the table, dancing and gambling. Her judgment may have been too severe,

[318] Quoted in English (Translator).
[319] Quoted in English (Translator).

because at that time Salvador had an Anglican chaplain as well as a cemetery, and an English surgeon and hospital for seamen. These characteristically British institutions were soon joined by an amateur theatrical society. In Rio, judging by the names of some English shops recorded by Maria Graham, British merchants tried as far as possible to retain the environment of their country of origin. Hence the nostalgically English touch of the signs identifying the 'pot-houses' that had already been established in the Brazilian capital in 1822: 'Union Jacks, Red Lions, Jolly Tars'. It was as if one were in Greenwich. The words 'London superfine' over English goods in the shops met the eyes all the time. Such goods could be purchased in the stores at prices little higher than in England. But Maria Graham noted that any object bought retail from an English or French shop in Rio de Janeiro was very expensive.[320]

On his way to Mr Price's house for dinner, the Reverend Walsh noticed that all the houses in the district – the commercial district in Rio de Janeiro – were closed and the streets deserted. The impression was of a city of the dead. At that time of day all businesses stopped for dinner and a siesta. All the lower floors of the English merchant's house were shut up; the master of the house and his family were at the very top of the building. Mr Price took his guest to the dressing-room, where Walsh got ready for dinner by removing his woollen or worsted coat and putting on a calico jacket.[321] That was a Brazilian custom from patriarchal times by then adopted by English merchants living in Rio. A custom perhaps of Muslim origin, it may be noted in passing, which survived in the more conservative cities in Brazil almost up to the present day. In any case, it was a feature of the Brazilian patriarchal complex adopted by agents of an industrial civilization like the British, which they may have taken from here to some of their tropical colonies, like the wise habit of wearing dust coats on long train journeys through dry and dusty regions.

Walsh is so reticent about the interior of the houses in which the English lived in Brazil that he does not even tell us about the furnishings of the house he himself occupied – a house in the Catete district, then 'at a considerable distance' from the city centre, from which it was separated by hills round which the inhabitants of that remote suburb had to wind their way.[322] He merely says that it had belonged to a former British naval officer, who had risen from the rank of lieutenant in HBM Navy to that of commodore in the Brazilian service, and it was a house fit for

[320] Graham, *Journal of a Voyage to Brazil*, p. 169.

[321] Walsh, *Notices of Brazil*, I, p. 86.

[322] Walsh writes, 'as you cannot climb over their summits, you must wind round their bases' (quoted in English – Translator). *Ibid.*, I, p. 88. (Walsh actually states that the house in which he stayed was on a street connecting the centre of Rio with Catete, i.e. in Glória district – Translator.)

an ambassador. It stood at the foot of a rock and faced the sea, the waves breaking beneath its windows on a beach of fine, white sand. He could see the ships entering and leaving the harbour, and the air was fresh.[323]

The English clergyman criticizes the economy of Brazilian homes in Rio de Janeiro, as he says they did not keep a larder (not for sugar, coffee, wine or any foodstuff) but purchased what they needed from local *vendas* in small quantities for immediate use – perhaps because if such produce was bought in larger quantities and stored in larders it might be stolen and consumed by the household slaves. One should conclude from that that English households were well supplied with food and drink, which they stored in larders and cellars. At the country house of an Englishman, Mr Willis, who was married to a Brazilian woman and lived in Irajá – his house being much visited by English merchants from Rio de Janeiro, who used to spend Sundays there, playing quoits and other energetic games in the hot sun and refreshing themselves with porter – Walsh partook of a huge dinner. Fish and *feijoada*, authentic Brazilian bean stew. The drinks were an Anglo-Brazilian combination: porter, port wine and cachaça, which was as transparent as water but in taste reminded him of Scotch whisky.[324]

Englishwomen's larders, ship-chandlers, smart restaurants and hotels run by or mainly for English people – such as the one that Horácio Messeri opened at Rua da Quitanda, No 14, between the Rua do Ouvidor and the Rua do Cano, which, according to an advertisement in English in the *Jornal do Commercio* on 5 November 1828, had

> clean, airy, well furnished and elegant apartments, where the lodger may be supplied with breakfast, dinner and supper,[325]

and also offered to supply 'dinners by the month, or by order [...] English, French and Italian style'[326] – would have been the almost immediate destinations of a large part of the European drinks and English preserves shipped over from Liverpool, as described in newspaper advertisements from the latter years of colonial Brazil and the early decades of the Empire: Yorkshire hams, pickled salmon, Jersey potatoes, flagons of Selters mineral water, like those sold at the warehouse in the Rua do Rosário;[327] rum spirit like that imported by Ch. Guimaud & Co. (Rua dos Ourives, No 51) for their more refined clientèle;[328] London cheese, mustard and hams 'very

[323] *Ibid.*, I, p. 89.
[324] *Ibid.*, II, p. 15
[325] Quoted in English (Translator).
[326] Quoted in English (Translator).
[327] *Gazeta do Rio de Janeiro*, 1 January 1820.
328 *Jornal do Commercio*, 12 July 1831.

good for eating cold', like those for sale at the warehouse 'in the street behind the Hospice in Rua dos Ourives';[329] boxes of Lisson and Uxin tea;[330] 'superior quality English potatoes, like those received by the warehouse in the Rua de São Bento;[331] 'English butter', which was the best at that time, selling for 350 or 370 réis a pound until 1835, whereas French butter sold at 280 or 300 réis a pound;[332] ginger like that brought to Pernambuco on 19 December 1836 by the brig *Sirius*, which also had on its manifest 100 kegs of beer, 1 crate of meat and peas, 2 barrels of butter, 1 crate of liqueurs and 5 casks of vinegar, among other goods.[333] It was these fine European – primarily English – foodstuffs, as well as porter, port wine, sherry, biscuits, sultanas and wheat flour, that filled the larders and cellars of well-stocked and well-run English and Brazilian households that did not send young slaves rushing out to the local shop to buy this and that when somebody of note suddenly turned up to dinner. And of course the English who ate or feasted in this way – setting the Brazilians excellent examples of 'fine living', which were soon imitated by the more refined members of society – were not to blame if a large part of the population of Brazil preferred – or were forced to prefer by their economic situation – salt cod, jerked beef and manioc meal to such delicacies. But since Brazilians had such a liking for cod – inherited from Portugal, in fact – the English did not neglect to supply the Brazilian market with this product: the shipping of Newfoundland cod to Brazil was almost an English monopoly for a while, just as jerked beef or *carne seca* from the River Plate to Brazil was transported mainly in English ships.

The shipping, mind you, and not so much the trade. English merchants in Brazil preferred to distinguish themselves as importers of fabrics and china, ironware and glass, ham and champagne. Goods more noble than salt cod or jerked beef, which were sold mainly by Portuguese; and more virile than the perfumes and knick-knacks sold mainly by Frenchmen or, rather, by Frenchwomen.

After dinner, as Walsh walked down the Rua dos Pescadores as far as the Campo de Sant'Ana, he was able to observe the commerce in Rio de Janeiro at its most colourful hour and to note the predominance of merchandise imported from England in this commerce. The shops had reopened. He observed them carefully: full of European, or English, articles, particularly 'Manchester shawls, handkerchiefs, cottons and calicoes of the most showy color, broadcloths, silks, hats, boots, shoes, and stockings, all

[329] *Jornal do Commercio*, 9 January 1828.

[330] *Jornal do Commercio*, 12 July 1828.

[331] *Jornal do Commercio*, 9 May 1828.

[332] *Diário de Pernambuco*, 'Preços Correntes' ('Current prices'), 14 February 1835.

[333] *Diário de Pernambuco*, 22 December 1836.

hung out in front of the houses',[334] since vitrines were still a rarity.

There was such a profusion of these articles, and the Rio de Janeiro market was still overflowing with them to such an extent – this was in 1828, now twenty years after British merchants eager to conquer Brazil commercially had first invaded this market – that Walsh, who was so meticulous in finding out the prices of British goods sold in Brazil, as Mrs Graham had been seven years before him, noted that they were being sold for less than in Cheapside.[335] He was forgetting, however, that that was the case of articles that were sadly hard to sell in the shops due to excess stock – some were already out of fashion in London or Paris; and he himself points out that the first shipments of goods that the English sent to Brazil even included ice-skates. In their initial eagerness to conquer the Brazilian market, English merchants had confused Brazil with Siberia.

But all those commercial ventures were protected or encouraged with duties paid by Brazilians. In fact, soon after signing the Decree of 18 January 1810, the prince regent called for the captains-general to be strict in fulfilling the contract between the two governments. As the Count of Aguiar[336] wrote to the captain-general of Pernambuco on 21 January 1810:

> Our Lord the Prince Regent has ordered me to send you two Copies of the Decree of 18th inst. laying down the Duties that his Vassals shall pay on all Foodstuffs and Merchandise of English Production and Manufacture that they import through the Customs Houses of the Kingdom, or State of Brazil, and overseas dominions so that you may enforce it in the Customs Houses of that City.[337]

Under the protection of His Britannic Majesty, British merchants revolutionized eating habits, dress and lifestyle not only for the well-to-do but also for the middle classes; and even for the mechanics, who lived in those timber-framed or mud-brick houses orientally fitted with lattice windows in Turkish style, which could still be seen after independence in Rio de Janeiro, Recife, Olinda and Bahia. Because the 1808 edict banning wooden or cane lattices, which were considered 'barbaric', 'gothic' or 'Turkish' and therefore unworthy of a city that desired nothing other than to Europeanize itself, did not apply to those smaller houses, which were barely any more solid or substantial than the huts or shanties of the very

[334] Walsh, *Notices of Brazil*, I, p. 86.

[335] *Ibid.*, I, p. 86.

[336] Fernando José de Portugal e Castro, Count and Marquis of Aguiar, who was the prime minister of the kingdom at the time (Translator).

[337] MS, Manuscript Section of the Biblioteca do Estado de Pernambuco.

poorest individuals or families. That, of course, was because the inhabitants of those smaller houses – the *petit bourgeoisie* – would have been unable to afford suddenly – within the six month period that wealthier houses were given – to get rid of the oriental archaism of the lattices and replace them with glass windows, as befitted a civilized city. That lets us now speculate about this measure, which was so violently adopted in the principal cities of Brazil soon after the arrival of the Court – together with English merchants – in Rio: was it simply a frenzied attempt to Europeanize the city aesthetically or for the sake of planning? A police precaution? Or due to subtle yet irresistible pressure on someone powerful in the Court by one or more of those more powerful merchants in the Rua da Alfândega or Rua Direita interested in importing and selling window panes, which appear in newspaper advertisements at the time?

In 1764, when Commodore Byron was in Rio, the only building with glass windows in the city, according to the English observer, was the viceroy's palace, while all the other houses had lattices.[338] An Englishman's keen eye had noticed it all those years ago. Lindley noticed the same thing some years later in São Salvador or Salvador: the houses had lattices. The windows did not have window panes. Neither panes nor paint – perhaps due to a lack of paint. In the words of this rather acerbic critic of Brazilian customs and affairs:

> Instead of glazed windows, they [the houses in Salvador] have wooden drop lattices, which want even the addition of painting to

[338] *Viagem feita à Roda do Mundo*, p. 24. (*A Voyage Round the World*, pp. 22-23 – Translator.) Koebel (*British Exploits in South America*, p. 31) remarks that 'Commodore Byron set out in 1764 in the *Dolphin* for the purpose of making discoveries in the South Seas. He was accompanied by the frigate *Tamar*, commanded by Captain Mouat. Having made the usual call at Madeira the two vessels proceeded to Rio de Janeiro, where the Portuguese – following a custom to which they had now become thoroughly addicted – enticed fourteen of the sailors away and succeeded in kidnapping five of them.' (Quoted in English – Translator.)
Byron was surprised by the lattices in Rio de Janeiro. Despite the strict order to replace them with iron bars or wooden balustrades 'within eight days' (11 June 1809), in 1820 there was still at least one town house in Rio with the primitive lattices (Luís Gonçalves dos Santos, *Memórias para Servir à História do Reino do Brasil*, Lisbon, 1825, I, p. 212, footnote). In 1833 Sir Charles James Fox Bunbury, an Englishman, still found a 'large number of houses that consist of only a ground floor, without glass windows, but in their place shutters fixed at the top and opening outwards' in the capital of the Empire ('Narrativa de viagem de um naturalista inglês ao Rio de Janeiro e Minas Gerais, 1833-1835', *Anais da Biblioteca Nacional do Rio de Janeiro*, 1940, vol. 62, p. 17). (This is a translation into Portuguese by Helena Garcia de Sousa of an unpublished manuscript by Bunbury; the quotation above has been translated from the Portuguese back into English – Translator.) A few years after Bunbury, Daniel P. Kidder, an American, noticed in the capital of Pará that latticed windows were more common than glass ones (*Reminiscências de viagens e permanência no Brasil (Províncias do Norte)*, translated by Moacir N. Vasconcelos, São Paulo, undated, p. 168). (Daniel P. Kidder, *Sketches of Residence and Travels in Brazil, Embracing Historical and Geographical Notices of the Empire and its Several Provinces*, London, 1845, vol. 2, p. 265 – Translator.)

enliven or preserve them.[339]

And he had previously remarked on the houses in Santo Amaro that: 'The houses are wholly destitute of casements to their windows, except a split-cane blind.'[340] Lindley not only remarked on the absence of glass and iron in house fronts: he also noticed that the lattices were poorly preserved, on account of a lack of paint. We shall see later that this was another area of trade that the English arriving after the opening of the ports came to dominate: the trade in paints for houses, windows and timbers. And, together with paints, they also traded in polishes.

Newspaper advertisements in the early decades following the establishment in Brazil of the Court and the English – because the latter event was almost as important as the former for Brazilian culture and, particularly, the Brazilian economy – mentioned the glass or glazing in mansions, houses and carriages for sale or to let so insistently that one can glimpse the aesthetic and psychological revolution brought about by the violent destruction – by order of the new government – of the wooden or cane lattices and the virtual imposition of glass in the houses of the bourgeoisie. Other advertisements by English merchants in Rio de Janeiro, Pernambuco and Bahia show us the importance of crystal and glass. There was plain glass – such as that imported from Liverpool in countless English brigs, one of them the *Mary Queen of Scots*, which entered Recife harbour on 19 November 1836 under the command of Captain W. Kelley, with a consignment for McCalmont & Co. of casks of ironware, crates and bundles of fabrics, tubs of china, casks of copper, four iron anvils, ten tons of iron, barrels of butter, crates of soap and other characteristically British goods, and thirty-six crates of glass[341] – and there was glass in the form of lamp-glasses, mirrors of 'excellent large glass',[342] compotiers, wineglasses or bottles, which frequently appear among the items imported and advertised by British merchants in Rio de Janeiro and Pernambuco. Might there not be some connection between these facts? Between the edict against lattices and this abundance of English glass in the shops and stores of Rio de Janeiro and Pernambuco, as revealed by newspaper advertisements? These facts are revealed but not explained, either by the newspaper advertisements themselves or by the manifests of the ships arriving from Europe. Nor is any light cast on them by the edicts or proclamations of the prince regent and captains-general against lattices made of simple local timber or cane. Might not the claim that lattices could be used as 'hiding-

[339] Lindley, *Narrative of a Voyage to Brasil*, p. 247 (quoted in English – Translator).

[340] *Ibid.*, p. 214, footnote (quoted in English – Translator).

[341] *Diário de Pernambuco*, 22 November 1836.

[342] *Jornal do Commercio*, 30 November 1827.

places for murderers' have been a mere excuse for their violent and sudden destruction? And the true reason the one that has already been suggested: pressure by one or more British merchants on one or more powerful men at Court, who agreed to that violence, apparently for the sake of security, aesthetics or town planning, but really to open up a market for English glass? Newspaper advertisements sometimes lead us to indiscreet economic interpretations of history.

Luccock says that the attention of a stranger arriving in Rio de Janeiro prior to 1808 was mainly attracted by the 'jealousies'[343]: they gave house fronts a 'heavy and suspicious appearance', made the streets dull and indicated that the inhabitants had little sociability.[344] The prince regent's order to abolish lattices, which meant replacing them with glass windows and balconies – balconies made of iron, another abundant English product of the time – is known to have been happily obeyed by some inhabitants but reluctantly by others.

The result was 'curious', as Luccock himself says. Without blinds, lattices or curtains at the windows, houses were suddenly left exposed to public view, so that some of their occupants felt ashamed of them – of their archaic interiors, that is to say – and tried to improve or modernize them by imitating European, that is, English and French, fashions. That would seem to suggest that, with the ban on lattices, the English suddenly gained a market not just for their glass and iron but for their furniture as well. The abolition of that oriental archaism seems to have ushered in a taste for European conveniences and fashions in the furnishing and decoration of Brazilian interiors.

Luccock says that the ostensible reason for the edict against lattices had been to improve the appearance of the city, but the 'real cause' for the abolition of lattices was the fear that they 'might become ambuscades for assassins'.[345] In this study, I have tried to suggest a deeper cause for such a violent and radical measure: the desire of British merchants to quickly open up the market that they needed in Rio for glass and iron of their own manufacture. Indeed, the lattices in well-to-do houses and mansions in Rio and other large cities in Brazil were soon replaced with glass imported from England. Glass and iron. A replacement process documented by newspaper advertisements.

As has been mentioned, Brazil began quite abruptly to receive crates of glass from England. Glass in large quantities. As well as iron: iron in abundance. And newspaper advertisements began to stress the quality and

[343] From the Portuguese 'gelosia' or the French 'jalousie', meaning latticework shutters (Translator).

[344] Luccock, *Notes on Rio de Janeiro*, p. 36.

[345] *Ibid.*, p. 37.

the almost moral – and not merely material – superiority that glazing and iron balconies imparted to houses, mansions and carriages.

On 24 July 1813 an advertiser in the *Gazeta do Rio de Janeiro* trumpeted:

> For sale in the Rua da Princesa Luz: a property of very well-built single-storey houses put up six months ago, each with one door and two windows, with large gardens, all with ceilings, flooring and glazed windows.

On 17 August 1811 the same newspaper carried this advertisement for houses with a glazed veranda:

> Anyone who would like to bid for dwellings consisting of single-storey houses, well arranged and in very good taste, each with a spacious terrace around it and a glazed veranda and its respective plot of land, located on the far side of *Boa Viagem* resting place, where they may be seen, should come to the Auctions held by the Judge for Orphans of this Capital City at his residence in the Rua *Direita*. Their valuation may be seen there or at the Office of the Clerk Carlos José de Jesuz at Rua do *Cano*, No 7.

Advertisements for glazed houses continued to appear even after Brazil's independence. An advertisement in the *Jornal do Commercio*, 10 January 1828:

> For sale: a country property in Tijuca, ground rent payable to the Viscount of Asseca, with a sea view, glazed masonry houses, outbuildings with slave quarters and stables, sixty thousand coffee bushes beginning to produce, virgin and second-growth forest, fields of manioc and plenty of water.

This advertisement shows that the area with glass-windowed houses was expanding and even reaching the vicinity of virgin forest.

And what happened in Rio and its surroundings also happened in other Brazilian cities where British influence was strongest: cities that had the lattices torn from their houses by order of the prince regent or his representatives. The mystique of glass and iron spread to those cities. And that mystique was reflected in newspaper advertisements. In Recife on 30 September 1839, the *Diário de Pernambuco* published an advertisement exalting as virtues of a town house located beside the River Capibaribe in Monteiro the fact that it was 'fully glazed' and was 'very close to the baths'. On 1 March 1840 the same newspaper carried another advertisement typical of the cult of glass: a 'very large dwelling-house' in 'large grounds on the road to Ponte d'Uchoa', which was recommended for being built of 'stone and mortar' and being 'fully glazed'. And on 19 September that year, another advertisement appeared in the *Diário de Pernambuco* for suburban houses – in Capunga – highlighting the same feature: that they were 'painted and glazed'. They were therefore recommended as houses where 'any family could decently spend a feast day'. The *Diário* for 17 August 1841 announced:

> To let: an elegant, glazed, single-storey house with many rooms and good grounds with plenty of fruit trees and two wells of drinking water, in the Rua do Cotovelo opposite the house that now belongs to the heirs of Captain Quaresma, the militia commander.

Since the days of Koster in Pernambuco, the 'shameful lattices' had been replaced in all the grand houses in the city centre with glass windows and iron balconies. So that any mention of a grand house in the city centre was understood to mean a house that not only had two or more storeys but was also glazed, and it balconies were made of iron. English glass. English iron. Between 1808 and 1830 few brigs sailed from England to Brazil without those four or five basic items of British trade with Portuguese America: glass, iron, cloth, china and salt cod.

Not just large amounts of glass, it bears repeating, but many different kinds. Plain glass. Fine glass. Door and window glass. Glass for tabletops. Crystal glass. Glass 'from Bohemia'. Cut glass. Glass in the form of spectacles, lenses and telescopes. There was even a shop in the Rua do Ouvidor that specialized in selling English glass. Another such shop specializing in English glass in Rio opened in the Largo de São Francisco de Paula in 1820.

> Anyone who wishes to purchase fine and plain glass [...] recently brought in from London should look in the Largo de S. Francisco de Paula, next to the black people's Cathedral, in a new shop that has opened there, [...] very affordable prices.[346]

On 28 October 1815 the *Gazeta* announced that the shop opposite Candelária church was selling 'window glass' and also – since it was one of

[346] Advertisement in the *Gazeta do Rio de Janeiro*, 5 January 1820.

the shops in which East and West met on good terms, instead of clashing – 'tea of all qualities recently brought from Macau by the ship *Maria I* to be sold wholesale and retail'. On 2 December 1815, the *Gazeta* advertised an auction of 'fine china and cut glass' in the Rua da Alfândega. And on 10 May 1821 the same newspaper informs us in an advertisement of another shop in Rio de Janeiro specializing in retailing tea 'in boxes of all sizes', together with 'glass and china'. And, moreover, it specialized in fitting 'glass in window frames'. All 'at affordable prices'. This tea and glass shop was at Rua de São Pedro, No 6.

The shop at Rua da Alfândega, No 5, dealt wholesale and retail in 'superior teas of all qualities', Chinese porcelain, English china, and modern crystal and glass, among other English and oriental goods. The information is from an advertisement in the *Gazeta* on 1 April 1821. And it seems that glass was also sold by another aristocrat of English trade in the Rua da Alfândega, Mr William ('Guilherme') Young, at his warehouse at No 4. He, according to an advertisement in the *Gazeta* on 14 August 1816, was also acting as agent for the Countess of Linhares:

> Anyone who wishes to rent the country house belonging to Her Excellency the Countess of Linhares at Alto da Glória until 1 April 1817 should speak to Guilherme Young at Rua da Alfândega, No 4.

At Rua do Sabão, No 23, another 'Guilherme' – William Watson – sold not only porcelain and china but '*English* cut glass', both retail and wholesale, according to another advertisement in the *Gazeta*, on 31 August 1816; the advertisement added that the upper floor of the same house always had 'an assortment of veneers, oddments and ironware for assortment of wholesale shops, everything always being *English*'.

There were numerous advertisements for carriages which, as with houses, made much of the fact that they were glazed. The following may be mentioned as typical examples of such advertisements: the one in the *Gazeta* of 14 September 1811 for a four-wheeled carriage 'with glass windows'; the one that appears in the same newspaper on 7 March 1821 for 'a good carriage with glass windows'; the one in the *Gazeta* on 3 August 1816 for 'a four-wheeled carriage, glazed body, with silver-decorated harness. It was a victory for the English carriage – glazed and light – over the curtained calash. Even the palanquin, in which the ruling classes used to be carried around the cities enveloped in heavy curtains, felt the impact of English glass: one that was for sale in Recife in 1836 was described as 'richly adorned and fully glazed'.[347] This marked the spread to Brazil of the

[347] *Diário de Pernambuco*, 18 January 1836.

age of glass, which, together with iron, characterized the beginning of the so-called palaeotechnical period of modern civilization.[348]

The widespread use of glass in houses and factories in Europe had improved light levels inside buildings and thus contributed to the extension of both domestic life and intellectual, manufacturing, commercial and administrative work. Professor Mumford emphasises the importance of this substitution of the window for the wooden shutter.[349] It was of considerable importance, of course, in countries with cold climates and many cloudy days in the year; but not in tropical countries to which glass, glass windows, skylights, window panes, stained glass and glass display cabinets were evangelically brought from Europe from the early years of the nineteenth century onwards as if they were such great necessities in the latter countries as in the former. It was, of course, the manufacturers of the articles who stood to gain the most if the mystique of glass took hold in those countries of hot sun and intense light. And in the nineteenth century such manufacturers were primarily English. That accounts for the prominence of English glass in newspaper advertisements in Brazil during the early decades of that century.

Where Professor Mumford seems to be right – from a human or universal and not just a northern European or North American point of view – in extolling glass so highly is when he stresses the importance of its use in the form of convex and, later, concave lenses for spectacles, with which science has corrected eyesight defects or simply age-related fatigue. Or in the form of telescopes, magnifying glasses, lenses, binoculars and spyglasses. In this respect, Professor Mumford recalls Singer's suggestion that the Renaissance – the revival of learning – might in part be attributed to the additional years of reading life that spectacles or glasses gave to human beings.[350] In Brazil, imports of reading glasses in fact peaked at the same time as the production and importation of books, magazines and newspapers. Including English books.

The invention of spectacles is attributed to an Englishman, Roger Bacon. And the English stood out in the production of spectacle glass, or spectacle lenses, before the Germans became the kings of this industry. The English had for a long time manufactured the best glass in Europe, and in large quantities; they had also devoted themselves to that speciality not only because they were Protestants and, as such, great readers of the Bible and other books, but also because they were a maritime people that needed glass for the improvement or safety of the science or art of navigation.

[348] See, for example, the work cited in the following note (Translator).

[349] Mumford, *Technics and Civilization*, p. 125.

[350] *Ibid.*, p. 126.

Brazilian newspaper advertisements from the times of Dom João VI and Dom Pedro I show that Brazil imported a not inconsiderable quantity of English magnifying glasses and telescopes, at least one of which was in Bahia by the end of the eighteenth or start of the nineteenth century. Brazilian imports of English glass, incidentally, seem to date back to the sixteenth century: Whital had included glass among the English products that would find a market in Portuguese America during the colony's first century. England produced a considerable volume of glass even then, and English manufacturers felt the need for foreign markets for their glass.

Glass had been made in England since the days of the Roman occupation. But for a long time the art of glass-making seems not to have progressed as much there as in other parts of Europe. It eventually developed with foreign assistance. In 758 the Abbot of Jarrow still had to ask the Bishop of Mainz to send him craftsmen who could make glass windows and vessels, since the English were very backward in the craft.[351]

It was in the sixteenth century that the fashion for ornamental glass spread from Venice to England and breathed life into the art and industry of glass-making in that country. In 1550 eight workers or technicians who were specialists in the art of ornamental glass-making moved from Murano – where the trade had declined – to London. One of them, Josepho Casselari, decided to stay in England, where another Venetian, Jacob Verzellini, made a powerful contribution to the development of the glass-making art and industry. Craftsmen from France and the Netherlands also helped to develop the industry in England.

But the factor that most especially favoured the industry among the English from the seventeenth century onwards was the use of coal to heat the furnaces for making glass. The new English technique of glass production was soon followed by a ban on importing glass into English markets. Within a short period, England was in fact exporting it on a large scale: one of many aspects of the vitality of its carboniferous civilization once it had begun to stabilize towards the end of the seventeenth century. By 1696 there were already eighty-eight glass-works in England, including thirty-nine making bottles, two mirrors, fifteen window glass and twenty-seven plain glass. In the eighteenth century the glass-making industry in England expanded rapidly: tumblers and wine-glasses from this period remain famous even today. In 1746 the industry was so prosperous that it attracted heavy taxes. With the help of German craftsman the art of cut glass was developed, for which English material proved to be superior to

[351] On this subject, see A. W. Franks, *Guide to Glass Room in British Museum*, London, 1888; Edward Dillon, *Glass*, London, 1907; Harry J. Powell, *Glass Making in England*, Cambridge, 1923; W. A. Thorpe, *English Glass*, London, 1935; and the recent essay by W. B. Honey, *English Glass*, London, 1946.

that from Bohemia. That English art is considered by specialists to have been at its peak of splendour between 1780 and 1810.

When Brazil's ports were opened up to foreign trade in general and British trade in particular, not only was glass-making one of the main industries in England, thanks to the availability of coal in the island and the technique of using it in that industry, but the art of cut glass was also at its height among the English, who had surpassed all their competitors in the field.[352]

It was therefore natural that glass would be one of the products of British industry that the English would seek to place on the Brazilian market without delay; and it was also natural that, in order to secure the market, they would lobby the prince regent, Dom João, to pass the famous edict against lattices. They could have done so through the brother of the powerful minister Dom Rodrigo de Sousa Coutinho, Dom Domingos, who lived in England and was apparently highly sympathetic to the cause or interests of British trade and industry.

Dom Rodrigo himself, the Count of Linhares, who had been educated in England, is known to have always been a fervent Anglophile; and we have seen that after his death in Rio de Janeiro an indiscreet newspaper advertisement showed that an English merchant was dealing with the Countess's affairs. Dom Rodrigo's passion for the English is seen as being to blame for the fact that the treaty of 1810 left Brazilian merchants in a position of inferiority compared with English traders in Brazil, as they had to pay twenty-four per cent duty on merchandise they imported from abroad, whereas only fifteen per cent duty *ad valorem* was payable on British goods entering the country. The Count of Anadia[353] stood up against such a scandalous concession to the English to the detriment of 'national trade' and tried to prevent Dom João from signing the treaty, as well as the act handing over the Island of Santa Catarina to the English Government, which Dom Rodrigo similarly favoured. The Count of Anadia is said to have gone to the Palace and remonstrated with the prince that:

> The reciprocal treatment mentioned in the treaty was illusory; the English would import everything into the Portuguese domains, and Portuguese nationals would only take to England raw cotton, brazil wood, diamonds, gold bars and dust, and coins; colonial products

[352] Honey writes (in *English Glass*, p. 38), 'By the 19th century, the English cut glass had secured a great market on the Continent. The brilliance of its lead-metal gave it an advantage over the Bohemian ...' And on p. 47 he adds, 'For this beauty of material no glass has ever surpassed the English.'

[353] João Rodrigues de Sá e Melo, Viscount and later Count of Anadia (1755-1809), had been the Portuguese foreign minister from 1803 to 1804 (Translator).

would be excluded by what were regarded as prohibitive duties; Portuguese industry, created with such difficulty by the Marquis of Pombal during the twenty-five years he was in office, would thereby be ruined; the impoverished and idle people would indulge in political discussions; and the final consequence would be a evolution that would prove fatal to the prince or his descendants.[354]

[354] C. G. (João Coelho Gomes), *Elementos de História Nacional da Economia Política em que se mostra as Diferentes Indústrias que havia no Brasil, etc.*, Rio de Janeiro, 1865, pp. 239-240.
Forty years before C. G. published his *Elementos de História Nacional da Economia Política* in 1865, another observer of Brazilian life, Francisco de Sierra y Mariscal, in 'Ideas Geraes sobre a Revolução do Brasil e suas Consequencias' ('General ideas on the Brazilian revolution and its consequences'), written in 1823, had highlighted the less favourable aspects of British influence over the Luso-American economy in somewhat scandalous tones, and more from the viewpoint of the former mother country than of Brazil: 'The immediate cause of the Brazilian Revolution should largely be attributed to the monstrous treaty of 1810. Since this treaty, I have seen, in the surroundings of Rio de Janeiro, Towns reduced to Ruins, and deserted; the same is happening in the Reconcavo of Bahia [the area around the city of Salvador – Translator]. This Treaty has brought death to Brazil, and to Portugal. The English have even carried out Coastal Trade. In exchange for the luxuries they have introduced to Brazil, they have taken the products of the Country and whatever money there was, and Brazil still owes the English many millions. The English are not like the other men of the European continent; although they suckle elsewhere, they love no other Country than England. They do not marry; they do not eat or drink anything but what is English. They are a Spider everywhere; any Nation should fear an English office in their Country more than all the English Artillery Pieces. I know Englishmen in Rio de Janeiro who send their Clothes to England to be washed and pressed, in short they are monsters for the Country in which they are staying, and they are the best English Citizens. With this treaty, ready-made Shoes, Furniture, Outfits and even Mattresses have entered Brazil; and I have seen, being unloaded in Rio de Janeiro, Coffins already fitted out for burying children.' (*Anais da Biblioteca Nacional do Rio de Janeiro*, vol. 43-4, Rio de Janeiro, 1931, p. 56.)
There is exaggeration on the part of Sierra y Mariscal when he warns that the English in Brazil never got married (to Brazilian or Portuguese women) and only ever ate or drank English food and drink. The Codex recently acquired by the Documentation Department of the Brazilian Ministry of Foreign Relations, referring to the year 1618 – 'Memorial de todos os Extrangeiros q. vivem nas Cap.[as] do Rio Grande, Parahyba, Tamaracá & Pernambuco e Bahia dos quaes se não pode ter sospeita' ['List of all Foreigners living in the Captaincies of Rio Grande, Parahyba, Tamaracá & Pernambuco and Bahia who shall not be held in suspicion'] – includes a certain 'Thomas babintão ingres' ('Thomas Babington, English'), of whom it states, in a characterization that does not sound exceptional: 'No 6. Came to this land 40 years ago is married to a Portuguese woman and has children and lives in poverty from his smallholding'. Several cases like that of Thomas will be considered in a forthcoming work – *Outros Ingleses no Brasil* – specially devoted to the study of Catholic and non-Catholic English people in colonial Brazil and traces of British influence on our country and our people gathered from documents from the colonial era. We shall then see that even before the opening of the ports of Brazil to foreigners some English people were already living in the country or turned up here to trade. Some were Catholic, others non-Catholic; some had the king's permission, others did not, and some became Brazilianized or converted to Catholicism here.
As for the privileges with which British trade had armed itself in Brazil since 1808, to the detriment of Portuguese and Brazilian interests, they were in fact privileges of an empire in relation to a colony. Some interesting information in that respect is given by Bento José da Costa, a Recife merchant, dated 7 March 1809, and by Captain-General Caetano Pinto de Miranda Montenegro on 18 May that year. They point out the expenses of an English ship in Brazil (Recife) in contrast

Anadia ended his remonstrance by denouncing the attempt to hand Santa Catarina over to the English.

According to the forgotten scholar of Brazil's economy and economic history whose words have just been transcribed,

> the prince, shuffling the papers that were on the table, indignantly tore up the paper abandoning the island; but Dom Rodrigo was there to instil in him the fear of Bonaparte, from whom only England could save the Portuguese royal house, and he succeeded in having the treaty signed. [...] The count left the palace with symptoms of the congestion that within a few hours was to kill him; and Dom Rodrigo later received a caning from the regent because of that treaty (when the news arrived that national ships had been captured by the English navy) and he decided to poison himself. [...] But the 1810 treaty remained![355]

That is what Coelho Gomes disparagingly states in his forgotten economic history of Brazil, and another historian of our economy, Aprígio Guimarães, Professor of Economics at the Faculty of Law in Recife in the mid-nineteenth century, did not hesitate to endorse Coelho Gomes on this and other points.[356] A sign that he was not a lightweight or anodyne writer,

to the expenses of an identical Portuguese ship in London. A 380-ton English ship paid 270$425 in Recife for three months, according to Costa, the merchant. An identical Portuguese ship in London, for the same length of time, paid 1:329$540! And, even so, James Gambier, HBM consul in Rio de Janeiro, complained about 'the elevated expenses' that English ships incurred in Brazil. See the correspondence between the Governors of Pernambuco and the Ministry of the Kingdom in the Rio de Janeiro National Archive. Manuscripts kept in the same archive reveal that, even with such privileges, as soon as the ports of Brazil were opened to foreigners some Englishmen devoted themselves to smuggling. The above-mentioned correspondence for 1810-1811 shows that the English galley *Leon* attempted to offload smuggled goods in Recife and the captain of the galley, James ('Diogo') Thompson, was arrested (Dispatch of 27 November 1810 from Governor Caetano Pinto de Miranda Montenegro to the Minister of the Kingdom). It should be pointed out, however, that in acting as vigorously as he always did against dishonest or insolent Englishmen, and even against the more arrogant British consuls such as John ('João') Lampriere, consul in Recife, Montenegro had the support of many British residents, such as those who visited him at Engenho Monteiro in 1813 (Dispatch from the governor to the Minister of the Kingdom, dated 4 January 1813, National Archive) to disapprove of the consul's attitude in the case of the arrest of an English galley captain, Robert Grasset, and to applaud the stance taken by the governor. Among these British residents in Pernambuco was Charles Bowen who, as we have seen, would later side with the revolutionaries in 1817 and would go on a mission to the United States on behalf of those rebels or patriots.

[355] *Ibid.*, p. 240. According to Luccock (*Notes on Rio de Janeiro*, p. 99), the Count of Linhares was 'taken off by poison' by his enemies.

[356] Aprígio J. da Silva Guimarães, *Estudos de Economia Política* (posthumous edition), Recife, 1902. Professor Aprígio Guimarães gave the following opinion on the work by Coelho Gomes: 'a work in which there is much useful information for our economic history, and many ideas that should

but one whom such an intellectually responsible scholar as Aprígio would not hesitate to support.

Oliveira Lima, in his monumental work *Dom João VI no Brasil*, sketches a portrait of the Count of Linhares (Dom Rodrigo de Sousa Coutinho) in such favourable tones that he sometimes gives the impression of being over-generous. Since that Portuguese nobleman was part of a court noted, as Dom João VI's court was, for the tides of corruption that almost constantly washed over it, and nothing suggests that the powerful minister tried very hard to swim against them – although nothing specific is known that might compromise his individual honesty – it would not be surprising if the count had acquiesced to some of the business undertaken at that time by Englishmen, or by intermediaries or agents or partners of Englishmen in Brazil and London. All the more so since he is known to have been an inveterate Anglophile, as has already been mentioned, and the brother of an even greater Anglophile who was particularly sympathetic to British interests in Portugal and Brazil. Such interests may well have included those of a manufacturer of glass – for door and window panes – and iron – for balconies, carriages and industrial and agricultural machinery – so hugely important were glass and iron in British industrial output at that time. What harm might there be if a minister of the prince regent of Brazil indirectly favoured the importation of English glass and increased amounts of English iron to Brazil by means of a simple edict, apparently purely for the sake of aesthetics, security, modernization or Europeanization? It was just a favour to the English. Certainly not a racket or anything at all shady that might dishonour a statesman.

It is a pity that the figure of Dom Rodrigo is still so poorly studied, since almost all the pages written about him are more like fervent apologias than critical interpretations. Or else diatribes by opponents of his anglophile politics, which, within limits, was what was most appropriate for Brazil at the time. Even Mr Tobias Monteiro, who is ordinarily so inclined to offer a severely critical interpretation of Brazilian people and events that his writing becomes embittered, does not judge or even portray the Count of Linhares in the truly masterful study in which he reconstructs and analyses the preparations for Brazilian independence. He confines himself to recording that Dona Carlota Joaquina[357] hated him and that Prince Pedro, ill-mannered as ever, did not hesitate on one occasion to allude to the dark-skinned grandparents of Dom Francisco, 'the son of the Count of Linhares'.[358] Professor Manchester merely points out that Dom Rodrigo

profit our statesmen' (p. 236). He acknowledges, however, that Coelho Gomes had 'protectionist prejudices' (p. 237).

357 The wife of Dom João VI (Translator).

358 Tobias Monteiro, *História do Império. A Elaboração da Independência*, Rio de Janeiro, 1927, p.

was energetic, quick-witted, impulsive, a lover of the new and grandiose, and a bitter enemy of the principles of the French Revolution, as well as decidedly pro-England and close to Lord Strangford.[359]

The prince regent's edict to abolish lattices merely created an immediate market in Brazil for a legitimate English activity: the trade in glass. And also for the trade in iron. According to Professor Manchester, that iron, together with other 'vested interests' (he only mentions fabrics and china, but not

141. We should not be taken in by the hasty or simplistic generalizations of those who label early nineteenth-century Portuguese and Brazilian Anglophiles as 'reactionary' and Francophiles as 'liberal', 'revolutionary' or 'progressive'. In his book *O Conde de Linhares* (Lisbon, 1908), a valuable study despite its apologetic tone, the Marquis of Funchal presents a well-documented discussion of the subject, pointing out with some exaggeration that members of 'the French party' in Portugal at that time were adepts 'of subservience to the orders of France and not to the ideas of the French Revolution' (p. 39). 'With respect to the ideas of liberty, equality and the rights of man, etc., [the Francophiles] neither possessed them nor were liable to assimilate them. If historians had only entered the homes of the political leaders of the early nineteenth century (some of which have remained intact until today), they would be convinced that their inhabitants had not evolved at all, at least since the time of Dom João V. If they also went into their libraries, which existed in all those homes, they would see that the new spirit had not found its way in there and only old codices occupied the shelves. If, however, they visited the homes of members of the English party, they would encounter libraries endowed with the works of the most notable thinkers of the eighteenth century, and they would find frescoes and furniture in the latest French Directoire style, which clearly demonstrates that French influence did not cross into the family sanctuaries of the leaders of the French party, not even when transformed into the material improvements accessible to the wealthy, as they were' (p. 40). Even if we accept that the Anglophile statesmen and politicians in Portugal and Brazil at that time either directly or indirectly favoured British economic interests, as well as their own private interests on the side, it would seem that they, and not the Francophiles, were the true liberals in the best sense of the term. They were the main reformers and modernizers in Portugal and Brazil, and had to fight reactionaries like Pina Manique and F. d'Almada, 'arch-enemies of Dom Rodrigo,' as the Marquis of Funchal says (p. 40). For Funchal, the French party represented 'precisely the traditional ideas of those Portuguese politicians who reacted against the Pombaline system ...' (p. 30). A considerable part of the opposition to the Count of Linhares and his brother in Portugal and Brazil may well have been motivated less by their leanings towards the English or their perhaps exaggerated connections with Englishmen, than by their connections with the 'Pombaline system', which was so detested by clericalists and reactionaries. And some of these considered themselves 'French'.

Apparently based on his intimate knowledge of the period when conflict between English and French influence in Portugal and Brazil was at its height, the Marquis of Funchal restores balance to the idea that for the Portuguese and Brazilians France then represented Revolution and Liberty while England was Reaction. The situation was not so simple. Nor does it seem that English influence at the time was solely economic, as Mr Afonso Arinos de Melo Franco assumes in his thought-provoking study 'O Visconde de Cairu' (*Digesto Econômico*, São Paulo, No 28, March 1947, p. 48), and French influence ideological. Everything suggests that English ideological – in the sense of liberal, democratic and reformist – influence on both Portuguese and Brazilians was then considerable, while at the same time, I repeat, it was opposed by the clerical or orthodox reactionaries, who seemed to be less afraid of the guillotines of France than of the bibles of England. And we should never forget that the economic and political rivalry between France and England was reflected in the competition between French and English merchants for Brazilian markets.

[359] Manchester, *British Preëminence in Brazil*, p. 27.

glass), led England to adopt 'a new commercial policy'.[360] Basing himself on Witt Bowden, whose book *The Rise of the Great Manufacturers in England, 1760-1790* is perhaps the most comprehensive study on the subject, the American historian points out that by the late eighteenth century the new English industrialists were feeling the need for wider markets for their growing output.[361] To secure new markets for this surplus, it is only natural that the agents for British producers tried to get as much as they could from politicians in other countries through the use of bribes or sweeteners, trickery or guile. That comes under what is generally termed the 'Jesuitic' method, but which has been employed by all the great dominators of individuals or peoples: the Jews and the English, for example; and more recently the Fascists and Nazis and, nowadays, the Soviet leadership in their political, if not economic, expansionism or imperialism.

As we have already seen, the now almost forgotten economist and historian João Coelho Gomes, in his *Elementos de História Nacional da Economia Política* – published in 1865 but dealing largely with the years of 1808-1812, a period that the author lived through in his youth and regards as decisive in the formation, or deformation, of the Brazilian economy – describes Dom Rodrigo de Sousa Coutinho in such an unfavourable light that he offers a caricature rather than a portrait. However, by contrasting his deformed image with the velvety portrait painted by Oliveira Lima we can find a sort of happy medium, from which the Count of Linhares emerges as a statesman of superior intelligence and an extraordinary capacity for action, but flawed in his make-up as a politician or statesman by having such a horror of the French Revolution and Napoleon I that, due to a surfeit of anti-French feeling, he became almost an accomplice of British imperialism in Brazil.

As an accomplice of British imperialism, he seems to have unintentionally helped to stifle the beginnings of socially and economically beneficial polyculture in this country at the end of the eighteenth century and in the early years of the nineteenth. This incipient polyculture was served by a trading system that had its own ships. The fact is that, when Dom João VI arrived in Rio de Janeiro, the country was beginning to produce some cloth and already appreciable amounts of bacon, pork, sausage, cheeses, tobacco, indigo, arrowroot, hides, tallow, grease, jerked beef, maize, cordage, piassava, beans and manioc. And not just the gold and sugar on which the country soon fell back once its markets were flooded with foodstuffs, baize, cotton, wool, leather, rope, glass, iron and even snuff, all brought from England and extolled in newspaper advertisements as truly messianic goods without which there was no salvation.

[360] *Ibid.*, p. 46.

[361] *Ibid.*, p. 48.

Alarmed by the prospect of this flood of imports, the 'trading body of Bahia' began in 1808 to protest against the establishment of trading houses by foreigners in Brazil. This anti-English outcry is clearly revealed in a document kept in the manuscripts section of the National Library: a *Representation* made to the prince regent.[362] 'Why do they not come to share in the labours of Agriculture but wish only to take pride of place in Trade?' asked the merchants from Bahia, referring to the Englishmen already on their way to Brazil, who would soon be sounding their invasion horns in the form of enticing advertisements in their unofficial *Gazeta* – clarions announcing their economic conquest of Brazil. The Bahian merchants warned against the temptation of these advertisements and the cheapness of English products:

> Everyone knows what their system is: there is no stronger argument than experience. Portugal has seen that at first the English sell cheap and buy dear; but later, once the country's production has declined and inertia raises the flag of their empire, they follow a different system... they save their Golden Fleece and the country's own merchants grow poor to make it rich.

The Bahian merchants sounded an even starker warning in their *Representation* to the prince regent against the dangers of giving the English privileges to establish their own trading houses in Brazil: 'And how did the English conquer Asia?' Yet it was all in vain. English trading houses and English ships soon acquired an almost imperial prominence in Brazilian cities and waters – and in the Kingdom's newspaper advertisements – completely overshadowing the Portuguese and Brazilian merchants.

Yet at the beginning of the nineteenth century Rio de Janeiro had shipyards – from Largo da Pracinha to Saúde – where shipbuilding techniques were not so archaic as to shame us in the eyes of northern Europeans. In any case, with their blacksmiths who made nails and bolts of copper, and their sail factories, these shipyards were able to build ships, equipped with typically Brazilian hawsers made of piassava, which plied up and down the coast of Brazil and to foreign ports laden with the products of that incipient industrial activity tolerated by the now decadent and excessively parasitic mother country.

It bears repeating that the exorbitant privileges granted to England in Brazil, apparently due in large part to pressure that Dom Rodrigo exerted on the prince regent, were responsible for stemming precisely those beginnings of industrial activity and inter-regional trade in Brazil, together

[362] Biblioteca Nacional, Manuscripts Section, I, 31, 28, 26.

with the likewise beneficial beginnings of polyculture. The beginnings of a less passive Brazilian economy than one based on sugar or tobacco, or even on gold or diamonds. Less passive and less dependent on foreign markets. Less colonial and more national.

Because he did not defend those interests effectively enough against the interests of English imperial expansion, which needed the Brazilian market for its surplus output, Dom Rodrigo is today regarded as a man who seems to have let himself be carried too far by the idea that defending Brazil against the political danger of the French Revolution or Napoleonic imperialism justified the sacrifice of its most precious economic interests to the all-absorbing demands of the British. That aspect of the political deeds of Dom João's eminent minister did not go unnoticed by either Coelho Gomes or Aprígio Guimarães. As Coelho Gomes writes of Dom Rodrigo:

> That minister had been educated in England where, alongside the English doctrines that he learnt, he naturally developed many close relationships in the country.

He had thus introduced to Brazil the economic ideas or doctrines of Great Britain, which, according to the Anglophobic economist, were subsequently received here in 'gilded books' and had become so widespread in our society that they had invaded 'some of our political luminaries'.[363] Apparently an allusion to the passionate Anglophilia of Silva Lisboa, with whom Coelho clashed in a polemic in the press, and who wrote the famous *Refutação das Reclamações contra o Commercio Inglez* ('Refutation of the Complaints against English Trade'), published in Rio de Janeiro in 1810, and the essay *Observações sobre a Fraqueza da Industria e Estabelecimento de Fabricas no Brasil* ('Observations on the Weakness of Industry and Establishment of Factories in Brazil'), which appeared in the same year.

The systematic Anglicization of the Brazilian economy had begun in Portugal: prior to the departure of Dom João and the royal family for Brazil,

> the royal spirit began to become indisposed against all men and wholesome doctrines of pure patriotism and of experience gained in the overseas provinces, principally those of Brazil.[364]

It was Anglicism against traditional purity; and, to secure its dominion

[363] Coelho Gomes, *Elementos de História Nacional da Economia Política*, p. 27.

[364] *Ibid.*, p. 28.

over Brazil, Anglicism – which had its primary advocate in Dom Rodrigo, as Dom João's minister in Rio de Janeiro – made use of Jesuitic intrigue against the purists by 'censuring such men as being supporters of Napoleon I'. In other words, anyone who was not an Anglophile was a supporter of Napoleon I and, as such, suspected of treason against king and country. By astutely developing this intrigue, Dom Rodrigo made the prince see him as 'the man he needed': the man able to keep the terrible Napoleonic peril away from Brazil, although at the expense of making very special political and, above all, economic concessions. Concessions that would mean acknowledging Portuguese America as being a virtual British protectorate.

According to Coelho Gomes, who is supported in this interpretation of Brazil's economic history by Aprígio Guimarães, Dom Rodrigo's plan – or the plan the English worked through Dom Rodrigo – 'was well conceived and masterfully executed'. That was as soon as the royal family had left Lisbon for Brazil. At that time,

> the Brazilian fleet or convoy lay at the bar of Lisbon, composed of a vast number of national ships laden with Brazilian products, which represented huge sums... When the Portuguese royal family left there for here, all the ships of that fleet lying at the Lisbon bar were handed over to the English admiral, Sidney Smith, who was then in Lisbon harbour with a British force.[365] [Coelho Gomes adds that] the delivery of the fleet into English hands was done by order and in the name of the prince. Admiral Sidney Smith received it in the name of the British Government and immediately dispatched it to the London docks. There the ships remained for three or four years. English commissions were appointed to deal with their administration. Who co-operated with those foreign commissions, as the shipowners' representative? Dom Domingos de Sousa Coutinho, the brother of Dom Rodrigo himself. It should be pointed out that Dom Rodrigo[366] had the good sense, or whatever you might call it, never to go to Portugal or come to Brazil.

And when the fleet was handed back to Portugal, it was done so 'with the corresponding account for enormous expenses...'[367] It was the beginning of the British economic protectorate of Brazil, the terms of which would be unmistakably expressed by the monopoly on imports to Brazil that was granted to Great Britain. Luso-Brazilian ships found

[365] *Ibid.*, p. 29.

[366] *Sic*; the writer presumably means Dom Domingos (Translator).

[367] Coelho Gomes, *Elementos de História Nacional da Economia Política*, p. 30.

it almost impossible to continue trading. According to Coelho Gomes, their crews were taken away, and they had to resort to making up their complement with slaves[368] as impromptu sailors. The English imposed laws on Brazil to protect workers and slaves even before they were applied to imperial Great Britain's own colonies or her factories at home: in what was in fact a fair provision (which seems to have spread to the major Brazilian farms and plantations, which until then had had no medical care for their slaves), they began to force those same ships to have not only a chaplain but a surgeon on board, and to meet other requirements, which together resulted in the near destruction of the Luso-Brazilian merchant fleet. That leads us to the interpretation that the purpose of those measures was not so much humanitarian as to stifle competition from Luso-Brazilian ships, and also to reduce the slave trade by indirect means, since if Brazil were well supplied with good African workers it might compete at an advantage with Britain's colonies in sugar production.

Another blow that the English then struck at Brazil's shipbuilding industry and, hence, its economy – clearly with the same imperial purpose of keeping the economy passively colonial – was that they succeeded in forcing Portugal, which was still the master of Brazil, to accept the right of a foreign vessel to become naturalized 'through the payment of fifteen per cent of its value'.[369] Again, it is Coelho Gomes who highlights this fact, full of the indignant purism that guides his whole interpretation of the economic history of Brazil, in almost violent contrast to the approach taken by Silva Lisboa: a theoretician of the extremely Anglophilic form of economic politics of which the two Sousa Coutinhos, one in Rio de Janeiro and the other in London, were the greatest practitioners, closely followed by the Duke of Palmela. Indeed, the latter is held to be responsible for the 1814 treaty, which, according to Coelho Gomes,

> further tightened the noose in which the 1810 Treaty had caught the country's forces. [To the extent that] the merchants in Rio de Janeiro, Bahia, Pernambuco and Maranhão sold ships, terminated transactions and liquidated their businesses. Just a small number of consignment offices and a few coastal trading houses remained.

That leads the Anglophobic economist to claim that 'Dom João VI effectively established himself as a consul for Great Britain.'[370] Those words almost confirm the predictions made by the Bahian merchants in their *Representation* of 1808 to the prince regent against the establishment of

[368] *Ibid.*, p. 32.
[369] *Ibid.*, p. 32.
[370] *Ibid.*, p. 41.

the English in Brazil with privileges that meant the weakening of Brazilian trade and shipbuilding: '... the Nation that merited such predilection had conquered Brazil without any shedding of blood'. No 'shedding of blood', indeed; but much shedding of printer's ink, used in the advertisements through which the English began to loom large in the eyes of a considerable proportion of the Brazilian population from 1808 onwards, as bringers of goods and products from British factories that were irresistibly tempting to the well-to-do classes awakened from their long sleep as people almost cut off from northern Europe: iron, glass, copper, wool and cutlery made in England,.

Areas in which there seems to have been gross racketeering by English merchants in Brazil during the first half of the nineteenth century – racketeering and not just commercial shrewdness – were copper and gunpowder. But we shall examine the question of copper in another chapter, and gunpowder too. In this one we shall merely point out that iron, either in its pure state or in the form of 'iron goods',[371] was even more important than glass in the early imports from or via England after the ports were opened in 1808.

Since the end of the eighteenth century, England had been 'producing iron in larger quantities and at lower costs than any other area', according to Shepard Bancroft Clough and Charles Woolsey Cole in their *Economic History of Europe*.[372]

Iron production in England had been favoured by that 'nice combination of economic factors' that those authors mention, to which the coal found under English soil should always be added. Hence the concentration of metallurgy in areas of Britain that had both iron and coal: the Midlands, South Wales and along the Clyde in Scotland. John Wilkinson, an Englishman and the first iron magnate, built the first iron bridge in England and the first iron pipeline stretching for forty miles; when he died, he was buried in an iron coffin.[373] And the English soon started using mainly iron to build their ships, which for so long had been made mainly of timber.

The English iron industry, closely followed by the Swedish but not exceeded or equalled by any competitor until the middle of the nineteenth century, was among those that arrived triumphantly in Brazil in the early decades of that century, and shone out in newspaper advertisements as much as the glass and steel industries. After 1808 English ships began to unload huge amounts of iron in Brazilian ports; this was the expression and symbol of a new civilization – that of iron, coal and glass – before

[371] Words used by Freyre in English (Translator).

[372] Boston, 1941, p. 349.

[373] Clough and Cole, *Economic History of Europe*, p. 413.

which Brazil could only bow in passive, colonial fashion. In exchange for that imperial, civilizing iron, whether in bars or in the form of the machines and instruments of civilization, as well as for glass, which was equally civilizing and came by the crate-load from English factories, and later for plain coal, it gave its rustic hardwoods, its gold, its diamonds and other precious stones, equally rustic, and its cotton, tobacco and other products, all of them rustic.

The importing of vast amounts of iron and glass into Brazil was bound to result in profound changes to the Brazilian landscape, which until then had been little marked by either. There were few iron balconies on its buildings, and glass windows in its houses were rare. That does not mean that it lacked an architecture already in harmony with tropical conditions and therefore ecologically well balanced, represented by buildings reminiscent of the Orient: buildings of stone and mortar supported by timbers that rivalled iron in strength and outclassed it in beauty.

As we have seen, that kind of building set amongst trees, either native or transplanted from other lands, had become a feature of the Brazilian landscape. English eyes fell in love with them, and many of the English preferred them – the ones closest to the main cities – for their residences, as we have seen. In newspaper advertisements in the first half of the nineteenth century, the voices of English sirens seeking to entice Brazilians to their transoceanic charms mingle with those of Brazilian nymphs seeking to attract foreigners to the sun, the shade and the native or acclimatized trees of Brazil: 'well-wooded' grounds with 'abundant fresh water' surrounding country houses with verandas or porches.

An advertisement like the one we find in the *Gazeta do Rio de Janeiro* on 14 December 1808 was almost certainly one of the first to arouse the lyrical and also practical – in the sense of health-seeking – interest of an Englishman fresh from Europe in the many ideal places to live in the surroundings of the main Brazilian cities. It is an advertisement for a house with

> five bedrooms, two verandas, patio, kitchen and area for preparing manioc meal [which could be converted into a wheat-flour bakery if the existing oven was not fit for that purpose], all covered with a tiled roof, with good equipment, wheel, oven, press and tub, troughs and mangers, etc.; furnished with chairs and some household goods; oven for making preserves and the necessary implements, with large orange and banana groves, rice field,[374] Vineyard, large area

[374] The Portuguese text has the unknown word *arnazal*, assumed to be a typographical error for *arrozal* (Translator).

> of coffee, two *quarteis*[375] of Manioc and some Maize and many other plants such as Figs, Pomegranates, Mangoes, Cashews, Indian and native Limes, sweet and sour Lemons, Tangerines, Calabashes, Malay Apples, Cotton, many Roses, a large pasture with good grass: all well fenced with new gates and plenty of water.

An ideal place for English horses and cattle. It just needed a coach house for 'the light carriage' introduced to Brazil by the English. There are numerous advertisements in the same vein, so it is no exaggeration to consider this one so representative or typical that it speaks here for hundreds of similar or identical voices extolling the trees, pastures and water of country properties.

Such houses surrounded by trees in the outskirts of the cities – houses where the Portuguese or rich Brazilians spent their feast days, as has already been mentioned – were where the wealthier English people gradually settled – the majority of them, at least – not just for love of the cool houses with verandas but primarily for love of the trees, rose bushes, plants and pastures for horses, sheep and cattle. Perhaps the 'Englishmen' who allowed themselves to stay in the cities, like many of the Portuguese and Brazilian merchants, living on the upper floors of the town houses in which they had their warehouses and avoiding the expense of travelling, were actually over-economical and even stingy Scotsmen. For the country houses – the *sítios* and *chácaras* – of Rio de Janeiro, far from the Rua Direita and Rua da Alfândega, or of Recife far from the Rua do Trapiche and Rua da Senzala, required light carriages to bring their inhabitants to the commercial centres and return them once the day's work was done to the shade of the fine suburban woods, where they could sleep peacefully, breathing the pure forest air and delighting in the scent of the jasmine and roses. That surely accounts for the large number of advertisements for 'light English carriages' in Brazilian newspapers at the time: they were indispensable to the Englishmen who lived in country houses. Palanquins and even calashes were unsuitable for those merchants-cum-'gentlemen farmers':[376] they were too lumbering and slow for people who lived a long way from their trading houses.

Once the English were installed in *chácaras* or *sítios*, they Englished them as much as they could. They tried to give grassy meadows the appearance of lawns. They extended the gardens. Some excelled at growing orchids. In time, such houses became genuine models for rich and elegant

[375] A *quartel* was a quarter of an *alqueire*, i.e. about 1.2 hectares or 3 acres in Rio de Janeiro (Translator).

[376] Words used by Freyre in English (Translator).

Brazilians, who began to admire the English not only for their science of houses but for their knowledge of gardens, estates and lawns; not only for their arrangement of drawing-room furniture, but for the modernization and sanitization of the kitchen, the WC, the yard and the stable. Without founding strictly English-style farms in Brazil, but instead wholeheartedly taking over old Luso-Brazilian country houses – the old, squat *chácara* houses with porches or verandas at the front or sides – the English made a great contribution in the first half of the nineteenth century to improving the hygiene and comfort of semi-rural living for the middle classes and even the wealthier aristocracy in Brazil. By turning to the English models not just of houses, furniture, dress, transport, cuisine and diet, but also of gardens, stables, WCs and suburban living, those more enlightened middle classes and wealthier rural aristocracy became highly Anglicized during the first half of the nineteenth century. It should not be overlooked that one of the processes by which this Anglicization occurred was imitation, which was largely developed through newspaper advertisements: the numerous advertisements for English goods, English products, English objects and English technicians that filled the papers of that period. A healthy accommodation was almost always found between such English innovations and Luso-Brazilian tradition.

There were of course some Englishmen among those who came to live and trade in Brazil after the opening of the ports who did not confine themselves to adapting the *chácaras* – the suburban or even rural houses that they found in this country – to their science of landscape gardening or art of domestic comfort; and they built suburban or rural dwellings in which they showed themselves to be not revolutionaries in the French style – that is, radical or absolutist – but the admirable contemporizing or conservative revolutionaries that the British have long been in all fields of culture or life. That is shown by Chamberlain's drawings of houses built by a countryman of his amidst the still untamed woods of the Glória headland in Rio: houses that looked traditionally Brazilian. In an explanation to one of the most significant illustrations in his album, the view of the church of Nossa Senhora da Glória, Lieutenant Chamberlain writes:

> The Houses on the point of Land Eastward of the Church are the property of an English merchant, who having first built one of these for himself, found the situation so desirable, that he soon surrounded it by others, and the Point of Gloria is become, as it were, an English Village.[377]

[377] Chamberlain, *Vistas e Costumes*, p. 193.

But this was an 'English village' – an assemblage of suburban domestic architecture – set in the outskirts of Rio de Janeiro without clashing with the tropical landscape of the region. A landscape assemblage and not just an architectural one.

That is what usually happened in Brazil after it was invaded by the English in 1808: the invasion was rarely marked by any radical replacement of the habits and styles of living, building, habitation, diet, transport or recreation encountered here by the invaders. That is suggested or illustrated by advertisements for auctions of houses occupied by English families, in which one can glimpse the gentle, velvet revolution that such families brought about in Brazil's social environment by introducing not only purely material values but also habits or customs of domestic life associated with such values. Sea or seawater bathing, for example. This form of bathing, at once hygienic and recreational, was a custom that Brazilians developed mainly through English influence; associated with it in newspaper advertisements are characteristically British residences, left partly on public display through auction announcements. Of all newspaper advertisements, this kind is perhaps the richest in significant details for the sociologist or social historian. And also in suggestions that cast light on areas of domestic living that would otherwise have remained in the dark or in shadow.

An advertisement placed by the 'Knight Diogo Gambier' (Sir James Gambier) in the *Gazeta do Rio de Janeiro* of 16 May 1811 informs us that the house in which that gentleman – who, incidentally, was HBM consul in Rio – had lived was for sale. Although that distant advertisement for an Englishman's house for sale is among the most discreet of its kind, it gives us an opportunity to pick out a few aspects of the gradual Anglicization of domestic lifestyles, which was so characteristic of the period of social transition in Brazil in the early nineteenth century. Everything in the eminent gentleman's house could be viewed 'upon application at said house'; 'bids for its purchase' would be received at the English consulate itself, in the Rua dos Ourives, by Thomas Spuring, secretary to the consul-general. Or, as a later advertisement adds:

> by Alexander Cunningham, Deputy Consul-General of the English Nation, every day from 10 o'clock in the morning until 2 in the afternoon, in Rua dos Ourives, at the English Consulate.

Sir James Gambier's country seat was in Botafogo: 'Bota Fogo', according to the advertisement. It consisted of

> well-laid-out buildings, with drinking water, fresh-water bath house, coach house, stables and many other comforts, both in the house itself and because everything is located in fine, fertile, spacious, well-fenced grounds supplied with fresh water, trees, fruit, vegetable garden and recreational garden, and very convenient, since it lies beside the small bay of Bota Fogo, for sea bathing, and in addition His Royal Highness has benignly seen fit to order that said Buildings and Grounds shall not at any time be requisitioned regardless of who becomes their owner, and also to waive the right to a tithe on the property...

Houses inhabited for some time by English consuls or other important Englishmen actually became known for that illustrious fact as 'the Englishman's house', ' the English consul's house' or 'the mister's house'. Sometimes they were advertised with that recommendation, as in the case of Sir James Gambier's house in Rio de Janeiro. Or the house of the 'English Consul' in Madalena, a smart Recife suburb. An advertisement in the *Diário de Pernambuco* on 31 August 1844 describes this 'very good house':

> For holiday or annual let: the country house in which the English Consul lived, in Passagem da Madalena, with very good house, coach house, stable, grass meadow, wells of very good water: apply to Delfino Gonçalves Pereira Lima at Rua Nova, No 44.

An old engraving of Recife dating from the time of the first emperor or the Regency marks out among the notable buildings of the city the English consul's house, which at that time was over towards Santo Amaro; it is perhaps the town house with a staircase at the side, in the style of certain old, rural residences in Portugal, the ruins of which can still be seen. All these houses were, of course, glazed, since prominent Englishmen must have been the first to set the example that really civilized Europeans only lived in houses with English window panes, and not surrounded by bars as if in a prison or convent.

Such houses were not usually rented out by the month or just by the year, but were apparently almost always leased for a long term. That is suggested by advertisements like the one placed by Mr Roope Brooking, who, on his return from Recife to England in 1845, announced in the *Diário de Pernambuco* of 13 February that year that he was transferring

> the lease of the house in which he lives, belonging to Senator Manoel de Carvalho, for a reasonable price, for the two and a half years that it has left to run...

All the contents of Mr Gambier's country house – to return to the advertisement for the house and furniture of that important Englishman in the time of Dom João VI – were also for sale and could be bought either separately or as a lot with the house, as the purchaser preferred. Unfortunately we have no details of the furniture and household ware in the country house that Sir James occupied.

Four years after Consul Gambier's auction, an even more important Englishman auctioned off his furniture and household ware: 'the Most Excellent Lord Strangford'. On 19 April 1815, the *Gazeta do Rio de Janeiro* announced that various articles, from books to a six-horse carriage harness, would be sold at the home of the representative of Great Britain in Brazil on 26 April at ten o'clock. The advertisement says:

> On the 26th inst. at 10 o'clock in the morning are to be sold at public auction in the house of the Most Excellent Lord *Strangford* the furniture of said house, kitchen utensils, chinaware, a carriage with harness for 6 horses, boots &c. The articles mentioned may be viewed at the house on the days preceding the auction.

The list of the items to be sold at public auction does not include the riding crop and boots with which the lord scandalized Araújo,[378] a gentleman who later became the Count of Barca, who was Minister of Foreign Affairs to Dom João VI. According to a gossip of the time, the British representative, who was accustomed to dealing with the Count of Linhares, asked for an appointment for a meeting with his replacement – Araújo. The appointment was arranged and he presented himself to the minister 'dressed in a riding jacket and boots and holding a crop'. Araújo entered the room, looked the English lord up and down and said something to the effect of

> I have a meeting arranged with His Britannic Majesty's minister. To you I have nothing to say.[379]

That is said to have made Lord Strangford request his passports and

[378] António de Araújo e Azevedo (1754-1817), a Portuguese politician and scientist, who died just before taking up the post of prime minister (Translator).
[379] Coelho Gomes, *Elementos de História Nacional*, p. 38.

abandon Brazil on the first ship, leaving behind his furniture, kitchen utensils, chinaware, books and the carriage and harness mentioned in the *Gazeta* advertisement. Who ended up with his almost regal carriage? Perhaps some *nouveau-riche.* Some Pinto da Fonseca made rich by the slave trade.[380]

Unfortunately – it bears repeating – advertisements in Brazilian newspapers during the first two or three decades of the press in Brazil seem to stop short of describing the furniture, utensils and objects found inside houses: whether out of excessive bashfulness or for some other reason, we do not know. In subsequent decades such furniture and utensils were minutely described in auction advertisements, affording us interesting glimpses of private life.

The advertisement in the *Diário de Pernambuco* of 30 April 1828 for an auction by Mr J. H. Otten, the proprietor of the English Hostel in Forte do Mato, is reticent. But it is far less so than the one about Sir James Gambier's house, and therefore more precious for my purpose, more than a century later, of trying to determine not only the extent but the nature of English influence on domestic lifestyles in Brazil. Because, from the beginning of the nineteenth century almost until today, English auctions were a major factor in the Europeanization or, rather re-Europeanization of Brazilian life, which the eighteenth century had kept so far removed from Europe. It became *chic* to attend such auctions, where Brazilians could effortlessly absorb the most modern European taste – the taste of middle-class, Nordic Europe, the Europe of machines and the Industrial Revolution. That Revolution with a truly capital 'R' had left Portugal, Spain and even Italy somewhat on the margins of carboniferous civilization,

[380] In 1844 'the famous *slaver* Manoel Pinto da Fonseca', as the historian Noronha Santos calls him, purchased 'land and a house with large orchards at Largo da Prainha, on the corner of Ladeira João Homem' valued at 16:000$000, which had belonged to Colonel Felippe Nery de Carvalho, a former member of the city council and a wealthy land and slave owner who, in 1842, when alighting from a carriage, was stabbed to death by a slave of his (Noronha Santos, *Meios de Transporte no Rio de Janeiro*, Rio de Janeiro, 1934, I, 92). Pinto da Fonseca appears to have moved house, or rather moved district, in his old age, to one of those parts of Rio de Janeiro made elegant by the English and to which one came and went in an English carriage.
When he moved to the mansion he had bought from the murdered councillor's widow, he would have therefore taken with him not just his scandalous notoriety as a *nouveau-riche* but also his taint as a slaver: 'the famous *slaver* Manoel Pinto da Fonseca'. Clearly, trading in slaves no longer afforded the slave trader, or slaver, the same social prestige as owning a large number of slaves, even though owning slaves could sometimes entail a risk or physical danger that might cost the owner his life, as it had Nery de Carvalho.
Neither trading in slaves nor selling cod gave a merchant that prestige. The satirical poets of the time began to smell the unmistakable stench of dried cod in the champagne drunk at the tables of men who had become rich by selling that fish. The odour of Africans cannot have been any less noticeable in the champagne drunk by slavers like Pinto da Fonseca.

tied up with minor, merely political revolutions of 'Liberals', 'Miguelists', 'Carlists', 'Republicans' and anticlericals. Copycats of another Revolution with a capital 'R' – the French Revolution – which the English one had exceeded in economic terms but could not equal in dramatic effect.

Those who went to Mr Otten's auction on Monday, 5 May 1828 at ten o'clock in the morning would have found not only old sofas and chests of drawers 'of all sizes', chests of drawers that were 'excellent quality and in very good taste' – which, however, were nothing new to those Brazilians with a more aristocratically patriarchal upbringing, who were used to large items of jacaranda furniture – but also canapés, tables and chairs in new styles, mirrors of various sizes and 'a Piano forte that has a very good sound'.

The English piano was certainly one of the most important items through which British imperialism affirmed its technical or industrial superiority in the eyes and ears of Brazilians who had only just escaped from a period of almost Chinese isolation. As for pieces of music, Brazilians could have them sent from other countries – Germany and Italy, for example – or even, as befitted lords who were still semi-feudal, commission them from 'composers of music' who had also come to settle in Brazil after the ports were opened, such as the Italian Pedro de Tardi in Salvador, who styled himself in an advertisement in the *Idade d'Ouro do Brazil* on 21 April 1818 as 'Master of the Royal Theatre of HM the King of Sardinia' and began not only to give 'Vocal Music lessons' but to compose and sell music of all kinds, as commissioned by the public. But in terms of pianos, there were none better than those made by British craftsmen, and they filled the drawing-rooms or music-rooms of many a town house and plantation mansion in the Brazilian Empire. 'Beautiful pianos by the eminent manufacturer W. Studart', such as those advertised by Charles ('Carlos') Crockatt in the *Jornal do Commercio* on 13 December 1827, together with 'violin strings', 'flutes made of [illegible] and ebony' with 'one to nine keys', and 'an elegant, well-ornamented organ, suitable for any church...'. And 'English jacaranda and mahogany horizontal pianos', like those being sold at Rua da Cruz, No 8, in Recife in 1841.[381] There were also English pianos to rent. An advertisement in the *Diário de Pernambuco* on 29 January 1842 tells us of a house in the Rua das Hortas, in the city of Recife, where they were hiring out not only 'a captive wet-nurse, without child... and good milk' but also 'an English piano'. Advertisements for auctions selling lots of English pianos can also be found, such as the one that appears in the *Diário de Pernambuco* on 25 May 1841. At their warehouse at Rua da Cruz, No 26, Gaskell, Johnson & Co. were auctioning no less than 'six pianos made of beautiful mahogany wood by the best

[381] *Diário de Pernambuco*, 14 July 1841.

English manufacturers'. Stodart pianos. Broadwood pianos. Clementi pianos. Pianos in abundance, in the face of which the old guitars that used to accompany lyrical songs gradually disappeared from drawing-rooms.

On 9 October 1827, in the Rio de Janeiro *Jornal do Commercio*, the English auctioneer 'Carlos' Cannell announced an auction 'in his house at Rua de Tras do Hospicio, No 11' on 'Thursday, 11th inst. at half past ten', of 'a rich and elegant set of new household furniture'. But these goods were made of jacaranda: Brazilian furniture that the English came to love with a particular passion. Jacaranda inlaid with brass. With seats 'of superior split cane'. And, apparently, in the natural colour of the wood, not painted in the Brazilian colonial taste that Luccock had observed, which seems to have changed under English influence.

Luccock thought the furniture in the Brazilian houses he visited in 1808 was 'poor and scanty'. He just accepts that the beds were almost always 'well-made, but far from modern'.[382] The alcoves he saw in Rio de Janeiro were not furnished with chests of drawers, which he says were rare articles, but with 'trunks and boxes made of hide, and baskets of various descriptions'.[383] Clearly an exaggeration by the Englishman. Or imperfect knowledge of Brazil. But the fact is that in Brazil at that time there were many houses in need not only of modernizing their furnishings in accordance with English or European tastes in furniture but also of becoming Europeanized or re-Europeanized in their styles, freeing themselves from the excessive use of mats – the mats on which ladies rested in oriental style during the day, thus not feeling the need for European sofas or canapés for the pleasures of the *siesta* or mere idleness.

An advertisement in the *Jornal do Commercio* on 11 October 1827 provides details on some furniture for sale, together with books, as there had been at Lord Strangford's auction:

> 2 sofas, 2 sofa tables, 2 card ditto, 2 side ditto, 1 forte piano, 1 large writing-desk, 1 wardrobe; and a large assortment of books of classical works (listed in a catalogue that may be viewed) [which the *Jornal* unfortunately does not publish].

On the 9th, Mr Cannell had held an auction in the Largo do Moura of 'a large quantity of defective iron pans brought from London on the Brigantine *Genii...*' And back in 1809, on 18 January, James 'Diogo' Gill had announced in the *Gazeta do Rio de Janeiro* that he had 'English chairs' for sale. English furniture brought from England.

382 Quoted in English (Translator).

383 Luccock, *Notes on Rio de Janeiro*, p. 120.

It should be noted that historians who specialize in studying the origins and development of furniture styles in Brazil consider the final years of the eighteenth century and the first decade of the nineteenth to be marked by the appearance here of the English Adam[384] style: an already rather Portuguese Adam style. One such scholar of the subject writes as follows about the Adam style in Brazil:

> It is characterized by very sober, dry lines, reminiscent of its English origins.[385]

The dryness to which Mr Ribeiro de Lessa refers contrasted with the somewhat sensuous, rounded lines of the baroque dominant in Portugal and Brazil, which even in sacristies, churches and convents left the legs of tables resembling those of plump oriental girls or women. But the specialist points out the characteristics of the English style introduced or acclimatized in Portuguese America:

> Forms with strictly utilitarian, yet delicate meanings. Surfaces stripped of ornament. Tables, beds, chests of drawers and wardrobes with prismatic, truncated pyramid-shaped legs and feet. Those of chairs, armchairs and sofas are also prismatic, sometimes straight, sometimes with an externally concave curvature towards the end. Chair backs and headboards of beds are simple and open, composed of two vertical prismatic columns and a variable number of cross-pieces perpendicular to them, likewise prismatic but slightly curved to make the back more comfortable. The arms of armchairs are rectangular in section, ending in incomplete scrolls.[386]

These lines in furniture, dry in the English manner, which appeared in Brazil during the regency of Dom João gradually evolved here 'over time and at the whim of furniture makers', as Mr Ribeiro de Lessa says. Thus 'Brazilian master craftsmen started working semi-cylindrical mouldings along the edges of furniture and little pyramidal squares in the corners'.[387] A piece of England evolving in Brazil. The English style of furniture rounding itself out in the Brazilian climate. Several of the 'English pieces of furniture' that appear in Brazilian newspaper advertisements in the

[384] A style (which Freyre calls the '*estilo Adams*') developed in London by the Scottish Adam brothers (Translator).

[385] Clado Ribeiro de Lessa, 'Mobiliário brasileiro dos tempos coloniais', *Estudos Brasileiros*, Rio de Janeiro, 1939, No 6, p. 14.

[386] *Ibid.*, p. 14.

[387] *Ibid.*, p. 15.

first half of the nineteenth century may actually have been made here and were English only in style. And even that had been modified 'at the whim of furniture makers', who in those days were almost all mulattos or Frenchmen, enemies of dry, straight lines and lovers of femininely graceful or baroque curves.

This Mr Cannell – who, we are led to believe, was, together with Mr J. J. Dodsworth, an auctioneer not only for the English colony but also for the most refined members of Rio de Janeiro society in the early years of the Empire – placed an advertisement in the *Jornal do Commercio* on 29 November 1827 in which, alongside 'household wares in the latest taste', which consisted of jacaranda furniture inlaid with brass, we find 'pictures including paintings of the King, Dom Pedro, Dom José and Dona Maria I, two table clocks, chandeliers with glass sleeves, bottle carriers for travelling', and also 'china services for tea, ditto for dinner'. Mr Dodsworth has an advertisement in the *Jornal do Commercio* of 15 October 1827 for an auction of 'a quantity of china' – probably English – 'for sale in small lots, for family use', and another on 17 October that year for 'oil paintings' and 'a collection of classics and superior books'. Unfortunately the classics are not listed, nor do we know the titles and authors of the 'superior books'.

Since 1818 a shop in the Rua do Caldeireiro in Salvador had been selling 'pictures in gilt frames' for the interiors of Bahian houses, as well as fully gilt tea services, pairs of teacups, also gilt, and a large, fully gilt dinner service.[388] It was as if, through this somewhat extravagant excess of gilding, these European articles were seeking to surpass the old oriental porcelain in richness of colour. Since in a future work I intend to deal with the clash that occurred in Brazil during the early years of the nineteenth century between European and oriental values of architecture and dress, tableware and transport, recreation and food, in this study I shall merely remark that English crystal and glassware, English and sometimes French porcelain tea and dinner services, and English kitchen utensils did not make Brazilians suddenly stop importing porcelain from the Orient or using earthenware pots and vessels – an oriental survival. Gradually oriental porcelain became rarer and English porcelain began, almost alone, to dominate merchants' advertisements and auction announcements. Eventually, as Brazil approached the middle of the century, auctions began to be held in which not only the glass, pianos, china and silverware were all English, but even the animals – bulldogs, cattle and horses – were as well.

On 21 April 1838, Charles ('Carlos') Saunders announces in the *Diário de Pernambuco* that he will hold an auction

[388] *Idade d'Ouro do Brazil*, 3 July 1818.

> on Thursday, 26th inst., in the country house where he lives in Mondego, of all his furniture, Piano, glass, porcelain, some silver items, a large four-wheeled carriage, a trap, a cart, an English cow, and a few more objects...

As we can see, many of the goods were English, even the cow. When the English who had lived in Brazil for a few years returned home, they left pieces of England behind. Even milch cows. Like the one in Charles Saunders's auction, and also like the one in Captain Killey's auction in Recife, organized by Oliveira the broker: 'a beautiful, very young cow of the best English breed (Devonshire), a good milker and suitable for improving the stock in this country', according to an advertisement in the *Diário de Pernambuco* on 12 November 1844.

The English were also responsible for spreading wallpaper for drawing-rooms around Brazilian cities, such as the wallpaper for sale at an auction held by Burle the auctioneer in Rio de Janeiro on 5 January 1830. The advertisement was published in the *Jornal do Commercio* on the 4th: wallpaper, china, crystal, books, pictures, mirrors – all English. It was with these pieces of England scattered around Brazil by auctions that the interior of many a Brazilian house was redecorated or refurbished in a mixture of traditional and new styles, until Brazil – the *grand-bourgeois* or aristocratic side of Brazil, that is, because the other, *petit-bourgeois* and proletarian side withstood the innovations much longer or was less affected by them – reached the middle of the nineteenth century with hardly any remnants left from the long period that it had spent as a more Moorish than European society in its most intimate customs, and more Eastern than Western in its domestic environment and many of its rituals of private life, and even in various of its methods of transport and work, in its principal means of recreation, and in a number of its foodstuffs and condiments to stimulate the palate: rice, pepper and cinnamon.

In the *Diário de Pernambuco* of 5 September 1837, a certain Mr Daniels announced an auction, to be held at ten o'clock in the morning at Rua da Cruz D. 51, of mostly English goods:

> Gilded and painted Porcelain Vases, tea and coffee services, washbasins, carafes, &c. &c., all in the best possible taste. [Also] 4 magnificent table clocks that keep very good time, which objects must be sold without fail, since their owner has to travel, and they will be sold for cash...

Brazil in the first half of the nineteenth century was filled not just with pianos but with English table or grandfather clocks. Not just with porcelain tableware, but with English washbasins.

There was more: even snuff then came here from England to the more aristocratic shops that were not content with the Bahian variety or were tired of the kind 'used in Asia'. In the *Jornal do Commercio* of 8 November 1827 is an advertisement for an auction by Charles Cannell that same day, in which he would sell

> a large assortment of woollen, linen, cotton and silk fabrics... [and] a large assortment of snuff. *Lafayette Snuff, Macobay Snuff, French coarse rapée.*[389]

In this area of trade too, the English article competed in Brazil with a product that, although not oriental, was recommended to the most fastidious of Brazilians as being the favourite snuff in Asia, for the reason stressed in newspaper advertisements at the time – in the *Gazeta do Rio de Janeiro* on 27 October 1813, for example:

> due to the excellence of its being the only variety that keeps in a hot, damp climate, without the slightest corruption, but rather it gets better the older it is...

On 18 May 1846 another typical advertisement appeared in the *Diário de Pernambuco* for English furniture and household items: the furniture and utensils of Charles Roope, who had to return with his family to England and was holding an auction

> of all the furniture in his house, consisting of consoles, sofas, chairs, card-tables, settees, round and long drawing-room tables, dining ditto and other small ones, English iron and wooden beds, wardrobes, secretaire and shelves, all in the best taste, a machine for pressing clothes, chinaware, glass, lamps, kitchen utensils and many other useful and necessary objects... as well as superior bottled wines and some silver items...

What wines might have been in this refined Englishman's cellar in the 'Rua da Seve, behind Aurora' in what seems to have been a Portuguese-style town house? French ones, perhaps: in 1809, James ('Diogo') Gill, the Englishman, was importing into Rio de Janeiro olive oil from Florence

[389] The names were quoted by Freyre in English (Translator).

and wines from Bordeaux for the English and the more refined Brazilians in the capital. And 'pots of magnesia', perhaps for the gluttons among them.[390]

On 29 January 1838 the *Diário de Pernambuco* announced the sale of the country house at Poço da Panela belonging to an Englishman, Mr Thomas Stewart, which perhaps had no cellar or bottled wine, but which must have been a delightful spot with its grapevines, orange trees and rose bushes.

> A very well-ordered country property, hedged throughout with lemon; a good house, stabling for 6 horses, coach house, walled paddock, large grass meadow, many orange and other fruit trees, highest-quality grapevines, a well of excellent water, a cow, a horse, a cart, two barrows, two stone troughs, various Garden utensils [and] all or part of the household furniture. [...] If not sold by private contract by 15 February, it will be sold on that day by public auction.

Mr Stewart's house must have been one of those fine houses belonging to Englishmen in Poço da Panela where afternoon tea was taken as religiously as in England: a habit that quickly spread to the Brazilian families living there, one of them being that of José Antônio Gonsalves de Mello, who, although a fan of comedies and theatre, lived in Poço da Panela almost all his life, unlike his relative Félix Cavalcanti de Albuquerque Mello, who was born on a plantation but spent all his adult life in Recife and Olinda, forever moving house as if none of them could satisfy his yearning for the big house in Jundiá where he had played as a child. Except that Brazilian tea was taken in the evening: tea or supper.

The frequency with which English or even French china 'tea services' appear in Brazilian newspaper advertisements in the first half of the nineteenth century attests to the speed with which the English habit of 'Indian tea' spread throughout the more refined or more policed – policed in the sense of where the *Ordenações*[391] were enforced – area of Brazil, which at the time was the part dominated by the sugar-producing complex. Tea became part of this complex. Auctions that let us see the interior of an elegant or merely decent Brazilian house in that area at that time rarely fail to show us that beside the card-table stands the tea-table with its porcelain tea srvice, sometimes fully gilt in truly *nouveau-riche* style. Koster, in fact, noted that in Recife in the early years of the century tea had quickly gone from being a remedy sold in apothecaries' shops under the name of '*chá*

[390] *Gazeta do Rio de Janeiro*, 18 January 1809.
[391] The codes of law inherited from Portugal.

*da Índia*' to being drunk in 'great quantities' by Brazilians, and not just by English residents.[392] That this habit in Brazil has English origins – despite the contacts between Portuguese America and the Orient – is shown by the fact that tea moved from apothecaries' shelves, where only the sick bought it, to appear as an elegant daily beverage in shops that sold both 'glass and tea'. In Rio de Janeiro in 1815, anyone who wanted to buy the finest-quality teas – *Aljofar*, *Pérola*, *Lisson*, *Uxim* and *Sequim* imported from China – was invited to go to the glass and window-pane shop opposite Rua da Candelária, No 18.[393]

Advertisements for auctions held not only by Englishmen but by other Europeans living in Brazil, and those placed by English auctioneers in Rio de Janeiro, Pernambuco and Bahia who dealt in British merchandise or objects belonging to Britons or Briticized Brazilians – advertisements published in the newspapers of the first half of the nineteenth century – reveal to us that such auctions were powerful forces in spreading new tastes, not only in styles of furniture and English styles of cutlery and chinaware – the English china that gradually took over from oriental porcelain in Brazilian sideboards and dressers – but also in reading matter: classics like Milton, novelists like 'the trusted Walter Scott', English essayists like Adam Smith, *Robinson Crusoe* and *Gulliver's Travels*.[394] And new techniques for cooking, pressing clothes and domestic hygiene, as well as new modes of work and transport, were propagated in Brazil by English auctions. In that they were more effective than mere warehouses, where machines and mechanical innovations sat lifeless. At auctions they were presented with all their living features, used and tested.

Auctions were practical lessons in Europeanization, which to a great extent meant Anglicization. Thus, when Mr Bieber – who, although not English, lived surrounded by English objects, like any refined European

[392] In *Travels in Brazil*, Koster writes: 'When the Englishmen, who first established themselves at Recife, had finished the stock of tea which they had brought with them, they enquired where more could be purchased, and were directed to an apothecary's shop. They went, and asked simply for tea, when the man wished to know what kind of tea they meant; he at last understood them, and said, "O, you want East Indian tea," "*Cha da India*," – thus considering it as he would any other drug. But at the time of which I am now speaking, great quantities are consumed' (p. 29, footnote). Koster adds that his guide who introduced him to Pernambuco 'was among the first British subjects, who availed themselves of the free communication between England and Brazil, and he even already observed a considerable change of manners in the higher class of people. The decrease in the price of all articles of dress; the facility of obtaining at a low rate, earthenware, cutlery, and table linen; in fact, the very spur given to the mind by this appearance of a new people among them; the hope of a better state of things, that their country was about to become of more importance; renewed in many persons, ideas which had long lain dormant; made them wish to show, that they had money to expend, and that they knew how it should be expended' (pp. 28-29).

[393] *Gazeta do Rio de Janeiro*, 9 August 1815.

[394] *Diário de Pernambuco*, 11 January 1836.

of his time – returned to Europe in 1850, he left wide open to the elegant people of Recife a house in which the innovations of English technology were gathered together as if in an exhibition. Including the 'clothes pressing machine', which, incidentally, had appeared in earlier advertisements, such as the one for Mr Roope's auction; and later we shall see that such machines had been for sale in warehouses of imported English goods in Rio de Janeiro since 1818. Apart from the clothes press, there were various modern examples of iron beds, lanterns, oil lamps, bathroom, washbasin, kitchen utensils, cutlery,[395] carpets, mirrors, card-tables, not to mention 'an excellent piano'. The inevitable English grand piano that so many now elderly Brazilians remember having seen in their grandparents' or great-grandparents' drawing-rooms, which it dominated with its British solidity – its almost brutal solidity – while it let itself be dominated in turn by the little, ring-adorned fingers of the pale daughters of the house, those delicate little girls of Imperial times.

Other highly characteristic advertisements are those for auctions of hulls, masts and cordage from British ships wrecked in Brazilian waters, like the one placed in the *Diário de Pernambuco* on 23 April 1846 by Oliveira the broker, by order of Dewsley & Raymond. Hull, masts, cordage and whatever else might be salvaged from the English galley *Wilmot*,

[395] Another important aspect of the early commercial relations between Great Britain and Brazil after 1808 was that one of the most important goods imported into Brazil from England – alongside iron, glass and domestic china – was cutlery, i.e. knives and forks, scissors, razors: items of cutlery that appear with some frequency among domestic wares in the first detailed advertisements for middle-class auctions. That perhaps accounts for the horror shown by several of the first English merchants to settle in Brazil after the opening of the ports, like Luccock, or to pass through, like Mathison, at the survival of the oriental habit whereby not only the slaves but the masters too would eat with their fingers, often from a communal dish or bowl or even a simple gourd or calabash, a habit that they even encountered among the less-refined Brazilian middle-classes in Rio de Janeiro, and not just among country people. Clearly, it would be in the interests of the English if that ancient oriental habit – which had formerly been European as well – could be replaced in Brazil with the widespread use of individual knives and forks. That would enable cutlery produced in Sheffield – 'the chief centre of the industry for the whole world' [quoted in English – Translator] to spread as widely as possible among the Brazilians. British cutlery soon won at least part of this almost virgin market, which started importing from England not only knives and forks for middle-class tables but kitchen knives, razors – associated with the adoption by more elegant Brazilians of the British habit for gentlemen to shave every day – scissors, surgeons' or doctors' lancets, surgical instruments, garden shears, butchers' knives, etc. Iron and steel items with handles made of silver, German silver, brass, horn, tortoiseshell, ivory or wood. Items to go with the iron and tinplate vessels replacing the rustic gourds and calabashes that until then had been used in vast numbers in Brazilian houses.
The widespread use of individual knives and forks among the Brazilian middle-classes, under the pressure of commercial advertising for those products or, alternatively, under the impact of English fashion on Brazilian habits, represents another victory for the West over the East in the struggle between the two, for which Brazil, with its lattices and mats, silks and palanquins, Chinese fireworks and litters, suddenly became the battlefield. An aspect of the contact between Brazilians and Europeans in the first half of the nineteenth century that we shall attempt to study in another work.

> where and as found, entirely grounded outside this bar, opposite the island of Nogueira; and furthermore some chains, sails, etc., salvaged from said galley and already on land.

That auction was to be held in the Praça do Corpo Santo in Recife, next to the Commercial Association, 'with the presence of HBM Consul' and perhaps the ship's commander, who may well have been upset at the sight.

Another auction of a grounded English ship was advertised in the *Diário* on 9 June 1846 by Deane Youle & Company: copper-bottomed hull, lower masts, bowsprit, cargo of coal and whatever else might be salvaged from the English brig *Elza* 'grounded in the area of shallows off Janga district'. In this case, however, it was to be sold

> all in a single lot, the purchaser being subject to the success or otherwise of the salvage of the objects mentioned. [To be sold in separate lots:] the sails, in excellent condition, cordage, dinghy and boat, topmasts, yards, anchors and iron anchor chains and various other belongings salvaged from said brig.

That auction lasted for two days and must have livened up the old city, the capital of what was perhaps the most Anglophile province at that time. Not only because of the already considerable number of skilled mechanics who lived there – for whom England in the first half of the century was like a toyshop for little boys – but also because of the importance of the cane planters and sugar manufacturers and wholesalers to the economy and society of the region. Those sugar barons were much sought after, both by agents for the British market, who wanted them to export their output to Europe, and also by engineers, technicians and representatives of British machine and tool factories, who wanted those Brazilian plantation and sugar-mill owners to purchase British innovations suited to that still prosperous regional industry. It was prosperous in Pernambuco and prosperous in Campos.[396] By 1818 there were advertisements such as the one for the still built by Sheares & Son of London that had 'recently arrived from London', according the *Gazeta do Rio de Janeiro* of 24 January that year, which added:

> It is already known in Brazil, where several of the same invention may be found that have proved to be of great profit and utility to

[396] Sugar-producing region in the north-east of Rio de Janeiro state (Translator).

Sugar Mill Owners, on account of their good features...

On 28 January 1818 the *Gazeta* announced another tempting novelty from London – tempting to the country's 'mechanics': a large quantity of woodworking tools 'which have been received from London in the latest taste and very modern'. On 31 January, Seaton Plower & Co., established at Rua Direita, No 14, advertised in the *Gazeta* that they had for sale 'a complete assortment of various Surgical Instruments' – an attractive novelty to the Brazilian surgeons of the time. Also in 1818, Charles ('Carlos') Durand, established at Rua Direita, No 9, had ordered from Europe,

> at the suggestion of several engineering officers of this city, 24 complete mathematical sets with the calibre of gun barrels according to the Ordinance of Brazil.[397]

L. Westin & Co. made it known to the public that at its distillery they were receiving spirit for rectification at the 'reasonable price of 5:000 per pipe'.[398] Jackson and Richardson announced that they had received from London

> riding saddles for all tastes as well as sugical instruments from the same manufacturer who supplied the Royal Hospital at Greenwich.[399]

Several of these novelties first sold by the importers were later resold at auctions held by Englishmen and Anglophiles, at which English ironware, clothes presses, riding saddles and carriages started to become common. In 1821, at the Viscount of Vila Nova da Rainha's auction in his 'noble house in Botafogo', among 'remnant furniture, slave planters and good planters of vegetable and flower gardens' – the viscount was Portuguese and was returning to Portugal accompanying the king – there was 'an *English* carriage' (the italics are from the advertisement in the *Gazeta do Rio de Janeiro* of 2 June that year) 'in very good use'. Later we shall come across other English carriages, but these will be new or 'just received from England'.

On leaving Pernambuco shortly after Mr Bieber, Mr D. W. Baynon also auctioned off his furniture and even items for his wife's use: pictures,

[397] *Gazeta do Rio de Janeiro*, 25 March 1818.

[398] *Gazeta do Rio de Janeiro*, 24 September 1818.

[399] *Gazeta do Rio de Janeiro*, 2 December 1818.

china, glass, a gold watch and diamond earrings. And a riding saddle, a side-saddle, card-tables and kitchen items. Many of these objects were English-made, and it should be noted that English riding saddles were highly prized in Brazil at the time, since not only animal-drawn forms of transport – carriages and carts – but also the actual techniques of riding and looking after horses in Brazil had been revolutionized by the English: a subject that I plan to develop in another essay. Among the kitchen items being auctioned by Mr Baynon – who seems to have preferred riding a horse to travelling in a gig – were iron pots and pans, which, mainly due to English influence, were replacing earthenware vessels in patriarchal kitchens in Brazil. Even so, earthenware vessels stubbornly resisted the invasion of iron.

Also in 1850 there is a long advertisement in the *Diário de Pernambuco* for an auction by Oliveira the broker, in which, alongside Afro-Brazilian products such as 'a young slave who works as a stonemason, another who is a cook and sugar refiner, another general worker, an 11-year-old slave girl seamstress and other skilled and unskilled slaves', or Asian-Brazilian items such as 'a sedan chair from Bahia', there were various products from European, especially English, factories: a canapé, a long tea-table, a double bed, washbasins, a table clock with bronze figures, bottles and glasses, and flower vases. Acculturation revealed in newspaper advertisements. The Industrial Revolution amid survivals of Brazilian agrarian feudalism. Clocks recently imported from London next to 'sedan chairs from Bahia'. Tea-tables also imported from London next to slaves imported from Africa. While Brazil mixed, blended and reworked all this in its own way. While Brazil not only Europeanized, Anglicized or Frenchified itself, but also converted many an Englishman who had arrived here full of holy wrath towards slavery to the almost nefariously sinful delights of owning slaves and, like any rich or simply middle-income white man, having himself served and even dressed and carried in palanquins by black men brought over from Africa.

Fletcher met many slave-owning Englishmen in Brazil. And that happened both before and after what is called the Lord Brougham Act (1843), which made it 'unlawful' for a subject of His Britannic Majesty to buy or sell slaves in any country.[400] An Act which Burton, forgetting

[400] Fletcher and Kidder, *Brazil and the Brazilians*, p. 137. In note 18 to the 'Diário do Capelão da Esquadra Imperial comandada por Lord Cochrane, Frei Manoel Moreira da Paixão e Dores' ('Diary of the Chaplain to the Imperial Squadron commanded by Lord Cochrane, Friar Manoel Moreira da Paixão e Dores', published in *Anais da Biblioteca Nacional do Rio de Janeiro*, 1938, vol. LX, p. 230) , it says that, while the English admiral's wife was in Rio in 1823, she, as any Brazilian woman would, resorted to the *For hire* section of a newspaper (*Diário do Rio de Janeiro*, 9 August 1823) to advertise: 'Lady Cochrane needs to hire two slave or freed black women, one who can wash, starch and prepare clothes: and the other to do the housework: apply at Lady Cochrane's house at Praia de Bota Fogo,

that he was a consul, did not hesitate to call 'absurd': 'the late venerable Lord Brougham's absurd Act of 1843'.[401] He justified the fact that English people living in the Brazilian Empire owned slaves by alleging that in Brazil only city dwellers could indulge in the luxury of having servants instead of slaves. Hence the number of English slave owners: necessity knew no law.

The English mining company in Brazil, whose main field of operation was São João del-Rei and whose shareholders were English, itself continued to own about 800 slaves after the 1843 Act, in addition to the 1,000 hired slaves it used in the exhausting work. If such Englishmen colluded in the slave-owning system in Brazil in this way, what moral authority did they have to fight it as if it were the basest form of degradation? Or to criticize Brazilians for not caring for the health or moral education of their slaves, when they themselves, bourgeois British residents of Rio de Janeiro, who had built a cemetery in Gamboa to bury their dead, for a long time neglected their duty towards a large proportion of their living fellows – the many sailors on English brigs who conducted the rich men's trade, helped make the merchants wealthy and constantly risked their lives for the greater glory of British civilization? Those sailors were abandoned in the ports to the depravity of the public houses. The duties of British chaplains – those chaplains that the English forced the Portuguese slave ships to retain – did not extend to the ordinary sailors, but just to the officers and engineers. In the middle of the nineteenth century, Fletcher was shocked at the disregard of British merchants for their own countrymen – the sailors on the many English brigs, schooners and frigates that then filled Brazilian harbours – and he sounded the alarm: 'the sailor is neglected'.[402] And it was not only sailors who were neglected by the well-to-do classes: so at first were the English workers hired to work in the mines and, later, on the railways, as I have pointed out before. Newspaper advertisements rarely mention those unimportant, or apparently unimportant, Englishmen, who had nothing to sell or hire out, save their own hands skilled at dealing with the sea and winds. But given the abandonment in which they lived for a time, it is not surprising that, while bourgeois British advertisements in Brazil sent out ideas of 'comfort' and 'hygiene' and especially the mystique of England's moral superiority, dozens of poor Englishmen abandoned here by their richer compatriots only appeared in the newspapers in reports of disorder, crime and arrests for drunkenness. But since this small study is far from being a lecture or a sermon, let us return to newspaper advertisements.

Advertisements for imported china, like those for furniture and cloth, cutlery and kitchen utensils, as well as auction announcements, are

or at No 79, Rua dos Pescadores, at 10 o'clock in the morning.'

[401] Burton, *Explorations of the Highlands of the Brazil*, p. 272 (quoted in English – Translator).

[402] Fletcher and Kidder, *Brazil and the Brazilians*, p. 202 (quoted in English – Translator).

particularly valuable in allowing us to keep track of English influence on domestic lifestyles in Brazil throughout the first half of the nineteenth century, in respect not only of technological changes but also of dominant colours. Advertisements placed by importers of British goods are in a way complemented by auction announcements, in which the same goods appear, but now domesticated or established through being used by Brazilians or in Brazil. Of all the advertisements by importers or sellers of English or British goods, it is those for chinaware that stand out in Brazilian newspapers in the early years of the nineteenth century as illustrating the new dominant colours in Brazilian life. English china, which was almost always white, or white and gilt, eventually overthrew the multicoloured china full of reds, greens, blues and purples from the Orient. The latter became rare – a bad penny pushed out by a good one? – and English china took its place, with its whites and golds, its greys and dark blues, although oriental porcelain did put up stout resistance against western varieties in Brazilian markets during the first half of the nineteenth century. This struggle between East and West in the Brazilian middle ground during that period of both conflict and accommodation is something that I have already pointed out in this examination of advertisements that are sociologically and culturally significant and not merely picturesque. I shall return to this topic in another essay.

An announcement that appeared in the Rio *Jornal do Commercio* on 10 November 1827 sounds rather romantic or exotic amidst all the advertisements for prosaically white, or white and gilt, or fully gilt chinaware from England:

> For sale at Rua dos Pescadores, No 2: Indian china, recently arrived from Macau on the Brigantine *Novo Dourado*, consisting of tableware of 172 and 174 cups and saucers, side plates and soup tureens, half-bowls for dinner from Nanking and Canton, entirely blue, as well as enamelled; plain white stoneware tea and coffee cups and saucers, at reasonable prices in bulk, in their respective crates... and also sold separately at a difference; in the same warehouse there is a batch of finest-quality blue nankeen, very good fabric, at a price, boxed, of 2200 réis cash.

But both the blue of the china and the yellow of the silks and nankeens from the Orient, like the earthenware pots and the jacaranda painted blue and red, were being ousted by the white, grey, black and dark blue of English taste in china, fabrics and furniture. For the kitchen- and tableware and the furniture in Brazil's houses, this was the beginning of the age that some sociologists today call the palaeotechnical period – as has already been mentioned in this essay – which began under English influence. China was white or, at most, white and gilt; pans were made of iron; furniture was black, brown, dark. Clothing for smarter gentlemen in the cities or even the countryside was likewise dark, brown, grey, navy-blue or dark purple. Their hats and shoes from England: dark. Their cravats: dark. Their carriages: dark. And their handkerchiefs were white, no longer the floral, bright, scandalously coloured ones with which snuff takers openly and jovially wiped their noses, clearing out bad smells and perhaps their sinusitis without compunction. For snuff taking was not a mere indulgence at that time: it was perhaps a prophylactic habit or a matter of personal hygiene, and in that respect it may not yet have been studied with the attention it deserves.

After 1808, it was unusual for an English brig to arrive at a major Brazilian port – Rio de Janeiro, Bahia or Pernambuco – without its bale of English china, glass, cloth, copper, iron and ironmongery, most of which was destined for houses, residences and kitchens. Items in black, grey and white– rarely any brighter colour. The carboniferously industrial West expelling those oriental archaisms – dazzling colours, reds, yellows and light-blues – from the Brazilian market. They had all become plebeian, rustic or outmoded.

Typical of the imported English goods that characterized the beginning of the palaeotechnical era in both domestic and public life in Brazil were the casks, crates and bales not only of glass and ironware but of copper sheets, bricks, steel, cutlery, white lead, pots and pans, tinplate tableware, scythes, scissors and kitchen knives. A variety of articles for domestic use.

From the time of Dom João VI onwards, Brazilian tables, cupboards, kitchens and coach houses started filling with English plates, pots and pans, glasses, jars, teapots and cups – as indicated by some of the auction announcements already mentioned in this essay – together with knives and cutlery also manufactured in England, as well as scissors, saddles and harnesses. Brazil's domestic economy dominated by British iron and steel, and not just by porcelain and glass 'made in England'.[403] In 1828 one of the importers of English goods established in the Rua Direita advertised in the *Jornal do Commercio* of 11 June that he had for sale:

> cutlery sets with ivory knives and forks, fine razors, scissors, pen-knives, spectacles, quadrants, together with 7-valve cornets and flutes of all kinds, beautiful gentlemen's and ladies' patented saddles, bits, trunks, church organs, Broadwood, Stodart and Clementi pianos, as well as stools, glasses, separate strings for them, clocks of

[403] Words used by Freyre in English (Translator).

> all sizes, some with drum and triangle with most parts Brazilian – all recently arrived from London.

So the warehouse at Rua Direita, No 25, alone could supply any well-to-do or aristocratic Brazilian of those days with the essentials – in terms of iron, copper, steel, wooden or leather goods – for refurbishing the interior of his house, from the drawing-room or dining-room to the kitchen, coach house or stable and from the chapel to the garden: pianos, tables, chairs, spectacles, binoculars, hammers, pins, needles, barometers, and gardening and farming equipment. And that was not all: in their almost magical factories the English even made copper ovens for the manioc processing sheds of Brazil's patriarchal old mansions, like those advertised in the *Jornal do Commercio* on 18 February 1828:

> 4 copper ovens made in England that have just arrived from there, suitable for roasting manioc meal...

And if the well-to-do or aristocratic Brazilian was forward-looking or loved innovations, he could also purchase patented machines 'for pressing clothes at great speed' for his house from English merchants in Rio de Janeiro or importers of British goods, such as the one advertised in the *Gazeta do Rio de Janeiro* on 28 February 1818 by Andrew Laurie of the Rua de São José, who also had for sale from London 'an engine for sawing all thicknesses and widths at great speed...', excellent for the interior of Brazil.

Other English goods occur in Brazilian newspaper advertisements in the first half of the nineteenth century, apart from fabrics, objects for domestic use, furniture, china and machines. Before we come to advertisements by importers and sellers of English carriages – with which we are already familiar from auction announcements – foodstuffs and books, pictures, pocket watches, and British teachers or teachers of English, let us stop for a moment and look at advertisements for paper and ink, paint, office equipment, soap and wallpaper. Several of these articles of English manufacture that are paraded in front of our eyes in Brazilian newspaper advertisements of the first half of the nineteenth century match those that the Reverend Walsh came across at the customs house in Rio de Janeiro – that building crammed with English goods that he visited more than once, as he tells us in his excellent book of impressions of Brazil in the time of Dom Pedro I. What I have not found in the advertisements gathered from newspapers from Rio de Janeiro, Pernambuco or Bahia is any mention of those English goods that the mischievous Anglican clergyman accuses his less geographically aware countrymen of having sent to Brazil in large quantities soon after the Brazilian ports and markets were opened up to European trade: blankets for polar nights and ice-skates.[404] Baize, certainly, and there is plenty of it in the early advertisements by Englishmen in Rio newspapers. But Brazilian cold can put up with baize: importing it was not as scandalous as importing ice-skates. It should be noted, as has already been mentioned, that the excessive amounts of baize and flannel imported into Brazil by English merchants in the early days seem to have given rise to the nickname '*baetas*' ('baizes') given to Englishmen by the Brazilians of the time. But we must not depart yet again from the advertisements, which have already been badly betrayed by other topics during this essay.

In an advertisement in the *Gazeta do Rio de Janeiro* on 29 August 1810, William ('Guilherme') March & Co., established at Rua da Alfândega, No 3, say they have paint for sale: 'ready-made paints in the following colours: black, yellow, white, red and purple'. And in 1809 Nathaniel Lucas advertised in the *Gazeta* of 14 June that year that at Rua do Ouvidor, No 46 – Lucas was one of the Englishmen established in the Rua do Ouvidor – he was selling

> a batch of linseed oil, ready-made yellow, red, black and white paints, patent varnish as used by the English Navy in black and yellow; also eight different carriages, and superior olive oil.

It was as if English paint manufacturers were hurrying to address Lindley's remark: that the timbers in Brazilian houses – in Bahia, at least – were deteriorating through not being painted regularly. Hence the advertisements for English paints that appear to show that the English not only dominated this area of trade in Brazil in the years following the opening of the ports, but had succeeded in impressing on Brazilians that it was necessary or useful to keep painting their houses, verandas, doors and windows. Everything – except their jacaranda furniture.

Paint for walls, timber and iron was not the only form of pigment that the English started importing into Brazil in large quantities at the time of Dom João VI. There was also writing ink. In an advertisement in the *Jornal do Commercio* on 31 March 1830, Mr Charles Hunt announces he has ink for sale at his warehouse at Rua da Alfândega, No 126: 'Real Japan Ink,[405] both retail and in casks of thirty dozen'. And other advertisements for ink suggest the English dominated this trade too: this and the trade in paper: '*Bath* heavyweight letter paper and many other kinds', as advertised

[404] Walsh, *Notices of Brazil*, I, p. 245 (Translator).

[405] Words quoted by Freyre in English (Translator).

in the *Gazeta do Rio de Janeiro* on 27 January 1821. And actual parchment for certificates and diplomas. At the time of Dom Pedro I, 'good-quality English parchment skins for diplomas or letters' were for sale in Rio de Janeiro, according to an advertisement in the *Jornal do Commercio* on 20 March 1820. The conclusion being that bachelors' and doctors' diplomas in Brazil at that time were written on English parchment in English ink from Japan.

Newspaper advertisements from the time also bring us English painters and plasterers, or people who used English techniques for papering drawing-rooms. Such as the painter Antonio Giorgi from Rome, who presents himself in an advertisement in the *Gazeta do Rio de Janeiro* on 12 September 1812 as qualified to paint any house and to decorate

> rooms with English paper on the dampest walls without said paper being affected [and also] to paste paper on said walls with a paste formulation that damp will never affect in any weather, be it cold or hot, due to said paste formulation and it will be free from all kinds of insects and termites.

The English thus had a direct influence on the Europeanization of Brazilian house interiors, some of which Maria Graham saw had been painted by Africans. English wallpaper, by the way, spread through middle-class houses in Rio de Janeiro. But not always to the applause of the hygienists of the time; and on this point it was perhaps the Brazilian hygienists who were right, rather than the English.

On 10 June 1847 an advertisement appeared in the *Diário de Pernambuco* by Duggan and Eton:

> painters and plasterers who have recently arrived from London [offering their services] to the public for any plain and ornamental painting, stucco and gesso work, all in the best European taste.

Another style of drawing-room painting and decoration that the English helped to introduce in Brazil.

English portraits and engravings often appear in advertisements, so it is strange that no English portrait painter competed with M. Letanneur, a painter of miniatures, who in the *Idade d'Ouro do Brazil* on 3 July 1818 informed the Gentlemen and Ladies of the City of Salvador da Bahia that he had arrived from Paris and established himself 'in *S. Raymundo* beyond the Praça da Piedade, house No 405'. A 'perfect likeness' would be found in

JOURNAL

OF A

VOYAGE TO BRAZIL,

AND

RESIDENCE THERE,

DURING PART OF THE YEARS 1821, 1822, 1823.

BY MARIA GRAHAM.

ONCE MORE UPON THE WATERS, YET ONCE MORE,
AND THE WAVES BOUND BENEATH ME AS A STEED
THAT KNOWS HIS RIDER.

LONDON:
PRINTED FOR LONGMAN, HURST, REES, ORME, BROWN, AND GREEN,
PATERNOSTER-ROW;
AND J. MURRAY, ALBEMARLE-STREET.
1824.

The frigate *Doris*, on which Maria Graham sailed from England to Brazil in 1821, illustrated on the frontispiece of her book on Brazil. (Collection of Sir Henry Lynch)

Maria Graham.

(Collection of Odilon Ribeiro Coutinho)

The English ship *Briton* in Rio de Janeiro harbour, where she arrived from England on 20 March 1813. The voyage of the *Briton* is narrated in a book, now rare, published in London in 1818: *A Narrative of the Briton's Voyage, to Pitcairn's Island, Including an Interesting Sketch of the Present State of the Brazils and of Spanish South America,* by Lieutenant J. Shillibeer.

(Collection of Sir Henry Lynch)

George March, an English merchant in Brazil during the first half of the nineteenth century.

(Collection of Sir Henry Lynch)

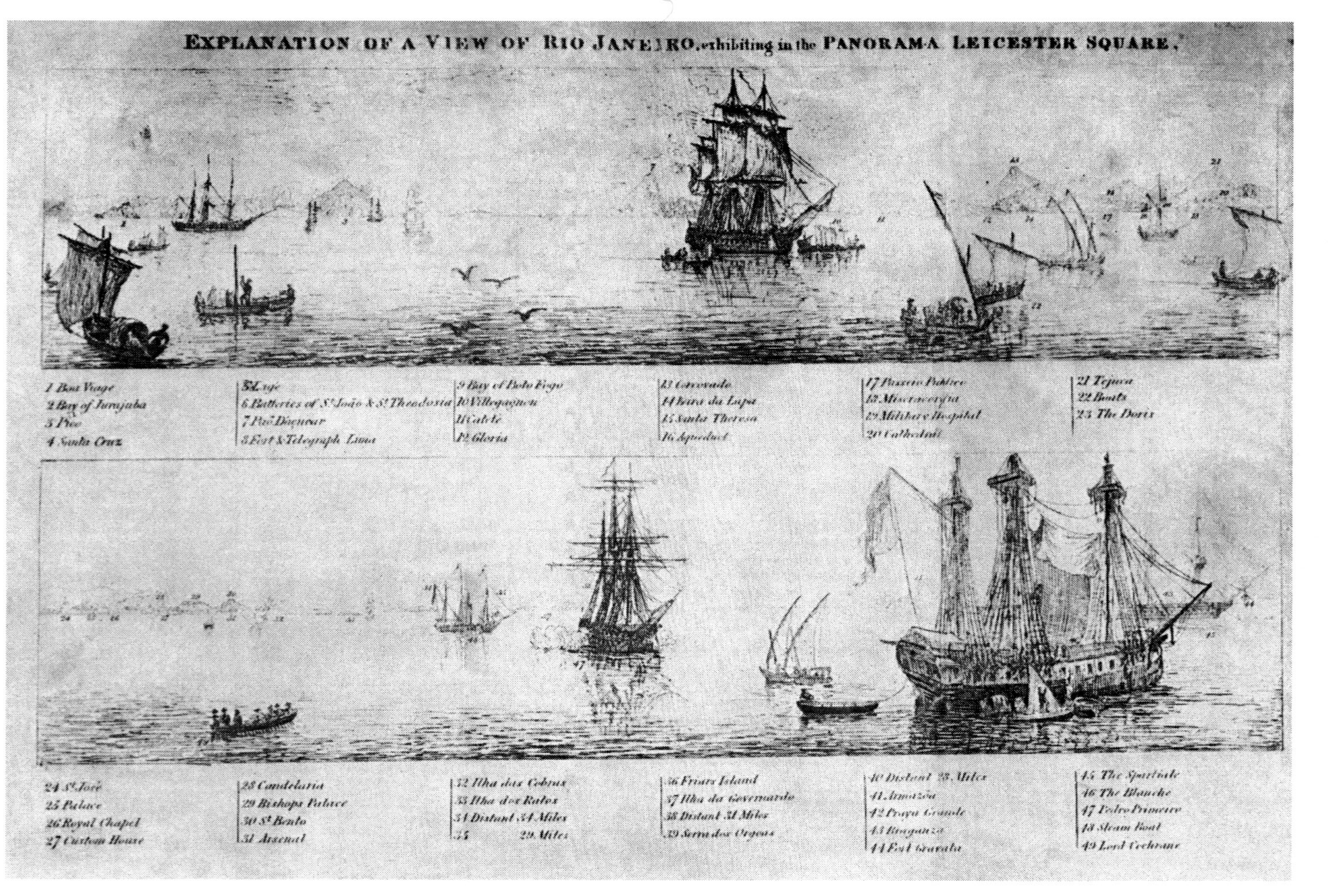


View of Rio de Janeiro, exhibited at the Panorama, Leicester Square, London, in 1828, drawn by Robert Burford, showing the *Doris*, the *Spartiate* and the *Blanche*, English ships than sailing on the Great Britain–South America line. The panorama also shows landmarks in the city, Brazilian ships and Lord Cochrane in a boat.

The *Thames*, a Royal Mail ship from 1841 to 1865. Drawing from the J. Sumpter Mitchell collection, reproduced in *"Royal Mail": A Centenary History of the Royal Mail Line, 1839-1939*, London.

The *Isis*, a Royal Mail ship (1842). Drawing from the J. Sumpter Mitchell collection, reproduced in *"Royal Mail": A Centenary History of the Royal Mail Line, 1839-1939,* London.

The *La Plata*, a Royal Mail ship (1852). Engraving from *The Illustrated London News*, reproduced in *"Royal Mail": A Centenary History of the Royal Mail Line, 1839-1939*, London.

The *Atrato*, the first ship built by the Royal Mail (1853). Engraving from *The Illustrated London News,* reproduced in *"Royal Mail": A Centenary History of the Royal Mail Line, 1839-1939*, London.

Advertisements relating to English activities in Brazil during the nineteenth century.

(Collection of the author)

Further advertisements relating to English activities in Brazil during the nineteenth century.

(Collection of the author)

*Baronesa*, the first locomotive in Brazil, which hauled the first trains to run on the Mauá Railway.

From an advertisement for the Recife–São Francisco Railway, one of the first railways built in Brazil with English capital, published in the newspaper *O Liberal Pernambucano* on 19 November 1858. The illustration records the first types of locomotive and rolling stock used by the English in Brazil

The Royal Mail fleet in Southampton in December 1841. A painting from that time in the Science Museum collection, London, reproduced in *"Royal Mail": A Centenary History of the Royal Mail Line, 1839-1939*, London

The north gate of Recife (from the balcony of Mr Stewart's house).

Drawing by Maria Graham from her *Journal of a Voyage to Brazil.*

The English burial ground (Rio de Janeiro) in a drawing by Maria Graham from her *Journal of a Voyage to Brazil*, London: Longman & Co. and J. Murray, 25 March 1824

The English burial ground, as seen by Alfred Martinet

The English burial ground (on the left, walled) in Gamboa, Rio de Janeiro, in a print by Planitz

The Padre, from the book by J. C. Fletcher and D. P. Kidder, *Brazil and the Brazilians*

Places in Brazil where the English first established themselves after the opening of the ports (1808), with institutions and agencies of economic, political and intellectual penetration. Map by Luís Jardim. **Key**: Consulate; Judge conservator; Commercial and/or industrial establishments; Cemetery; Surgeon or doctor; English language teacher or school; Library; Chapel; Hospital; Governess or housekeeper; Protestant chaplain; Newspaper in English; Consul; Technician.

his portraits. Sometimes the English-made portraits or prints displayed for sale in Brazil look more like British propaganda material than art for art's sake: such were the portraits of the Count of Linhares (Dom Rodrigo de Sousa Coutinho) that, perhaps by mere coincidence, were put up for sale next to those of Wellington and Beresford and a print of the *Embarkation of the French*. The portrait of Dom Rodrigo cost 2:400, Wellington also 2:400, Beresford 2:560 and the *Embarkation of the French* 2:000. That is what we are told in an advertisement in the *Gazeta do Rio de Janeiro* on 11 February 1815.

An advertisement placed in the *Diário de Pernambuco* on 2 January 1845 by a merchant established in the Rua da Cadeia de Santo Antônio, No 19, in Pernambuco, mentions '24 English cartoons'. Unfortunately, there are no further details on these caricatures. Who might they have depicted? Who was the cartoonist? And in 1843 there appeared in Recife a certain Mr Evan who announced to the public in the *Diário de Pernambuco* of 16 May that he took 'admirable and perfect portraits'. He had already taken several to 'general satisfaction'. He was a 'Daguerreotype artist'. He advised gentlemen who wished to 'obtain from him a true copy of themselves or a second image and likeness' to seek him out 'as soon as possible', for he had already stayed in Pernambuco 'for longer than he had intended when he arrived here'. I cannot guarantee that that Mr Evan was English.

In a recent study published in the 9 November 1947 issue of *Letras e Artes* (the literary supplement to *A Manhã*, Rio de Janeiro) under the title 'Os primeiros fotógrafos no Brasil' ('The first photographers in Brazil'), Mr Sílvio da Cunha writes that in 1847 an Irishman, Frederick Walter, disembarked in Ceará with a daguerreotype apparatus and various magical instruments. Incidentally, to account for the presence of an Irish portraitist and magician in such a remote province as Ceará in the first half of the nineteenth century, it should be noted that Ceará appears to have been attracting the attention of the English since the end of the eighteenth century. According to Tomaz Pompeu de Sousa Brasil, in his essay *A cultura do algodão, especialmente no Ceará* ('Cotton cultivation, especially in Ceará' – Fortaleza, n.d., II, p. 165), from 1778 to 1801 British merchants purchased Brazilian cotton, then considered 'excellent', at a good price; and the Brazilian cotton that they most prized seems to have been from Ceará, although it was only in 1809 that the people of Ceará were able to make direct contact with the London trade. In 1810, as Mr Raimundo Girão recalls on page 70 of his *História Econômica do Ceará* ('Economic history of Ceará – Fortaleza, 1947), Hughes, an Englishman, told Governor Barba Alardo de Meneses that the tatajuba wood of Ceará was 'highly esteemed in England by dyers', although this timber, commonly and rather obscenely known as '*pentelho de inglês*', 'Englishman's pubic hair', does not seem to have grown in Ceará.

But while purchasing cotton and tatajuba in Ceará, the English did not neglect to sell the people their china and cloth; nor to portray them in daguerreotypes, for the first men to do so, combining their art with magic, seem to have fascinated the simpler or vainer people in Brazil. Newspaper advertisements show that they attracted a huge clientèle in the northern provinces, which were generally the richest at that time. Including Maranhão.

And there was more. In the early years after Brazil's independence, Ceará was also the destination for

> ship after ship from England laden with copper because of the great profit they made by exchanging 5 or 6 patacas of their copper for our silver coin worth 960.

That is also information from Girão, on page 260 of his above-mentioned economic history of Ceará. Those Englishmen were neither pirates nor smugglers. They were merely shrewd. And as such I do not know if they could be called 'poor' cousins of those against whom the governor of Pernambuco raised the alarm in a circular letter to the magistrates of the districts of Alagoas, Recife, Paraíba and Juiz de Fora de Goiana on 22 November 1799. The alarm was less his than the prince regent's, whose 'royal advice' on the issue was echoed in that letter, today kept among the colonial manuscripts in the manuscript section of the Pernambuco Public Library, where it was patiently and generously copied for this essay by José Antônio Gonsalves de Mello Neto. To that same researcher I owe a copy of another manuscript letter, sent from Recife on 13 September 1815, in which the governor of the captaincy sent the magistrate-general of the district of Alagoas the information he had received from the marshal-inspector-general of the Militias that an Englishman had appeared in the countryside around the town of Anadia, a major centre of slavery (there had recently been a slave revolt in Alagoas), 'parading as a clock maker or repairer in a land where there are very few clocks'.

It was not just the cotton of Ceará that attracted English attention to that part of the country in the first half of the nineteenth century. There was also 'Ceará scrap'.[406] And Mr Raimundo Girão, who furnished this information on p. 380 of his *História econômica do Ceará*, also mentions on p. 375, based on the monograph on the carnauba palm by Marcos de

[406] A form of latex, also known as 'Ceará rubber', produced by the tree *Manihot glaziovii* (Translator).

Macedo (*Notice sur le Palmier Carnauba*, Paris, 1857), that in the early nineteenth century the Count of Galvêas had sent

> to Lord Grandville in England a sample of wax, regarding which, on 9 May 1811, William Thomas Brand read a detailed paper to the Royal Society of London 'to see if this product could be used as a substitute for beeswax and become a branch of commerce between Brazil and England'.[407]

The English extended their trade to any place where they could exchange the products of their industries for Brazilian raw materials, and they turned up even in remote areas in the form of portraitists, magicians and clock makers or repairers. It was in Rio de Janeiro and the capitals of Bahia and Pernambuco, however, where they found the largest number of purchasers for their finer goods and more elegant arts during the first half of the nineteenth century.

An advertisement by the English broker J. J. Dodsworth in the *Jornal do Commercio* on 11 December 1827 talks of

> shaving kits, sewing boxes of all kinds with music and without, writing desks, harnesses for gigs and buggies, chandeliers, pictures with fine prints, double-barrelled shotguns, a gig with its accessories, boxes for liqueurs, men's cambric shirts, leather and satin capes for ladies, fustian trousers and waistcoats, ladies' parasols.

An advertisement in the *Diário de Pernambuco* on 19 May 1838 mentions 'beautiful cases of fine English razors'. English razors dominated the Brazilian market; and the gentleman's habit of shaving every day or nearly every day spread with them among fashionable men.

Although several of the clocks imported from Europe in the first half of the nineteenth century already came from Hamburg – some of them with musical chimes – British-made clocks, and particularly pocket watches, sometimes appear in Brazilian newspaper advertisements in the first half of the nineteenth century. We have already seen some clocks. Pocket watches mainly appear in announcements of objects lost or stolen. One in the *Gazeta do Rio de Janeiro* on 15 April 1809 tells us that on Maundy Thursday, in one of the churches in the city, someone lost

[407] Quoted by Freyre in Portuguese and French, from Girão (*História econômica do Ceará*, p. 375). Girão (followed by Freyre) transcribed the name as 'Lloyd Grandville', whereas Macedo's original has 'Lord Grandville'. Freyre also added the error 'brande de commerce', for 'branche de commerce' (Translator).

> a pocket watch, gold case numbered 5055, made by Vale, an *English* watchmaker, in the City of *Coventry*, with a purple ribbon with two seals attached to it, one of stone and the other of glass, both with letters inscribed, lost on Maundy Thursday evening in Carmo Church.

Another precious English watch was lost in Rio de Janeiro in December 1815: a gold watch 'with the name of the maker on it, namely Rob. Koskell, and the number 21,926', according to an advertisement in the *Gazeta* on 16 December that year. And another had been lost in 1813: 'a patented watch with the name *Litherland Liverpool*', as detailed in an advertisement in the *Gazeta* on 24 July 1813.

In the 'Miscellaneous announcements' section of the *Diário de Pernambuco* on 29 May 1837, there is another advertisement, not for an English watch for sale, but for one that had been stolen, which is a document not only of cultural interest but also of psychological significance. English sentimentality can be glimpsed in this advertisement, alongside British sobriety, stoicism and dignity:

> On 24th inst. there disappeared from the house of Crabee-Heyworth & Co. (presumed stolen) a gold watch with an inscription in the Latin language on the cover thereof stating that said watch was bequeathed by Doctor John Adamson of St Andrews to his wife and also stating the date of death of said Dr, the maker's name is Cha. Summers of London; the person who brings said watch or news thereof to the house of the above-named will be well rewarded; note that it is not so much the intrinsic value of the watch as the fact that it is a family heirloom.

Another watch was stolen in Recife on 12 June 1836, as we are told in an advertisement in the *Diário de Pernambuco* signed by Antônio Leite de Pinho, the owner of the watch. This one was

> an English patented watch; mechanism, cover and case of silver, not light, somewhat large; works well; made by Setherland Davis, with the number 11,706 inside the case; with two keys attached to it by an old ribbon, one for the watch itself, made of yellow metal; the other made of iron for a padlock.

Anyone who had the watch offered to him or had any news of it should go to the house on the right-hand side of the Rua dos Martírios or should advertise, and he would be generously rewarded. In those days, people who owned an English watch in Brazil had a treasure, but it is unknown to what extent a correlation can be made between those Brazilians who owned such a treasure – an English watch – and the cult of so-called 'English time', that is, punctuality, precision and strict fulfilment of obligations or commitments. In short, the cult of the 'Englishman's word', which, incidentally, was made easier to keep by the fact that the English established in Rio de Janeiro after 1808 made use of 'light carriages', contrasting with the calashes and palanquins in which the lords of the land were carried.

English carriages often catch one's eye in newspaper advertisements from colonial times and the early years of the Empire, and it is nearly always their lightness that is emphasised. We have already come across some in auction announcements: used carriages. Now let us admire some of those freshly brought over from England or built here by English craftsmen, still gleaming new, like the one advertised in the *Gazeta do Rio de Janeiro* on 18 January 1809 by James ('Diogo') Gill, who lived at Rua da Candelária, No 7: 'an English carriage and some English chairs, all in the latest fashion'. In the *Gazeta* on 8 February 1809 it is Mr Standfast who announces he has a 'very light' English carriage for sale, though it is almost as golden and colourful as the palanquins still in use at that time:

> Whoever wishes to buy a very light, English, four-wheeled carriage, with yellow body, patented lamps, upholstered in pearl-coloured fabric, with red morocco cushions, and with its respective harnesses: speak to George Thomas Standfast, who lives at Rua Direita, No 35, [and he adds in the same advertisement, without changing tone, that he has] also a few Barrels of Butter and prime-quality cheeses for sale.

The *Gazeta* on 12 May 1810 has an advertisement for 'a smart English trap with its harness for one horse'; on 22 May 'a carriage from London in the latest taste'; on 8 September 'an English carriage in very good condition with harnesses for two and for four'; on 13 June 1811 'a fine, new, English carriage'; and on 6 September 1809 there was an advertisement by Kingstons, Lamberth & Co. for 'a 4-wheeled cushioned Carriage and harness for 4 animals'. On 24 May the same year, the same English merchants had advertised in the *Gazeta* that they had for sale 'in a shed beside the Cathedral at the end of the Rua do *Rosário* where there is an *English* farrier [...] a four-wheeled cushioned carriage; and two two-wheeled English Traps'. The *Jornal do Commercio* of 16 March 1832 advertises an 'English carriage with cushions and a removable seat with harness for 4', an innovation of the time that may have escaped the notice of the eminent specialist in the subject, the historian Noronha Santos. In 1844, according to an advertisement in the *Diário de Pernambuco* of 6 June that year, there was for sale in Recife

> a four-wheeled English carriage, nearly new and made by one of the most famous gig builders in England ... very light and with all the harness needed for one or two horses...

And several mentions of 'carriages with glass windows' in advertisements from the same period have already been highlighted. Carriages with glass windows were an English innovation that contrasted – as has already been pointed out – with carriages that had curtains in the style of oriental palanquins.

Even before Brazil became independent of Portugal, there was a carriage factory in Rio de Janeiro: an English initiative. On 31 March 1821, James ('Diogo') Adamson, an Englishman,

> who has recently arrived in this Capital City... announces to the public [in the *Gazeta*] that in the Largo de São Francisco de Paula, opposite the Church, he has set up a large Factory in which he makes all kinds of carriages, traps and gigs, and also performs repairs of all kinds, all for very reasonable prices, and he has a landau for sale in good condition as well as various carriages that have just arrived.

With Adamson thus established in Rio de Janeiro and with Dyson Brothers and Finnie – and not just James Gill and Kingstons, Lamberth & Co. – selling English carriages to the well-to-do in Brazil since 1809, the rule of the palanquin or sedan chair carried by slaves could be regarded as being over in the capital of the Kingdom of Brazil. Only the most stubborn traditionalists continued to have themselves transported by their black slaves: more trustworthy animals than horses.

In the *Jornal do Commercio* and the *Diário de Pernambuco* during the early years of Empire, a variety of English carriages were offered to persons of taste or those who required speedy transport: little two-wheeled traps for a single horse; large four-wheeled carriages for two horses; luxury carriages; tilburies. 'English Tilbury for sale,' says an advertisement in the *Jornal do*

*Commercio* on 22 January 1830. This democratic form of transport spread readily in Rio de Janeiro.

Within a few years after Brazil's independence, European carriages, especially English ones – for which there were countless newspaper advertisements at the time – had made palanquins and sedan chairs a thing of the past in the streets of the capital of Pernambuco just as much as in Rio de Janeiro. In Bahia the palanquin survived longer, and the European – principally English – carriage won a slower victory over the old oriental mode of transport, which had been acclimatized in Brazil since the earliest days of colonization.

Perhaps in no other area of English technical influence over Brazil in the first half of the nineteenth century did newspaper advertisements show the change in Brazilian habits brought about by contact with British people in as much concrete detail as in this one: draught transport; transport technology; the carriage.

In a recent study, Mr Adolfo Morales de los Rios Filho states that

> the first large workshop of this kind [carriages] to be set up here – in 1833 – was that of João Ludolfo Guilherme Röhe from Altona.[408] Knowing that carriages in Brazil were imported from Europe, he came here with the firm purpose of founding the carriage industry. And he succeeded, for he brought materials, modern machines and new ideas.[409]

Professor Morales de los Rios Filho appears to be unaware that there had been a carriage factory in Rio de Janeiro more than ten years before Röhe's. The advertisement transcribed above for James Adamson's carriage factory – established in Rio back in the days of Dom João VI – shows that when Röhe arrived in the capital of the Empire in 1833 the carriage industry had already been founded in Brazil. Röhe may have improved it; and it is not denied that he achieved 'primacy in the transport industry'. The glory of having founded the industry, however, should apparently go to the Englishman. If confirmed, that will be perfectly natural, given the technical advances in building carriages for the middle classes and even the aristocracy that had been achieved in England, whence so many English types of light carriage had spread throughout the civilized world, their origin marked by their English names: phaeton, tilbury and victoria.

[408] A port and suburb of Hamburg that belonged to Denmark until 1864. According to the *Encyclopaedia Judaica* (2008), Portuguese Jews had settled there in the seventeenth and early eighteenth centuries, some of them involved in the South American trade (Translator).
[409] Morales de los Rios Filho, *O Rio de Janeiro imperial*, p. 262.

It is possible that Adamson's 'factory' was just a small workshop. The fact is, however, that exaggeration was not characteristic of English advertisements in Brazil during the first half of the nineteenth century. As Adamson described his workshop as a Factory with a capital F, it is almost certain that carriages were actually built there.

Incidentally, Professor Morales de los Rios Filho's claim is virtually a repetition of one made by the historian Noronha Santos in his excellent *Meios de transporte no Rio de Janeiro – História e legislação*. There, omitting the English founder of the carriage industry in Brazil entirely, Mr Noronha Santos writes: 'In 1831 came the foundation of the first large carriage workshop, organized by J. L. G. Röhe, whose business achieved primacy in the transport industry.'[410]

An interesting point that Mr Noronha Santos makes in his essay concerns carpenters who had been employed in 'the vehicle industry' in Rio de Janeiro since the end of the eighteenth century. One of them, Antônio José Pereira, a Portuguese, who had qualified as a carpenter of carriages and gigs on 4 March 1797, had come from the mother country 'with a reputation as a repairer of *packet boats* and *coaches*, which were carriages with seats for more passengers than a gig', as the historian explains on page 90 of the first volume of his work.

It seems to be a matter of basic justice, then, to include the Englishman, who has been overlooked or omitted by the two historians, between those carpenters who worked on gigs or coaches and Röhe, the great Danish modernizer of the carriage industry in Brazil (whose praises are sung by Mr Noronha Santos, accompanied by Mr Morales de los Rios Filho). Otherwise, the development of the carriage industry in our country will be without its 'missing link',[411] the necessary intermediary between the carpenters of the slow-moving colonial vehicles, in which only viceroys, bishops, magistrates and rich noblemen could swan around, and the manufacturers of the light carriages that were mainly English inventions or English in style: cars,[412] cabs, dog-carts, tilburies, victorias and phaetons.

That intermediary might not have been an Englishman but just someone who introduced English models and techniques to this speciality: the carriage industry. A modernizer who adorned himself with labels or adjectives in English for the greater prestige of his art or trade, in the manner of that French tailor pompously titling himself as '*fashionable*', in English, who on 18 October 1843 appears with an advertisement in the *Diário de Pernambuco* promising the elegant residents of the old

[410] Santos, *Meios de transporte*, I, p. 191.

[411] Words used by Freyre in English (Translator).

[412] The original has 'caps', presumably a misprint (Translator).

province to do 'everything within his power to obtain the same acclaim in Pernambuco as he was able to attract in Paris'. It happens, however, that in Brazil the intermediary between the colonial art of vehicle carpentry and the new technology of carriages created by the Industrial Revolution was both chronologically and logically an Englishman. We should not forget that. We should not distort the historical sequence in such a case where chronology and logic are fraternally united. It was logical for an Englishman to be the first manufacturer of modern carriages in Brazil, just as an Englishman was the manufacturer of the first locomotive to run in this country, on rails also manufactured in English workshops. And in the case of carriages, logic is matched by history. We should respect the fact that history and logic coincide and restore to long-overlooked Adamson the glory he deserves, as the first manufacturer of modern carriages in Brazil.

Another point to observe is that the advertisements by British merchants in Brazil show that, as well as being importers of grease for carriage wheels and polish for shoes, they became famous for selling oils brought from London for softening all kinds of leather. An advertisement in the *Gazeta* on 5 July 1820 says:

> oil used by all leather workers and tanners in England and very suitable for cleaning gig and calash harnesses and curtains and preventing them from drying out in the sun or with age.

This advertisement is by Jackson and Richardson, established at Rua do Ouvidor, No 31, where they also sold bits, saddles, coach lamps, spyglasses, sets of mathematical instruments, brushes, combs, razors, perfumes, soaps and clothing dyes. They were almost next door to José Belieni, who in the same period used to import picture frames, prints – 'including some by famous artists' – theatre glasses and maps from Europe. We are told that in an advertisement in the *Gazeta* on 11 August 1820. The major importer of 'English shoe polish' at the time seems to have been Cyrus ('Cyro') Bridge, whose advertisement for a 'large assortment of shoes that have just arrived' appears in the *Gazeta* on 16 January 1819.

Large quantities of English foodstuffs – which have already been mentioned in this essay – were also imported into Brazil in the first half of the nineteenth century. Customs records and the manifests of ships arriving from Europe are in many respects complemented, filled out and clarified by Brazilian newspaper advertisements of the time. The advertisements give us a better idea of people's preferences in terms of brands, tastes and flavours; they also lay bare some aspects of the problem of English influence in Brazil that are merely outlined or hinted at in those official documents. And only a newspaper advertisement could tell us that it was an English merchant in the Rua Direita, a certain Mr R. Hamilton, who in 1830 supplied the residents of Rio de Janeiro who had a more refined palate or more demanding taste with not only Imperial and Hysson teas but 'little bottles of Cayenne peppers'. All 'superior quality', says the advertisement in the *Jornal do Commercio* on 20 January 1830.

The English did not dominate the supply of wheat flour, crackers and biscuits to Brazilian colonial markets for very long, as they were soon overtaken by the United States. The English were, however, largely responsible for passing on a taste for bread to Brazilians, who until the end of the eighteenth century had almost exclusively consumed manioc meal.

Although outdone by the Americans in the wheat-flour trade, as well as in tar and other products,[413] the English in Brazil continued to sell some of that flour, which in regions of Brazil more attached to the past is even today called *farinha do Reino*, 'Kingdom flour', a memory of colonial times before the arrival of Dom João VI in Brazil, when wheat flour came here via Portugal. 'Kingdom flour', as well as 'Kingdom cheese' and 'Kingdom pepper'. And we have already seen that Sir Sidney Smith's English squadron sold spoilt flour or biscuit in Brazil on more than one occasion.

Now and again the purser of the English squadron in Rio de Janeiro announced that he was auctioning spoilt wheat or barley flour and biscuit. In the *Gazeta do Rio de Janeiro* on 16 June 1810 there is an advertisement by the purser for an auction to be held

> on Thursday 21 inst. at 10 o'clock in the Customs Warehouses on Ilha das Cobras of 21 barrels with 190 quarters of wheat flour, 4 barrels with 30 bushels of barley flour and 5,077 sacks with as many hundredweight of biscuit, all spoilt; the condition of these provisions may be viewed on the days before the Auction.

A further advertisement by the purser-general of the English squadron for an auction of '210 hundredweight of spoilt biscuit' to be held in the same customs warehouses on Ilha das Cobras appears in the *Gazeta do Rio de Janeiro* on 24 October 1810. At that time, we should remind ourselves

[413] Manchester, *British Preëminence in Brazil*, p. 97. Typical of US trade with Brazil in the decades immediately after Brazil's political independence is the following manifest of an American brig – the *Lexington* – which entered a Brazilian harbour on 25 August 1838, according to an announcement in the *Diário de Pernambuco* on 28 August that year.: '853 barrels of flour, 200 crates of spermaceti, 100 barrels of tar, 100 ditto of bitumen, 100 ditto of pitch, 500 small casks of crackers, 100 sacks of pepper, 390 crates of tea, 1 barrel of corn flour, 4 crates of drugs, 251 barrels of potash. Off the Manifest: 12 parasols for men, 6 ditto for Ladies.'

again, Brazil was still a colony. But advertisements of the same kind can be found in newspapers from the early years of the Empire, some of them even in English.

Brazil was then so fanatically patriotic that nativism went as far as people's palates or diet. Being Brazilian for some patriots almost meant belonging to a sect whose diet should be restricted to manioc meal and sugar-cane spirit, excluding 'kingdom flour', wheat bread, wines made from grapes and beer from barley.

It appears that the English were the main popularizers of beer and tea in Brazil, just as much as they were of bread, beef,[414] lamb and champagne itself. Until the time of Dom João VI's arrival in Rio de Janeiro in 1808, English influence in Brazil had come indirectly and somewhat amorphously via Portugal, which the Methuen Treaty had made a particularly beneficial ally of the British nation and a guaranteed market for the cloths, fabrics and flour that overflowed from England, or from other producer nations through England, to England's colonies or quasi-colonies. After 1808, however, English influence in Brazil became clear-cut and direct, and it brought about a veritable overhaul of Brazilian eating habits. The only resistance it encountered was from those more radical patriots; or from the poorest section of the population.

English butter deserves to be singled out from the rest of the English produce imported by Brazil in the first half of the nineteenth century. It became an essential item on the tables of middle-class houses in the cities and the best aristocratic mansions on plantations and farms. It infiltrated recipes for the finest Brazilian cakes of aristocratic or middle-class origin. Such recipes often include the expression 'English butter', meaning superior butter, table butter or dessert butter, contrasting with 'French butter', which was for cooking or seasoning. Barrels of English butter appear in countless newspaper advertisements during the time of the Kingdom in Brazil, though rarely alone: they almost always stand next to casks of glass and sometimes alongside the most unlikely goods. In an advertisement by James Gill in the *Gazeta do Rio de Janeiro* on 18 January 1809 – mentioned above – in which he has 'an English carriage and some English chairs' for sale, we unexpectedly come across butter: 'butter in barrels of 1 and 2 quarters'. In Standfast's advertisement in the *Gazeta* on 8 February 1809 (also mentioned above), another luxury English carriage comes with 'a few barrels of butter and cheeses of prime quality for sale'. If the advertisement were not by an Englishman, it would give the impression that the butter and cheese were soiling the morocco leather of the carriage. Barrels of butter continue to roll through newspaper advertisements during the time

[414] Word used by Freyre in English (Translator).

of the first emperor and the Regency, sometimes together with casks of flour, like those received from England in 1836 by McCalmont & Co., English merchants in Pernambuco: 250 barrels of butter and 250 casks of flour. Or together with barrels of beer, bales of woollen fabrics and bundles of household goods, such as those that arrived in Rio de Janeiro in October 1821 on board the English ship *Agnes*, according to a news item in *O Espelho* on the 17th of that month. Sometimes a ship arrived in Rio from England with a cargo just of English butter, like the *Cyclops* with '100 barrels', as *O Espelho* informs us on 14 November 1821. But butter usually came with beer, china or ham; butter with woollen fabrics; butter and salt cod; butter and potatoes, ropes and sailcloth; butter and coal, gunpowder and iron. Butter for people's mouths, and gunpowder less for the mouths of cannons or firearms than for making fireworks.

The food item that the English specialized in transporting in their relations with Brazilian markets in the first half of the nineteenth century, as we have seen, was salted and dried Newfoundland cod; Brazilian newspaper advertisements are full of it at that time. One English ship alone, the *Nelson*, entered Rio de Janeiro harbour in October 1821 with 1,330 casks and 672 crates of salt cod, which were soon advertised for sale in *O Espelho*, a newspaper that reflected the economic – and not just political – events of the time.

In that respect – bringing Newfoundland cod to Brazil – the English did not try to revolutionize Brazilians' traditional eating habits by replacing local foodstuffs with British produce, but preferred for commercial reasons to adapt to a Portuguese dietary tradition that flourished in Brazil: the taste for and habit of eating salt cod. This tradition reconciled religious precepts of abstaining from meat on certain days with the fact that the famous dried fish could be bought easily and more cheaply than meat in nineteenth-century Brazil. When interpreting almost all aspects of Brazil's economy, lifestyle and diet at that time, we must always bear in mind the effects of the plantation monoculture, which made it difficult for the vast majority of townsfolk to find fresh meat, as well as vegetables, milk or eggs, to eat. The middle classes could vary their diet of dried or fresh meat by eating lobsters, shrimps, prawns, farmed mullet, or salmon or ham imported from London. The vast majority of people had nothing with which to vary their monotonous diet of dried meat and manioc meal other than salt cod. Cod with manioc meal prepared as a mush (*pirão*) or fried (*farofa*).

Hence the large amounts of Newfoundland cod imported into Brazil on nauseatingly laden English brigs sailing into the harbours of Rio de Janeiro, Bahia, Pernambuco and Maranhão. We have already seen the huge cargo of salt cod with which the *Nelson* arrived in Rio on an fine October day in 1821. And, like the *Nelson*, dozens of other English ships brought cod and nothing else to Brazil. On 19 December 1846, the English brig *Meteor* brought 2,830 casks of salt cod for Henry Christophers & Charles Roope, English merchants in Pernambuco. Almost at the same time, another English brig unloaded a consignment in the same port for another English firm that we have already come across, McCalmont & Co., consisting of two barrels of meat, a crate of salmon, a crate of hams, another crate of pickled meat, two casks of hams and four crates of preserves. The salt cod was for the ordinary people of the towns and the slaves on the sugar plantations, on some of which the masters even asked the bishops to increase the number of days for eating fish – which was mainly cod – and abstaining from meat to help them solve the problem of feeding their slaves. The pickled meats and, in particular, the hams were for the fine gentlemen.

We have already seen that English ham often appears in Brazilian newspaper advertisements in the first half of the nineteenth century. Sometimes, as in the *Diário de Pernambuco* on 12 April 1836, it is mentioned with English sweet biscuits and tea – three articles particularly associated with the sugar complex in Brazil. It was precisely in the cities where colonies of English people sprang up after the arrival of Dom João VI – Rio de Janeiro, Salvador in Bahia, Recife in Pernambuco and São Luís in Maranhão – that the habit of tea, ham and sweet biscuits from England spread, as may be seen from newspaper advertisements. The area over which these three products spread comprised those more important cities and the regions around them dominated by the agrarian aristocracy, that is, the sugar-cane planters: the Fluminense region around Rio, the Recôncavo around Salvador, the area known as the *zona da mata*[415] in Pernambuco and the region of Maranhão occupied by the more noble plantations. Throughout the first half of the nineteenth century that aristocracy took pains to adopt English and French manners, and several of its members sent their sons to study in Paris, Montpellier, Edinburgh, Aberdeen and London. Elsewhere, not only did Indian tea remain a remedy nearly up until the present day, but hams and English biscuits were almost products from another world.

On the subject of remedies, it should be noted that it was an area of trade in which the English did not stand out so much as the French in Brazil in the first half of the nineteenth century. Except with regard to magnesia: English magnesia frequently appears in the newspaper advertisements of the time. In an advertisement in the *Gazeta do Rio de Janeiro* on 18 January 1809, the pioneering James Gill (whom we have

[415] Literally 'forest zone', the formerly forested coastal strip in north-eastern Brazil (Translator).

met as a seller of English carriages and furniture, olive oil from Florence, wines from Bordeaux, raisins and butter) announces that he has 'tins of Magnesia' for sale. As in the case of other British products, magnesia too is spelt in Mr Gill's advertisement with a capital letter. It was not just magnesia, but Magnesia with a capital M, like the Butter, Iron, Steel and Glass that came from England.

Calomel is another remedy that the English seem to have brought to Brazil – and the whole of Hispanic America – in the first half of the last century, as a kind of sacred, messianic, imperial remedy, the virtues of which should not be doubted. There was almost a diplomatic incident between Peru and Great Britain over it, when the Peruvian Government issued a decree banning the use of calomel in the treatment of dysentery. The note sent in 1836 by HBM consul in Lima to the Peruvian foreign minister defending the application of calomel against dysentery had reverberations in Brazil, which proved to be highly persuasive publicity for the now famous remedy, such was the image of calomel put forward in that interesting document, supported by the testimony of experienced English naval doctors and by cases observed in various hospitals. A summary of the note sent by HBM consul in Lima appeared in the Rio de Janeiro newspaper *O Patriota* on 16 April 1836.

An advertisement in the *Jornal do Commercio* on 18 January 1828 says:

> Seidlitz Powders for sale at Rua da Alfândega, No 18, this refreshing drink is highly recommended by doctors.

Another advertisement for a remedy from London appears in the same newspaper on 12 September that year:

> At Rua dos Pescadores, No 46, there is a small amount of sulphate quinini of excellent quality that has just arrived from London, and it is for sale at an affordable price in one-ounce bottles.

And on 11 January 1830 there is an advertisement in the *Jornal* for soda and Seidlitz powders, and Cheltenham salts, which had arrived from London three days previously together with 'some pianofortes and fortepianos in the modern taste'; the powders were being sold 'in very affordable portions'.

It should be noted in passing that advertisements placed by English merchants established in Brazil sometimes describe oils and polishes for leather and grease for machines in such endearing language that it is as if they were describing powders, pomades or ointments for a person's skin, body or wounds. That is the tone of the advertisement in the *Jornal do Commercio* of 12 June 1828, in which importers of English articles inform the public that they have received

> a quantity of the very old and genuine No 30 polish from London, in small, medium and large pots, which they are selling at a reasonable price. The fact that this polish is not yet well known in this City is the only reason why its very superior quality does not yet find that esteem that it well deserves, its greatest virtue being in nourishing and softening the leather, since it is free from that great quantity of *vitriol* that most of the other kinds have, which dries and scorches footwear. In England its fame has increased greatly, and the advertisers are asking for no more than a single demonstration and they are certain that within a very short time it will have the same fortune here, as it is the unique, genuine, English No 30 polish by the eminent maker *Robert Warren*.

One gains the impression that the use of such mellifluous polish must have resulted in shoes that were happier than their wearers' feet; just as the use of some English oils advertised in Brazilian newspapers left certain machines or engines imported from England into Brazil in better health – if one can talk about the health of a machine – than the workers looking after them. Men that the bosses did not always look after as well as they did their machines; or as well as slave owners did their slaves, or ships' captains did the captives they brought over from Africa.

Those slaves were treated with 'disinfectant water, very good [...] for cleansing the putrescence of wounds', which was then sold in apothecaries' shops such as the one at Valongo, together with 'moss lozenges, very good for coughs'. That information is given in an advertisement in the *Jornal do Commercio* on 26 November 1827 aimed especially at the 'Captains of Ships that sail in the slave trade'; but equally of interest to other men as responsible for maintaining the health of African workers as the ships' captains themselves; as responsible for maintaining their health – let me now reverse the way I said it above – as factory owners were for maintaining their machines, and the owners of shoes – at a time when wearing shoes was a sign of being a free man – were for preserving the English shoes that lent, if not absolute comfort, then middle-class or aristocratic dignity to their feet and their walk.

Advertisements for other English medicines together with articles of personal hygiene appear in Brazilian newspapers in the first half of the nineteenth century. The *Diário de Pernambuco* of 4 June 1844 carries an advertisement for the main ones placed by the 'drug warehouse' in the Rua de Madre de Deos, No 10, which specialized in importing British products: Windsor soap, sparkling lemonade, Bermuda Arrow Root, patented elastic trusses, toothbrushes and tooth powders, lozenges of muriate of morphine and ipecacuanha, soda powders, and lozenges of bicarbonate of soda and ginger. And the majestic king of all remedies at the time, Gregory's Powder, the virtues of which are praised by the vendor in the style of an Anglican but not entirely Victorian sermon: 'excellent purgative, stomachic and very useful for diseases of the liver, spleen, &c., &c.' In the Indies – the advertisement gravely asserts –

> where these diseases progress so far and constantly cause such damage, rare are those persons who have no knowledge of the good effects of this remedy. A child, a decrepit old man and, in short, a man at any age in life can without fear make use of this medicine, the salutary effects of which lead us to judge it a divine inspiration of the wise and philanthropic genius of its inventor.

Again in the *Diário*, on 7 November 1841, there appeared another intriguing advertisement for an English remedy, in which the manufacturer, a certain Mr Johnson, said that he had heard that his syrup was being faked in Pernambuco. And he had therefore decided to change the labels on the bottles of his remedy.

Another English remedy that kept its reputation in patriarchal Brazil for a long time was Todd's Potion. A characteristically English remedy: rum, syrup, tincture of cinnamon and distilled water. It was taken by the soupspoon in acute infections.

Fowler's Liquor and Holloway's Ointment were famous in Brazil until the middle of the nineteenth century and even during the second half of the century; the latter came from London – 244 Strand – and was sold here in 'little pots' at 800 réis each. This ointment was said to work wonders in the treatment of thousands of diseases, from prosaic 'corns' to 'cancers'; from 'mouth ulcers' to 'ailments of the anus'; from 'fistulas of the abdomen' to 'chilblains'. Nobody in Brazil should doubt the efficacy of this English remedy, because many people in England had already declared the 'beneficial results' they had obtained from it to the 'Lord Chancellor and other magistrates'. That is what we are told in an advertisement in the *Diário de Pernambuco* on 6 July 1851.

The remedies that most stand out in the newspapers of the time, however, are French. They are the ones most noisily advertised by their sellers. No advertisement for an English remedy can compare with the 'Anti-choleric elixir for Ladies and Lords', by Monsieur Gillié, in the *Jornal do Commercio* of 2 November 1827:

> A purgative so gentle that it very particularly should serve for nervous persons and those of a delicate complexion, whose stomach has not the plebeian and brutal vigour of a Galician...

In an advertisement in the same newspaper on 26 October 1827, the seller had already said that this elixir had 'the property of purging abundantly without irritating the stomach or the intestines'. Hence it was the ideal purgative for 'Ladies and Lords'. The way in which certain manufacturers or importers of remedies in Brazil in the first half of the nineteenth century recommended them for one class or another, sometimes for the nobility and sometimes for slaves, is another topic that I shall try to address in another essay.

Advertisements by English doctors are not uncommon, though none of them attained the level of scientific prestige enjoyed by Dr Sigaud, a Frenchman, in Rio de Janeiro during the first half of the century. Neither Dr Abbott, or Abbot, in Bahia, nor Dr Loudon in Pernambuco; none achieved the standing of Dr Sigaud. It is clear, however, that both Dr Loudon and Dr Abbott contributed substantially to the development of medicine in Brazil. Neither of them, however, left an advertisement in that affirmative, not to say bombastic or even charlatanic tone, in which a certain Dr K., 'trained in the University of Copenhagen and approved by the Academy of Bahia', announces in the *Diário de Pernambuco* on 3 December 1844 that he is 'ready to perform any operation necessary to cure ailments of the eyes'.

Other more modest men were the English physicians Dr Richard Daunt, Dr William ('Guilherme') Ellis and Dr Thomas Whatley in São Paulo; and Dr William ('Guilherme') Taylor March in Rio de Janeiro, where he became famous as the 'father of the poor' well before any moneybags or dictator of our days.

In connection with British doctors in Brazil, we should not forget that there was already an English doctor in Rio de Janeiro in colonial times. That is shown by the origin of the former name of the section of street between the then Rua do Carmo (now Rua Sete de Setembro) and the Rua do Ouvidor. According to the tradition collected by the venerable Vieira Fazenda and recorded by him in 'Antiqualhas de Memórias do Rio de

Janeiro'[416] the name of that stretch – *Sucussará* – was derived from the fact that a certain English surgeon who had lived there was quaintly associated with the following episode:

> a neighbour of his having spent a bad night 'due to his discomforts' [says the chronicler] for which modern medicine uses preparations of hamamelis virginica, the Englishman reassured the patient, telling him 'Oh! that is nothing... Do this [and he recommended a remedy to the patient] and your ... will get better – *seu ... sarará.*'[417]

Because the English doctor expressed himself in Portuguese that was not only vulgar but also poorly pronounced, the street became known by that odd name: *Sucussará.*

The most emphatic of the advertisements by English doctors in Brazil was perhaps one by the man who, in colonial times, presented himself to the people of Rio de Janeiro as knowing the secret or technique of the true English vaccine, causing protests from local and Portuguese doctors. I repeat, however, that the English doctors in Brazil are a topic for a separate study. They were an institution.

The advertisements placed by Englishmen in Brazilian newspapers during the first half of the nineteenth century were, with one or two exceptions, real lessons in good taste, sobriety and professional ethics, contrasting with the emphasis, exaggeration, effusion and sometimes evidence of charlatanism found in a large number of advertisements by Europeans of other origins and of various professions. Some of those professions were adopted by these hoaxers in Brazil. There were some who passed themselves off as engineers, and others who presented themselves as doctors without having qualified in medicine anywhere.

The most common advertisements by English technicians established in Brazil were certainly those of engineers. Some, like Alfred de Mornay (an Englishman of French origin) offered his services in the *Diário de Pernambuco* on 16 August 1844

> to sugar-mill owners and other persons who might wish to use his skills in measuring lands, improving and constructing modern waterwheels, obtaining the necessary power even with the least possible amount of water... and also in drawing up plans of

[416] 'Relics of memories of Rio de Janeiro'– *Revista do Instituto Histórico e Geográfico Brasileiro*, tome 95, vol. 149, p. 458

[417] Since *Hamamelis virginiana* (witch hazel) is used to treat piles, among other disorders, the word omitted is clearly '*cu*' ('arse'), hence the street name (Translator).

machinery and any work of his profession; [and later, in 1852, he invited Brazilians to purchase] shares in the Recife to Agua Preta Railway, passing through the sugar-growing zone of the province.

Other engineers, like Bowman, a partner in the MacCollum & Co. machinery factory, announced in the *Diário de Pernambuco* on 25 October 1845 that he was accepting orders for

> one of the principal foundries in England of steam engines, iron waterwheels, with or without grindstones, and all other objects of this nature, [and he invited] sugar-mill owners or their agents to come and examine the steam engine built at said foundry in England, installed to drive the lathes and other apparatus in the factory in the Rua do Brum, since its power is suitable for a sugar mill and the model has the advantages of being very simple, powerful and safe, and easily adapted to mills currently worked by animals.

As early as 1818, John ('João') Gilmour announced in the *Gazeta do Rio de Janeiro* on 21 August that he had arrived from London, sent by a firm in that city that manufactured all kinds of engines,

> to see the engines ... that are in use in this country in sugar manufacturing and distilling, and for any other purpose, and has brought with him two complete, newly invented engines for milling sugarcane, and he has assembled one in the new Ordem customs warehouse, where he invites all gentlemen interested in engineering to examine it; and he offers to take down accurately any order for engines or machines and send them to the factory in *London* to be made, so as to prevent the occurrence of mistakes and delays, as have occurred with some orders sent to his firm previously without due intelligence.

In the same period another English technician, Thomas Reed, arrived in Rio de Janeiro from Jamaica; he was a specialist in reforming 'the style of the ovens for making sugar...' by cooking 'with bagasse or firewood, placed under one boiler to make all the others boil', according to an advertisement in the *Gazeta* on 8 December 1818.

We should remember that some Englishmen began to set themselves up as plantation owners in Brazil around that time. Some did so in Campos. In Pernambuco there was Henry Koster, who owned the Amparo plantation in Itamaracá. It is not recorded that he himself made any impression in this activity as a reformer of sugar-making engineering. He must, however, have contributed to that urge to reform sugar production techniques through the use of English methods and English-made machines for which Campos and Pernambuco stood out in the first half of the nineteenth century. Hence the advertisements for sugarcane grinding machines in the newspaper advertisements at that time, such as the one that appears in the *Diário de Pernambuco* on 22 September 1841, placed by one of the most important British firms in Recife – Johnstone, Pater & Company: an advertisement for 'a high-pressure machine of a model not before seen in this province'. Or the one by Alexander Gilfillan & Co., established at Rua Direita, No 88, in Rio de Janeiro, who announced in the *Gazeta* on 10 May 1821 that they had for sale

> an eight-horsepower steam engine for a sugar mill, with horizontal cylinders, for grinding sugarcane.

Or the one by McCalmont & Co. in the *Diário de Pernambuco* on 2 January 1850 for

> English ironware for sugar mills, as well as cast- and wrought-iron boiling pans of different sizes and models, grindstones for mounting on both wooden and iron wheels powered by animals or water, and four-horsepower high-pressure steam engines.

There were chemists too: English chemistry shines out of newspaper advertisements from the beginning of the nineteenth century, alongside engineering and mechanics. In 1811, Dr Gardner appears to us in the *Gazeta do Rio de Janeiro* on 27 July thanking

> with great pleasure and satisfaction all the Ladies and Gentlemen who did him the honour of attending his latest Lectures; and at the same time advising the public that his 'Chemical Laboratory' would open every Thursday afternoon to repeat his Lectures which he had the honour of giving in the Presence of HRH Our Lord the Prince Regent and His August and Royal Family.

An advertisement in the *Gazeta* on 27 June 1810 had already introduced 'Mr Gardner, Dr of Medicine, Member of the Mathematical and Philosophical Societies of London' to the Rio de Janeiro public; or, as the advertisement says in somewhat Brazilian style – that is, with surprising cordiality on a first meeting – 'to his Friends in General'. Mr Gardner then informed the *Carioca* public that

> he was to begin his lectures on 'Chemistry and Natural Philosophy' on Friday 29 June at 6 o'clock in the evening without fail, hoping to be honoured by an audience able to co-operate with the great labour and expenses that he has incurred in chemical apparatus suitable for making the lectures more complete. [The advertisement added that he was publishing] a printed compendium of the Lectures, which may be acquired at the Introductory lecture.

The note of thanks by the chemist and philosopher from London shows that he did attract the desired audience in colonial Rio de Janeiro in 1810; and that Dom João VI himself – so unjustly accused of being stolid by superficial historians – listened patiently, and perhaps with interest, to Mr Gardner's lectures, in this way foreshadowing his august grandson – whom he 'shared' with Marcus Aurelius[418] – Emperor Dom Pedro II; a scholar who did not always have good taste but did have a genuine passion for lectures by wise men and philosophers, and whom panegyrists generally contrast with his grandfather. As if poor Dom João had done nothing else in his life than devour roast chicken and listen to the litany sung in churches. But at least a newspaper advertisement comes out in favour of the maligned regent and shows us Dom João listening not to one of the castrati in the Imperial Chapel but to the resounding voice of an English chemist and philosopher lecturing on Chemistry and Natural Philosophy.

There is another aspect of Gardner's advertisement that is relevant to the aims of this little study: to show that Brazilian newspaper advertisements in the first half of the nineteenth century yield not only significant information on the extent and nature of English trade in Brazil at the time, but also sometimes surprising evidence of the influence of English technology and scientific and intellectual culture on Brazilian life. Mr Gardner's lectures are a piece of such evidence of England's scientific and intellectual influence on early nineteenth-century Brazil, which some assume to have been dominated intellectually from the outset by France, and only commercially by England.

The colony, having barely emerged from a long period of segregation and dread of anything heretical, was soon following English lessons not only in political art but in natural philosophy. Not only in chemistry but

[418] Victor Hugo famously described Pedro II as a grandson of Marcus Aurelius, on account of his magnanimity to his subjects (Translator).

in laboratory methods.

We will find other evidence of English intellectual influence in advertisements for English teachers, both men and women, and teachers of English. And for governesses, English schools, English teaching methods and English books.

The dread of anything that might seem heretical – which was so strong in Brazil until the end of the eighteenth century, when one or two of the more restless priests or graduates began to let themselves be contaminated by the 'natural philosophy' of the English and French and by the political ideology of the United States – was so great that the French language itself is known to have been considered suspect, and studying it extremely suspect. An effect of the pedagogical policy of the Jesuits: keeping Brazilians as intellectually segregated as possible within the confines of Latin and Portuguese. English must have sounded even more suspect to orthodox ears; the study of English, the language of countless heretics and freemasons, would have seemed more suspect still to those responsible for colonial pedagogy, faithful to the traditions of the Jesuits and the Holy Inquisition.

Under Dom João's regency, the two taboos were finally broken, and French and even English began to be taught openly. The newspapers were filled with advertisements by teachers of French and English. One of the pioneers of French teaching in Pernambuco was José Antônio Gonsalves de Mello at his house in Poço da Panela, where, according to an advertisement in the *Diário de Pernambuco* on 16 June 1827, he received boarding pupils 'to teach them reading, writing, counting, Arithmetic, Portuguese Grammar, practical Geography and French'. Incidentally, although he was very fond of the classics and gave his children the names Thales, Cícero and Ulysses, José Antônio belonged to a family of Francophiles, and one of his more daring relatives during the first half of the nineteenth century gave his son, who was to die in the Paraguayan War, the highly suspect name of Voltaire. Those were excesses committed in the revolt of the liberals against the retrogrades. The sacrifice of children to the 'Goddess of Reason' represented by Voltaire's France or to the 'Goddess of Science' represented by Newton's England.

In the *Gazeta do Rio de Janeiro* of 8 February 1809 we already find an advertisement by an 'English lady teacher', who a few years previously might perhaps have been burnt alive for her audacity:

> An English lady living at Rua dos Ourives, No 27, has a house of education for girls who want to learn to read, write, count and speak

English and Portuguese, sew and embroider, etc.

An English woman teacher offering to teach English to the girls of Rio de Janeiro. The more orthodox heads of families must have been scandalized to read the advertisement in the *Gazeta*. It may well have made some grumpy old man in his pigtail and nankeen breeches, sniffing his comforting snuff, exclaim, 'These English are devils!' The same exclamation that Luccock, in his book on Brazil, heard from a rather more demonstrative Brazilian at the beginning of the nineteenth century,[419] and that other Englishmen in our country have heard since then.

But there was not only the Englishwoman at Rua dos Ourives, No 27. Miss Catherine ('Catharina') Jacob appears in the *Gazeta do Rio de Janeiro* on 6 January 1813 with an advertisement of a similar kind. This time, however, it was an actual school that was being advertised:

> Miss Catharina Jacob takes the liberty of making it known to the Public that she has established an Academy for the instruction of Girls in the Rua da Lapa, opposite the house of Her Excellency the Duchess, in which she will teach reading, writing and speaking the Portuguese and English languages grammatically; all kinds of sewing and embroidery; and Housekeeping. She is hopeful that, as a consequence of her care, her attention in education, Religion and Morals will forever merit the protection of the Parents, relatives and persons who grant her this honour; each girl shall bring complete bedding, three hand towels, a full set of cutlery and a silver cup; they shall pay for each girl 18 mil-réis per month, quarterly in advance.

The advertisement goes on as if to lay open almost all the school's house rules to public gaze:

> Likewise all persons who wish their girls to learn Music, Dance and Drawing, it shall be paid for separately; they shall send their servants to the school every Saturday with a change of clothes; likewise persons who so wish may fetch their girls every Saturday afternoon or Feast Day eve provided that they return to the School by eight o'clock in the evening on the Sunday or

[419] Luccock, *Notes on Rio de Janeiro*, p. 108 (Translator).

> feast day; there may be modifications for families who, on account of the distance from their residence, find it inconvenient to supply clothing and anything else weekly; for which a special adjustment will be made. The opening of the School shall commence on the first of January 1813.

English discipline thus entered the houses of the Brazilian middle-classes or aristocracy to remodel education for girls. There was perhaps no more subtle form of English influence on Brazilian life than that shown by advertisements like those we have just seen, taken from the *Gazeta do Rio de Janeiro* in the early years of Dom João in Brazil.

But it was not only education for girls. The newspapers of the first half of the nineteenth century show an even larger number of English teachers for boys and grown men; English lessons; and English schools for boys. Even schools run by priests started including English language teaching in their curricula; and English gradually lost the taint of being a language of heretics. On 20 January 1811 Father Felisberto Antônio de Figueiredo e Moura announced in the *Gazeta* that, at Rua do Senhor dos Passos, No 18, in Rio de Janeiro, he had opened

> a House of Education, whose pupils, pursuant to a notice of 8th inst. issued by the State Secretariat of Foreign Affairs and War, by order of HRH Our Lord the Prince Regent, would be exempt from arrest and recruitment on condition that they were assiduous and full of good conduct.

In this semi-official school run by a priest, Latin Grammar and the 'Catechism of Our Holy Religion' were now taught alongside English:

> In this same House there will be Teachers to teach English, Arithmetic, Painting, Drawing and Rhetoric. All for the premium of 4$ per month.

The period when Dom João VI was residing in Brazil saw veritable revolutions in the intellectual as well as the economic and social life of Brazil, some of which are not mentioned or pointed out by the historian Oliveira Lima in his masterful study of the subject. The beginnings of coeducation in our country, for example. It cannot be claimed that it was an English initiative; it does, however, coincide so well with the change or reform in Brazilian habits and methods of teaching and literary culture – even the shape of written letters – brought about by the presence and actions of English people in the main Brazilian cities that it is only fair to link this almost scandalous innovation to British influence. An advertisement in the *Gazeta do Rio de Janeiro* on 24 June 1815 highlights this innovation: 'a house of instruction for the Youth of both sexes...' teaching 'Latin and Portuguese Grammar, French and English Language'. Teaching for girls was in a 'separate Classroom' and consisted of 'Basic Letters, Grammar, sewing, embroidery and cutting of all kinds of ladies' clothes'. The new school was also for boarders: ' We accept boys to live in the house itself.'

It should be noted in passing that it was not only the shape of handwritten letters that changed in Brazil due to the presence of the English in the main cities, going from stiffly upright – the old Portuguese style – to the thirty-five degree slant characteristic of English writing. Typefaces changed too – although they had rarely been used in the country before the arrival of Dom João. The *Gazeta* of 3 November 1816 carries this significant advertisement for the history of the graphic arts in Brazil:

> Manoel Antonio da Silva Serpa, proprietor of the Typography of Bahia, who is at present in this Capital City at Rua da Prainha, house No 16, first floor, makes it known that anyone who wishes to have any work printed or reprinted in good English type at reasonable prices may come to his house...

Having made this observation on typefaces, let us return to schools, where not only English letter shapes were introduced during this period but also English teaching methods, such as Lancaster's, and methods of discipline, such as Mr Gardien's.

Mr Gardien's book, which was full of both French and English innovations in pedogogy and was translated into Portuguese at the beginning of the nineteenth century by Joaquim Jerônimo Serpa, under the title of *Tratado da Educação Physico-Moral dos Meninos*,[420] was perhaps the first serious warning to appear in Brazil about the dangers of abusing the paddle and the whip in the education of children. Which does not mean that crates of whips of the kind then used for breaking horses, slaves and children did not arrive in Brazil from England. On 2 July 1841, an advertisement in the *Diário de Pernambuco* advises the public of the arrival of a consignment for Gaskell, Johnston & Co., on the English brig *Windsor* from Liverpool, containing not only bundles of cotton and woollen fabrics, casks of ironware, crates of soap, barrels of beer, kegs

[420] 'Treatise on the Physico-Moral Education of Children'. The original work may have been by Claude-Martin Gardien, a French doctor who published several works on science and medicine in the late eighteenth and early nineteenth centuries (Translator).

of lead shot and seven tons of iron machinery, but also English whips, some of which must have had that sad fate: of being instruments for the domestication not only of animals but of slaves and children as well.

In 1827, an advertisement in the *Jornal do Commercio* on 5 October tells us of an 'English School' in Rio de Janeiro, 'established until now at Rua dos Barbônios [*sic*], No 98', which had just moved to 'Matacavallos, No 94, on the corner of the Rua dos Invalidos'. The curricula followed a new plan for Brazil at that time, emphasizing practical and even commercial studies:

> Latin, Portuguese, English, French and Spanish languages, grammatically, History and Geography, Logic, Rhetoric and Written Elocution, Arithmetic, and double-entry Bookkeeping, Algebra and Geometry, Drawing and Dance.

Dance is known to have been very much in fashion in England at the time. In an advertisement from the same period, Valentim José da Costa tells the public – in the *Jornal do Commercio*, Rio de Janeiro, on 10 November 1827 – that his school of public education has been established at Rua da Prainha, No 132, for three or four years. And his school taught 'writing in English-style letters'.

In the *Diário de Pernambuco* of 24 October 1835

> an able person offers to give English and French lessons in private houses; those interested may apply to the house of Mr Catão, who will tell them who the advertiser is.

By about this time, English was already appearing in official courses: in the same newspaper on 26 February 1836 the schoolmaster Father Miguel do Livramento Lopes Gama makes it known

> to whom it may concern that the examination of candidates to replace the Chair of English and French in the School of Arts of this Academy will take place on 29th inst. at 8 a.m. in the Meeting Room.

He was referring to the Academy of Olinda.

Another advertisement in the *Diário de Pernambuco* – on 30 June 1838 – is by an 'English-language Teacher of the Pernambuco Lyceum by order of His Imperial Majesty, may God protect him, etc.': his name was Carlos Van Nes. By then there was already a large number of English teachers advertising in newspapers in Rio de Janeiro. Back in 1809 the *Gazeta* had carried this rather mysterious advertisement in the issue of 23 August that year:

> Anyone who wishes to learn the English Language grammatically with perfection in a short time should speak to *Francisco Ignacio da Silva,* who will give him a card with the name of the teacher, who is from London. [And in the same issue of the *Gazeta* was an advertisement that John Laurence ('João Lourenço') Toole] ... *English* Language teacher, is establishing a Class of said Language, which he teaches grammatically, as well as Arithmetic and double-entry Bookkeeping.

It seems, however, that it was not as easy to find a native English teacher of English in Rio in 1830 as it had been in 1809. That is what this advertisement in the *Jornal do Commercio* of 21 January that year seems to suggest:

> It is desired to be known whether in this Capital City there is an English class, whose teacher is also English; please announce his address through this Newspaper, so that arrangements may be made to teach a boy who has now been learning that language for one year.

Note the insistence that the teacher must be English. There must, however, have been not just one but several native English teachers of English in Rio de Janeiro in those days. The appeal made by the boy's parent or guardian did receive an immediate response. On the 26th of that month, the *Jornal do Commercio* announced:

> There is a person who has recently come from England who wishes to teach the English Language grammatically in private houses, and knows the Portuguese language with perfection.

In that same year, 1830, there is an advertisement by an 'English Lady' – in the *Jornal do Commercio* of 6 March – which does not seem to conform to the code of gentility of the then approaching Victorian period:

> Any single or widowed Gentleman who wishes to hire a very capable English Lady to look after a house should enquire at Rua da

Pedreira da Gloria, No 24.

An advertisement by a housekeeper? But why would this English lady only be interested in running the house of a bachelor or widower?

There are other advertisements in the *Jornal do Commercio* by English housekeepers or ladies who wished to lodge in family homes. The following one appears in the *Jornal* on 28 April 1832:

> There is an elderly English lady who wishes to lodge in the house of a widowed lady or a single man or anyone with a small family. [Another on 13 August that year says:] Whosoever requires an English Lady to look after and run a family home, at which she has much practice, should place an announcement in this newspaper so as to be sought out. [And on 23 January 1833:] There is an English Lady who understands the Portuguese language and has sufficient skills and all the necessary qualities to take care of the running of a house; anyone who wishes to utilize her services should apply at Pateo da Pracinha, No 1, ground floor, where there is a plaque written in English, and there he will find the person with whom to treat.

This was one of the English institutions in Brazil during the first half of the nineteenth century: the English housekeeper or governess. English governesses and English doctors had considerable influence on Brazilian society at that time. English governesses were not only found in Rio de Janeiro: there were also some in noble households in the north. The Reverend Daniel P. Kidder came across one in Ceará, in the household of a 'prominent merchant', whose two eldest children were being educated in Portugal: 'for the younger, an English governess was employed in the house.'[421]

And we should not forget the most eminent of the English governesses who lived in Brazil during the first half of last century: Maria Graham. She was governess to Princess Maria da Glória.[422] But only for a short time, because 'the foreign woman' or 'the Englishwoman' was soon the target of a conspiracy of intrigue, gossip and spite by the ladies and the

[421] Daniel Parish Kidder, *Sketches of Residence and Travels in Brazil*, London, 1845, II, p. 219. Freyre quotes from the Brazilian translation: *Reminiscências de viagens e permanência no Brasil (Províncias do Norte)*, translated by Moacir N. Vasconcelos, São Paulo, n.d., p. 138 (Translator).

[422] Maria da Glória (1819-1853) was the eldest daughter of Dom Pedro I. On the death of Dom João VI in 1826, Pedro, already Emperor of Brazil, briefly became King of Portugal as well, but after two months he abdicated the Portuguese throne in favour of Maria, who became Queen Maria II of Portugal (reigned 1826-28 and 1834-53) (Translator).

all-powerful barber of the Palace, who succeeded in turning Dom Pedro I himself against her. Her life with the imperial family allowed Maria Graham to observe many interesting details of Luso-Brazilian customs and human nature itself. Hence the value of her correspondence, published in the *Anais da Biblioteca Nacional do Rio de Janeiro* (1938, vol. LX).

The first advertisement genuinely for an English governess in a Brazilian newspaper seems to have been one in the *Jornal do Commercio* in 1830:

> an English Lady who has recently arrived from her country wishes to find a position in a family where she may provide her services in the education of girls, having for that sufficient knowledge as she can certify principally in the English and French languages, Music and Drawing, and Geography, this Lady is still not perfect in the national language and cannot offer her services to an English family.

There was also an English school then in Rio de Janeiro for English children. That is what we are told by an advertisement in the *Rio Herald* on 8 March 1828: M. J. Maze, former private tutor to the children of Mr Maxwell, a rich Englishman of the time,

> respectfully informs such English families in this city that have children to be educated, that not being longer engaged with Mr. Maxwell by reason of his son's going to England, he will on the first of May gladly receive into his school the children of such families, shall they then offer.[423]

And in 1843 there was already someone in Recife offering to give 'English lessons in the mornings in private houses'. This was Mr 'José de Maya, British subject', who in the *Diário de Pernambuco* of 4 December that year also announced an English language class at his house in the Rua da Praia, in the evening, from 6 to 8, on alternate days, for 'persons employed in commerce'. People who wished to learn English from Mr Maya could register their names at the advertiser's house or at Witch Bravo & Co., apothecaries, Rua da Madre Deos, No 1.

Incidentally – to add a marginal note to these advertisements about English teachers – someone who seems not to have had much luck with his first English language teacher was His Majesty the first emperor. When the Reverend Walsh went to visit Dom Pedro I in Rio, the latter received him speaking French. He was learning English from Father Tilbury, but

[423] Quoted in English (Translator).

still very much in the early stages. The Reverend Walsh heard, however, that the Emperor of Brazil had an English groom from whom he had acquired a vocabulary in Shakespeare's language that was not exactly fit for the salon or court, although it was perhaps the kind that best suited the temperament and brig-master's manners of Dom Pedro I.

Grooms improvising as English teachers[424] are not easy to identify through newspaper advertisements of the period. A period when polyglots arriving from Europe 'with knowledge of the English, French and Portuguese languages' and offering their services as butlers or cooks – like a certain advertiser in the *Jornal do Commercio* on 15 October 1827 – did not always seem to have resisted the temptation of leaving the kitchens and pantries to the slaves. Some of them, free, white and perhaps fair-haired, seem to have suddenly adopted more illustrious or more profitable professions than cooking or serving at table. One such profession must have been teaching English.

It should be noted that Father Tilbury, who taught Dom Pedro I English, was not just a teacher of his difficult language. Judging from newspaper advertisements, this eminent priest was something of a real humanist. As well as English, he offered – in the *Gazeta do Rio de Janeiro* of 3 January 1821 – to teach Brazilians 'French, Geography and *Belles-Lettres*'.

We must not overlook the advertisements in which English firms offer young Brazilians positions as office boys or junior clerks in trading houses that functioned in some ways as schools. Such is the advertisement in the *Jornal do Commercio* on 11 February 1830: 'Wanted: a junior clerk for an English trading house...' It was precisely in that romantic year of 1830 that a young Brazilian from Rio Grande do Sul became a junior clerk in an English establishment in Rio de Janeiro belonging to Richard ('Ricardo') Carruthers. That Brazilian was called Irineu Evangelista de Sousa.[425] According to Alberto de Faria, that trading house acted as a real school for the future Baron of Mauá:

> Carruthers taught him accountancy, gave him an English grammar, English books... Mauá became an English merchant... He *counted* only in English and expressed his anger only in English; he explained the latter quirk by saying that he did not like to utter rude words in his mother tongue. In the British colony, his name, with the consonant doubled and the vowel modified, was nationalized and popularized – *Sinhôr Irrenéu*.

[424] Walsh, *Notices of Brazil*, II, p. 251.

[425] See footnote 169.

And the author of this well-known biography of Mauá continues his apologia for both the man and the British Empire:

> He received everything from this English school – his feeling for commerce, the broad sweep of his industrialism, the spirit of (p. 69) enterprise, the long flights of his dreams of greatness, his plain speaking, the cult of credit and that nobility of processes through which, in the latter quarters of the nineteenth century, trade made the British Isles the greatest of Empires.[426]

Mauá was just one of many poor boys in Brazil who, as clerks in English warehouses, were influenced by the English directly. The same happened to boys from rich or comfortably-off families who attended English classes or schools – of the many that appear in newspaper advertisements at the time; and to boys and girls from even richer families who had English governesses or private tutors. One such girl was a plantation owner's daughter called Flora Cavalcanti de Albuquerque; at the end of her life, now the elderly widow of Oliveira Lima, she confessed to me: 'I only know how to pray in English.'

And let us not forget the slaves and *moleques* of English people, who must also have learnt from them at least how to swear in English, if not how to pray or count. Some of them even dressed in English style, borrowing their masters' trousers, shirts and hats. In 1844, an Englishman in Recife, Mr August Corbett, was robbed of

> a *Crioulo* called Capucá, aged 8 or 9... light-brown, good-looking, his upper eye-teeth missing as he is beginning to change them, when he smiles he has a dimple in his right cheek... very bright and curious... sackcloth trousers and shirt and a blue cloth cap, [who must have been highly prized by his owner, such was the appeal he put out for the missing *moleque* to] all the police authorities, captains of vessels, slave-catchers and private individuals.

That is given in an advertisement placed in the *Diário de Pernambuco* on 16 September 1844 by the anxious English owner. I trust everyone helped him get his precious little black boy back. Perhaps Capucá already spoke some English: enough to carry out his master's orders.

Some of the runaway slaves of the time appear in newspaper

[426] Alberto de Faria, *Mauá*, Rio de Janeiro, 1928, p. 70.

advertisements dressed not in coarse sackcloth but in '*English* striped shirt and trousers', like the Congo *moleque* whose escape was announced in the *Gazeta do Rio de Janeiro* on 3 January 1821; or like José, a black Angola *Crioulo*,

> a good cook, well spoken, ordinary stature, somewhat lighter brown, thin, long face, small eyes, mouth and nose, a mark on one of his legs from having worn shackles, wearing an *English* striped shirt, white trousers.[427]

Perhaps these slaves belonged to English merchants who imported cloth. Indeed, the English gained a reputation in Brazil for treating not only the people but also the animals employed in their domestic service better than anyone else. So when we see a newspaper advertisement – as in the *Diário de Pernambuco* on 12 March 1840 – describing a chestnut horse 'with all the gaits and in very fine condition', we can be almost sure that it is a horse kept by an Englishman.

Nathaniel Lucas, an Englishman established in Rio de Janeiro, began to trade in horses in 1809, particularly saddle and carriage horses.[428] Such horses must have been an important factor in the Anglicization of Brazilian habits, not because the animals were English – which is uncertain – but because they had probably been trained by Mr Lucas to trot and gallop like good horses from England. Trotting and galloping were gradually adopted by the more refined Brazilians, just as the use of horses was spread through English influence to areas of Brazil until then dominated by human or ox-drawn transport. But this subject will be examined in another study, in which I shall especially consider the influence not only of the use of the first modern machines but also the greater use of horses on Brazilian life during the nineteenth century, in the sense that they freed people from a number of tasks that had been regarded as inseparable from slaves, and consequently were, if not causal, at least conducive to the existence of slavery or servile or forced labour in our society or milieu. We shall see then that the English appear to have contributed more powerfully to abolishing servile work in Brazil by increasing the popularity of horse-drawn transport and beginning the mechanization of agriculture and industry than through their immense but often frustrated, if not hypocritical efforts to stamp out the illegal trade in Africans to this country.

That increased popularity seems to have stemmed largely from advertisements not only for tempting machines from England but also for

[427] *Gazeta do Rio de Janeiro*, 28 September 1816.
[428] *Gazeta do Rio de Janeiro*, 25 February 1809.

saddle and carriage horses: those sold by Mr Lucas, for example; or those that occasionally gallop out of newspaper advertisements to praise such as this: 'a good, handsome horse, very fat, trots and canters, and very good natured'.[429]

Horses of that quality would have to have harnesses and saddles like those that came from France and especially England, from where merchants also received excellent whips, as well as fabrics like the so-called 'devil's skin' or bombazine, a cotton and wool weave that was thicker than canvas, generally with dark-coloured patterns, which for all those reasons was considered ideal 'for riding'. At least, that was the opinion of the fabric importers of the time, one of whom was established in the Rua do Colégio in Recife, facing the Arco de Santo Antônio, and placed an eye-catching advertisement in the *Diário de Pernambuco* on 4 August 1846.

I have found few advertisements for English breeds of dogs, though English pedigree dogs became even more famous in Brazil than cattle or horses. It is possible that they only became common in advertisements during the second half of last century.

Even so, here are a few advertisements relating to English dogs that can be linked to the changes that English culture brought to the Brazilian. They suffice to show the importance that English dogs gradually gained in Brazilian life from the early decades of the Empire.

On 20 September 1839, someone – apparently an English person – advertised in the *Diário de Pernambuco* that they needed 'a guard dog...'. On 11 July 1846 the *Diário de Pernambuco* printed a notice about an English dog lost by an important person in the Province:

> Lost from the house of the brigadier commander of arms, a bulldog: would the person who has taken it in please send it back.

That must have been a rare event. But not so rare that it would surprise Pernambuco for its rarity. Two years previously another dog had been lost or stolen in Recife:

> a Scottish dog with the following marks: short legs, white all over except for its head, which is half white and the other half chestnut coloured; will whoever finds it please bring it to Aterro da Boa Vista, No 4, where he will be generously rewarded.[430]

[429] *Diário de Pernambuco*, 24 November 1843.
[430] *Diário de Pernambuco*, 17 March 1844.

And an English pedigree dog went missing from another house in Boa Vista, as well:

> large, very young, vinegar coloured... ears cropped, chest all white. Whoever finds it, please return it, for as it is a well-known dog... it cannot remain hidden very long.[431]

Yet another English dog went missing at almost the same time: 'an English dog, very intelligent, black with tan-coloured feet and muzzle... [and] a wound on its back, now closed'.[432] And perhaps the strange-looking dog that had disappeared from a house in the Rua do Livramento in Recife, according to an advertisement in the *Diário* on 3 August 1843, was English too: 'a long, whitish cross-bred dog...'

The *Jornal do Commercio* published the following advertisement in 1833:

> Lost on the afternoon of Wednesday 5th inst. in the Rua da Alfândega: a young dog, English breed, white with black ears and tail and a tortoiseshell collar with a padlock; whoever finds it and takes it to Rua dos Pescadores, No 39, will receive a good reward.

It must have belonged to someone rich or a nobleman at court to be wearing a 'tortoiseshell collar'.

Mastiffs or bulldogs had been in this country – especially Pernambuco – for a long time. They date from the seventeenth century, unless they first arrived here with adventurers or pirates like Lancaster, people who were nearly always fond of dogs, monkeys and parrots, unlike sedentary and peace-loving people, who are more inclined to own cats and canaries. We know that cats were imported from Europe in considerable numbers by the Dutch, who used these animals to catch rats and mice in stores, warehouses and homes in Brazil.[433] They also brought English bulldogs to this country at the same time. A seventeenth-century document discovered by Mr José Antônio Gonsalves de Mello Neto, a patient researcher, states that 300 'English bulldogs' were sent to Brazil to 'help Dutch soldiers in capturing Indians and blacks'.[434] A less savoury fate than awaited the cats.

It will be a topic for a chapter in another work to chart the presence of

[431] *Diário de Pernambuco*, 25 June 1844.

[432] *Diário de Pernambuco*, 19 August 1844.

[433] José Antônio Gonsalves de Mello Neto, *Tempo dos Flamengos. Influência da ocupação holandesa na vida e na cultura do norte do Brasil*, Rio de Janeiro, 1947, p. 184.

[434] *Ibid.*, p. 185.

these animals in newspaper advertisements and other documents that have been largely ignored or forgotten, despite being valuable for reconstructing and interpreting the more intimate aspects of Brazil's patriarchal past. And not only the presence of cats, dogs, horses, cows, goats, sheep and oxen; but also that of monkeys and parrots, marmosets and agoutis, parakeets and canaries. Oral history tells us that monkeys and parrots were particular favourites of the English as living souvenirs of Brazil. And in the ports of northern Brazil some parrots fetched high prices when sold to English travellers or sailors, who particularly admired their ability to swear in English and Portuguese. I have been unable to find any mention of such parrots intended specially for English owners in newspaper advertisements, perhaps because the trade in them was something of a racket and was one of the main swindles and confidence tricks to which the English fell victim in Brazil, at the hands of quayside tricksters. One of the most common of such tricks was to sell parakeets to naive or inexperienced English travellers as young or baby parrots.

Even so, there are advertisements in the newspapers about parrots which perhaps belonged to English people: the one advertised in the *Diário de Pernambuco* on 28 June 1844, for example: 'a very large parrot with an iron ring on its leg...' And the 'talking parrot' wanted by an advertiser in the *Diário*, who received a reply from someone else on 14 July 1840, was perhaps bought by an Englishman.

The advertisement in the *Diário de Pernambuco* on 5 August 1843 must surely have caught the attention of at least one of the many English people living in Pernambuco at the time: 'an amusing tame monkey, very charming...'

A significant advertisement by James Grabten & Co., English importers of animal products, appeared in the *Diário de Pernambuco* on 11 October 1844. These merchants had received 'a consignment of bird manure, known as *guama*, very suitable for manuring land...' Like other English merchants in Recife, Grabten & Co. had their warehouse in the Rua da Cruz, where they sold many items of interest to the farmers of the region, and not just to the fine people in the capital.

Advertisements for English books in Brazilian newspapers in the first half of the nineteenth century are not nearly as prominent as advertisements for Latin books are during the early years of that period, or French ones in the later years. But they are not exactly lacking. On 22 October 1827, Mr Dodsworth was holding an auction at Rua da Alfândega, No 38 – according to an advertisement in the *Jornal do Commercio* on that day – of 'a large collection of books belonging to The Most Excellent Marquis of

Sabará', among which were several English books: *Grove's Military History and Ancient Armour*; *Chemistry* by Thomson, in five volumes; the *English-Portuguese Dictionary* by Vieyra, in two volumes; and the complete works of Walter Scott. In 1815 the same auctioneer had held another important auction of books, advertised in the *Gazeta do Rio de Janeiro* on 5 April that year: 'a large collection of books in different languages', together with 'pianofortes' and 'household goods'. In 1815 there had also been an auction of 'books in various languages', advertised in the *Gazeta* on 13 September: books, French engravings, whether 'galant' or not nobody knows, 'a phantasmagorical magic lantern, some beautiful tea services, a complete telescope made by Gilbert, oilcloths for drawing-rooms and various household goods'. Evidently an auction for some humanist or philosopher in the eighteenth-century mould who lived in Rio de Janeiro surrounded by English and French books, a telescope, scientific innovations and perhaps 'galant' engravings. Some Francophile abbot or Anglophile graduate.

There were many English books, or books translated from English, that the inhabitant of Rio de Janeiro could purchase at the '*Gazeta* shop' during the time of Dom João VI. One of them, the '*Philosofo Inglez, ou Historia de Mr Cleveland, filho natural de Cromwell, escripta por ele mesmo*,[435] 9 volumes of 8 [parts], for 12$000', according to an advertisement in the *Gazeta* on 23 September 1815. Another book then for sale in that shop sounds to our ears like a work of British propaganda or apologia: *A Voz da Verdade e Gratidão ou Elogio gratulatorio ao immortal Heroe da nossa Idade, o Ilmo. e Exmo. Sr. Arthur Wellesley, Duque de Ciudad Rodrigo, Lord Marquez de Wellington*,[436] by Friar Joaquim Rodrigues.

And some advertisements for books in English are truly amazing. On 6 March 1830 the *Jornal do Commercio* announced: 'For sale, the Novel *Paulo e Virgínia*[437] translated into English and some household goods'.

Bentham is perhaps the English author whose name appears most frequently in book advertisements in Brazilian newspapers during the time of Dom Pedro I and the Regency. After Bentham, writers who stand out are Pope – advertised in translation from the days of Dom João onwards – Locke, Swift, Defoe, Walter Scott, Milton and Adam Smith,

[435] This novel was actually written in French by Antoine François (Abbé) Prévost in 1731-39, and translated into English as *The Life and Entertaining Adventures of Mr. Cleveland, Natural Son of Oliver Cromwell, Written by Himself* (Translator).

[436] Literally 'The voice of truth and gratitude or gratulatory eulogy to the immortal hero of our age, the Most Illustrious and Most Excellent Sir Arthur Wellesley, Duke of Ciudad Rodrigo, Lord Marquess of Wellington' (Translator).

[437] An English translation (*Paul and Virginia*) of Jacques-Henri Bernardin de Saint-Pierre's *Paul et Virginie* (1787) (Translator).

not to mention strictly technical books or journals such as *The Lancet* and *Outlines of Midwifery*. Or the *Sistema de Leis sobre Seguros Maritimos*,[438] translated from English into Portuguese and published in 1821, which was being sold that same year by Paulo Martin in his shop at Rua da Quitanda, No 33, according to an advertisement in the *Gazeta* on 2 October. Or the *Exposição Anatomica do Utero Humano Gravido e dos seus Contheudos*, by Hunter,[439] translated from the English by Antônio Lopes d'Abreu, which was advertised in the *Gazeta* on 24 November 1813. Didactic books also appear, such as the *Spelling Book* in an advertisement in the *Diário de Pernambuco* on 22 November 1841.

We are given some interesting information in a notice by Father Miguel do Sacramento Lopes Gama, director of the Law Course in Olinda (*Diário de Pernambuco*, 7 January 1848) that the English authors then required in the examinations of prospective bachelors of law were Goldsmith (*Roman History* and *The Vicar of Wakefield*), in prose, and '*The Seasons* by James Thomson' and 'the *Paradise*', in verse.[440]

On 19 November 1836 Messrs McCalmont & Co. of Pernambuco received from Liverpool a crate of books and another of office supplies. The books may have been blank books or ledgers, which at that time seem to have been imported from England in larger numbers than books of literature, philosophy or science. In any case, it is still significant that English authors of the standing of Milton, Bentham, Locke and Pope were being advertised for sale in a country barely out of its colonial isolation, and, of course, were being bought and read, albeit by only a small number of people.

It does not matter that Luccock, who was severe and often unfair in his criticism, observed that few of the English works sold at a 'Sale of Books' in Rio de Janeiro in 1818 – he believed – fell into Brazilian hands, and that neither the Glasgow edition of Homer's *Iliad* in Greek nor other works in Greek and Hebrew published in England found buyers at that sale.[441] The fact is that there were people in Brazil at that time who could read a little Greek, as well as a lot of Latin; and people who were beginning to read a little English as well as French. Literary English and scientific or technical English. Works by Milton or Pope, and works about surgery and other sciences, translations of which were also coming out.

[438] Literally 'System of laws on marine insurance' (Translator).

[439] William Hunter, *An Anatomical Description of the Human Gravid Uterus, and its Contents*, 1774 (Translator).

[440] Freyre gives these four titles in Portuguese, so it is not clear whether the students were expected to read them in English or in translation (Translator).

[441] Luccock, *Notes on Rio de Janeiro*, p. 574.

Other English items of an intellectual or scientific nature in the newspaper advertisements from the period considered in this little study deserve to be specially highlighted: those relating to nautical matters, dominated then as now by British science and technology more than by any other. Such were the *Ensaio de Tactica Naval* and the *Construcção e Analyse das Proposições Geometricas*, works translated from English,[442] which appear in an advertisement in the *Gazeta do Rio de Janeiro* on 24 January 1810. And in the *Gazeta* on 21 July that year is an equally characteristic advertisement for articles for sale at Rua da Alfândega, No 2 – the street of English merchants:

> *Nautical Almanacks*, Telescopes, Achromatic Spyglasses, Ditto for day and night, Mathematics Sets of various kinds, Hydrographic Charts and other Machines for Nautical Astronomy, etc.

It was to books and instruments of this kind that the classics – such as Sallust, Tacitus, or the old 'Quintillian annotated in the margins' that appears in an advertisement in the *Diário de Pernambuco* on 31 March 1836 – began to yield some of the space that they had been sovereignly or exclusively occupying on the shelves and desks of Brazil.

Other traditional, classical or 'pure' articles also shrank away from the new goods. The English invasion extended to almost the entire cultural sphere: the patriarchal trunks, chests or cupboards, which were gradually emptied of the oriental silks, nankeen breeches and oriental gowns worn by judges, and were filled with 'English dress coats, frock coats and trousers', like those advertised in the *Diário de Pernambuco* on 4 February 1829; the kitchens, where the earthenware pots were being replaced with iron ones; the hat-stands, where the three-cornered hats were being replaced with round ones, and the swords and canes with parasols; the dining-rooms, drawing-rooms, bedrooms, lavatories and all the outhouses; the dining-tables, where 'sets of English knives and forks'[443] started appearing; the drawing-room walls, where the religious prints gradually disappeared, replaced by gleaming mirrors and pictures with 'the history of Mary Stuart in 8 pictures'[444] or portraits of Wellington; the china cupboards, where china from the Orient gradually gave way to English ware; the larders,

[442] John Clerk, *An Essay on Naval Tactics, systematical and historical*, London, 1790, 1797. George Atwood, 'The Construction and Analysis of geometrical Propositions, determining the Positions assumed by homogeneal Bodies which float freely, and at rest, on a Fluid's Surface; also determining the Stability of Ships, and of other floating Bodies', *Philosophical Transactions of the Royal Society of London*, vol. 86, (1796), pp. 46-278 (Translator).

[443] *Diário de Pernambuco*, 4 February 1829.

[444] *Ibid.*

in which boxes of tea and olives, 'English sweet biscuits',[445] hams, tinned peas and cheeses from London and raisins from Gibraltar triumphantly took their places; and the wooden window lattices, replaced almost overnight with glass in the more noble houses in the cities. There was such a dramatic change in the city environment in Brazil during the early decades after the ports were opened up to foreigners (a change that newspaper advertisements proclaimed with the shouts of auctioneers) that it was like a theatre or a stage set in which the entire scenery was being changed in order to put on a lively play. And while that play was not exactly Shakespearian, it did involve some comedy and a touch of tragedy, with plenty of ridiculous things to laugh at and many a sad detail to make the sentimental cry, like the far-from-trivial fact that the greatest Anglophile of the times, Dom Rodrigo de Sousa Coutinho, the Count of Linhares, died apparently not from natural causes but poisoned by his enemies, who were also opposed to British expansion in Brazil. That expansion was loudly proclaimed in the newspapers every single day, in their advertisements for British merchandise and products.

In fact, the advertisements for English merchandise and products in Brazilian newspapers during the first half of the nineteenth century are like a theatre or a classroom in which the lesson is dramatized, showing us the replacements or half-replacements that occurred in that period in the habits and lifestyles of the Brazilian middle classes and aristocracy in the areas of diet, hygiene, dress, transport, recreation and medication. It was not only the triangular or three-cornered hat that was quite suddenly replaced with the round or 'English' hat, and the sword with the cane and especially the parasol or umbrella. The palanquin was also replaced with the carriage; home-made remedies, such as 'cow's tongue syrup' or 'tamarind purgative', with calomel, Gregory's powder and apothecaries' potions; rustic toys, such as puppets or paper kites, with little John Bulls and blond-haired dolls; the 'guitar that has a very good sound' with jacaranda pianos from London; the Latin dictionary with the English dictionary; the *Hours of the Virgin* with novels by Defoe, Walter Scott and Ann Radcliffe; Voltaire's works with Bentham's; rice pudding as a dessert with Gibraltar raisins; manioc meal with wheat flour; sugar flowers with sweet biscuits; cane juice with punch; lattices with glass windows; and urinals with water-closets. All these replacements supply the historian or sociologist with material for studying the penetration of one culture by another. Sometimes the same newspaper that advertises a palanquin from India or a fully curtained sedan chair from Bahia also announces the arrival from Europe of a phaeton or a fully glazed English carriage. A newspaper that reports the disappearance of a lame horse is soon followed by another, like the *Gazeta* of 31 January

445 *Diário de Pernambuco*, 12 April 1836.

1821, with an advertisement for a 'new farrier ... in both the *English* and the *Portuguese* style, according to the physical principles of hoof anatomy'. Or one that recommends the patriarchal virtues of 'cow's tongue syrup' is soon followed by one extolling the palaeotechnical qualities of Gregory's powders.

Several of these replacements or half-replacements did not happen all of a sudden, of course, as soon as the ports were opened up to foreigners or the *Gazeta do Rio de Janeiro* and *Idade d'Ouro do Brazil* to advertisements for English innovations. The more sophisticated Brazilians in Pernambuco and Bahia had long had a taste for English goods, which had been known and valued since early times. It was just that it had been difficult to satisfy that taste other than by unlawful means: smuggling, clandestine trade and dealing with freebooters. The more sophisticated Brazilians in the north of the country had had English hats and shoes, for example, since the seventeenth century, as they were common here during the years of Dutch occupation.[446] They had also had cheese, butter and bread from northern Europe since that time, as the Dutch had introduced those products as well. Since the seventeenth century they had also had English bulldogs: a good imperial breed for helping white rulers control the unsubmissive brown and black masses; an aristocratic breed for helping landlords control their defiant slaves.

But it was at the beginning of the nineteenth century that Brazilians really made contact with the values and technology from northern Europe in general, and from England in particular, which until then had almost only been obtained by unlawful means. Except by the people of northern Brazil during the three decades of Dutch occupation, which was also to some extent an English and French occupation, and not only Dutch and Jewish.

446 Gonsalves de Mello Neto, *Tempo dos Flamengos*, p. 186.

## CHAPTER III

# OFFICIAL CORRESPONDENCE OF HBM CONSULS

## (First Half of the Nineteenth Century)

> *The consul general, Sir James Gambier, was creating yet more trouble for Strangford by his efforts to participate in the social life of Rio despite the strict etiquette of the Portuguese court.*[447]
>
> (*Alan K. Manchester,* British Preëminence in Brazil, *Chapel Hill, 1933, p. 82, referring to* Dispatch from Strangford to Canning No 33, *Foreign Office, 63/ 61.*)

> *... the abolition of the slave trade, given the position that England had adopted on this matter, would greatly facilitate the recognition of Brazilian independence. That was Canning's view, which was expressed to José Bonifácio by Chamberlain, the British consul in Rio...*
>
> (*Octávio Tarqüínio de Sousa,* José Bonifácio – 1763-1838, *Rio de Janeiro, 1945, p. 209.*)

[447] Quoted by Freyre in English (Translator).

Either of those terms – *official correspondence* or *consul* – suggests dreary bureaucratic routine, contrasting with the adventure, action and surprise conjured up by the expression *diplomatic papers*, which one immediately imagines are full of intrigue, political mystery or merely gossip[448] from the times of statesmen with lace cuffs or just gold cuff-links. We just need to remember, however, that men of the intelligence, scholarship and spirit of adventure of Richard Burton were His or Her Britannic Majesty's consuls in Brazil to reconcile ourselves to this arid kind of bureaucracy, although it seems that no man of dispatches appointed as consul of his country anywhere in the world has ever become noted for his official correspondence or reports.

Some consuls fully integrated into the consular routine did become known for their official reports, such as Sir Roger Casement, who was HBM Consul in Rio at the beginning of this century and left us documents on the situation of the Indian rubber-tappers in the Amazon that are of sociological value and not merely bureaucratic interest.

But one can also see that even Sir Roger, who was so expressive in the way he drafted his correspondence and reports, was not purely a consular official. Within the apparently orthodox bureaucrat lay a heretic. A terrible revolutionary. And the cause that the revolutionary served was precisely that of the enemies of His Britannic Majesty: the Irish republicans, who were allies of the Germans in the 1914-1918 war. Casement was eventually punished by British justice. And punished with a death sentence: a surprising fate for a consul, who almost always comes across as an inoffensive, peace-loving bourgeois, when inside him there may be a spy in the service of his own government's enemies, as in Sir Roger's case; or, at least, a man eager for worldly glory or ostentation like Sir James Gambier, HBM consul in Rio de Janeiro at the time of Dom João VI, about whom Strangford

[448] Word used by Freyre in English (Translator).

complained in a dispatch to Canning, the British Foreign Minister at the time, saying that the consul was trying to live the life of an ambassador or diplomat.

It is to HBM consuls in Brazil – middle-class bureaucrats who were not always inoffensive or peace-loving, even when they were staunch servants of the Crown and orthodox Anglicans – that we owe a great deal of interesting information on this country, scattered throughout a vast amount of official correspondence, first with the captains-general and later with the provincial presidents. It is also scattered throughout general or specialist reports, some of which, despite their arid appearance, surprise the curious reader with the richness of the documentation they contain and the sometimes dramatic human interest that gives life to this documentation. Since we have to content ourselves with those copies of dispatches sent by British consuls to Brazilian authorities that a layperson can still find, examine or consult in our provincial archives, why should we think about extraordinary papers written by consuls? Well, some of the consuls posted to Bahia and Pernambuco must have sent their secret or confidential little reports to Rio de Janeiro, if not to London. But these secrets must have been savoured only by the eyes of Britons, and of Britons high up in the consular or diplomatic service – the bishops or canons of the Foreign Office, so to speak, in charge not just of commercial but of political relations with what were for a long time Britain's semi-colonies in South America. We must content ourselves with the trivial; or with the occasional bonus of noble dispatches from consuls who, as *chargés d'affaires*, sometimes stood in for ministers or ambassadors; one such was Chamberlain, who more than once came to terms with José Bonifácio[449] on the question of the slave trade, a topic closely linked to the recognition of Brazilian independence.

First of all, we should establish the nature of those trivial dispatches. They are not exactly diplomatic correspondence of the kind centred on Rio de Janeiro, which was the royal court of Dom João VI and then the emperors – correspondence from which Professor C. K. Webster of the University of London extracted substantial material for his recent work *Britain and the Independence of Latin America (1812-1830)*,[450] and which is calling out for someone like Alberto Rangel to gather from it all the indiscretions or gossip of particular interest to Brazil. The consuls'

[449] José Bonifácio de Andrada e Silva (1763-1838) held a position equivalent to prime minister in Brazil in 1822-23, after D. João VI had returned to Portugal, and to a great extent engineered Brazilian independence in 1822. He later became guardian of the five-year-old future Pedro II on the abdication of his father Dom Pedro I in 1831.

[450] C. K. Webster, *Britain and the Independence of Latin America (1812-1830), Selected Documents from the Foreign Office Archives*, London, 1938.

correspondence consists instead of administrative and commercial papers, which now and again take on a political slant. Much less noble, therefore, than the papers sent from the capital of the Kingdom, later the Empire, of Brazil, which referred to mainly political matters. But since the English were in Pernambuco and Bahia from the outset, setting up warehouses, shops and workshops in these two main cities of northern Brazil as soon as the country's ports were opened up to foreign trade in general, and English trade in particular – because English trade enjoyed the benefits of its very special status for several years, as everyone knows – the surviving volumes of the copies of correspondence between the governors and HBM consuls in these two old cities give us glimpses of significant aspects of those early relations of the commercially and technically most advanced country in Europe with a Brazil that lay almost orientally stagnant in its culture of European origin.

Aspects that we would be unlikely to find captured in strictly diplomatic communications. Almost always concerned with politically important matters, diplomatic correspondence rarely descends to the trifling details of relations between the peoples, as consular dispatches do: seen from the viewpoint of a century later, those trifling details sometimes take on greater human meaning than grandiose episodes.

The correspondence of European diplomats in Brazil – their reports or communiqués to their respective governments – has been lauded by such notable historians as Oliveira Lima and Alberto Rangel, who have already brought those documents to the notice of Brazilian scholars. The late Alberto Rangel, in particular, extracted many points of interest to Brazil from old diplomatic papers stored in European archives. Some years ago, that eminent researcher enriched the *Documentos Brasileiros* collection with a volume of invaluable comments on Brazilian society during the Regency and Empire by French ministers and *chargés d'affaires* in Rio de Janeiro, which he gathered from the Quai d'Orsay Archive.[451] He did not forget to include in his preface the now classic phrase by Froissart on ambassadors: '*espions sûrs et honorables*'.[452] Which to some degree extends to consuls – spies of commercial life, at least.

The correspondence of provincial governors with English consuls during the Kingdom of Brazil and the first phase of the Empire of Brazil – sometimes with copies of dispatches from the consuls to the governors – that I have been able to examine does not, I repeat, have the same dramatic interest as diplomatic papers and does not offer the same precious material

[451] Alberto Rangel, *No rolar do tempo (Opiniões e testemunhos respigados no arquivo do Orsay – Paris)*, Rio de Janeiro, 1937.
[452] 'sure and honourable spies' (Translator).

for the biographies of outstanding figures from that period in Brazilian life as the correspondence between foreign diplomats and the great men of the Empire. Its value, interest and utility is for those who are preferably looking through old papers to find a document that will clarify or illustrate the social process rather than the exceptional occurrence, although it is not always possible to prise the two apart without damaging the vitality that lies in the whole.

Diplomats in the strict sense of the word generally only dealt with noble or distinguished issues, which are almost always so-called 'one-off' facts or occurrences. For their part, consuls mainly record recurrences – repeated events – in their reports. For the scholar of social processes illustrated by the relations between different peoples or cultures – accommodation, subordination, assimilation, etc. – it is in the recurrences that the illustrative material of greatest value is to be found, and not in what seem to be one-off occurrences, however sensational or important they are or appear to be from a strictly political point of view. It would never occur to a British ambassador in Brazil to record the decline in imports of English porter or ale,[453] outsold by lighter German lager that was better adapted to the tropical climate. That decline was, however, noted by the consuls in their reports. A minor, unimportant point at first. Repeated, it becomes sociologically significant. One of the sociological interpretations of this particular recurrence relates to the Anglomania of Brazilians – it was not so extreme that Brazilians preferred the heavy beer of the English to the light beer of the Germans, which was more suited to the palate of the people and the climate of this country. Another interpretation: the relations between the two countries, which for many years had been marked by the subordination of the Brazilians to the British, changed, with the triumphal appearance of other economic imperialisms that rivalled the British in their South American ambitions, from relations of subordination to relations of accommodation. The British could no longer imperially impose their tastes in goods on the Brazilians, but now had to compromise with Brazilian tastes to some extent and accommodate their products to the conditions of life in Brazil. The travelling salesman, charged with enquiring about his customers' tastes or preferences and satisfying them as much as possible, became an important figure in the relations between the two peoples; while the functions of British consuls in Brazil became less imperious than they had been during the early decades of the Brazilian Empire, and came to resemble somewhat those of the travelling salesmen – enquiring, obsequious and accommodating – given the new environment of accommodation that governed the relations of European manufacturers with their South American consumers; and given the new situation – of

[453] Words used by Freyre in English (Translator).

competition between equally powerful imperialisms – that superseded the former one: that of the days when British ministers and consuls in Brazil represented the only imperialism of which Brazilians were truly aware.

Therefore, writing at the beginning of the twentieth century, Koebel wanted British candidates to the diplomatic service – and with even more reason the consular service – in South America to familiarize themselves with the conditions under which their countrymen did business with South Americans. Any such candidate should be prepared for hard work 'in his shirt-sleeves'; apart from which, he should be something of a detective.[454] That is, he should know how to enquire, probe, find out, pry and anticipate, and not just solemnly sign bureaucratic papers or appear at official events in frock coat and top hat, or white dolman and pith helmet. And not just know how to descend the steps of imperial consulates to ostentatiously protect subjects of the British Crown whose lives were in danger or to intervene in the illicit slave trade, which, as we know, was for many years a cause of friction and even conflict between British imperialism and the Brazilian Empire.

In this theatrical clash with the Brazilian Empire and with Dom João VI's government, British imperialism seemed to play the part of the most lofty Christian civilization horrified at the exploitation of black people by their white brothers; whereas Brazil represented the sordid economic interests of the last white exploiters of their black brothers in the Americas. One HBM consul, however, Richard Burton, who had had close contact with slavocratic Brazil, came to the following conclusion in 1868:

> ...the Brazilian negro need not envy the starving liberty of the poor in most parts of the civilized world.[455]

And an English historian who tends to praise rather than criticize his people reports the following scandalous episode that happened in Rio de Janeiro in 1853 – in the middle, therefore, of the conflict between British imperialism and the Brazilian Empire – which reveals that the British were not always the masters of Christianity or civilization and the Brazilians constantly the erring disciples. In that year, the director for the month of the Rio de Janeiro commercial exchange, who was British, scandalized the people of the city by expelling a black Brazilian from the building. That black Brazilian happened to be none other than a seaman who had heroically risked his own life to save the lives of passengers when a steamship of the Brazilian Steam Packet Company went down. He had

[454] Koebel, *British Exploits in South America*, p. 544.

[455] Burton, *Explorations of the Highlands of the Brazil*, I, p. 271.

just been received by the emperor, who had not hesitated to shake his heroic hand. But an English merchant ejected him from the commercial exchange for being black.[456] Simply for being black.

Contrasts such as this between the official attitude of HBM government and the personal one of Britons regarding not only the issue of slavery but that of the relations between whites and blacks reinforced the reputation that the British gained in Brazil, not always fairly but often deservedly, of being hypocritical, a reputation that marks the British among both their neighbours and distant peoples. Punctual, certainly, like no one else; and true to their word. But also hypocritical. The supposed champions of the redemption of Africans have not always shown themselves capable of treating them with the humanity or human sympathy that many foreign observers, including Britons, glimpsed in the relations of masters with their slaves and of whites with blacks in Brazil.

Even so, some of the best evidence for facts as honourable for most Brazilians as they are dishonourable for many Britons comes not only from private observers – British scientists, missionaries and merchants – but from His or Her Britannic Majesty's consuls or official observers. In alluding to such evidence, I refer to the part of the *British and Foreign State Papers* relating to Brazil, a valuable source of information on the slavocratic regime in our country, in which the English do not hesitate to officially compare the Brazilian regime with that of the British colonies, only to conclude that, in contrast to the slaves on plantations in the West Indies, those in Brazil were treated in a patriarchal manner by the Brazilians.[457]

Similar evidence in favour of the slave regime in Brazil compared with the system that predominated in British colonies is given with greater emphasis in reports by parliamentary committees, especially the Select Committee on Sugar and Coffee Planting, 1847-1848;[458] and the fact is that HBM consuls seem to have played a major role in helping British politicians and the general public understand the conditions of labour in Brazil, which were patriarchal rather than characterized by crude exploitation of blacks by their masters. They and other British official observers were to do the same with regard to the problem of replacing black workers with white settlers in Brazil: they were to play an important role by submitting objective, well-documented reports that established the true situation, which differed from both the exaggerated version of Brazilian propagandists and the deformed version of European anti-propagandists. The *Reports Respecting the Condition of British Emigrants in Brazil*, a model

[456] Koebel, *British Exploits in South America*, p. 370.
[457] *British and Foreign State Papers*, London, XXXII, p. 126.
[458] *Parliamentary Papers*, London, vol. 23.

of precision and objectivity, came out in London in 1873.

The English had been studying the subject of working conditions in slavocratic Brazil for many years. As well as the position of the English with regard to those conditions. And the moral environment created in Brazil by the dominance of the slaveholding system. The result of those enquiries was the above-mentioned *Reports*, a synthesis of somewhat monumental proportions in the genre of bureaucratic literature, but they were preceded by works such as that by Robert Walsh, the first chaplain to the British legation in Rio, who in his own way was a bureaucrat himself: a employee of the Crown and not just a minister of God.

Although the Reverend Walsh, who was in Brazil at the beginning of the nineteenth century, points out a number of cases of cruelty by Brazilian slaveholders towards their Africans or Afro-descendants, he does not absolve his own countrymen. Of all the incidents he observed in Rio de Janeiro, where he was a kind of ecclesiastical *attaché* to the British legation, none seems to have aroused greater indignation in him than having seen a pretty, fair-haired boy with blue eyes and very pale skin playing in the garden of a house on the road to Tijuca with some black children of his age. Walsh asked the owner of the house whether that angelic-looking child was his son. The owner of the house replied that he was not; he was his slave. As for the fair little slave's father, he was an Englishman, a 'mister', perhaps an Anglican, whose full name was mentioned to Walsh. The fair little slave was not just an angel: he was also an Angle. An Angle through his father.

'Shocked and incredulous'[459] to hear that, Walsh then learnt further, equally horrific information about his countryman: he used to sell his 'white' children together with their mothers! That fair-haired child on the road to Tijuca was not the only case of an 'English boy' who was a slave in Brazil through the fault or depravity of his parents. Technically, a consul or an *attaché* to the British legation in Rio de Janeiro had nothing to do with such cases, but they could not fail to affect someone like the Reverend Walsh, a minister of God and not merely a British government employee. Someone who had also seen a desire for liberty in black slaves who had no English blood at all: 'The yearning after liberty is the strongest feeling of a negro's mind.'[460]

The system of slavery clearly degraded the best feelings of slave owners: hence the case of that Englishman, who in England would perhaps never have stopped being a good Christian father, a good Anglican or a good Presbyterian. But abroad, and in contact with slavery, he sold his own

[459] Walsh, *Notices of Brazil*, II, p. 194.

[460] *Ibid.*, II, p. 193.

children and their mothers. And he sold them, Walsh mused, 'with as little compunction as he would a sow and her litter of pigs'.[461]

That case of the Englishman corrupted by being a slaveholder is one of many that can serve to illustrate the tendency of all men, when displaced from their usual conditions or situations – even the British, who seem to remain particularly attached to their principles and habits when they are abroad – to become accommodated to new situations, such as owning slaves, by becoming almost different people in such situations, and even becoming more extreme than individuals already habituated to those situations in performing acts like those that Walsh classed as 'incredible'. HBM consuls in Brazil and elsewhere must have seen thousands of examples of this tendency among the English people registered in their books; and they must have noticed traces of the influence of the exotic environment in themselves and their own feelings, although it should be noted that a nineteenth-century British consul, more than any ordinary Briton or a consul of any other nation, almost always lived abroad within an imperial glass case, with the royal coat of arms and standard reminding him all the time of his extraordinary or extraterritorial condition.

That does not mean that they were all-powerful or that all Brazilians and Portuguese bowed to their will, even in those days when Brazil was a virtual colony of Great Britain. Not even the most arrogant ministers of His or Her Britannic Majesty in Rio, like Mr Christie, attained that status. In the early years of the nineteenth century, some black men murdered an English sailor in Botafogo Bay and then threw his body overboard. The Englishman's wife witnessed the crime, and HBM consul took immediate steps to have the murderers punished. The black men were arrested. But a year after the crime, the Brazilian judge called on the consul to produce his countryman's body as indispensable evidence of the crime. It was impossible to produce that evidence – even for a consul of the British Crown, ostensibly a more powerful mistress of the waters than Iemanjá.[462] But Iemanjá, protector of Africans, won the contest by having the owner of one of the black men – 'a stout athletic man, and so a valuable slave' – protect his property by slipping the judge 500 mil-réis to put an end to the process.[463]

In this case, HBM consul had done his duty and was within his rights to protect the interests of a British subject: the widow of the Englishman murdered by the black men. But since the early years of the nineteenth century, that is, since British consuls began acting in the Kingdom of

[461] *Ibid.*, II, p. 195.

[462] The Afro-Brazilian *orixá* (deity or spirit) of the sea (Translator).

[463] Walsh, *Notices of Brazil*, II, p. 199.

Brazil, some of them had gone too far and abused their authority by trying to intervene, or sometimes actually intervening, in matters outside their jurisdiction. Hence the clashes or conflicts that certain consuls had with Portuguese authorities in Brazil. With the Count of Arcos, captain-general of Bahia, for example. And, as we shall see later, also with Caetano Pinto de Miranda Montenegro and Luís do Rego Barreto, two other captains-general. But especially with Brazilian authorities, after independence.

In 1812, having received a complaint from HBM consul in Salvador regarding 'a so-called new Duty' being imposed in the Bahian customs house 'on the provisions and spares of British ships', the count did not hesitate to point out in a dispatch to the consul, dated 2 January, that he had it on record

> in all truth that the Customs Houses of England did not deliver free of Duties to the Portuguese those provisions and Goods that they stated were for the personal use of their households, and families...[464]

He thus quashed one complaint with another. And almost three years later, in a dispatch of 9 December 1814 responding to a note from the British consul regarding an American corsair, the Count of Arcos did not hesitate to tell him quite plainly that it was not the British consul's business to have knowledge of what was contained in the 'very revealing observations of that note of Your Lordship',[465] that is, the note the consul had sent to the governor.

This firm and sometimes rather ironic way for a governor to stand up to the imperial arrogance of certain British consuls was to become accentuated by the authorities of the Empire of Brazil, after the declaration of independence, even though British politicians like Canning had in fact been highly enthusiastic and supportive of Brazilian independence. Hence dispatches like those exchanged in 1827 between HBM consul in Pernambuco and the president of the province. Until then, the gaoler in Recife would receive sailors arrested merely on the consul's orders. In a dispatch of 10 February 1827 from the vice-consul John James Smith to the provincial president José Carlos Mayrink da Silva Ferrão, the representative of His Britannic Majesty protested that his authority was being diminished by the gaoler's demand that he would only receive sailors arrested on the president's orders. But he ended up requesting – merely requesting – His

[464] Manuscript (*Correspondência da Corte, No 25*) in the Manuscripts Section of the Pernambuco State Library.

[465] Manuscript (*Correspondência da Corte*) in the Manuscripts Section of the Pernambuco State Library.

Excellency to give orders to the gaoler to 'receive and keep in custody' any British sailor sent to him by a 'competent authority'.[466]

Another British consul in Recife, Mr John Parkinson, had his authority diminished even more severely in 1822, though unjustly so. That is what he reports in a dispatch dated 1 March that year, addressed to the 'President and other members of the Provisional Government Junta':

> ... yesterday [the consul writes] a man accompanied by a corporal appeared at his house, claiming to have the authority to examine and verify the contents of two hogsheads of white wine, which had been purchased that day at the Customs warehouse in this City. The pretext of this examination was that said hogsheads might contain spirits. Since the undersigned was not at home at that time, his servant did not feel authorized to resist the power that those men had usurped and therefore the casks were tasted by them, and they found that they contained white wine. Having made this investigation the two men asked for a drink and left... Although the undersigned is persuaded that such an outrageous measure that is at the same time so greatly in violation of the existing Treaty between the two Nations could not be committed with the consent of any part of this Government, he finds himself obliged, both to the Position that he has the honour of filling and to preserve his rights and privileges and to maintain an express article of the above-mentioned Treaty, to expound the case to Your Excellencies fully trusting that an immediate enquiry will be set up and the perpetrators punished.[467]

In the days of Dom João VI and the Count of Linhares, the governor might well have been dismissed for such an affront to a British consul, even if perpetrated by impostors and not by government agents. This, in 1822, was a new era. American power was emerging besides the British. And French imperialism was again confronting the British, giving Brazilians the impression that the world was not simply the property of Great Britain.

On 27 August 1830, Consul Parkinson's successor in Pernambuco, Mr Henry Cowper, did not behave like a conqueror in an occupied land when marking the death of His Majesty King George IV, but had the goodness to inform the president of the province that

> His Britannic Majesty's Frigate, the *Druid*, anchored at Lamarão all morning will at daybreak raise the Flag to half-mast and

[466] *Consuls' Correspondence*, Manuscripts Section of the Pernambuco State Library.
[467] *Ibid.*

> immediately after eleven o'clock will fire fifty guns at one-minute intervals in witness of the grievous event that afflicts the British Nation due to the death on 26 June last of HM King George IV of Glorious Memory.[468]

We were no longer in the days of Sidney Smith and the effrontery of the *Agamemnon*.

Expressive of the new relations of mutual respect between the British and Brazilian governments, which gradually took shape with Brazil's consolidation as a politically independent empire, is the dispatch of 25 October 1833 sent to HBM consul in Bahia by the president of the province of Bahia, Joaquim José Pinheiro de Vasconcellos, sending him

> the documents you require in your Dispatch of 20th inst. relating to the conduct of the Justice of the Peace of Conceição da Praia against the British Merchant James Buckanan; [but he concludes haughtily:] This manner of conduct is in accordance with the Laws, which I am bound to enforce not as Your Lordship wishes but as they provide. May God keep Your Lordship.[469]

In a dispatch of 8 August, Parkinson had protested that his countryman had been arrested 'without an arrest warrant being approved or signed by the Judge Conservator...', who was the only 'legal authority' indicated in Article 6 of the treaty of 17 August 1827. According to the decree of 23 October 1667 – Parkinson maintained, basing his argument on antediluvian laws – the judge conservator was 'the only authority with the power to arrest British subjects except in cases of *flagrante delicto*'.

Consul Parkinson fought like a lion in Bahia to uphold the authority of the judge conservator of the English. He wrote to the president of the province on 31 July 1832:

> I am persuaded that Your Excellency has not the slightest desire knowingly to use that official influence to invade or curtail the privileges guaranteed to His Britannic Majesty's subjects by Article 6 of the Treaty of 17 August 1827, which states that the Constitution of the Empire having abolished all special jurisdictions it is agreed that the place of the Judge Conservator of the English Nation shall subsist only until such time as some satisfactory replacement for that jurisdiction is established that may likewise assure protection

468 *Consuls' Correspondence*, Manuscripts Section of the Pernambuco State Library.

469 Manuscript in the Manuscripts Section of the Bahia State Public Archive.

> for the persons and property of HBM subjects. [He concluded rather threateningly:] I do this with every respect for Your Excellency and with the conviction that the discussion has reached a point at which I must interrupt it and refer the whole question to higher powers.

On 22 September 1832, Parkinson returned to the subject in relation to the arrest of some Irish subjects of His Britannic Majesty:

> Having heard that three British subjects were detained in the prison for criminals of the worst kind, that they were in heavy irons and compelled to arduous daily labours, it was my duty to go to the Galé, or Shipyard prison, and there I verified that they are three Irishmen by the names of Ricardo Dalton, John Cavench and Patrick Lee, belonging to the unfortunate class of the so-called 'Irish Settlers', who are currently in the situation described. On enquiring into the cause of their detention I was informed that about three weeks ago they were arrested by the Municipal Guard for sleeping in the street and, having been brought before the Justice of the Peace of Conceição da Praia he sentenced them to six months' imprisonment with forced public labour in irons.

HBM consul protested 'in the name of justice' against the sentence handed down by the justice of the peace, and also protested against 'the deplorable state of hunger and misery of those sentenced without trial' and against the fact that the judge conservator had not been consulted.

On 17 October 1832 a somewhat euphoric dispatch from Parkinson to the president of the province informed him of the election of the new judge conservator, which had taken place at a public meeting of the English merchants in the consulate. 'Magistrate Thomas Xavier Garcia d'Almeida' had been 'unanimously elected to replace Mr Ignacio Accioli de Vasconcellos, currently President of Alagoas'. The euphoria of the consul who fought hardest for the authority of the judge conservator of the English not to be diminished was short lived:

> It is my sad duty to inform Your Excellency that on the night of 22nd inst. Mr Ricardo Micholson, a British Merchant, residing on his farm on the island of Boa Vista in the neighbourhood of this city, was robbed and barbarously killed by a gang of murderers. The crime was perpetrated and accompanied by circumstances of unbridled barbarity in his dwelling and within the family of the unfortunate man, but his wife and children escaped.

That is from another dispatch from Parkinson to the president of Bahia, on 25 January 1833. Evidently, crimes of that magnitude would not occur if Brazilian justice were equal to that of England. In a dispatch of 1 August 1833 Parkinson reappears, claiming compensation of £400 for

> Charles ['Carlos'] Bill, doctor (medical officer) of HBM Packet *Lady Mary Pelham*, who, together with four sailors and one passenger, was detained by the Justice of the Peace of São Pedro on 13-11-1832; they were thrown into a common prison and missed their ship, which had to sail for Rio.

Just because of the consul's intervention, the case was passed to the judge conservator – the 'true channel' – and 'the persecuted people were set free'. A real victory that Parkinson had won for his holy cause: the judge conservator of the English.

British consuls stood up to Brazilian authorities on a number of occasions, not out of pure imperial arrogance but in defence of what seemed to them as sacred as a life itself: the rights of a British subject. Such is the case of the British consul in Pernambuco who, in a dispatch dated 28 January 1834, sent the vice-president of the province

> some Documents under the Signature and Seal of the undersigned and his predecessor by which Your Excellency will see that João Zurich is a subject of His Majesty and as such enjoys all the privileges laid down in Article 6 of the Treaty of Commerce of 17 August 1827. Under said article Your Excellency will know that no subject of HBM may be arrested without charge and without a warrant signed by the legal Authority except in cases of *flagrante delicto* and that he shall be free of any restraint in all cases in which the law allows for bail. The undersigned is also honoured to inform Your Excellency that according to the Instructions of his Government the subjects of the Ionian States are in all respects protected as British Subjects. And as the said João Zurich was yesterday arrested without charge, which is a clear Infringement of Article 6 of the aforementioned Treaty of Commerce, the undersigned hopes that Your Excellency will do him the justice of ordering that he be immediately released, to remain ready to answer any accusation made against him before the competent Court.[470]

[470] *Consuls' Correspondence*, Manuscripts Section of the Pernambuco State Library.

That lesson in law was given by Mr Henry Cowper to the then vice-president of the province, Manoel de Carvalho Paes d'Andrade. And as the vice-president only published part of his correspondence with the British consul, the latter again stood up indignantly to ask His Excellency to do him 'the justice of divulging everything to the Public and through the Press'. Even so, João Zurich remained under arrest. Duly so, according to the provincial government. Unduly, according to HBM consul, who on 17 May addressed vice-president Paes d'Andrade again, this time not to deal with the now irritating Zurich case, but simply to bid His Excellency farewell. He did so in an extremely courteous dispatch, full of 'ingenuous [*sic*] sentiments for the civil manner in which' he had always been treated by the Brazilian authorities. And Mr Cowper concluded, perhaps with a touch of irony:

> I would be failing in my duties of Gratitude and of that due to Justice and Truth if I were not also to add to these sentiments a confession of the constant conviction that I have long held that the Brazilian People has to an eminent degree all those qualities that form the [illegible] of Social Life and of those Elements that, well governed, form the Basis of Independence and National Prosperity.[471]

Perhaps those words 'well governed' contain a barbed remark against bad governors of the Brazilian people like Paes d'Andrade – who were capable of keeping a British subject in prison without charge. In any case, on returning to England with his family – his wife, two children and two servants – on board the English brig *Rochelle*, Mr Henry Cowper did not neglect to refer the case of João Zurich to his country's minister. And on 4 August 1834 the vice-consul wrote to Manoel de Carvalho Paes d'Andrade informing him that he had received

> a dispatch from the His Britannic Majesty's Minister at the Court of Rio de Janeiro demanding to know the measures that the government of this Province has taken regarding João Zurich, a subject of HBM.[472]

Poor João Zurich, 'born on the island of Cepahlonia in the Ionian States and a subject of HBM', was to have a sad end in Brazil. After causing a veritable storm with his imprisonment – it was not confined to the provincial teacups but reached the capital of the Empire and maybe even London – he was murdered in Olinda on 3 January 1836, 'near the

[471] *Ibid.*
[472] *Ibid.*

Convent of São Bento'. Who might this foreigner, João Zurich, have been, to have incited the hatred against him that he did: imprisonment, persecution and eventually his murder in Olinda, 'near the Convent of São Bento'? He must have had at least one good side to him: he treated his slaves well. For it transpires from a dispatch of 11 January 1836, in which HBM consul informs the government of the Province of

> this fatal catastrophe violating the Laws of this Country which must be enforced on similar occasions, [that] the dead man's slave had been wounded while defending his master's life and is presently imprisoned in Olinda...[473]

João Zurich may have been a ne'er-do-well, unworthy of the protection of the British Crown. But, despite that, he was a man who inspired that kind of dedication in his slaves.

These scraps of correspondence show that in 1834 Great Britain took pains, through the voice of one of her consuls, to protect and uphold the rights of a Greek who was a British subject. And the principle that Consul Cowper maintained in his correspondence with Vice-President Paes d'Andrade seems to have been correct. Correct both legally and ethically. That does not always seem to have been the case with other consuls in their give-and-take with Brazilian authorities.

One of the most common reasons for such friction was the smuggling of African slaves, for which HBM consuls were ordered by their government to keep their eyes wide open after the treaty between Great Britain and Brazil to stop slave trafficking. For years, British consuls in Brazil were constantly writing to the provincial presidents to inform or warn them of smuggled slaves or of ships suspected of taking part in the dirty but profitable trade. The presidents – many of whom apparently found it in their interests to turn a blind eye to such smuggling, since that illicit and unlawful trade was considered by pragmatic men at the time, including statesmen, to be vital for the Brazilian economy – sometimes dismissed their warnings as mere rumours. When in 1833 the British consul in Bahia brought it to the attention of President Pinheiro de Vasconcellos that news was circulating of smuggled slaves brought in by the Portuguese schooner-brig *Atrevido*, the president replied, somewhat annoyed, that he had demanded 'precise information from the Customs Inspector', who had assured him that 'the most scrupulous Examinations were carried out on each Vessel in accordance with the existing Legislation in that respect' and that they had found 'no reason to suspect that the treaty had been infringed'. The

[473] *Ibid.*

president concluded by asking the consul for 'more exact news on this subject', and then quickly made their correspondence public.

That irritated HBM consul. He wrote a sharp dispatch to the provincial president on 23 December 1833 complaining that His Excellency had

> violated the solemn promise ... not to publish the outcome of his investigations into the landing of new Slaves...[474]

The president quickly replied to his dispatch, explaining that he believed that he had promised secrecy only regarding the person who had given the consul the information,

> so that he would not be troubled by the perpetrators of the crime. I feel rather pained, both as a Public Servant and as a mere citizen, to be regarded by the Consul as having breached a confidence and, what is worse, a promise! But the English Consul should believe me and restore to me that good opinion that in justice I deserve.[475]

In 1831, when a foreign vessel – the French schooner *Clementina* – was seized in the port of Goiana by the justice of the peace of Taquara with a cargo of contraband new slaves, the president of the province communicated the episode to Minister Carneiro de Campos 'to be presented to HM the Emperor' in a dispatch of 26 January, confirmed by one of 28 February of that year. In the second dispatch he informed the minister: 'The English Consul notified me of this transaction in the manner described in copy No 2, to which I replied as in copy No 3...'[476] Which shows that HBM consuls were keeping watchful and alert for slave smuggling.

Papers found on the French schooner showed that she had left Saint-Pierre in Martinique to conduct coastal trade. But the ship's course, which the provincial government had had examined at the naval inspectorate, showed that nothing had forced her to come to the Brazilian coast, as all the winds were against that. The crew were detained and held in custody on board the barquentine *Vinte e Nove de Agosto*. As for the slaves, since they had begun to die

> through lack of care and food, the Public Treasury Committee ordered the Inspector of the Navy to victual them through that Office until such time as some Private Individual might take charge of

[474] Manuscript in the Manuscripts Section of Bahia State Public Archive.

[475] *Ibid.*

[476] *Consuls' Correspondence*, Manuscripts Section of the Pernambuco State Library.

their keep and expenses, to be paid eventually by whoever is legally liable.[477]

It was not only the ordinary consuls in Bahia and Pernambuco who remained vigilant against the illegal trade in black slaves, but also the consul-general himself, His Britannic Majesty's *chargé d'affaires* in Rio de Janeiro. In 1816 the captain-general of the captaincy of Pernambuco received a dispatch from the Marquis of Aguiar showing how far such vigilance went. In the dispatch, the marquis states that that consul-general and *chargé d'affaires* had informed him in an official note that

> a reliable person who had recently come from Pernambuco had assured him that he had seen a good sailing Vessel in that Port ready to depart for the Coast of Africa with the intention of conducting the Trade in Slaves on the part of that Continent situated above the Equinoctial Line, where it is prohibited, and also that two other Ships had already departed with the same design, one of them having arrived back successful in her criminal enterprise. Any My Lord His Majesty the King wishes Your Lordship to inform with all haste and with precise [illegible] what there is on this subject. May God keep Your Lordship. Palace of Rio de Janeiro, 3 April 1816.[478]

The English kept up intense action against the unlawful trade in slaves from Africa to Brazil throughout the first half of the nineteenth century. From 1821 to 1829 alone, British cruisers along the coast of Africa apprehended the following Brazilian vessels suspected of engaging in the illicit trade in slaves: the brig *Gavião*, belonging to Elias Coelho Cintra; the brig *Conde de Villa-Flor*, belonging to Manoel Antônio da Silva Brandão, from Pará; the smack *Esperança Feliz*, belonging to Manoel José Freire de Carvalho, from Bahia; the brig *Dez de Fevereiro*, belonging to Maria Vitória Carolina de Cerqueira, from Bahia ('had no slaves on board'); the schooner *Novo Forte*, belonging to Venceslau Miguel de Almeida, from Bahia ('bad catch'); the brig *Cerqueira*, belonging to José de Cerqueira Lima, from Bahia; the smack *Crioula*, belonging to Antônio Pedroso de Albuquerque and Vicente de Paula, from Bahia ('no slaves', 'released by the captain with no formality at all'); the smack *Diana*, belonging to Joaquim Carvalho da Fonseca, from Bahia; the brig *Activo*, belonging to Francisco Antônio de Oliveira, from Pernambuco ('bad catch'); the brig *Perpetuo Defensor*, belonging to João Alexandre de Silva Pinto, from Rio de Janeiro ('bad catch'); the galley *São Benedicto*, belonging to Joaquim José

[477] *Consuls' Correspondence, No 32*, Manuscripts Section of the Pernambuco State Library.

[478] *Court Correspondence*, Manuscripts Section of the Pernambuco State Library.

de Oliveira, from Bahia ('bad catch'); the schooner *Eclipse*, belonging to Antônio de Pádua da Cunha Pimentel, from Bahia; the yacht *Três Amigos*, belonging to Joaquim José Teixeira, from Rio de Janeiro; the brig *Venturoso*, belonging to Antônio Pedroso de Albuquerque and João Alexandre da Silva Porto, from Bahia; the schooner *Tentadora*, belonging to Luiz Antônio do Passo, from Bahia; the schooner *Carlota*, belonging to José de Cerqueira Lima, from Bahia; the brigantine *Providencia*, belonging to Joaquim José de Oliveira, from Bahia; the schooner *Independencia*, belonging to José de Cerqueira Lima, from Bahia; the brig *Trajano*, belonging to José Alexandre da Cruz Rios, from Bahia; the schooner *Conceição*, belonging to Francisco Mamede de Almeida, from Pernambuco; the brig *Bahia*, belonging to José de Cerqueira Lima, from Bahia; the schooner *Coproba*, belonging to Francisco Pinto de Luna, from Bahia; the smack *São João Voador*, belonging to João José de Sampaio, José João da Cunha and Antônio Dias Coelho, from Bahia ('bad catch'); the schooner *Vencedora*, belonging to Antônio de Pádua da Cunha Pimentel, from Bahia ('bad catch'); the schooner *Terceira Rosalia*, belonging to Manoel Franco Moreira, from Bahia; the schooner *Esperança*, belonging to José Alexandre da Cruz Rios, from Bahia; the schooner-brig *Voador*, belonging to Geraldo José da Cunha e Simão, from Rio de Janeiro; the brig *Andorinha*, belonging to Joaquim José de Oliveira, from Bahia; the schooner *Estrela do Mar*, belonging to Joaquim Mattos Costa, from Rio de Janeiro; the schooner *Sociedade*, belonging to João Pereira de Araújo França, from Bahia; and the schooner *Ismenia*, belonging to Manoel Ribeiro Guimarães, from Rio de Janeiro.[479]

The large number of 'good catches' among the Brazilian ships captured by British cruisers in less than ten years shows that HBM consuls' system of information on the illicit slave trade from Africa to Brazil was already at a level to be expected of a people who were to become famous for Scotland Yard and their Intelligence Service. Consuls at that time were detectives as well as prosaic bureaucrats. But police detectives, not merely commercial ones as Koebel wanted them to be.

Bahia, more than Pernambuco, seems to have been the main focus of activity of large-scale slave traders in the early nineteenth century, one of whom is claimed to be of particularly noble descent. It was therefore natural that HBM government should send its best consul-detectives to Bahia at that time – because after the middle of the century the centre for the most intense trade or contraband in slaves had shifted elsewhere: to Rio de Janeiro.

In 1830 the English consul in Salvador addressed an official note to the president of the province, drawing his attention to the arrival in the

[479] Manuscript, Documents Section, Historical Institute of Bahia.

harbour of the schooner *Baiana* 'bringing on board slaves from Kaongo[480] after a ninety-three day voyage...'. And on 17 July 1832 HBM consul wrote to the same authority with an even greater wealth of precise details to inform him, or pass on to him the report received by the consulate, that the brig *Tereza* was intending to sail for the African coast the following day under the Portuguese flag. She belonged, however, to a Brazilian: Manoel Cardoso dos Santos. And she was going to fetch African slaves to land them on the Bahian coast, as she had already done on the coast of Havana. If the government of the province had that schooner-brig unloaded forthwith, they would find, inside a crate, which was supposed to be a load of fabrics, 'the Cauldron for cooking the slaves' food and more ironware for said purpose'.[481] On 23 October of the same year, the consul-detective addressed the president of Bahia again with further information about 'the illegal trade': he had information that 'two ships that had recently arrived from the coast of Africa had successfully landed a considerable number of slaves in the vicinity of this city...'.[482] Might His Excellency be aware of such an event?

British consuls gave the provincial governments such precise descriptions or characterizations of the ships suspected of smuggling or privateering that some of those mysterious ships almost sail out of the dispatch papers into the ocean. That aspect of British consular activity in Brazil during the early decades of the nineteenth century appears somewhat romantic to our eyes. The bureaucratic papers suddenly seem to lose their dullness to gain the colour, movement and sparkle of passages from adventure stories.

> A large, 150-ton Lugger sometimes converted into an Hermaphrodite Brig with a 24 calibre piece, full of Spanish, Portuguese and French crew, and it is very likely that she recently robbed some Ships since she has many injured men on board, and many Quadrants, Sextants and Chronometers.

That is how the then vice-consul Henry Cowper, in a communication to the president of the province of Pernambuco dated 10 July 1830, 'for the Commercial intelligence of His Imperial Majesty', describes 'a Pirate ship that recently appeared on this Coast', which on 13 April that year robbed the British brig *Prompt* 'at Latitude 2° South, Longitude 27° West'.[483]

Sometimes the mysterious ships were merely English brigantines that had run out of drinking water on the voyage and put in to the Brazilian

480 *Sic*, presumably Kongo (Translator).

481 Manuscript, Manuscript Section of the Bahia State Public Archive. The historian Luís Viana Filho refers to this document in his recent work *O Negro na Bahia*, 1946.

482 Manuscript, Manuscript Section of the Bahia State Public Archive.

483 *Consuls' Correspondence*, Manuscripts Section of the Pernambuco State Library.

coast to refill their casks with fresh water. That was the case of one that appeared at about eleven o'clock on a September day in 1819 off Barra Sage, 'which lies more than twenty leagues South of this City', according to a communication from Natal addressed to Luís do Rego Barreto. When three sailors from the unknown brigantine were questioned by the governor of the captaincy, it was found that she was English, was called the *Rochdale*, had sailed from Liverpool for Pernambuco, was laden with trade goods, had a crew of nine men including the officers, had no arms at all, and was 'consigned to Mitchele'; 'after seventy-two days' voyage they had sighted the Coast of this Captaincy and, as they had only ten cartloads of Water on board, the Captain had sent the Ship's Boat ashore with three casks to fill with water'. That is what John ('João') Forsshale, first pilot of the suspect brigantine, told the governor. The seamen John Lithgow and David Peacock confirmed it.[484]

We should not forget, however, that a considerable contraband trade was carried on along the coasts of Brazil on the pretext of taking on water, by ships coming from Europe or the Orient or Africa to conduct illicit trade with Brazil. Walsh, always well informed, mentions the fact that 266 English ships, 151 American, 39 French, 14 Swedish and 35 from other nations entered Rio de Janeiro harbour in 1827,[485] and points out that the goods most imported by Brazil at the time – dried fish from Newfoundland, wheat flour almost entirely from the United States, beeswax from Africa, iron from Sweden and wine from Catalonia – included 'India goods', so that there were 'five East Indiamen trading from the harbor of Rio',[486] yet prior to 1808 no foreign ships at all were seen in the harbour. Apart from those allowed in to take on water or repair damage, 'which, under that pretext, contrived to carry on some contraband trade'.[487] Including, we may well suppose, contraband in 'India goods', which were always highly prized by Brazilians in colonial times. It is therefore impossible to calculate the volume of goods from foreign lands – including Asia – imported into Brazil in those days just from the figures for goods imported legally through the colony's customs houses. The careful watch that honest authorities kept on ships that looked like pirates was therefore well founded, even when the ships pretended to be in need of water or repairs.

That does not mean that there were no pirate ships like the one described by Vice-Consul Cowper. The smack *São João Diligente*, on its

[484] *Revista do Arquivo Público* (Pernambuco), 1st Semester 1946, p. 114.

[485] Walsh, *Notices of Brazil*, I, p. 250. Walsh also reports that 90 foreign and 760 [Freyre has '750' – Translator] Portuguese ships had unloaded at the customs house in Rio de Janeiro in 1809, and 422 foreign and 1240 Portuguese in 1810 (I, pp. 100-101).

[486] *Ibid.*, I, p. 248. See footnote 295 regarding Freyre's mistranslation of 'East Indiamen' (Translator).

[487] *Ibid.*, I, p. 100.

way from Jaraguá to Bahia laden with sugar and cotton, was captured by one off Miaé, between the Pebal and Coruripe, in September 1819. At dawn on the 4th of that month, the master of the smack sighted

> a Sail that had looked like that of a raft, which he only made out to be a Schooner when, through being becalmed, she put out her oars and came and seized him at about seven o'clock that same morning, having on the Main Masthead a Pennant with a yellow band between two white ones.[488]

Also in 1819, regular vessels were captured by 'Insurgent Corsairs', resulting in

> orders to our Minister to the United States to make the necessary Complaints, since it is reported that those Corsairs are armed and crewed by Citizens of the United States itself...[489]

That information may have come from HBM consuls in dispatches similar in tone to the one Cowper sent in 1830.

On 14 July 1831, HBM consul in Pernambuco wrote that he had the honour of communicating to His Excellency the president of the Province, 'in order to inform Brazilian Trade', that the British brig *Norma* had been attacked on 17 April by a pirate ship 'at Latitude 4° 23' North and Longitude 31° West'[490]... 'After a gallant fight that lasted two hours, the Pirate was defeated.' The *Norma* had had one man killed and one seriously injured. A description of the pirate ship that had attacked the *Norma*, '309 Tons, Captain John George Lezett, coming from Liverpool to this port', followed:

> A 120-ton Schooner, with a bow *savec* and *bolaso*,[491] copper-bottomed, painted black with a broad white stripe. It had an eighteen-calibre swivel piece and other guns, forty or fifty men, including English and Americans, but most seemed to be Brazilians or Portuguese, to all appearances a Vessel intended for Slaving, being very filthy. After the engagement it sailed towards NE Maranhão.

[488] *Revista do Arquivo Público* (Pernambuco), 1st Semester 1946, p. 264.

[489] *Ibid.*, p. 81.

[490] The Portuguese has 'Norte' ('North') (Translator).

[491] These two words may have been miscopied from the dispatch (Translator).

This document is in the manuscript collection of the Pernambuco State Public Library.

On 18 July 1832, HBM consul notified the Brazilian authorities of another mysterious ship 'that appeared off this Coast' which was 'highly suspicious in appearance and character'. On 8 July, two American merchant ships had set sail from Bahia: one, the *Eugenio*, bound for Recife, where it had already arrived; the other, a schooner on its way to Baltimore. On the 9th, some fifty miles from Bahia, the suspicious ship 'set course after the *Eugenio* and, after sailing in a direction parallel to her' about 250 yards away, without signalling to her, left the *Eugenio* and followed the schooner. According to information gathered by the consul-detective from passengers on board the *Eugenio*, the suspicious ship could be described as follows:

> Schooner Brig of about 150 Tons, apparently built in Baltimore, painted Yellow with a white stripe on either side, it had a Swivel piece and two more Guns, the Piece is easily seen because it is very high up. It has about Forty Men on board and was Flying the Spanish Flag.

This document is also in the Pernambuco State Library manuscript collection.

Sometimes, however, it was the eyes of the Brazilian authorities that, rightly or wrongly, saw something suspicious – even 'sinister motives' – about British ships, even when at anchor in some harbour. The barque *Diana* was, in fact, accused of 'sinister motives' while anchored near the Brum fortress in Recife harbour in 1832. In a dispatch of 19 June 1832 HBM consul rebutted the accusation: the barque, he could assure the president of the province, was anchored there merely 'through ignorance of the exact limits of the harbour'. Her consignees were well-known merchants: Smith & Lancaster. She would not continue her voyage until 'the question of the damage suffered by the barquentine *São Christovão*' had been resolved, says the dispatch from HBM consul to the president of the province of Pernambuco, which is kept in the manuscript collection of the State Library.

Two other English vessels can only have been considered pirates in appearance: seen through the Brazilian authorities' lenses, they gave a watchful justice of the peace the impression that they were taking part in the political struggle that split Bahia in two in 1837. In a dispatch of 12 December 1837 addressed to the vice-president of the province, which is now in the State Archive manuscript collection, Hermes Correia de Moraes, justice of the peace of the parish of Vitória, informed His Excellency that one afternoon the previous week he had observed through his spyglass that

> two sailing boats ... were coming hither from the Reconcavo and, seeing that they turned as soon as they reached the level of the batteries, I sent the whalers to apprehend them as they were becoming suspicious: they indeed approached them and, when they fired two musket shots, one of the sailing boats obeyed straight away, and as the other did not obey but rather tried to escape, thus confirming the suspicion, it gained the attention of the whalers, which boarded it and even so to take it to the harbour they found it necessary to cut the halyards of its sails. On one of the boats were '8 oxen'. [The long dispatch concludes:] The whalers finally succeeded in taking on board and bringing to my presence thirteen foreigners (leaving the boats at anchor with the oxen), who, as I saw straight away, were English Subjects, and I learnt that they had been to buy cattle for the company of the Frigate. I sent them away and told them to take the boat with the oxen; which I believe they did, because it was not in the harbour in the morning.

Even so, there were some complaints by those that considered themselves the legitimate Brazilian authorities about the attitudes or movements of English vessels. Antônio Pereira Barreto Pedroso, on board the corvette *Sete de Abril*, wrote to HBM consul on 22 December 1837 – in a dispatch now in the manuscript collection of the Bahia State Public Archive – telling him that he had been informed that British warship commanders were under instruction from HBM government

> to maintain the strictest neutrality in circumstances such as those in which this province finds itself. Since this neutrality is what the Brazilian Government also wishes to see practised, I must bring it to your attention that the protest and threat contained in your latest dispatches do not accord at all with that promised restricted neutrality, insofar as the purpose in which Your Lordship is engaged of making good the transactions undertaken with the rebels and recognition of the validity of the passports given by their leaders and of the payment of duties made to them, when they can only be validly paid to the recognized authorities established by the Imperial Government, to the point of wanting to use force to uphold said validity, visibly amounts to an offence to the Brazilian Government and assistance to the sectarians that have rebelled against said

> Government. In addition, the Government of this Country recognized by yours has the right to move public establishments to wherever it sees fit and, the Customs House and the Board of the Consulate having been moved to the Town of Itaparica, as I notified you, a measure that having been taken here had also been taken by the Imperial Government, as Your Lordship will see from the enclosed copy of the Notice, which I have just received, it is clear that Your Lordship could not recognize any other authorities employed in said establishments without breaking the bonds that link the two Governments. I consider it redundant to develop further considerations. On this occasion I again request Your Lordship to have the Warships and Merchant Ships of your Nation anchor immediately at such a distance from land that the Imperial Warships may lie between them and said land out of range of the fortresses. In giving this opportunity for Your Lordship to prove the neutrality ordered by Her Britannic Majesty's Government in that keeping your Ships close to land amounts to aid given to the enemies of the Imperial Government I address to Your Lordship the protests of my consideration and respect.

It was a case of the biter bitten:[492] British ships, which had been sworn enemies of pirate ships since the beginning of the nineteenth century, were now suspected by Brazilian imperial authorities of the dreadful sin of piracy, which they had given up back in the sixteenth century. What seems to have happened is that, when the province of Bahia split into two equally powerful halves, British trade wanted to continue as far as possible to maintain relations with both Bahias and not just with the side that considered itself the only one capable of dealing with foreigners: the legitimately imperial, legal Bahia of the Reconcavo. That was the view of the imperial government, as declared from Rio by Miguel Calmon du Pin e Almeida in a dispatch of 28 November 1837 to the president of Bahia, a dispatch that may be read in the State Archive. Since 'the Capital City of the Province' was controlled by the 'rebels', it was necessary

> to deprive them of all the means that might enable them to persist in the revolt. The most important of the resources that must be cut off from them is the Collection of Public Revenue and Customs Duties, revenue that may in fact be received outside the City, as was done to a small extent during the war of Independence. When, therefore, Your Excellency considers the time to be right for such a measure,

[492] The Portuguese saying '*o feitiço a cair sobre o feiticeiro*' translates literally as 'the spell falling on the wizard' (Translator).

> the Acting Regent on Behalf of the Emperor authorizes you to set up Customs and Consulate Commissions to collect Import and Export duties, according to the inspection and accountancy rules laid down in the respective Regulations. Furthermore the Government deems it highly appropriate for Your Excellency to make it known to the inhabitants of said City that the Administration will take no account of taxes of any nature that may be paid by them to the rebel authorities.

It was economic war between the two Bahias. And British trade was violently caught up in that economic war, since neither of the two Bahias was strong enough to guarantee British merchants the entirety of their interests and their profits. As observed by an English lady, the English living in Bahia were particularly fond of their businesses, their interests and the material side of life. That was in 1821. It had been the case since earlier times. They sometimes appeared to be meddling in political struggles among Brazilians, when they were really only interested in continuing to make their pots of money.

Englishmen had also been found apparently involved in political activities during the political struggles in Bahia that followed the Cry of Ipiranga[493] – for example, carrying 'Dispatches and letters from the enemies of the Portuguese Nation to others that remain in hiding within the City', according to a dispatch of 28 March 1823 from Carlos Damasceno Rozado, adjutant at the general headquarters in Bahia, to HBM vice-consul, which is now in the manuscript collection in the State Archive. That archive also contains a dispatch – or fragment of a dispatch, since the end with the date and signature is missing – from a Portuguese authority in 1822, denying the English merchants established in Bahia permission to trade with 'the insurgents of the Reconcavo'. In yet another, the Portuguese authority Ignacio Luiz Madeira de Mello addresses Mr Wm. Follet, HBM consul, on 22 May 1823 informing him that Jesuíno José Alves had been publicly and privately insulted by William Augustus ('Guilherme Augusto') Kentish, a British subject, because said Jesuíno José Alves had carried out

> an order issued by a higher authority to seize certain fabrics, [and he asks the consul] to reprimand said Guilherme Augusto Kentish for that conduct; warning him that if he reoffends he will be liable to being punished according to the Portuguese Laws to which he is subject while he resides in this country, hoping that no other English subject will be apprehended in the transgression of the established

[493] The declaration 'Independence or Death', uttered by Dom Pedro at Ipiranga, São Paulo, on 7 September 1822, taken officially to be the moment of Brazilian independence (Translator).

> orders which absolutely forbid any communication with the insurgent areas, with no permission to transport thither provisions, merchandise or drugs of any kind.

The crime of which Kentish was accused by the Portuguese authorities – who in 1823 were still established in Bahia, when almost all the rest of Brazil had already become an independent empire or nation – was that of trading unlawfully with the part of the Brazilian population that was now victorious in its revolt against the Portuguese yoke. Consequently, it is difficult to characterize it clearly as piracy, since the last Portuguese established in Brazil as masters of the colony were by then in a highly precarious situation. So much so that, on 2 May in that same year of 1823, they were forced to take the ridiculous step of seizing the chickens that were part of the cargo of the English brig that had just dropped anchor in the harbour, on the pretext that in the city of Salvador there was 'a total lack of this article for provisioning the Military Hospitals and, therefore, the sick are deprived of that food...' That transpires from a dispatch of 2 May 1823 sent to HBM consul, again by Ignacio Luiz Madeira de Mello from the general headquarters in Bahia. It seems that there was a lack or a shortage of food not only in the hospitals but also in the barracks, offices and residences of the Portuguese officials, and therefore that English brig arriving in port full of probably fat chickens would have been a godsend. The Portuguese, still the apparent masters of one or two pieces of Brazil, were in an unsustainable situation, yet they were trying to pretend they were 'legitimate' in the eyes of the English: trying to look strong, when in the capital of Bahia they were forced to seize chickens from the English to sustain themselves. In the military hospitals, at least. Perhaps nobody knew better than the English that the entire area of Bahia still dominated by the Portuguese was a military hospital writ large, in need of chicken broth and other care or support of the kind given to the seriously ill.

In Bahia, as elsewhere in Brazil, the English always excelled in their exact knowledge of the colonial or national situation. The Portuguese, and later the Brazilians, might create masterful deceptions of the 'for-English-eyes' kind,[494] but no matter how deceived the English pretended to be they always managed to sniff out the other, hidden side of things. Consuls did so because it was their job. Merchants did so for commercial interest or gain. Women, like Mrs Kindersley, did so out of feminine curiosity, which in Englishwomen sometimes results in works of genius. Captains of HBM war frigates did so for the old spirit of adventure. Scientists like Gardner did so out of so-called scientific curiosity. Clergymen like Walsh did so

[494] *Para inglês ver*, 'for English eyes' (literally, 'for an Englishman to see'), is a common expression in Brazil meaning 'just for show'.

for the pure pleasure of broadening their knowledge of human nature, a reflection and sometimes a negation, or deformation, of God's image.

We should not be surprised, therefore, that the poles flying flags of Great Britain on English houses in Bahia were not always innocent flagpoles, like those used for flying saints' standards on country people's homes or on church terraces in Brazilian cities at the time, but were lookout posts and, in particular, a means by which the English on land could communicate with the English at sea.

A dispatch to HBM consul in Bahia dated 16 July 1821, in the State Archive manuscript collection, said that the provisional junta was informed that

> many of your Nation residing in this City have poles erected on their houses with flags which they use to make certain signals to sea, which is absolutely forbidden by the laws of the Kingdom, and there is no record of it being permitted by any treaty. [The Junta made it known that] such a procedure was forbidden, expecting that Your Lordship's honour and acknowledged probity will ensure full enforcement of this provision.

And in a dispatch of 23 July that year, sent on behalf of the junta by José Lino Coutinho to Mr Wm. Pennell, HBM consul, the Portuguese authorities returned to the subject:

> The Most Excellent Provisional Junta of this Government having been made aware of your dispatch of 18th inst. regarding mine of 16th, notifying me that Your Lordship had afforded every attention to the orders issued in respect of the prohibition of flags which in many places continue to be raised by many English citizens residing in this City, with a view to enforcing them, and also explaining the duty that you have of having the flag raised as granted to you by your official status on Sundays and on the two birthdays of our respective sovereigns, the Most Excellent Junta wishes me to thank you for the promptness with which Your Lordship has acted in that matter and to notify you that permission is granted exclusively to Your Lordship to have your respective flag raised on those days.

Neither I nor my research associates have been able to discover an official or approved list of the eighteen English merchants – eighteen is the number given by Mrs Graham – who in Bahia in 1821 kept themselves so abreast of events on land and at sea by means of their flagpoles that they could be considered predecessors of the English Telegraph, that powerful British institution in Brazil and other semi-colonial countries during the second half of the nineteenth century. The list of members of the *Sociedade de Agricultura, Commercio e Industria da Bahia* – the Society of Agriculture, Trade and Industry of Bahia – of 30 March 1832, now in the documents section of the State Public Archive, tells us of the British merchants living in Bahia eleven years after the episode of the flagpoles, who perhaps kept up their observations using the excellent spyglasses then manufactured in England, through which consuls and captains of HBM frigates must have caught sight of more than one slave ship or pirate in Brazilian coastal waters. The list shows that the merchants then flourishing in Bahia around the consul, John Parkinson, were Abraham ('Abrão') Peyster, Arther & Peter Lowe & Co., Clegg & Jones, Dalgrish Macnab & Co., Drop Asthey, Gelfillan Miller & Co., G. R. Foster, William ('Guilherme') Evans, Harrison, Lathan & Co., Heyworth Crab & Co., J. H. Tarlton, Ironside Illives & Co., John Gillmer, Mellors Russel & Co., Moore Dickinson & Co., V. H. Witt & Co., Sealy, Walker & Co., Stewart & Brother, and W. W. Benn & Co.

It would be rash to definitely sort these out into good and bad: those who had slid into some form of dishonest activity – such as smuggling copper and gunpowder – and those who assisted the consuls and captains of HBM naval frigates to rid the seas and beaches of Brazil of those forms of piracy that were crudest, roughest and most harmful, not only to the vast imperial interests of the British Crown and Commerce – with two capital Cs – but also to the safety and regularity of Brazil's small coastal trade. A small trade that was, in effect, barely tolerated by the large, all-absorbing, imperial trade conducted, or to be conducted, in Brazil by the British, under the privileges granted to it by absolute Anglophiles like Dom Rodrigo de Sousa Coutinho.

In 1837, the small Brazilian ships that sailed the coastal waters of the Empire were still being attacked and plundered by pirate ships. According to information gathered from the commander of HBM war corvette *A Mosca*[495] by the English consul in Pernambuco, Mr Edward Watts, and passed on by him to the president of the province on 17 June that year,

> On about the 12th of May ult., a Launch with twenty armed men, all speaking the Spanish language, boarded and plundered a Brazilian coastal vessel between Cabo Frio and Rio de Janeiro, stealing all its cargo and a Slave, and then towed it to the high Seas, threatening to

[495] 'The Fly' – it is unclear whether this British ship had a Portuguese name, or whether the name was translated into Portuguese in the dispatch, or indeed by Freyre himself (Translator).

> kill the crew at the slightest resistance: at daybreak the next day the Launch signalled to a schooner accompanying it by means of a flag marked as follows:

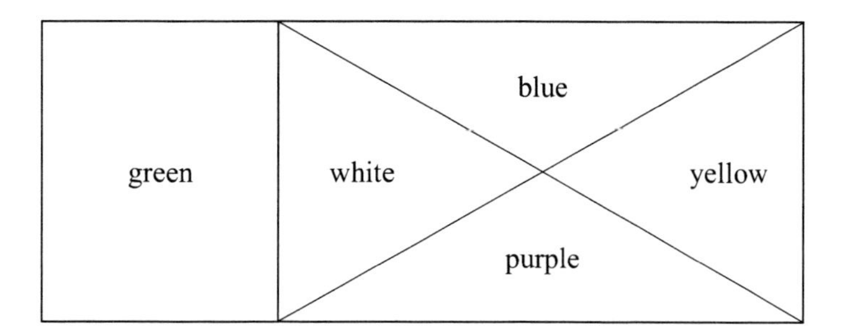


> and having taken fright at the appearance of another ship it hastily abandoned its prey.

The above-mentioned HBM war corvette had just put into Recife harbour. Consul Watts was passing the corvette commander's message on to the president of the province of Pernambuco since it was 'news... of interest to the shipping relations of each nation'. He was also doing so – it may be added – as a sign or reminder of the fact that it was HBM warships that policed the Atlantic waters along the Brazilian coast, thus allowing the then young Empire to carry on its coastal trade, which, although reduced to almost nothing by the English, would not exist were it not for the mighty British navy.

A number of legal disputes occurred over the seizure of pirate ships. Such as the one resulting from the case of the Spanish brigantine *Almirante*, suspected of engaging in the slave trade. On 12 August 1830 the president of the province of Bahia, Luiz Paulo Araújo Basto, sent HBM consul a dispatch maintaining with a lawyer's passion an argument totally opposed to the one upheld by the British legal experts. For Basto it was necessary to distinguish between a 'crime of piracy' (of which the brigantine had been cleared by the competent court) and 'commercial speculation'. In addition, the Empire of Brazil was not

> bound by any Treaty to keep watch over the conduct of other Nations in that respect (the slave trade) and it would therefore be against the Law of Nations and a breach of the duties of hospitality, and everything else in that sense performed against said Brigantine; finally, Your Lordship's assertion is not accurate in saying that the slave trade must be condemned and treated as piracy by all Subjects

> of Brazil, Great Britain and the very Nation to which the Brigantine in question belongs because what is laid down by the Convention between His Imperial Majesty and His Britannic Majesty Article 1 is that the continuation of the Trade in slaves after the three years stipulated, by any subject of His Imperial Majesty, shall be considered and treated as piracy; but this article only relates to the two High Contracting Parties [and] neither gives other Nations any right nor binds them because by law contracts bind only the contractors. In view of all these reasons grounded in the principle of known evidence Your Lordship can clearly see that in the Ports of Brazil no other Conduct can be taken towards the above-mentioned Brigantine without violating the Law of Nations; if that Brigantine indeed engages in the trade in question, which it will only be possible to ascertain in the act, it will then be for the protectors of humanity to proceed as the Laws allow and as the circumstances permit.

The principle upheld by HBM consul in a dispatch of 5 August 1830 to the president of the Province of Bahia had been that the slave trade should be

> deemed and treated as piracy by the subjects of Brazil, the Subjects of Great Britain & the Subjects of the very nation to which the Brig in question belongs.[496]

The president of the province of Bahia returned to the subject in a dispatch to HBM consul on 18 August 1830 in order to insist on the point:

> ... to deny a Vessel entry and freedom to leave a Port when she has and exhibits her respective Passports judged legal by the competent Authority and not to allow her to carry on lawful Trade in the products of the country is not an act that Justice and the Law of Nations can ever authorize on mere suspicion of a future unlawful act; in such a case the means are others.

We should not forget that, at the time when President Basto was so assuredly advocating the slave trade whenever it was possible to release it from the technically legal constraints that hindered it and even to justify it under the principles of Justice and Law, with capital letters, ships whose

[496] Quoted by Freyre in English (Translator).

piracy was confined to taking part in that trade were seen as rather romantic and even heroic by a large number of Brazilians. In about 1840, Captain Hill, of the English frigate *Cleopatra*, published a kind of report on the repression of the African slave trade, which was translated and published in *Minerva Brasileira*, No 3, in December 1844. Referring to a Brazilian pirate ship apprehended by the English, Captain Hill said:

> The captain of this slave ship laughed at the idea of being considered a criminal in Brazil... He had been an officer in the Brazilian navy. I believe that in that country, far from than regarding the smuggling of slaves as a criminal act, they think of it as a suitable career for bold, entrepreneurial men.

The frontier for smuggling as an heroic activity had shifted from Minas Gerais to the coast of the sugar-producing area of the Empire, from where it would later, almost in our own days, move on to the borders of Rio Grande do Sul with the River Plate republics. The same sociological phenomenon but based on different materials – gold, slaves, cattle. The same phenomenon: economic interests not only reducing a heinous crime to a peccadillo, but exalting the dangers of illegal activities as deeds of 'bold, entrepreneurial men'. In the case of Minas Gerais, smuggling had to some extent become a justifiable reaction by colonial people to the abusive exploitation of the colony by the distant metropolis. In the case of the contraband in slaves, it was agrarian Brazil that was trying to defend itself in any way it could against the excesses with which the British Empire was seeking to stop competition with the free – and relatively expensive – labour of its tropical colonies from countries where labour was still slave-based and regarded as cheaper than free labour.

In the early nineteenth century, according to the author of an article on the right to reciprocal visits between Brazil and Great Britain, in which he justifies the smuggling of slaves, Great Britain had since 1808 been trying to limit the agrarian output of Brazil, where the 'prodigious vegetation' just needed 'manpower' (i.e. slaves to encourage it):

> ... in the end Brazil realized that it was dying; vested interest promoted smuggling. [And he added:] The Empire of the Holy Cross will die without agriculture; agriculture will disappear where there is no manpower; free workers are not appearing; slaves are banned; where will we end up?[497]

[497] *Ao Commercio Brasileiro*, n.d., p. 12.

Significant words. They reflect the dilemma in which Brazil found itself. Its personality was split. The slave trade, condemned by Great Britain and the more advanced part of Europe, began to disgust its Christian conscience and its feelings as a sub-European or quasi-European society. But without the trade in Africans the Brazilian economy would crumble. That curious adjustment between feelings and interests then occurred: Brazil began to reject the trade, not only officially but also through other manifestations of how it felt; on the other hand, however, in the eyes of many Brazilians the smuggling of slaves began to take on hues of romance and adventure, not in the figure of the slave-trader who raked in the dirty profits in his comfortable merchant's house, but in that of the slave-ship captain, glorified as an heroic figure, who confronted the commanders of mighty English frigates on the high seas.

One should not think that all the English shunned the risks and rewards of the 'evil trade' in the nineteenth century or that the whole race of former pirates stood loyally on the side of Saint George against the Dragon, that is to say on the side of the Law against Crime, Piracy and Smuggling. On more than one occasion, consular dispatches reveal the names of Englishmen involved in the trade in Africans and other banned or illicit goods.

On 7 January 1836, a petition from Lyon & Parkinson – now in the manuscript collection of the Bahia State Archive – arrived at HBM consulate in Bahia, run at the time by Mr John Robilliard, asking the consul to allow a brig to depart under the British flag without the customary clearance from the consulate. The consul opposed this absurd request from his two countrymen, as he suspected them of trafficking in African slaves, and also because the crew included some slaves, in clear breach of English law. He would only allow the brig to set sail if all the passengers presented their passports as usual. The incident shows that English ships, or ships flying the British flag, could also be involved, if not in blatant piracy, then in half-piracy: disguised or deceitful piracy.

Brazilians were not always set the best examples of honesty or discipline by the English ships that anchored in the ports of the Empire during the first half of the nineteenth century. On the contrary: mutiny and insubordination of English sailors against their officers sometimes erupted in Brazilian waters in those days. One example occurred in 1836 on board the barquentine *Golden Fleece*[498] in Bahia harbour, according to a dispatch from HBM consul to the president of the province on 27 December that year, now in the manuscript collection of the State Archive.

[498] Freyre's spelling of the name is '*Golden Fluce*', presumably miscopied from the dispatch (Translator).

The insubordination was put down by the officers of the Brazilian corvette *Sete de Abril.* As the consul says:

> ... I believe credit is due to the officers of His Imperial Highness's Corvette *Sete de Abril* for the prompt and effective assistance rendered by them; it is regrettable, however, that one of the crew of the *Golden Fleece* was killed, although it appears that it happened by chance and not intentionally, and that he had been the ringleader of the malcontents and deserved the fate that he met.

Also in 1836, according to documents kept in the Bahia State Archive, the Englishmen Elliott, Roberts, James, Youds and Wilkinson were in custody in that province as smugglers or suspected of smuggling. In a dispatch of 8 February that year, the inspector of customs stated that those Englishmen were known as being

> the first persons who leave this port for the Vessels that are entering, often going to meet them beyond the Fortress at the Bar. Last year, on one of those occasions, one of them on being pursued landed at the Port of Victoria a number of packages brought from the ships that were entering...

In July the same year, there was another clash between Englishmen and 'guards of the Anchorage watch' of Bahia: a boat from the English brig *George & James* tried to avoid the inspection that those guards were about to perform on it; the guards pursued and caught it; on being caught the English boat was slightly damaged by 'the grappling iron used on such occasions'. The damage gave rise to a complaint by HBM consul. The damage was so minor, however, and it was so obvious that the guards were carrying out their duty against the Englishmen from the brig that the provincial government took no action. As the president stated in his gentle dispatch to the consul, 'the best relations fortunately exist between the Subjects of this Empire and those of Great Britain.' If that was so, why upset them just because of a boat damaged by the grappling-iron of another, when that other boat was manned by guards who were simply carrying out their duty of policing the anchorage and stamping out smuggling of all kinds: slaves, gunpowder, copper or iron?

A strange coincidence: if the Youds arrested in February 1836 on suspicion of the crime of smuggling was in fact a smuggler and was getting rich from this unlawful means for a British subject established here as a merchant to promote trading relations between Brazil and Great Britain, then it was Bahian criminals rather than the police who settled the score with him by boldly breaking into his house and stealing valuables. Perhaps they were valuables the smuggler had brought off English brigs in mysterious boats that reacted against any inspection by the anchorage guards. The local criminals were thus putting into practice the old adage that says 'it is no crime to steal from a thief'.[499]

A Mr John Youds, in fact, wrote a dispatch – now in the manuscript collection of the State Archive – to HBM consul in Bahia on 4 December 1829 informing him of

> an attempted murder and robbery perpetrated at my house in Victoria yesterday at about midnight, a gang of armed men surrounded the house and after some effort broke in through the door and made a hole in the side of the house large enough for a man to pass through. After four had got inside they seized two Englishmen, William Gould and Richard Price, and wounded them both, leaving them with seven wounds in different parts of their bodies, which appear to have been made with a bayonet, and they are at present in the British Hospital in a critical condition; then, after a terrible fight, the injured men succeeded in escaping, leaving the Thieves and Murderers to do as they liked. This is not the first time in the last fifteen months that my houses have been broken into and robbed, since in that period my stable has been broken into, two horses have been stolen with their saddles, bridles etc., and all kinds of livestock worth a considerable sum, to the extent that as this country property is so unsafe I think it prudent not to keep livestock any more.

The fact that Youds was only detained on suspicion of smuggling in 1836 and the daring robberies of which he was a victim in his country house in Victoria happened in 1829 suggests that the Englishman perhaps resorted to the illicit trade to make up for the losses he had suffered at the hands of robbers in Bahia. But it is also possible that the Bahian police were quite wrong to suspect Youds and his companions of smuggling; in that case, may their souls forgive any flippancy in these pages, which were written by someone who does not have absolute or Muslim[500] trust in what documents say or claim, no matter how official they may be. Since I do not blindly trust such papers, I always try to add to any simply literal 'truth' in documents a psycho-sociological interpretation of the facts – or of what 'is written' about the facts – as I am convinced that, when subjected to

499 The Portuguese version is '*ladrão que rouba ladrão tem cem anos de perdão*', literally 'a thief who robs a thief will have 100 years' forgiveness' (Translator).

500 Freyre uses the term in the sense of 'unquestioning' (Translator).

such an interpretation, that truth can sometimes contract and sometimes expand. Sometimes it contracts so much that it vanishes.

But it was not just arrests of British subjects and the appearance of pirate ships that HBM consuls in Brazil had to worry about: there were also official ceremonies or festivities. And questions of etiquette.

Both British and US consuls seem to have avoided as far as possible appearing at such ceremonies in the presidential palaces in Bahia and Pernambuco, where etiquette required guests to bow to the effigies or portraits of the emperors as a sign of obedience and respect. In the eyes of nineteenth-century Anglo-Saxons, almost all of them strictly Protestant and intransigently antipapal, the ceremony must have seemed somewhat popish and perhaps even idolatrous. Did the Scriptures not warn against the cult of images? Why, then, should a British consul bow to a mere portrait of a Brazilian emperor? Koebel, the historian, perhaps basing himself on papers he examined in London, records the distaste felt by the consuls of his country for this Brazilian ceremony.[501] Kidder had already referred to the matter in his book on Brazil – a work continued by Fletcher. He had regarded the Brazilian ritual as a mixture of 'Chinese obeisance to the portrait of the monarch and reverence to the Catholic saints...'[502]

HBM consuls' distaste for that ceremony, known as '*cortejo*', is confirmed by dispatches in which the consuls themselves apologize for being unable to attend the event, almost always claiming to be unwell. The dispatches of 17 August 1840 from HBM consul in Recife at the time, Mr Watts, apologizing for not being able to attend the '*cortejo* at the Government Palace' on the 20th, commemorating 'the proclamation of Dom Pedro II by the General Legislative Assembly', and of 1 December 1841 from the British consul – no longer Mr Watts but Mr Cowper – informing the president of the province of Pernambuco that it would be impossible for him to attend the *cortejo* on the emperor's birthday on account of an 'unfortunate illness'[503] confirm the precedent established by their predecessors for the absence of British consuls at such an important ceremony in the Empire of Brazil as the *cortejo*, which was described as follows by the Reverend Kidder:

> Presidents of provinces, as the special representatives of the Crown, follow the example of their sovereign, by holding levée in the several provincial capitals; but they do not presume to receive Imperial honours in their own person. The place of honor in their

[501] Koebel, *British Exploits in South America*, p. 317.

[502] Fletcher and Kidder, *Brazil and the Brazilians*, p. 492. (The phrase quoted is not in fact from this work – Translator.)

[503] *Consuls' Correspondence*, Manuscripts Section of the Pernambuco State Library.

> *sala de cortejo* is always allotted to the portrait of His Majesty. Near by, as the special representative of the throne, the President takes his place, accompanied perchance by the bishop. Before these, in measured step, pass the dignitaries invited, in the order of their rank and distinction, paying their obeisance severally to the Imperial portrait.[504]

The same ceremony was held for the prince on his birthday.

Some years before, in 1826, John James Smith, HBM vice-consul in Pernambuco, oozed courtesies in a dispatch (dated 4 December) that could almost have been written on pink paper to the president of the Province (who was Francisco de Paula Cavalcanti de Albuquerque that year), begging forgiveness for his absence at a palace *cortejo*:

> John James Smith, Vice-Consul of His Britannic Majesty in this Province of Pernambuco, was honoured to receive the dispatch that Your Excellency the President addressed to him on 22 November, inviting him to attend the *Cortejo* for the Most Felicitous Birthday of His Imperial Highness the Prince of Brazil, which honour he was unable to enjoy since on that day he was indisposed through ill health, which he sincerely laments and for which he considers it his duty to give Your Excellency due satisfaction as a sign of respect and consideration.[505]

Which shows that not even vice-consuls were willing to bow to the effigies or portraits of the members of the Imperial family of Brazil on the occasion of their birthdays or other commemorations. They were Britons, not Muslims.[506] Anglicans independent of the cult of images, and not papists who worshipped figures or effigies.

That does not mean that the emperors of Brazil were not admired or respected by the British: the British of the times of George IV and Queen Victoria. They were. We know that several Englishmen were in their personal service or served the Empire, including men of the stature of Taylor and Grenfell, to both of whom our navy owes a great deal. In 1808, Forbes, a general from an eminent Scottish Catholic family, died in Rio de Janeiro as he accompanied the royal family to Brazil. He was buried with

[504] Fletcher and Kidder, *Brazil and the Brazilians*, p. 492.

[505] *Consuls' Correspondence*, Manuscripts Section of the Pernambuco State Library.

[506] As before, Freyre uses the term 'Muslim' in the sense of a devoted, unquestioning follower, but it is a painfully inappropriate metaphor in this context of icon worship (Translator).

full honours in the Convent of Santo Antônio.[507]

But there were also Englishmen who hired out their services as good sea-dogs to the enemies of the Empire or the emperors, if not of Brazil itself. In 1838 the president of the province of Bahia received confidential information from the Brazilian consulate in London that the Englishmen Henry ('Henrique') Sinclair, Thomas Henderson, Charles ('Carlos') K. Wise and Moses Hugues had set off from England for Brazil, 'where they will side with the rebels, whose agents hired them here in secret, each of them having received 300 pesos for the voyage'. All of them had served in a previous war: 'in the navy of Buenos Ayres against the Empire'; and the president of the province of Bahia should be aware that they could do serious harm to the legal order 'because they are professional officers and, experienced in privateering as they are, they will cause considerable damage to our trade'.[508]

As we have seen, Brazilians still lived in dread of privateers in their waters during the early decades of the nineteenth century. Mysterious ships were occasionally seen by fishermen. Or they attacked honest ships. And they were not just ships smuggling black slaves, to which the beaches of Rio de Janeiro, Bahia and Pernambuco eventually became accustomed in the nineteenth century, so common were they despite British vigilance; or smuggling goods: copper, gunpowder or cloth. There were also corsairs. Ships that sometimes so worried both the English masters of the seas and the Brazilian masters of the lands that they rashly approached such ships as if the nineteenth or late eighteenth century were still the seventeenth or sixteenth: times of unbridled piracy and insolent privateering. When mysterious foreigners put ashore by nobody knew which schooner, brig or ship started appearing in Brazilian cities in the late eighteenth and early nineteenth centuries, they alarmed the authorities and the local population. They must have come from one of those suspicious ships.

Before the treaty of 1810, the Englishmen who appeared in Brazil without anyone knowing their origins or their intentions must have been included among the suspicious. In 1795 one such Englishman turned up in Pernambuco. He was called 'João Henrique de Londres' – John Henry of London. At least, that is the name that appears in the old manuscript in the Pernambuco Archive which reports the event: an old paper from a time prior to that of the consuls. According to this dispatch, in which the colonial governor addresses the metropolitan authority, informing him of the appearance of the mysterious Englishman with the commotion of someone reporting the appearance not of a man but of a soul from another

507 Walsh, *Notices of Brazil*, I, p. 192.

508 Manuscript, Bahia State Public Archive.

world, João Henrique de Londres turned up in Recife in Pernambuco

> saying that he had come as a Sailor, in an English Ship, and after he fell overboard a Portuguese Ship picked him up and put him ashore in a place of which he did not know the name, so he had walked 300 leagues to reach this Town. And because such individuals must not reside here as determined by the Royal Orders, and the narration of his travels seems to me entirely suspicious, I took the step of having him seized and sent to Your Excellency as I say, for Your Excellency to do with him as you see fit. May God keep Your Excellency for many years. Recife de Pernambuco, 30 September 1795.[509]

A few years later, this 'Londres' would have had HBM consul to look after him, even if he were an adventurer. In that year, however, he was summarily sent to Lisbon without a Cowper to defend him, as he later defended Zurich the Greek, from the possible excesses of the Portuguese authorities.

It is not surprising that that was the situation in Brazil in 1795, since Brazil was then almost like the China or Tibet of the Americas. It is not surprising that the Portuguese authorities in Brazil even mistrusted subjects of a nation so particularly linked to Portugal, and consequently Brazil, as Great Britain, whenever there seemed to be anything irregular, amiss or mysterious about the circumstances in which such individuals landed in the colony. Only once the prince regent was installed in Rio de Janeiro and Great Britain was favoured with such privileges that made her almost a metropolis to the South American kingdom did that distrust shift its focus to other foreigners, such as the French – suspected of being agents of the great Revolution or partisans of Napoleon I – or the North Americans, still green but already substantial rivals of the British.

The Americans could only compete with the British in Brazil by irregular means. Thus on 5 December 1811 the Count of Aguiar informed Caetano Pinto de Miranda Montenegro, governor of the captaincy of Pernambuco, that 'Our Lord the Prince Regent' was aware 'that in the ports of that Captaincy, principally in the less visited ones', the Americans were engaged in 'great contraband of Fabric from Asia, especially Nankeen', causing notable damage to trade and Royal Revenue. And the count concluded his dispatch:

> It pleases Our Lord that Your Lordship shall, without delay, take the most forceful Steps to destroy such grave abuses; expecting that

509 *Court Correspondence*, Manuscripts Section of the Pernambuco State Library.

> Your Lordship's zeal and intelligence will ensure the success of the measures that you adopt to this end, the implementation of which Your Lordship shall report to this Secretariat.[510]

Shortly before receiving this dispatch, however, on 14 October 1811, the governor had received from the count, Dom João's minister, a dispatch that came with a petition from McCrohon & Fleet, merchants in Pernambuco and consignees of the American brigantine *Free Love.* In their petition the merchants asked for the Pernambuco customs house to agree to release

> the fabrics from Asia that were impounded by it, brought on said brigantine despite the prohibition made in the Order of 4 February of the current year, on the grounds that she is a foreign vessel and put in there just a few days after the publication of said Order.

And, trusting the good faith of the Americans who, despite the order, brought fabrics from Asia to Brazil, the prince concluded, through his minister's hand:

> It pleases Our Lord to order Your Lordship to arrange the release of the aforesaid Fabrics from Asia, which are in that Customs House, transported by the above-mentioned American Brigantine *Free Love.*[511]

This favour granted by the prince to the Americans perhaps irritated the English, who were now comfortably installed in Brazil as masters of its trade. And that irritation may explain the dispatch of 5 December from the Count of Aguiar ordering the governor of the captaincy of Pernambuco to act forcefully against American smugglers. Unfortunately I have been unable to find any note or dispatch from HBM representative in Rio de Janeiro that might clarify the matter from the British point of view.

What we find in the dispatches of British consuls in the following years are signs that they were increasing their vigilance in relation to smuggling or corsair ships. The war between Great Britain and the United States must have led the English to step up their watchfulness against their new rivals, the citizens of the United States of America, who were as clever as the English themselves in matters of trade and merchant shipping. And

[510] *Court Correspondence*, Manuscripts Section of the Pernambuco State Library.

[511] *Court Correspondence*, Manuscripts Section of the Pernambuco State Library.

as bold as they were in matters of naval warfare.[512]

As Professor Rippy says in his study on the origins of the rivalry between Great Britain and the United States, commercial competition between the two nations soon became more acute than any other, although the products sold by the English to South Americans were from their factories and shipyards, whereas those sold by Americans were from their farms and ranches. There was, however, competition in terms of transport: both the English and the Americans wanted the advantage of shipping goods to young nations that did not yet have their own merchant fleet.[513] Or those whose fleet was small, as in Brazil's case.

Professor Rippy stresses the efforts made by the English to maintain their prestige as masters of the seas in Latin America against the United States and, in this respect, highlights pronouncements like that made in 1824 by Lord Liverpool, the British prime minister from 1812 to 1827.[514] Rippy seems, however, to overlook facts such as the one mentioned here, which suggest that the British government was putting pressure on the Brazilian authorities – or the Portuguese authorities in Brazil, when it was semi-independent of Portugal under Dom João VI – not to tolerate any shipping of goods from Asia to Brazilian ports in US ships. Some of the alarms raised by British consuls in dispatches to Brazilian authorities during the reigns of Dom João VI or Dom Pedro I concerning mysterious ships seen in Brazilian waters may have been directed against American vessels, which they wanted to paint in the most garish and even scandalous colours as being illicit, suspicious and intruding.

In 1814, however, it was Englishmen and not Americans that the governor of the captaincy of Pernambuco was forced to detain in the Fortaleza das Cinco Pontas as insolent sailors or even corsairs, for having unduly seized the Portuguese brigantine *Boa-União* with a 'cargo of slaves' from Cabinda intended for Brazil. The harassment of the brigantine had been carried out by the English frigate *Niger*, 'which had hoisted the American Flag'. Since this was an important arrest – involving English officers and men – the captain-general hastened to report the fact to the now Marquis of Aguiar.

[512] In *Sea-Power & Empire* (London, 1940), Professor F. J. C. Hearnshaw points out that, during the 1812 war between the United States and Great Britain, English ships suffered a series of humiliating defeats at their enemy's hands. 'In the end, however, British sea-power prevailed. Every American port was blockaded and American commerce entirely swept off the ocean (1814)' (p. 176). His statement is perhaps an exaggeration. US international trade was not entirely destroyed as a result of that war, since Brazil, for example, continued to receive wheat flour for its consumption mainly from English America.

[513] Rippy, *Rivalry of the United States and Great Britain over Latin America*, p. 108.

[514] *Ibid.*, p. 110.

> I ordered the detention of the English Lieutenant, Midshipmen and Seamen in the Fortaleza das Cinco Pontas; and when the Consul sent me dispatch No 3, I replied to him with Nos 4 and 5. In these dispatches Your Excellency will not fail to notice that the consul appears to try to question the formality of the arrest and that although I had satisfied him with regard to the Lieutenant and Midshipmen, I did not mention the fact that the Seamen were taken handcuffed. The order that I gave was as follows – that the Lieutenant and Midshipmen should be taken by an officer with every decency and the Seamen by a military escort: but the person charged with the act took them in handcuffs on his own decision, for greater security. That decision, given the quality of the persons and the reason for the arrest, I mean the insult done to the Portuguese Flag, did not appear to me worthy of punishment or to the consul as requiring satisfaction... As a consequence of my reply the consul wrote back to me the letter copied as No 6, to which I replied with No 7; and when the English Lieutenant asked me on 31 October to allow him to leave the Fortress on his word of honour, and the two Midshipmen, as Your Excellency will see from his own letter No 8, I immediately granted him his request and copy No 9 contains the reply that I gave him.

And somewhat fearful as to the manner in which the prince regent, who was such a great friend of the English, would receive his measures against the frigate *Niger*:

> In new or extraordinary cases, it is not easy to combine the rules of Justice and of prudence. I shall therefore be thankful if what I have done in this respect merits His Highness's Royal Approval; as well as my sending the prisoners by Your Excellency's Order on the Portuguese brigantine named *Mãi de Deos*, the commander of which is Luciano Miguel da Silva. May God keep Your Excellency for many years. Recife de Pernambuco, 17 November 1814. To the Most Illustrious and Excellent Lord the Marquis of Aguiar – Caetano Pinto de Miranda Montenegro.[515]

The governor's forceful action won the prince's approval. As a result, years later, in 1820, after a further clash – this time between the captain-general of the captaincy of Pernambuco, Luís do Rego Barreto, who was

[515] *Court Correspondence*, No 18, Manuscripts Section of the Pernambuco State Library.

an authoritarian, violent man notorious for his outbursts, and the same HBM consul in Recife – Barreto wrote in a dispatch to Thomaz Antônio de Villanova Portugal[516] that the consul was the same one with whom his predecessor had had

> the argument that I am honoured to place before Your Excellency in which he [the consul] attacked him in ... immoderate terms ... and his repulse was approved by his Majesty as may be seen in these same documents. [And the arrogant captain-general concluded:] I do not know whether on that occasion the English Consul was reprimanded as befitted his crime, I know that he did not learn from the first episode, that this case deserves satisfaction and that the Country's Authorities should not be subject to the recklessness and hauteur of Foreigners.[517]

This dispatch from Luís do Rego Barreto is dated 22 April 1820 and comes from book 25 (1817-1821) of the *Court Correspondence*. The same correspondence also includes a dispatch sent from Engenho Monteiro on 20 January 1813, in which Caetano Pinto de Miranda Montenegro informed the Royal Court:

> I have just had a disagreeable altercation with the British Consul, which he caused with the offence he gave in the arrest of Roberto Grosset, who had been the Captain of the Galley *Dart*, by giving in writing an arrest warrant for him to be taken to a public Prison on his order by an Officer of Justice that the Magistrate inconsiderately gave him, without said Clerk or the Consul notifying me thereof in any way.

The English captain complained to the captain-general about his own consul's outrageous behaviour. The captain-general had Grosset released. 'For this reason,' wrote the governor of Pernambuco in the same dispatch to the Count of Aguiar, 'the Consul wrote to me very haughtily...'[518] Unfortunately, no copy has been found of the consul's dispatch. We just know from Miranda Montenegro's communication to the Count of Aguiar that in 1813 there was an exchange of vehement dispatches between the captain-general and HBM consul in Recife: the governor replied to

[516] Thomaz Antônio de Villanova Portugal (1755-1839) was Dom João VI's chief minister from 1817 to 1821 (Translator).
[517] *Court Correspondence*, No 25, Manuscripts Section of the Pernambuco State Library.
[518] *Ibid.*

dispatch No 1 from the consul with his own dispatch No 2:

> and when he sought to justify his conduct in dispatch No 3, I refuted his arguments in No 4, and he put an end to the dispute in No 5.[519]

The fight between the two authorities was bitter. The British colony seemed to be divided; at least, according to a communication from the governor to the Count of Aguiar, Montenegro had been thanked 'by the English residing in this captaincy'. In his words,

> The English residing in this Captaincy sent a Deputation of six (6) merchants to thank me at this Country Residence where I am now, for having protected them against the outrages of that very person who should protect them.

And the dispatch concludes in a very interesting way for those who seek to interpret and understand the history of Brazilian culture and institutions, which were so abruptly shaken up in pace and style by the opening of the ports to foreigners in 1808:

> I am convinced that I acted as I was duty-bound to act; and if I failed in my duty in any way, that resulted from not having instructions as to how to proceed correctly, because since Brazil opened herself up to Trade and Communication with Foreigners in 1808 I have not yet received any orders on the policing of the Ports, and jurisdiction of the Consuls, and there are no documents in the Government Archive by which I can guide myself, for the old Order that existed was not to admit Foreigners, excluding them from all Trade, and Communication.[520]

We should not be surprised, therefore, at the many clashes of Portuguese or Brazilian authorities with representatives of His or Her Britannic Majesty: the many conflicts of authority between consuls and captaincy governors or provincial presidents. What is surprising is that those clashes and conflicts were not even more common, since a great many new problems must have arisen without warning in the relations between Brazilians and Britons, who had previously been rare in this part of the Americas but were suddenly living here in the capital and main cities in their dozens. In the capital they had a special judge; in Pernambuco and

[519] *Court Correspondence*, Manuscripts Section of the Pernambuco State Library.
[520] *Ibid.*

Bahia they were primarily protected by the authority of consuls. Initially, these consuls must have felt as embarrassed at exercising an authority that in some way exceeded that of ordinary consuls – given the privileged position of the British in Brazil at the time of the prince regent – as the Portuguese and, later, Brazilian authorities felt at that intrusive yet unavoidable power. More than any others, the British in Brazil in the early decades of the nineteenth century represented what today we would term the impact of the part of Europe that had been most profoundly revolutionized or modernized by the Industrial Revolution, in terms of its technology and its whole culture, on the China or Tibet of the Americas that was Brazil at that time. A Brazil that had been kept isolated from the other peoples of Europe – especially the Protestant peoples of northern Europe – by the Portuguese metropolis, which was jealous of the gold from the mines and protective of the orthodoxy of Brazilians' faith and customs, for such a long time that to European eyes it had almost lost the qualities or characteristics of a sub-European society to acquire those of an exotic one.

Before 1808, Caetano Pinto de Miranda Montenegro had known how to deal with intruders – those heretics, British or otherwise, who disembarked here without permission. He would have done with any suspicious Englishman who turned up here what a former governor of the captaincy had done in 1795 with that 'Henrique de Londres' – Henry of London. Miranda Montenegro himself had not hesitated to do his duty when five Englishmen appeared in Pernambuco in 1805, transferred with a letter and passport from the captain-general and governor of Angola, who wrote that they had been cast ashore on that coast by a Spanish corsair. Like a good feudal lord who was also a bachelor in law and scrupulous in complying with the formalities of the law, Caetano Pinto de Miranda Montenegro ordered each one

> provided with a ration of porridge as well as one *cruzado's*-worth of victuals per day, which according to the practice established here must be given, firstly because they are officers of the esteemed Nation.

He had them sent to the metropolis on board the transport ship *Príncipe da Beira.*[521] In his dispatch of 17 October 1805 informing the Viscount of Anadia of this measure, the captain-general wrote:

> The crew of said transport ship includes two other Seamen of the same Nation who jumped ship from another English corsair that had put in here, regarding which I carried out strictly that which the Law

[521] *Court Correspondence*, Manuscripts Section of the Pernambuco State Library.

> of Nations permits and which the Royal Decree of 3 June 1803 lays down, reducing the innocent aid that I gave her to a little water and some fruit, and a repair to the pump, because she was making water. Said corsair was named *Scorpion* and her Commander Guilherme Dagge.[522]

People like Montenegro, who had been accustomed to fulfilling clear, positive laws about foreigners in Brazil and to dealing with those English who put in or turned up here in the manner of a Christian lord who was generously sparing the lives of heretics by giving them some porridge and a few *cruzados*, and only allowing them what was laid down in the Royal Decree of 3 June 1803, must have found it difficult to adapt to the new status granted to the English in Brazil in 1808 and especially in 1810.

In a dispatch dated from the Palace of Rio de Janeiro on 17 January 1815, Montenegro received a message from the Marquis of Aguiar that must have calmed his anxiety, uncertain as he was about the way in which the markedly Anglophile royal court of Dom João VI would receive his not always gentle ways of dealing with the English after 1808. Including those responsible for capturing a Portuguese brigantine. The Marquis of Aguiar informed him:

> I took into the Royal Presence of My Lord the Prince Regent the dispatch that Your Lordship addressed to me numbered 91 with all the further Papers accompanying it regarding the Brigantine – *Boa União* – which, coming from Cabinda and being seized by His Britannic Majesty's Frigate – *Niger* – was restored by the Master and Crew manning it. It pleased His Royal Highness to approve not only the correspondence that Your Lordship had with the English Consul João Lempriere [*sic*] in respect of the Officers and Seamen of said Frigate who arrived at that port as prisoners of the aforementioned Brigantine, but also the manner in which Your Lordship sent them to this Court and all the further actions you took in this matter, which I mention to Your Lordship for your intelligence.[523]

His successor, however, soon started receiving instructions that may be regarded as contrary to that dispatch approving a way of dealing with Englishmen that was clearly not within the spirit of the 1810 treaty. That suggests that the British consul in Recife had been in communication with HBM consul-general or *chargé d'affaires* in Rio on the subject. And the latter seems to have made the king realise that the English were not

[522] *Court Correspondence*, Manuscripts Section of the Pernambuco State Library.

[523] *Court Correspondence*, Manuscripts Section of the Pernambuco State Library.

receiving the same treatment from the authorities in Pernambuco as they were in Bahia: the treatment that was due to them under the famous treaty. Hence the dispatch received by Luís do Rego Barreto, dated 6 August 1817, in which the king's minister informed him that

> It pleases Our Lord the King, in accepting the representation made to him by His Britannic Majesty's Consul-General and *Chargé d'Affaires* to the Court, that the English Packets that call at that Port both coming from and going to England be received and treated there as they are in the Port of the City of Bahia, in view of the convention on Packets of 19 February 1810. I mention all this to Your Lordship for your intelligence and so that you may at once adopt the measures and give the orders that may be necessary for the full execution thereof.[524]

Luís do Rego Barreto had begun his government with orders not to create any hindrance to the English in Pernambuco in what was most precious to them: their shipping trade. But since 'two refractory spirits will never agree',[525] it was not long before the arrogant Portuguese general clashed with the arrogant British consul in Pernambuco, where, incidentally, the figure or institution of the judge conservator had never taken hold, as it had in Rio de Janeiro, and also to some extent in Bahia. There are in fact frequent references to the 'Conservator of the English Nation' in the correspondence of HBM consuls in Salvador with the provincial authorities. In 1827, a certain José Gordilho de Barbacuda, a subject of HBM who was the 'victim of an unprecedented ... injustice by the Governor of the Island of Itaparica', sought redress from the conservator, according to a dispatch from the British consul in Salvador to the governor of the province on 29 November 1827.[526]

And on 20 July 1832, HBM consul himself was furious about an insult to a certain British subject in his domestic service – John ('João') Alkins – and invoked in favour of the offended party the judge conservator of the British Nation, an institution that in fact was already rather outdated, although in theory still in existence and legally valid. According to a dispatch from the consul dated from Bahia on 20 July that year,

[524] *Court Correspondence*, Manuscripts Section of the Pernambuco State Library.

[525] Freyre uses the Brazilian proverb '*dois bicudos não se beijam*', which literally means 'two large-beaked birds do not kiss'. It is close in meaning to the Latin proverb '*durum et durum non faciunt murum*' (which has direct equivalents in Portuguese and other Romance languages). The translation suggested here is taken from Robert Burton's gloss of the Latin proverb, in *The Anatomy of Melancholy* (London, 1621), 2nd partition, section 3, member 7 (Project Gutenberg online edition, http://www.gutenberg.org/files/10800/10800-h/ampart2.html, consulted on 25 April 2010) (Translator).

[526] Manuscript, Bahia State Public Archive.

> the man [John Alkins] was going to the City on horseback under my orders with a dispatch on His Britannic Majesty's Service under cover for an English gentleman who was then about to depart for Liverpool. In the public street at the Fort of São Pedro he was interrogated by four men who by force and personal violence pulled him from the horse and despite his admonitions [illegible] carried off with the horse, saddle, bridle and whip, all my own personal property. After this shameful outrage, if not robbery, had been committed, a fifth individual in uniform with a crown on the left sleeve of his jacket wrote the insolent anonymous note enclosed herewith desiring my servant to take it to the Consul his Master. For the personal injury the courts of Justice offer recourse, but for the public offence against a peaceful British subject bearing official papers in the King's Service and for the likewise public insult of having my property detained without observance of the forms of the Law and in disregard of the jurisdiction of the Judge Conservator of the English Nation, I am compelled to turn to Your Excellency, not doubting in the slightest your prompt and unequivocal assistance both for the detention of the criminals and so that, as British Consul in this Province, I may obtain full and public satisfaction, as was the offence.[527]

The consul was John Parkinson, who also served as consul in Pernambuco.

Since he was not given this satisfaction and the steps he had requested were not taken, Parkinson returned to the subject in a dispatch of 31 July, reminding the Brazilian authority of 'the privileges guaranteed to His Britannic Majesty's subjects by Article 6 of the Treaty of 17 August 1827, which stipulates in Article 6:

> The Constitution of the Empire having abolished all special jurisdictions the place of the Judge Conservator of the English Nation has been kept and shall subsist only until such time as some satisfactory replacement for that jurisdiction is established that may likewise ensure protection for the persons and property of HBM subjects.[528]

However, argues Parkinson in his long dispatch, since he, the

[527] *Ibid.*

[528] *Ibid.* (Freyre transcribed this part of this dispatch with a few minor differences earlier in this chapter – Translator.)

consul, had suffered a 'public outrage', the government of Bahia was not 'competent' to act in the sense of giving satisfaction to a British authority. Did the mandate of the official who had seized his, the consul's, property have the 'knowledge or approval of the Judge Conservator of the English Nation?' He was still awaiting the satisfaction due to him. If, however, the opposite was the case, he wished to be 'distinctly informed' on this point:

> whether it is the intention and determination of this local Government to protect the practice of bringing suits or handing down sentences of fines or imprisonment on HBM subjects without the sanction or confirmatory signature of the legally established Judge Conservator of the English Nation.[529]

In a subsequent dispatch to the president of the province – on 31 July – Consul Parkinson said that the justice of the peace had been poorly informed when he said that he, the consul, had received 'everything' – that is, all the items of his property that had been seized from his servant. No: 'a postillion's strap' was missing, and 'the horse itself came back with some bruises...'[530] Finally, on 4 August 1832, in a dispatch addressed to the president, Parkinson protested against 'the principle established by Your Excellency and the consequences that may ensue therefrom', and considered that discussion of the subject by him, the consul, had reached a point at which he had to 'interrupt it and refer the whole question to higher powers'.[531] What is clear is that the figure of the judge conservator of the English Nation had, in practice, now become a kind of hangover from the time of the Old King that was abhorrent to the new statesmen and judges of Brazil. Nonetheless, the consul did not stop arguing hard in favour of the institution: according to the treaty of 1827 between Brazil and Great Britain it still existed. Ever since the final days under Dom João, however, the figure of that judge solely for the English, dressed in his gown of exception, had in practice been withering away in those places where it had flowered: Rio de Janeiro and Bahia. In Pernambuco, as I have said before, it had never even sprouted, alongside those other institutions solely for the English that appeared in Brazil after 1808: chapels, hospitals, cemeteries, clubs and libraries.

It must be emphasised that the institution of the judges conservators – one of the impositions of the 1810 treaty – had only ever been tolerated by the Brazilians with deep resentment and against their will. As Professor Manchester points out, those special judges 'were to try all cases involving

[529] *Ibid.*
[530] *Ibid.*
[531] *Ibid.*

British subjects according to the laws established in Portugal for such jurisdiction since the 1654 treaty. English subjects residing in the port or city where the tribunal was to be set up should choose the magistrate by a plurality vote, subject to the ratification of D. João or his successors.'[532]

Article 6 of the 1827 treaty considered the fact that the constitution of the Empire had abolished all special jurisdictions and that therefore the position of judge conservator of the English Nation should only remain until such time as a satisfactory replacement for that jurisdiction could be established. But it took the denunciation of the treaty as a whole by the royal court in Rio de Janeiro to abolish once and for all the institution that English politicians had tried to maintain for as long as possible and which, as it was a form of extraterritorial jurisdiction of Great Britain in Brazil, seemed to be flaunting British imperial power over a colonial territory – something that Brazilians proud of their new status as a politically independent nation would inevitably reject.

In 1842, during the negotiations of a new treaty – when, according to Pereira da Silva,[533] Henry Ellis, who had come to negotiate for Great Britain, attracted the people's curiosity for the pomp and splendour with which he disembarked and came to live in the then modest town that was the capital of the Empire: with an eight-horse carriage, liveried servants and almost prince-like luxury – the British merchants living in Rio themselves made it clear to HBM special envoy that they had no interest in the continuation of the 1827 treaty and no great desire to maintain the judges conservators. Ellis quickly communicated the fact to Lord Aberdeen in a dispatch dated 16 December 1842.[534] The merchants said that traders of other nationalities established in Brazil were not suffering injustice in the way the law was enforced, and they were not protected by the privilege of extraterritorial jurisdiction as the English alone were. On 9 November 1844, the Foreign Minister of the Brazilian Empire informed the provincial authorities that the Anglo-Brazilian Treaty of 1827 had expired and that the institution of judges conservators, which in practice hardly existed any more, had been abolished. Hamilton, Ellis's successor, had tried in vain[535] to maintain that leftover from the regency of Dom João, who had in fact inherited it from Portugal. In Portugal, only the audacious Marquis of Pombal, King José's prime minister, had fearlessly confronted this form of British imperialism by passing a law on 30 October 1752 to invalidate the right granted to the English living in Portugal by the Charter of Special

[532] Manchester, *British Preëminence in Brazil*, pp. 87-88.

[533] J. M. Pereira da Silva, *Memórias do meu tempo*, Rio de Janeiro and Paris, n.d., I, pp. 98-99.

[534] Manchester, *British Preëminence in Brazil*, p. 292.

[535] *Dispatch from Hamilton to Aberdeen, No 88*, Foreign Office Archive, quoted by Manchester, p. 296.

Privileges in 1647 and confirmed by the treaty of 1654: the right whereby an English subject could not be arrested without the consent of the English judge conservator.[536]

Hamilton's efforts in the capital, like Parkinson's in his provincial consulate, to retain the judge conservator are understandable. It was less a matter of upholding the privileged status of the English in Brazil, should they commit crimes, than of keeping up the prestige of the British Crown itself, which the Foreign Office certainly did not want the New World to shun in favour of the exclusive privilege of the republican United States. Professor Harold Temperley, in his book on Canning's foreign policy,[537] shows that one of that eminent statesman's constant concerns was to maintain British prestige in the New World, particularly in monarchic Brazil. And outward displays had their value in maintaining it. Acting on Canning's recommendations, Consul-General Chamberlain was almost childishly delighted to inform the British minister of the fact that the news of the United States' recognition of the independence of Brazil had been greeted in Rio with just a cannon salute and that 'there were no illuminations'.[538]

As an affirmation of Great Britain's imperial prestige in Brazil, there could be no more forceful or impressive institution than that of the judge conservator. At the same time, it represented a constant threat to good relations between the two countries. There was no less of a threat when, for lack of a 'special judge of the English', overbearing and arrogant consuls acted imperially in favour of the English against the Brazilians, such as the one who clashed with the equally overbearing and arrogant Luís do Rego Barreto.

As people who live in glass houses should not throw stones, it was not long before Barreto's wish that the country's authorities should not be 'subject to the recklessness and hauteur of Foreigners' backfired on him: he himself was a 'foreigner', that is, a Portuguese, who was considered by the authorities set up by Brazilian patriots to be too 'reckless' and 'haughty' to govern a spirited, freedom-loving people like the Pernambucans.

That is clearly another story. But since a large part of it is narrated in very lively terms by an Englishwoman, Maria Graham, I am not betraying the subject of either this book or even this chapter by mentioning it. For it is precisely through the Englishwoman's notes that we learn not only that

[536] Manchester, *British Preëminence in Brazil*, p. 41.

[537] Harold Temperley, *The Foreign Policy of Canning, 1822-1827*, London, 1925, pp. 18 and 143-149.

[538] *Dispatch from Chamberlain to Canning, 29 August 1824*, Foreign Office Archive, quoted by Rippy, *Rivalry of the United States and Great Britain over Latin America*, p. 129.

Luís de Rego Barreto had served in Portugal under the English general Lord Wellington – information that any biography of the Portuguese general can give us – but also – and here is an assessment or judgment of Barreto's personality by an impartial observer – that he was a distinguished soldier, although 'perhaps too little yielding to the people and the temper of the times';[539] and he was more accustomed to being feared than loved.[540] It was natural, therefore, that Barreto should be disturbed by something in the British consul with whom he had to deal in Pernambuco that he would later be disturbed by in the Pernambucans themselves: the fact that neither the consul nor, later, the Pernambucans feared him like the bogeyman.

Maria Graham knew the Portuguese governor and his family well. The general's wife was the daughter of an Irishwoman: she spoke English naturally and had an admirable voice. The Englishwoman thought her two daughters were fine, well-bred young women.[541] But not even 'Do Rego', as Maria Graham calls the famous captain-general, with all his energy, would be able to keep the captaincy loyal to Portugal. Neither to Portugal nor to himself, Luís do Rego Barreto, and he eventually gave up fighting the Pernambucans and embarked on a French ship for Europe.

He did Brazil one particular service, among others, during his days as captain-general: like the Count of Arcos, he with his arrogance helped to temper the insolence of HBM consuls, some of whom perhaps imagined that all the captaincies of Brazil were governed by men as accommodating and over-tolerant of British 'recklessness' and 'hauteur' as Dom João VI. Luís do Rego Barreto was neither accommodating nor a man who easily tolerated 'recklessness' and 'hauteur' from foreigners. Not even the English. And several Brazilian presidents of provinces were like him.

Times of political crisis in Brazil, such as the most troubled days of Luís do Rego Barreto's government in Pernambuco, were almost always difficult times for relations between the Brazilian authorities and HBM consuls. In 1824, John Parkinson, the consul in Pernambuco – Parkinson was also HBM representative in Bahia – had to approach the president of that province to ask His Excellency to take steps 'against the repetition of insults and outrages',[542] which the dispatch unfortunately does not detail. He would not let himself be taken in by the president's subterfuges regarding the measures requested; he could see no reason for the president to refer him 'to his Conservator' for such measures, meaning the private judge conservator of the British. For even if such a judge had existed, or might still exist in Rio de Janeiro, as one of the British privileges

[539] Graham, *Journal of a Voyage to Brazil*, p. 59.

[540] *Ibid.*, p. 98.

[541] *Ibid.*, p. 103.

[542] *Consuls' Correspondence*, Manuscripts Section of the Pernambuco State Library.

guaranteed by Article 10 of the Treaty of Commerce between Brazil and Great Britain, that Article 10 had never been implemented in Pernambuco 'and consequently never to this day has such a Magistrate been recognised by the successive Governments of the Province of Pernambuco'. That is how Consul Parkinson expressed his feelings in a dispatch of 14 January 1824.[543]

In the capital of Maranhão that same year, Brazilian authorities had burst into the house of an English merchant named Hasketh. That was all it took for a British warship, the *Eclair*, commanded by Captain Johnstone, to approach the port so that she could control the city with her guns. The authorities offered an apology.[544]

The same captain reappeared in Pernambuco some months later, commanding the frigate *Doris*. Here he was accused by the republican patriots of 'victualling' the imperial ships commanded by Captain John Taylor. On 16 April, the president of the province, Manoel de Carvalho Paes d'Andrade sent a dispatch on this matter to HBM consul in Recife, who replied on the same day to the republican president. In his dispatch, Consul Parkinson wrote:

> as the British Government has absolutely forbidden each and every one of its subjects to intervene or take any part in the domestic arguments or war of nations other than in the strictest neutrality and, on considering with justice, it could not persuade itself that His Excellency the President of the Province would officially argue a case of such weight without being quite certain of the truth thereof and moreover possessing evident proof of the facts against the aggressors. [And he concluded:] I therefore beg that it please Your Excellency to have me informed of the names of the British subjects that, by means of the Frigate *Doris*, as is expressed in Your Excellency's dispatch, have supplied victuals to Capt. John Taylor, because only thus can the means be indicated to curb this traffic and bring to conviction and punishment those guilty of such irregularities.[545]

[543] *Ibid.* In this respect it is worth repeating the information given by Henry Koster in his *Travels in Brazil*: 'A *Juiz Conservador*, Judge Conservator, of the British nation has been appointed for Pernambuco, but at the period of my departure from Recife, he was not arrived. Very soon after the commencement of a direct commercial intercourse with Great Britain, a vice-consul was appointed for Pernambuco, by the consul-general at Rio de Janiero [*sic*]; this person was superseded by a consul sent out direct from England, who is subject to the consul-general of Brazil, but the place is disposed of by the government at home' (p. 30, footnote). (Quoted in English – Translator.)

[544] Koebel, *British Exploits in South America*, p. 302.

[545] *Consuls' Correspondence*, Manuscripts Section of the Pernambuco State Library.

Whether or not the accusations against Johnstone were true, the fact is that he was transferred from the waters of Pernambuco to those of Bahia, where he finished taking on the provisions that he had begun to acquire in Pernambuco, thus depriving the city of Recife, according to an English historian, of 'the transaction and its profit'.[546] That, however, would not be the only time when the Pernambucans, and particularly the people of Recife, would see their economy suffer because of the frankness of their political opinions. And Johnstone was not so sure of being respected by the republicans in Recife as he had been by the rebels in Maranhão. In that same year of 1824, on Tuesday, 24 January, John Gill, a British subject and first mate on the English galley *Kelton*, had been removed from his ship and thrown into a public prison by the Brazilian authorities. As a dispatch from the British consul on 2 February 1824 states:

> arrested, removed from the ship and thrown into the public prison, without the undersigned receiving any notification at all of the warrant for his arrest, that being contrary to the customary attention.[547]

Months later, the commander of the English schooner-brig *Josefina* informed his country's consul, who hastened to communicate the fact to the Brazilian authorities, that while his ship was flying the English flag, on the afternoon of 2 March, she had been 'visited by a military force' which had arrested seven of the crew. Consul John Parkinson's dispatch of 4 March 1824 explains:

> Seven seamen from her crew were arrested and taken to the Inspectorate prison, where they remained the whole night, and all this was performed under the direction and authority of the Customs officer João Cavalcanti.[548]

It seems the Cavalcantis of the time even tried to ride Englishmen.[549] But not without an angry protest from HBM consul. Not without his vehement assertion of authority in respect of arrests which, in his view, were of the kind classed as 'vexatious' in the Treaty of Commerce between

[546] Koebel, *British Exploits in South America*, p. 302.

[547] *Consuls' Correspondence*, Manuscripts Section of the Pernambuco State Library.

[548] *Ibid.*

[549] A pun on the name Cavalcanti (a powerful family in north-eastern Brazil) and the verb *cavalgar*, to ride a horse (Translator).

the two nations of Great Britain and Brazil. It was his duty, said Parkinson in his dispatch of 4 March 1824, 'to impose in the feelings of the His Britannic Majesty's subjects the most respectful adherence to the Laws of this Country'; but it was equally his duty 'to ensure that the administration of these Laws insofar as they regard the person and property of British subjects' was not of the kind described in the 1810 treaty as 'vexatious'. The *Josefina's* sailors had been released the following morning without any inquiry into the grounds for their arrest. Without their having been given a chance to 'show their innocence and obtain due satisfaction for being groundlessly deprived of their freedom'. That was inconceivable for the British. The consul therefore complained strongly:

> In order to avoid future doubt the undersigned has the honour of begging Your Excellency to be pleased to have him informed of the accusation made against the above-mentioned seven seamen and whether it is with Your Excellency's sanction that visits are made on board English ships and British subjects are put in prison without his being in any way notified as Consul.[550]

The fact is that British seamen were sometimes caught up in the Pernambucans' nativist hatred of Portuguese seamen. In the middle of 1822, prior to Brazil's independence, the house of Mr Thomas Gardner, a British resident of Recife, was forcibly entered by local soldiers who were looking for a Portuguese, who was Mr Gardner's assistant. When reporting the case to the president and members of the provisional junta, Consul Parkinson said that he was persuaded that 'the measure had been taken without any authority whatsoever'.[551] That is revelatory of the state of confusion and lax authority in Pernambuco in the final days of the colony.

On 21 August that year Consul Parkinson found himself obliged to write to the same authorities about another offence to a Briton residing in Recife, Mr Carlyle Holmes. This time, however, the almost sacrosanct person of a Briton in Brazil had been offended not by mere soldiers 'without authority', but by minor officials of the courts of justice, who thus presumed

> to usurp such extraordinary powers... taking their presumption to the extent of breaching the privileges safeguarding His Britannic Majesty's subjects through 'visits and vexatious searches'...

[550] *Consuls' Correspondence*, Manuscripts Section of the Pernambuco State Library.
[551] Dispatch of 5 August 1822, *Consuls' Correspondence*, Manuscripts Section of the Pernambuco State Library.

Such excesses appeared to the consul to constitute 'a matter too serious in nature to be treated with indifference...' He therefore called on the Brazilian authorities not only to take steps against the offenders but to adopt other measures that 'in their wisdom they deem effective to prevent the repetition of such a breach of the Treaty'.[552]

Consul Parkinson was in fact an intransigent enforcer of the 1810 treaty in Brazil, in which the lion's share had clearly gone to the British lion. In 1823, when the English brig *Irene* under Captain Tidmarsh arrived in Recife from Buenos Aires laden with dried beef, the captain was informed, after he had been given leave to enter the harbour free of charge to unload, that 'in addition to the Customs Duties, he would be required by a private individual to pay him 160 réis per quarter hundredweight'. In response to which the consul argued:

> The undersigned cannot persuade himself that the provisions in question might by some principle be subject to payment twice over of the Duties applied to them, notwithstanding any private contract where such a contract runs absolutely counter to the Spirit of the Treaty of Communication between two nations while said Treaty is in force. [That being so,] in the present case the provisions in question should only be subject to the Customs Duty or to that payment of 160 réis per quarter hundredweight, by virtue of some contract or privilege.
> I would call on the president, in this case, to make 'the necessary entries in the registers to avoid delay...'[553]

In the same year, 1823, the representative of Sealy, Walker & Co., of Bahia, lodged a protest with HBM consul in Recife against the provisional junta of the province of Pernambuco for the

> seizure of 500 casks of salt cod loaded in Lisbon by Henry Fielding Junior in the Galley *Nicolau Augusto*, ... as said casks are legitimate British property.

A curious fact is that this person appears to be the son of Henry Fielding, the great English novelist who died in Lisbon. If that is true, it shows that there is no logic in the succession from father to son: a novelist

[552] *Consuls' Correspondence*, Manuscripts Section of the Pernambuco State Library.
[553] Dispatch of 7 January 1823, *Consuls' Correspondence*, Manuscripts Section of the Pernambuco State Library.

father can be succeeded by a son who trades in salt cod.

An interesting case that happened at the same time in the centre or focus of Brazilian nativism that Recife or Pernambuco was in that period – as it had been, in fact, since the seventeenth century, when the king's governor was thrown out of the captaincy by the local grandees – was the question of the property or assets of Englishmen involved in the property or assets of Portuguese forced to leave the former colony. The affair is recorded in one of the most important dispatches issued by the then HBM consul in Recife, dated 10 January 1823:

> The undersigned, His Britannic Majesty's Consul in the Province of Pernambuco, is honoured to notify Your Excellencies the President and Members of the Provisional Government Junta that, a representation having been made to him by the principal British merchants residing in this City regarding a recently promulgated edict ordering an embargo[554] and deposit of the assets of the Europeans who have emigrated or have been obliged to leave this province by Order of the Government, he has also been informed that a large proportion of the property that is thus threatened by the execution of the Edict is English property sold on credit to the individuals in question in full confidence that its owners[555] would at all times be liable for their legal debts. The undersigned is persuaded that there is no intention to confiscate either directly or indirectly His Britannic Majesty's subjects' property held in good faith: since the interests involved here are so considerable he hopes that it will please Your Excellencies to make the necessary entries in the registers for the purpose of removing any doubt and confirming the feelings that he is honoured to hold that the just claims of His Britannic Majesty's Subjects here resident will be guaranteed against this unexpected measure.[556]

Actual cases soon started appearing. One was the confiscation of the ship *Joaquim Guilherme*, against which a certain João Abrahão Mazza, representing John Fletcher in Recife, duly lodged a protest at the British consulate. As the consul pointed out in his dispatch of 6 October 1823, this ship was

> nominally Portuguese, yet virtually and in good faith English property, if the solemn oath of the consignee, Captain, Pilot and

[554] The Portuguese has '*embarque*', literally 'embarcation', assumed to be a miscopying of '*embargo*' (Translator).

[555] The Portuguese has '*suas Propriedades*', literally 'their properties', assumed to be a miscopying of '*seus Proprietarios*', 'its owners' (Translator).

[556] *Consuls' Correspondence*, Manuscripts Section of the Pernambuco State Library.

> other persons of character deserves credence.[557]

And on 12 February 1824 HBM consul in Recife put before the president of the province the petition that had been submitted to him by the English merchants established in that city on the question of the British property involved in that of Portuguese who were to be deported from the province. In this new dispatch on the subject, the consul insisted that

> the number of persons to be deported is so great, and they are so extensively indebted to the petitioners that their sudden expatriation threatens to cause serious, grievous damage to a body of respectable merchants who could never be suspected of interfering in political opinions of the country in which they reside and in which they have deposited their considerable capital, and who in their commercial transactions have always had in mind the protection of the Law with regard to debtor and creditor, and aware of the good harmony that has for so long existed, and happily still exists between Brazil and Great Britain, they naturally entertained the hope that measures or regulations would never be adopted against their debtors whereby their property would be exposed to the inevitable danger that must ensue from their expulsion, which has been done in such a short period of time that it is absolutely impossible for them to arrange or settle their accounts with them, and which is also a measure that places the greatest burden of punishment on innocent men who are subjects of a nation that is beyond doubt Brazil's best ally.[558]

Having expounded 'the reasons for the petitioners' concern', Consul John Parkinson – who was, incidentally, one of the most able and most diplomatically skilled men who passed through the British consular service in Brazil, at a particularly difficult time for a British consul in a country like this, that is, in the early decades of the nineteenth century – concluded by hoping that the period of time that the Portuguese merchants indebted to the British were allowed to remain in Pernambuco would be extended. A measure of moderation that would be received by the British with 'feelings of gratitude'.

The British did not meet with any good will on the part of President Manoel de Carvalho Paes d'Andrade, who could only see the political side of the matter: the necessary deportation – deportation with confiscation

[557] *Ibid.*

[558] *Ibid.*

of assets – of those wealthy Portuguese whose presence was a cause for concern to the Brazilians of Pernambuco. Hence the consul's dispatch of 14 February expressing his position: his primary concern was the 'loss and damage' threatening the property of His Britannic Majesty's subjects. As he pointed out,

> It is certainly not the place of the undersigned to question the need for a political measure of State adopted by a friendly, independent state; but it is part of his special duty to call on behalf of the British merchants for protection for the large mass of capital that they have transferred on trust, guaranteed with the good faith of the Law.

It happened that 'in the present case' said merchants would be unable to realize their 'just hopes...' if the state, 'without prior notice or basis in law', 'ferociously' expelled 'a body of men' who owed them 'a considerable sum that could well be calculated at 500 to 600 *contos de réis*'. The consul therefore asked the president of the province to inform him of the security measures with which His Excellency intended to replace the bond between those debtors and their properties, a bond formed in law which had been broken as a result of 'political measures of State'. And he concluded rather dramatically:

> Insisting on this measure of justice the undersigned takes this opportunity to say that he does not claim on behalf of his countrymen any privilege other than that which the Laws and practice of Great Britain would concede to Brazilian subjects: this is so strictly correct that not even the King's Government nor even the King himself has the authority to expel a foreigner against whom there is a just claim of debts.[559]

It can be seen that John Parkinson was not a man to leave a claim half-done if in his view as His Britannic Majesty's consul it was just. The conflict between his internationalism – of a characteristically British complexion – and the perhaps exaggerated nativism embodied in Manoel de Carvalho Paes d'Andrade, when he was president of the province of Pernambuco in 1824, is one of the most interesting episodes to be found in the correspondence of British consuls with Brazilian authorities.

It is also interesting to see in this correspondence of British consuls with Brazilian authorities that, after the precedent set by Rio de Janeiro in the early days of independence – when the streets of the capital, bloodied

[559] *Consuls' Correspondence*, Manuscripts Section of the Pernambuco State Library.

by the encounters of Irishmen and Germans with black men and *moleques* filled with a strange, black hatred against those pale whites, were finally restored to order thanks to the intervention of the sailors put ashore by English and French ships at the request of the imperial government – some of those authorities did not hesitate to request the same kind of help from the British navy against the same threat: the insubordination of the *capoeiras* or coloured people. In Bahia in 1837, the justice of the peace João Lourenço Seixas approached HBM consul in Salvador to ask for his help by having men put ashore from the English frigate then anchored in the harbour, since that was the only way he could guarantee the 'safety of the property of Her Britannic Majesty's subjects' in the parish of Conceição da Praia, which lay 'entirely unprotected'. There were 'well-founded suspicions' that 'in the current crisis' there might occur 'some excess on the part of the masses, especially the coloured population...'[560]

This dispatch is from 13 November 1837. A few days previously, the president of the province, Francisco de Souza Paraizo had sent a dispatch written in his own hand to the consul – the representative of 'a friendly Nation' – asking him, in view of the prospects of 'terrible anarchy' facing the province of Bahia, 'to have the British Brig of War currently in this Harbour remain some time longer here so that it may serve as support in case of need'.[561] It was an appeal by white Bahians to white Britons to lend them their ethnic solidarity in the event of any insurrection by the black population, who had already got the better of the white people's police on more than one occasion in that part of Brazil.

Yet it seems that the *Sabinada*[562] also had the support of some Englishmen. The fact that some Englishmen came from England to Brazil at this time to fight as very well-paid mercenaries against the legitimate government has already been mentioned. A dispatch received in December 1837 by HBM consul from the president of the province of Bahia says that the government was 'reliably informed' that a cutter in the service of the warships of the 'Reconcavo dissidents' was crossing the bay carrying water and was also seen in daily communication with the corvette *Sete de Abril*, which was flying the English flag. The forts and armed vessels in the government's service were respecting the cutter because of the English flag she was flying. It was consequently the consul's duty to ensure that the neutrality 'mutually promised by Your Lordship and this Government' was not being abused under cover of that flag.[563]

[560] Dispatch of 13 November 1837, Manuscript, Bahia State Public Archive.

[561] Manuscript, Bahia State Public Archive.

[562] The federalist revolt in Bahia in 1837, named after its leader, Francisco Sabino Álvares da Rocha Vieira (Translator).

[563] Manuscript, Bahia State Public Archive.

It is in fact possible that the government of Bahia was using the 'threat of a further insurrection by coloured people against the whites' in order to bring the English over to the side of the legitimate government. In order to merge its cause with that of European civilization itself, most powerfully represented in the eyes of the whole world by the English. To merge it with the very defence of the 'white race' against revolts by black or mixed-race groups.

In the Balkan confusion[564] at which Brazilian politics excelled at the time, especially in the north of the Empire – in Bahia, Pernambuco, Maranhão and Pará: provinces that in those early years of Brazil's independence were spattered with the blood of *Sabinadas*, *Balaiadas* and *Cabanadas*[565] – the English seem to have played the same kind of part as they did in the fighting in the real Balkans: though almost always courted by both sides in the disputes, they never fully committed themselves to any of the causes in question. Always seeking to defend their own interests and not specifically those of Brazilians against the Portuguese, they supported Brazil's independence from Portugal as it was in Britain's best interests. They almost always took the same stance: in the struggles of imperialists against republicans, and in the fighting in Bahia in 1837 between 'legalists' and the 'Reconcavo dissidents', their attitude was nearly always one of neutrality and a lack of interest in the political doctrines that divided Brazilians.

Although in the Pernambucan Revolution of 1824 the British residents in Pernambuco, with their consul out in front, seem to have been against the revolutionaries and nativists and for the 'Portuguese' and imperialists, the fact was that the Portuguese owed them five or six hundred *contos*. Of course, there were exceptional cases, such as that of the English merchant Charles Bowen, who was one of the revolutionaries in Pernambuco in 1817. Or the case of those Englishmen drawn to a life of adventure and fighting – men like Cochrane – who fought for Brazil's independence or the consolidation of the new empire more for money than for idealism, and more by taste or temperament than by conviction.

Those English merchants living in Recife thus showed a characteristically British attitude when, in response to the agitation in the capital of Pernambuco in 1831, they met at the consulate to lodge their protest against all the damage they may have suffered when their houses and stores were ransacked by 'armed soldiers of the Brazilian Government';

[564] The Portuguese has '*confissão*' ('confession'), which must be an error for '*confusão*' ('confusion') (Translator).

[565] The *Balaiada* (1838-1841) was a popular liberal uprising in Maranhão; the *Cabanada* (1832-1835) was a revolt in Pernambuco and Alagoas by poor people disillusioned with the Regency government, after Dom Pedro I's abdication. Similar unrest also occurred elsewhere in the 1830s and 1840s (Translator).

and also to enquire as to the fate of the agitators. When this protest was passed on to the president of the province, Joaquim José Pinheiro de Vasconcelos, by HBM consul, Mr Henry Cowper, the president replied in a dispatch dated 23 September that year that he would not take the protest into consideration. He did so 'on the advice of the Council, which I consulted on the content of Your Lordship's dispatch of 19th inst.' He judged the English merchants' protest to be 'absolutely devoid of Right'. The president assured the British merchants residing in Recife, via the consul, that the agitators were on board vessels and that they would be 'held, tried and punished according to the laws of this Empire...' He also assured them that the government of the province was working 'incessantly to maintain public safety and peace and, as is its duty, ensuring the full enforcement of the Treaties that guarantee Foreigners the enjoyment of their rights and Properties'.[566]

The attitude of the English merchants who made the protest – imitated the following day by the French – was the subject of adverse comments in a 'letter to the editor' that appeared in the *Diário de Pernambuco* on 6 October 1831; it was interpreted as arrogance by foreigners who wanted to dictate the law to Brazilians.

> Now what? [the letter asked.] Does it by any chance behove the English Merchants to ask the Brazilian Government what it intends to do about this or that? Without calling this protest impudent, we consider it pretentious that its authors, without the slightest knowledge of the Law, have the vanity to presume anything. [The letter went further:] Whereas the Independence of Brazil was a vain title with which Pedro Bourbon sought to entertain the credulous Brazilian People the more surely to enslave it, it became a reality on 7 April this year of 1831 when the Nation, knowing of the perfidies of this Portuguese, expelled him from its Territory, establishing a Homogeneous Government which does not aspire, like him, to be absolute. But since the Foreigners are accustomed to laying down the Law to us, as they did during the time of the tyrant, who needed them, they still do not want to accept that those times have gone and that Brazil is of the Brazilians, who will not suffer them to come and dictate the Law to them, as the protests made by the so-called Body of British Commerce and various consuls... and the French Merchants... make us believe.

It is interesting to note that the consuls who backed the protest did not include either the English consul, Mr Cowper – who merely passed it

[566] *Consuls' Correspondence*, Manuscripts Section of the Pernambuco State Library.

on to the provincial government – or the US consul; nor did the British merchants include Thomas Gardner & Company, Smith & Lancaster, Johnstone, Pater & Company, Harrison, Lathan & Co. or William Collins Cox. A minority of important merchants refused to join the somewhat hasty majority in their initiative, which was indeed impertinent; instead, they maintained the same discreet attitude as the consul, who now no longer felt like a kind of brig master or fusilier lieutenant in a conquered land, as some of those early British consuls in Brazil had. Those violent clashes between arrogant consuls and authoritarian captains-general such as the Count of Arcos or Luís do Rego Barreto had, I repeat, served some purpose.

As for the English merchants living in Brazil, not all of them were always both Angles and angels: some of them left their consuls in difficult positions in relation to the Brazilian authorities. In 1838, Cipriano Henriques de Faria complained to the government of his province, Bahia, that 'about ten Casks of Wheat Flour' had been removed from a house he owned in Bonfim 'by the Foreigner Garret, Assistant to the British Merchants Robson Co. ...' Since the English had not paid the Brazilian for the precious flour, the provincial government asked the consul in a dispatch dated 27 January 1838 to take steps to ensure said casks were returned to Faria or were paid for.[567] And that is not the only complaint against English merchants, signed by Francisco Sabino Alves da Roxa and addressed to Her Britannic Majesty's consul. On 8 March 1838 he addressed the same consul, sending him 'a copy signed by the chief officer of this Secretariat' – the provincial government secretariat – of

> the dispatch with which the Most Excellent Minister for the Treasury sent me a list of Foreign Merchants of this Province who have not paid the overdue amounts of the Customs bills that they have signed as subscribers, which includes Harrison, Lathan & Co. and Franside & Co. I am writing to Your Lordship to request that, as Consul of the Nation to which they belong, you advise them of how indecorous and even dishonourable it is for a Merchant to fail to strictly fulfil the agreement to which he is bound by his handwriting and signature; this Government therefore hopes that the Bills that they have signed, and are now overdue, will be settled forthwith.[568]

The head of the Bahian government must have smiled when he sent such a dispatch to HBM consul. For, only some six years before, the president of the illustrious province had received a dispatch from London

[567] Manuscript, Bahia State Public Archive.
[568] *Ibid.*

dated 5 December 1832 on a matter of a similar nature, signed simply 'Rothschild'. Jewishly mellifluous, the banker said to the president that he had not recently been 'honoured with letters from Your Excellency...' He was therefore taking the liberty to

> repeat my request for the continuation of remittances on behalf of the Imperial Government. Such remittances are much to be desired so that Brazil's credit may be maintained in the present quarter... Is there hope of soon receiving a communication from the Illustrious Treasury Committee of that Province?[569]

The dispatch from the Ministry of the Treasury on the affair is perhaps one of the most sharply worded ever issued in the history of that venerable institution, which has been compared to an ecclesiastical establishment run by bishops in frock coats: the famous 'bishops of the Treasury'. This time, the bishops surpassed themselves with a thundering sermon against merchants who were late in paying their customs bills, referring to 'scandalous conduct' dishonouring 'their own signatures', in 'the strictest legal process to the point of forgoing the sacred deposit entrusted to them when they were attributed that good faith, which they have betrayed'. For the purposes of being forwarded to the consuls – including the British consul in Bahia – the dispatch was sent to the Minister and Secretary of State for Foreign Affairs. It was signed by Joaquim da Silva Freire and the copy was certified by the chief officer Ignacio José Aprigio da Fonseca Galvão.[570] Insignificant details recorded here for no real reason, except for the fact that this was in fact an extraordinary case: Englishmen being severely reprimanded by Brazilian authorities for failing to make payments guaranteed by their signatures. This was more than extraordinary – almost fantastic – in a country where, as we have seen, the expression 'an Englishman's word' had come to mean the same as word of honour, and 'Englishman's time' the same as absolute punctuality.

But there is no rule without exceptions, as the grammar books say; and as is also said even more loudly than those books by that other grammar full of irregular verbs that is the character or behaviour of the British people. And not only the British people, but humankind itself. Everything human is contradictory, and there are no absolute laws that define human character or the history of a people. While the history of Brazil's relations with Great Britain during the nineteenth century is filled with countless cases in which the English appear as the heroes in the quasi-romance of chivalry played out on the sea and the beaches that was the repression of the slave

[569] *Ibid.*
[570] *Ibid.*

trade by British warships and consuls, with the Portuguese or Brazilians as the villains, we can also find in the correspondence of the Portuguese or Brazilian authorities with HBM consuls evidence or traces of villainy carried out by individuals of the 'race of Heroes' in the lands or waters of the 'villains'. Even Englishmen suspected of dealing in counterfeit money. Police traditions in Rio de Janeiro, as mentioned in an earlier chapter, hold that the first counterfeiter in Brazil was an Englishman. And in 1830 an adventure story unfurled on the coast of Pernambuco with Englishmen playing the main roles; but I am not sure whether they were the kind that would have interested the Anglophile Joseph Conrad for one of his books on British sailors battling the waves in tropical seas. In August that year the justice of the peace of Itamaracá seized ninety sacks, not of wheat flour but of copper coins with a face value of 80 réis, each sack holding an amount worth 100$000. They were seized from

> 'a Raft or *Jangada*, which was forced by bad weather to put in to that place on its way to Parahyba do Norte, as the raftsmen stated to said Judge, claiming that they had received that money from an English Brig off Pao Amarelo, and their Raft had been hired for that purpose by some Englishmen residing in this city of Recife.[571]

The justice of the peace saw grounds for suspecting it was counterfeit money. Perhaps he knew that the English firm involved in the matter of sending sacks of copper from Recife to Paraíba – Mitchel, Smith, Lamberth & Co. – had been in trouble with the customs in Bahia the year before because of a load of gunpowder that had arrived from the brig *Quebec Packet*, which the firm wanted to reload 'duty-free'. On that occasion, according to a dispatch from said merchants to HBM vice-consul in Salvador, dated 6 May 1829, the purveyor of Bahia had made 'allegations against our character', to which they were responding by stating they had always 'acted in the most perfect good faith'; the information against them that the purveyor had given to the president of the province was 'full of misrepresentations'.[572]

The justice of the peace immediately had the 80 sacks held 'for Deposit, at the Treasury Committee Building, forwarding all clarifications in that respect to the General Magistrate of Crime for him to proceed according to the Law'. The magistrate, however, admitted to being unable 'to perform a legal examination on which to base the competent criminal procedure', in view of which the justice of the peace sent to the president of the province himself

[571] Manuscripts Section of Pernambuco State Library.

[572] Manuscript, Bahia State Public Archive.

> one of the above-mentioned sacks, the one with the mark H. & C.ª n. 42, which contains the sum of one hundred mil-réis, and it is inside another sack sealed with the mark F. P., to order that the Mint in that Capital perform the necessary examination of the coins so as to fulfil the purpose required by that magistrate.

The justice names the English merchants mentioned by the raftsmen and reports the explanation they offered for that mysterious shipment of sacks of copper coins: a shipment of copper to 'their partners in the City of Parahyba'. Suspecting a crime, however, the justice of the peace remained inflexible: 'Nothing may be decided before the Investigation is concluded.' That comes from the dispatch on the affair sent to the Marquis of Barbacena[573] by President Pinheiro de Vasconcelos, dated at the 'City of Recife de Pernambuco on 31 August 1830'.[574]

The justice of the peace in Itamaracá was suspicious of the copper coins because copper was then so suspect a material that British consuls would give their 'official protection' to imports or re-exports of 'copper of British manufacture' to distinguish it from transactions for doubtful purposes. That is what we find HBM consul in the city of Salvador doing in a dispatch of 18 February 1832, addressed to the government of the province. He tells the Brazilian authority that

> a British establishment in this city had sent a representation to him alleging that in the Customs House they had eight crates of copper of British manufacture for furnaces and for Boilers that they wish to re-export to Pernambuco. They also inform me that they are ready to ship them in a Brazilian Packet and give the greatest guarantees that they will be duly delivered to the Customs House in Pernambuco. [And the consul solemnly concludes:] May I at the same time assure Your Excellency that I would never lend my official protection to a transaction that appeared suspicious.[575]

A sign that any importing or re-exporting of copper at that

[573] Felisberto Caldeira Brant Pontes de Oliveira Horta, Marquis of Barbacena (1772-1842), was Minister for the Treasury at the time (Translator).
[574] Manuscripts Section of Pernambuco State Library.
[575] Manuscript, Bahia State Public Archive.

time was a sensitive subject. We shall find further evidence of this in the correspondence between that consul and that government. For the president of Bahia replied to HBM consul's dispatch of 18 February with objections based on the lamentable state that the circulation of copper in that part of Brazil had reached, because of the production and distribution of counterfeit coins.[576] The consul, in turn, argued against that, understanding that the president's justifiable reflections were not a response to his dispatch but instead 'applicable to the country's police rather than the importers'.

> The copper of British manufacture to which I allude [he added] was imported to Bahia as a regular and legal object of trade under the Treaty between Brazil and Great Britain.

Since an impediment had been placed on the release of said copper in Bahia, the owner was seeking to re-export it on a Brazilian ship to another part of Brazil. Detention of the copper under those circumstances, according to the consul, was tantamount to confiscation. Hence he insisted on a new pronouncement from the head of the Bahian government on the subject, which he repeated in a dispatch of 14 March 1832. He wished to know whether there was any legal prohibition preventing HBM subjects who were merchants from re-exporting goods of British manufacture from Bahia to Pernambuco or any other part of the Empire.[577]

The consul eventually won, and the copper was re-exported. And on 6 August of that year, 1832, the same consul reappeared, arguing for another British firm established in Bahia to be allowed to re-export twenty crates of copper of British manufacture to Rio de Janeiro

> subject to the same precautions and guarantees under which the firm of Moore & Co. recently exported with the sanction of the His Excellency the President of the Province.[578]

It was the police that should investigate the use or abuse of that copper.

Although these notes are limited to the examination and attempted interpretation of certain aspects of the relations between the British and Brazilians, as revealed or suggested by old dispatches from HBM consuls or their correspondence with Brazilian authorities in the last years of

[576] *Ibid.*
[577] *Ibid.*
[578] *Ibid.*

colonial Brazil and the early years of the Empire, while the examination and attempted interpretation of other aspects of those relations are reserved for another little study, it would be an injustice to the subject to interrupt it at this point: the importing and re-exporting of English copper, which seems to have been used by someone in Brazil to produce counterfeit coins, perhaps with the complicity of certain British importers and re-exporters. It is difficult to resist the temptation, however. So let us for a moment leave the consuls' dispatches to gather information from other sources on copper smuggling in Brazil during the times of Dom João VI and the early years of Empire.

'In 1821 there was only copper that was largely counterfeit and banknotes' in circulation.[579] A reflection of the disarray of honest activities in the country caused by the presence of adventurers in Rio de Janeiro eager for quick profits, some of them men of prestige at Court. Mathison, who was in Brazil at the time and observed our economic life through the eyes of an expert, says that the period of Dom João VI in Brazil was one of poor administration. Few improvements had resulted from the vast sums collected in taxes,

> yet, at the same time, it is remarked that large fortunes have been realised by many official personages.[580]

Much corruption in official and semi-official circles. Huge fortunes suddenly amassed by eminent dignitaries. Many irregularities in the customs houses:

> The collection of the customs was ... notoriously ill-conducted, and smuggling systematically pursued on a large scale. ... [With all the smuggling:] the regular course of trade was very much impeded, and an undue advantage given to the smuggler over the fair and honorable trader.[581]

The king issued paper currency without any scruples: to buy small

[579] Victor Vianna, *O Banco do Brasil – Sua formação, seu engrandecimento, sua missão nacional*, Rio de Janeiro, 1926, p. 116.
[580] Mathison, *Narrative of a Visit to Brazil...*, p. 134 (quoted by Freyre in English – Translator). The historian Tobias Monteiro points out that 'the venality of men of position' in Dom João VI's court was the subject of remarks by the Austrian Minister, Baron Stürmer, the scientist Saint-Hilaire and Silva Arêas, who chronicled that period in his letters, writing: 'it is impossible to have more prevarication, more dilapidation and more madness' (Tobias Monteiro, *História do Império – A elaboração da Independência*, Rio de Janeiro, 1927, p. 245).
[581] Mathison, *Narrative of a Visit to Brazil...*, pp. 134-5 (quoted by Freyre in English – Translator).

items in the shops a person had to carry a bagful of copper coins, as that was all there was, apart from the over-abundant paper money.[582]

In such a situation, it is not surprising that some of the English merchants in Brazil allowed themselves to be seduced by the adventure of smuggling copper, a product that soon began to be regularly imported from Great Britain into Brazilian ports. Or even by the risks of counterfeiting coins.

Therefore, despite all their austerity, the dispatches from HBM consuls do not always succeed in dispelling our impression that there really were some British merchants in the Brazil of Dom João VI and the early years of the Empire who were involved in smuggling copper and even counterfeiting coins. Such British merchants, smugglers or counterfeiters played their part alongside Portuguese and local people – and other foreigners – in flooding Brazil with fake copper coins by 1833. As Victor Vianna says in his work on the Banco do Brasil:

> The fake coins, clandestinely minted, amounted to 5,000 *contos*. Law No 52 of 3 October 1833 provided for the complete replacement of the copper coinage in circulation.[583]

Walsh remarks on page 251, volume I, of his book on the Empire under Dom Pedro I that the copper coins circulating in Brazil at that time were large, excessively heavy and therefore inconvenient.[584] They were made of copper imported from England, but a considerable part of that English material was wasted because of poor technology. A British merchant then had the idea of buying the copper waste and sending it back to England, where it was remade into copper sheet which was then imported again by Brazil. The merchant thus managed to make a fortune from the leftovers of the copper used to mint Brazilian eighty-réis coins, until the imperial government realized what a loss it was making and started purchasing copper from England already cut to the size of the Brazilian coin. That did not stop copper sheet from coming illicitly from England to Brazil. There was not always a Brazilian consul in London with such a sharp eye for such irregularities as Manoel Antônio Galvão, who on 6 April 1836 communicated to one of the authorities in his country that he had been informed of the preparation of a 'large quantity of copper sheet to be sent to some of our ports'. The consul hoped to 'thwart that purpose', according to a dispatch sent by him to the president of the province of Bahia, which

582 *Ibid.*, p. 145.

583 Vianna, *O Banco do Brasil*, p. 179.

584 Walsh says that the most common coin in use was an eighty-réis piece, worth four English pence at that time (Walsh, *Notices of Brazil*, I, pp. 250-251) (Translator).

is now among the manuscripts in the State Archive.

These manuscripts also include documents relating to the compensation to which English merchants established in the capital of that province felt entitled 'for false copper coins deposited by them in the House of Exchange for recall...' On 18 October 1828 the then acting HBM consul in Bahia, Carlos Weis, asked the president of the province to declare

> that part of the money that has recently arrived from the capital of Rio de Janeiro is intended for the payment of more than 500,000$000 owed to the British Merchants of this City for copper coin deposited by them in the House of Exchange...

Faced with such a request, repeated in a dispatch of 29 October that year, the president of Bahia, Manoel Ignacio da Cunha e Menezes, wrote to acting consul Weis on 26 October 1828:

> ...in view of the content of said [dispatch] I cannot respond to Your Lordship better or more satisfactorily than by sending you the enclosed copy of the Provision of the National Treasury dated 18 August of the current year, in accordance with which we must act in this matter.

The procedure that had been adopted since May that year by the provincial government of Bahia, which was apparently confirmed by the Provision of the National Treasury, seems to have been established by José Egídio Gordilho de Barbacuda in a dispatch of 25 May 1828 to the acting consul, in which he responded to the request of the

> English Merchants who have deposited various sums of false coin to be exchanged [so as to effect] the prompt payment thereof. I have personally informed Your Lordship and some of those Merchants that, since the abundance of copper coin that was in circulation exceeded all expectations, there will consequently be insufficient means to pay for it in full and that although the Commission finds itself in the difficult position of making use of extraordinary coins these will not be enough to cover the receipts for deposits that it has issued. The English Merchants are well aware of the good faith with which the Commission has acted in this affair, and therefore it does not believe it deserves the slightest blame, hoping that His Imperial Majesty will soon hand down the measures that are urgently needed

> in this respect. ... The recall amounted to more than 5,000 *cruzados*, the loan did not exceed 224 *contos de réis* [and] the amount of the receipts issued by the Commission totalled 900 *contos de réis*.

With regard to another concession relating to copper that English merchants in Bahia claimed – to be able to re-export it outside the province – the president of Bahia had already written to HBM consul, Mr William Pennell, in a dispatch of 8 January 1828, saying that although he was aware

> that the Order of May 1812 favours their claims, I can equally appreciate how extraordinary is the crisis in which this Province has found and still finds itself: for which reason it is impossible for me to accede to their desires without justly incurring censure for ignoring the fact that public salvation is the first of all laws.

A dramatic declaration from a government which, nevertheless, had not the means or the skills to resist the insistent demands from British commerce, through the words and deeds of HBM consuls, to re-export copper from one port to another in the Empire, thus facilitating illicit trade and the counterfeiting of coins.

It should be emphasized that the part of the Brazilian population most hurt by the counterfeiting of copper coins was the poor. 'It was the poor classes that suffered most from this state of affairs,' wrote the German Eduard Theodor Bösche in 1835, in his *Wechselbilder*,[585] referring to the early years of the Empire. 'They went hungry because they only had copper and nobody wanted to take it,' adds Bösche, who also gives us the information that the main speculators or smugglers of copper coins in Brazil in those days were not English but Americans:

> American speculators at that time smuggled shiploads of copper into Brazil and received the most precious metals in return.

By pushing the lower classes into destitution, this must have contributed to 'the robberies and attacks on houses...'[586] Including the

[585] Eduard Theodor Bösche, *Wechselbilder von Land- und Sittenschilderungen während einer Fahrt nach Brasilien*, ('Alternate impressions of descriptions of the country and customs during a journey to Brazil'), Hamburg, 1836; published in Portuguese as 'Quadros alternados de viagens terrestres e marítimas, acontecimentos políticos, descrição de usos e costumes de povos durante uma viagem ao Brasil, de 1824 a 1834', *Revista do Instituto Histórico e Geográfico*, 83 (1919), pp. 133-241.
[586] *Ibid.*, p. 219 (Brazilian edition).

houses of those rich Englishmen whom the most impoverished Brazilians saw as profiting from their distress.

In 1829 it was irregularities in the importing not of copper but of gunpowder from England that led to somewhat acerbic dispatches from the president of the province of Bahia – the Viscount of Camamu that year – to HBM consul. One of them was the dispatch of 5 May 1829 in which the president of the province told the consul that the merchants Mitchel, Smith, Lamberth & Co. had

> misinformed Your Lordship regarding the aversion they have shown to having the gunpowder currently on board the English brig *Quebec* unloaded, as the Customs purveyor has just notified me in a dispatch... [And he concludes in authoritarian tone:] in view of which, and since the Brig's lingering is yet further proof that she had no other destination than this Port, she must immediately have the gunpowder in question deposited, as I have already notified Your Lordship, of whom I again demand prompt action since I wish to act in all things in accordance with Your Lordship in order not to employ the coercive measures that this Government has at its disposal.

Together with copper, gunpowder seems to have been a product that was widely smuggled from England into Brazil in the first half of the nineteenth century. The smuggling was sometimes carried out by Englishmen, who thus took revenge for the smuggling of Africans by Brazilians against the sacrosanct interests of the British, rather than against their Christian sentiments.

Why was so much gunpowder smuggled? What was special in Brazil during the last years of the Colony and the first decades of the Empire that made this secret trade so profitable: trade which, although not appearing in newspaper advertisements, does emerge in the correspondence of the Brazilian authorities with HBM consuls? It seems there were two factors that encouraged the smuggling of gunpowder in Brazil at that time: the conspiracies, minor revolutions and rebellions that threatened to and sometimes did break out; and the fireworks (another oriental survival in Brazil) for church festivals, saints' processions, novenas, Saint John's days and Easter Saturdays – festivals that were only enjoyable when vast amounts of gunpowder were used. Without counting the official use of gunpowder for salvos on royal birthdays, arrivals of illustrious dignitaries, funerals and investitures; or for the equally commemorative rockets fired on all such occasions.

Ferdinand Denis, who was in Brazil in the early nineteenth century, mentions the 'discharges of rockets fired in front of the churches'. The French observer, whose *Brésil* is one of the best books written about our country, although much of it merely repeats Reverend Walsh in an elegant style, adds that to these rockets

> are attached crackers, which explode and fill the air with a cloud of white smoke dotted with little sparks.[587]

In fact, there was hardly a day in the year when people in some district or suburb of Brazilian cities were not celebrating some saint or our-lady. And not just with plenty of wax, but with plenty of gunpowder as well. The wax was imported from the coast of Africa 'expressly for this use', says Denis; the gunpowder appears to have been mainly from England. According to the calculations of a friend of Walsh – who concerned himself with the subject before Denis did, with his accustomed objectivity – the amount of money that Brazil spent on this wax and gunpowder was enormous;[588] and those who profited most from this excess of 'popery' seem to have been the Protestant English gunpowder merchants – or smugglers. Walsh does not say as much: it is little-known documents from the period that indicate this irregularity.

Why the contraband in gunpowder? Perhaps because buying from smugglers worked out cheaper for the brotherhoods, which were the main organizers of the religious festivals and commemorations. Perhaps because at least some of the gunpowder was, as I have already suggested, intended for revolutionaries or conspirators, under the blanket – who knows? – of the then powerful Freemasonry movement, the enemy of absolutism and the friend of liberal movements, which was full of English merchants. The fact is that on 13 August 1818, the Portuguese representative in England wrote from London to Thomaz Antonio de Villanova Portugal:

> It is also my honour to pass into Your Excellency's hands the original Letter that Antonio Julião da Costa has written to me, in which, giving further proof of the zeal and activity with which

[587] Ferdinand Denis, *Brésil*, Paris, 1839, p. 131. Here Denis repeats Walsh, who writes: 'The eve of a saint's festival is always announced at twelve o'clock the day before, by a discharge of three sky-rockets, in front of the church. These rockets are filled with crackers, which explode high in the air, and then descend in showers of white smoke, on the roof of the building. [...] the whole year is an uninterrupted succession of these explosions, in some part of the town' (Walsh, *Notices of Brazil*, I, p. 210). (Quoted by Freyre in English – Translator.)

[588] Walsh (*Notices of Brazil*, I, p. 211) writes: 'there was annually expended one hundred contos of reis, or about fifteen thousand pounds sterling, in wax and gunpowder, as essential requisites to the worship of God.'

> he performs his duties, that consul informs me of the attempt to smuggle gunpowder from Liverpool to Pernambuco, which has in all probability happened on several occasions. Before receiving this dispatch I had already received information that another attempt was being made here intended for other Captaincies of Brazil, including even Rio de Janeiro, and sometimes in small Barrels apparently of Beer, and released as such... After assuring Your Excellency that I shall recommend this inspection to the activity of our Consuls, I must explain to Your Excellency that this and other forms of smuggling are performed, I am told, by means of the Volumes that I believe are called *Canastros*[589] there, which do not go to the Customs House and merely on the basis of a verbal declaration of their contents are released even on board without any inspection; I therefore take the liberty of reminding Your Excellency of the convenience of ordering that in future such *Canastros* or volumes of the nature of those that pass through in that manner be taken to the Customs House and there examined before they are released. May God keep Your Excellency. London, 13 August 1818 – Rafael da Cruz-Guerra.[590]

As a result of that, the customs officers and port police in Brazil started carrying out stricter inspections of the loads brought in by ships arriving from Liverpool. And at least one English firm established in Bahia and Pernambuco, with a branch in Paraíba as well, was suspected of being involved in gunpowder smuggling. On 9 August 1833 the president of the province of Bahia wrote a rather sharp dispatch to HBM consul, who had complained to him about measures taken by the port authorities regarding an English brig, the *Hero*, suspected of carrying contraband.[591]

After Brazil became independent, the customs houses raised their charges on the orders of His Imperial Majesty's government, to the indignation of the British merchants or importers established in the country. Those in Bahia, at least, who met to protest against the change,

[589] Literally, large baskets or hampers (Translator).

[590] *Consuls' Correspondence*, Manuscripts Section of the Pernambuco State Library. While travelling in the interior of Brazil in 1818, Luccock met a woman who had some smuggled gunpowder. He writes: 'Considering the laws against the private sale of gunpowder, and the jealousy of the government with respect to that article, I could not notice, without surprise, that, as we passed along, an old woman offered us as much as three pounds of that article for sale; she had it concealed, indeed, among her clothes, and made the offer to us, as strangers, with some little secrecy; but it seems as though the laws were relaxed, or exercised with less strictness than formerly; and this supposition is confirmed by the fact, which we afterwards learned, that much powder is secretly made, ...' (Luccock, *Notes on Rio de Janeiro*, p. 517).

[591] Manuscript, Bahia State Public Archive.

which they considered harmful to their just and honest interests. The protest was sent to the provincial government by HBM consul in the city of Salvador, and President Luís de Araújo Basto replied in a dispatch on 21 June 1830, pointing out that Article 19 of the Treaty of Commerce between the Empire of Brazil and Great Britain laid down the procedures for reviewing the valuation of any item: through representations by the relevant consul and not protests by merchants. As for the new charges:

> it is not the English Merchants who will be harmed by such excessive charges, because the consumers will bear the burden of all the duties imposed on goods that they need and which the Merchants themselves do not sell without calculating their real cost and a profit proportionate to the market circumstances.

In a further dispatch on 11 August that year, replying to one in which HBM consul insisted that the protest was legitimate, the president of the province of Bahia declared that it was not in his power 'to make any decision contrary to that which is determined in the Imperial Provisions that order that said charges be implemented'. And, returning to the subject again at the consul's provocation, the president of the province of Bahia contrasted the Empire of Brazil with British imperialism, stating that 'the lists of articles valued too highly in the new Charges' should be sent up 'to the August Presence of His Majesty the Emperor'.[592]

The consul and the English merchants in Bahia must have felt avenged towards the provincial government or the Brazilian imperial authorities when, in a dispatch of 23 September the following year, they submitted to the president

> a documented representation from the British Merchants established in this City regarding fraud discovered in some sacks of cotton and Boxes of Sugar exported from here to Europe...[593]

That fact should also be taken up to the august presence of His Majesty the Emperor. But, documented as the complaint was, it made the Brazilian exporters look bad compared with the British importers.

The grievances were constantly being offset on either side, however; and it is surely because of such give-and-take that cordial relations between the two peoples were able to grow through mutual tolerance. If contraband gunpowder came from Liverpool to Brazil, then sugar mixed with soil or

[592] Dispatch of 17 August 1839, Bahia State Public Archive.

[593] Manuscript, Bahia State Public Archive.

cotton mixed with stones went from Maranhão, Bahia or Pernambuco to England. If Brazilian customs officers mistreated British merchants, then sailors off British frigates were so disorderly in the ports that the people lost their patience and forced the local police to take strong action against the unruly sea-dogs.

In 1831, sailors from English frigates anchored in Bahia harbour ran riot to such an extent that they tried

> to force a poor washerwoman, and started mistreating her as well as a son of hers, and another woman with a child who came to help was actually injured...

That was the information given to the president of the province by the district judge of Vitória parish. The president sent that dispatch to HBM consul together with another dated 22 December 1831. In this dispatch he wrote:

> And I must add that, as this is not the first time that disrespect has been shown when cutters from English Frigates have landed in such places, it will be convenient to avoid coming ashore in areas that are deserted and unsuitable for disembarking, where all kinds of crime may be committed with impunity.[594]

But it was not only in deserted areas that British subjects ran wild – there were vagabonds who jumped ship or ill-intentioned sailors like those who on 14 July 1833 came ashore from ships anchored in the harbour, went to the house of Miguel dos Anjos Garcia and 'broke into this Citizen's house on the pretext that some women they knew lived there...', according to a dispatch from the justice of the peace, Francisco Exequiel Meira, to the president of the province on 30 June that year.[595] They sometimes even ran riot in the city centres. Or in the more elegant suburbs. Watched by more respectable people from their town houses or country residences.

The justice of the peace of Conceição da Praia had already been forced to arrest disorderly Englishmen who were wandering the streets of his parish, 'sleeping under the arches of Santa Barbara or in the dockyards, or under the covers and in the works on the quayside'. He himself, the justice of the peace, had been disturbed by those ruffians:

594 Manuscript, Bahia State Public Archive.

595 *Ibid.* (There seems to be an error with one of these dates, as the dispatch reporting the event appears to precede the event itself – Translator.)

> ...I have often been disturbed out of hours by fights that they were having with others whose money they had stolen from their pockets while they were asleep, which resulted their exchanging many punches and ending up with broken noses and lips...

He would then have some of those ruffians held at Ribeira until morning, when he would release them; others who were drunk were taken to the Arsenal and kept there until they sobered up; and the justice of the peace would always tell them to work and accept 'any way of earning a living, however small, so as to abandon such a bad life'. In his dispatch to the president of the province – who passed on the magistrate's information to HBM consul – the justice of the peace continued:

> And they answer that they do not need to work in this country, that the climate itself takes care of them, and that they live like that in their own land where the extreme cold alone forces them to work to clothe and feed themselves and to have a house for shelter and to buy firewood to keep themselves warm by the fire, in fact the cold alone would be enough to kill them, but here they do not need much clothing and they sleep very well anywhere in the street without feeling cold; finally some inhabitants of the Reconcavo have enticed some to take them elsewhere, and there they have given them work, but they put up with it for very little time and as soon as they can they run away to this City and prefer to live this wretched life here...[596]

Clearly, these northern men left on quaysides by their country's ships were not ideal settlers for nineteenth-century Brazil, with its monoculture and plantations. Nor were they the 'English rural workers' that José Bonifácio so wanted for Brazil, according to the historian Octávio Tarqüínio de Sousa in his recent study of this great Brazilian's life and works – a study in which the art and science of biography reach heights rarely attained in our literature.

In addition, some of those maladjusted British subjects gave HBM consuls themselves a good deal of trouble. There are dispatches from British consuls to Brazilian authorities asking them to take action against unruly or insubordinate Englishmen. On 20 January 1825, Mr Parkinson, HBM consul in Pernambuco, sent a dispatch to Brigadier-General Lima e Silva,

[596] Manuscript, Bahia State Public Archive. José Bonifácio's efforts to attract 'English rural workers' to Brazil resulted in first fifty and then 200 such workers embarking for Brazil in 1822 (Octávio Tarqüínio de Sousa, *José Bonifácio – 1763-1838*, Rio de Janeiro, 1945, p. 208.

who was in charge of the provincial government, asking His Excellency to hear from his secretary Joaquim Pereira Branco

> the exposition of the unruly conduct of an Englishman named Philipps, an assistant at the House of Henry Worths & Co., hoping that it will please Your Excellency to adopt the necessary measures to prevent the repetition of such scandalous conduct.[597]

On 13 January 1823 the same consul had informed the president of the province that

> a certain Cuthbert Marx, supercargo of the brig *London*, had behaved with violence and animosity in this consulate, using threatening and insulting language to the undersigned in the performance of his duties...

And, again in Recife, one of those ruffians even punched an English clergyman. That information is from a dispatch of 11 July 1826 from HBM vice-consul in Pernambuco to the president of the province, who at the time was Francisco de Paula Cavalcanti de Albuquerque. He had just received a serious letter from the 'Rev. John Penney, Chaplain of the British Chapel': the clergyman was complaining that he had been 'attacked and mistreated by Robert Singlehurst, a British merchant...' The vice-consul therefore asked the head of government to 'adopt the appropriate measures' to ensure that 'that insult' would not happen again.[598] Singlehurst seems to have been an Englishman with a fiery temper – perhaps with red hair to match – as his name appears in reports of violence or aggression on more than one occasion.

It seems there is no doubt, however, that in the first half of the nineteenth century the Brazilian police committed many abuses against well-behaved Englishmen like Mr John Carrol Junior, another Recife resident. One fine day, Mr Carrol, a well-mannered man, found himself thrown into the Calabouço prison alongside thieves. He was told the reason for his arrest was to make him 'serve in the National Guard'.[599] He was thought to be a vagabond, like those who worried the justice of the peace in Conceição da Praia and even aroused the interest of sugarcane planters, who were eager to find replacements for African slaves, who were becoming scarce and difficult to find after Britain's suppression of

[597] *Consuls' Correspondence*, Manuscripts Section of the Pernambuco State Library.

[598] *Ibid.*

[599] Dispatch from HBM consul to the president of the province of Pernambuco of 6 March 1842, *Consuls' Correspondence*, Manuscripts Section of the Pernambuco State Library.

the trade. And what replacements would they like to employ to work in their cane fields and sugar mills more than 'British vagabonds'? But that subject is too vast to be addressed here in the middle of a variety of topics: it requires a separate study, which has in fact already begun, for a work in which I shall try to examine and interpret the transition from slave to free labour in this country.[600]

Other topics that I must also leave for a separate study are almost like episodes from a romance of chivalry which unexpectedly spring out at anyone who today examines old dispatches from British consuls in Brazil. One example is the case that we can glimpse in a certain dispatch sent in 1824 by HBM consul to the president of the province of Bahia. On 6 May that year, the president replied to the consul, referring to the 'conduct of the master of the British Vessel, who seeks to take with him secretly a girl who has run away from her parents' house'. And he praised 'the honourable feelings' of the consul, sending him an order 'for the Inspector to grant him the necessary powers for such a purpose'. It is a case that begs clarification, if clarification is possible, since it is such a mysterious and personal subject.

That part of the correspondence of British consuls in Brazil that deals with the 'hiring of engineers' will also remain for another study, as will consideration of the reports left for us by HBM representatives in Brazil on colonization and immigration issues. Here I shall merely suggest that at a certain point in Brazil – during the first transitional decades that followed the arrival in Rio de Janeiro not only of His Royal Highness the prince regent but also Their Royal Highnesses the English merchants – there was real excitement not only about the goods or products of English industries – especially machinery – but also about British fashions and technical methods, particularly the methods of engineers. If people expected miracles from machines and instruments of British manufacture, which were so often advertised in the newspapers of the time, then they also expected that English engineers, whom governments and individuals then sought to hire for public services or private industries, would work wonders here as if they were magicians and not mere human beings. In fact, Brazilian adolescents in the nineteenth century saw magic in certain symbolic initials, such as 'hp' (horsepower); certain words such as 'kilowatts'; and various other signs of British dominion over facts or things in physics, mechanics and electricity. In the eyes of those adolescents, Saint George had got off his horse and onto a locomotive: he had taken on the shape of an English engineer. And the consuls' correspondence allows us to see significant aspects of this new cult or new mystique. But let us not get ahead of ourselves with regard to either engineers or British doctors in

[600] *Ordem e Progresso*, to be published shortly. (In fact, it was only published in 1959 – Translator.)

Brazil during the last century.

The fact is that the matters revealed in consuls' dispatches are not only prosaic – or novelistic merely in the sense of adventure or detective novels, such as the hunting-down of Brazilian slavers by English ship captains, with the constant co-operation of HBM consuls turned detective, or the pursuit of real or supposed English smugglers or counterfeiters by the more zealous or honest Brazilian authorities. There are also episodes that even today touch our feelings, rather than merely excite our imaginations or our curiosities. Such was the interest that HBM acting consul in Bahia in 1829 took in a certain John ('João') Davies, 'a free black from the Coast of Africa and a British subject', whom a local trickster named Vicente enticed off the schooner-brig *Venus*, on which Davies worked, only to 'try to sell said João Davies as a slave of this country...', according to a dispatch that the vice-consul addressed to the president of the province on 18 February that year. At that time, incidentally, the official interpreter at the British consulate in Bahia was Jonathan Abbot – the poor little Englishman who was to become one of the greatest medical doctors in Bahia. It was he who translated into Portuguese the vice-consul's correspondence with the president of Bahia about the free black man called John Davies. The police had arrested not only Vicente but Davies too. The vice-consul then made every effort to the British subject set free. He insisted on his release in a dispatch of 5 December. And he finally obtained the order for Davies's release, 'his arrest being considered unfounded'.[601]

Another interesting episode reflected in HBM consuls' correspondence with Brazilian authorities, with which we shall close this chapter, concerns the play put on by the English residents of Bahia in the city's theatre on the evening of 29 November 1831. They set aside the takings from the show for the Orphanage Charity. HBM consul in Salvador soon received a dispatch from the president of the province that was almost lyrical, or sentimental, in its effusion and almost rose-tinted in its tenderness:

> ... I must beg Your Lordship to tell them [the English residents of Bahia] that this Government, bearing in mind said benefice, cannot fail to thank them for this act of charity towards a group of Brazilians who, in their innocence and state of Orphanhood, are worthy of Humanity's assistance. May God keep Your Lordship.[602]

Yet another rosy aspect of the correspondence between presidents of Brazilian provinces and HBM consuls was that concerning plant seeds

[601] Manuscript, Bahia State Public Archive.

[602] *Ibid.*

brought by English people and offered to Brazil by British consuls. On 11 July 1834 the president of the province of Bahia thanked HBM consul for that, saying he held the offer 'in the greatest esteem': it would enrich the Botanical Garden, established by his government in the Public Promenade, with exotic plants. Which shows that the English did not confine themselves to transplanting giant water-lilies and orchids from Brazil to the greenhouses of England: they also brought to this country plants that could grow in the botanic gardens and scent the foul air of Brazilian cities at the time of the Kingdom or Empire. And such an offer made to His Excellency the president of a Brazilian province by His Lordship HBM consul suddenly breaks down the bureaucratic aridity of the correspondence between those authorities to give it a sweet, almost feminine tenderness: the tenderness of humankind towards flowers, trees and plants.

# CHAPTER IV

# THE CHRONICLER OF THE *WARSPITE* (1831)

*... he [Dom Pedro I] turned to Mr. Aston, the British chargé d'affaires, and, indicating the British fleet at anchor in the bay of Rio de Janeiro, exclaimed, "Let us send to Admiral Baker for some boats!"*[603]

(*W. H. Koebel,* British Exploits in South America, *New York, 1917, pp. 340-341.*)

*The emperor had completely lost the popularity he had had at independence, and in the eyes of the liberals he looked like a foreign usurper, a Portuguese king governing Brazil supported only by the Portuguese merchants and the clique surrounding him. Disorder soon spilled onto the streets of Rio de Janeiro.*

(*Octávio Tarqüínio de Sousa,* José Bonifácio – 1763-1838, *Rio de Janeiro, 1945, pp. 281-282.*)

[603] Quoted by Freyre in English (Translator).

Political historians of Brazil owe a great deal to Englishmen like Walsh, Mathison, Koster, Sidney Smith, the Earl of Dundonald and Bryce – and not only to Southey and Armitage.

Those Englishmen did not write histories of Brazil. Just 'narratives', 'diaries' or 'travels'. Nevertheless, they helped to elucidate people and events in Brazil through their valuable statements or observations.

In Pernambuco, an Englishwoman, Mrs Graham, witnessed the preparations for one of the passionate anti-Portuguese revolutions that would result in the independence of Brazil, and was also Cochrane's emissary to Paes d'Andrade; and she left us a wealth of accurate information on Brazilian personalities and events in the early nineteenth century. Without her notes, our knowledge of some of those events would today be incomplete, or deformed by the passions of the political chroniclers of the time.

The same is true of the notes left to us by two other English observers of political events in our country, whose narratives, however, remain almost unknown to Brazilians. The first of these, Lieutenant Count Thomas O'Neil,1 published in 1810 *A Concise and Accurate Account of the Proceedings of the Squadron under the Command of Rear Admiral Sir Sydney Smith, K. S. &c. in Effecting the Escape of the Royal Family of Portugal to the Brazils, on November, 29, 1807;* and also the Sufferings of the Royal Fugitives, &c. during their Voyage from Lisbon *to Rio Janeiro: with a Variety of Other Interesting and Authentic Facts.*

The other is the chronicler of the *Warspite*, His Britannic Majesty's ship on which Dom Pedro I and his family – except for the future Dom Pedro II – took refuge in 1831 before sailing on to Portugal. This 'naval spectator',

[1] His name is misspelt 'O'Beil' by Freyre (Translator).

as Koebel[2] calls him on the pages where he reports the observations made by the *Warspite's* chronicler, apparently from originals kept in a special archive,[3] perhaps overuses the humorous tone, which it is so easy for someone from a powerful nation to do when dealing with incidents in which the main players are individuals or groups from a secondary and somewhat exotic nation. But another chronicler would have been unlikely to record the aspects that he did.

That naval officer was his ship's interpreter or linguist. He knew Portuguese and French. He even knew Latin. He was therefore able to witness many an interesting scene. And to understand what was said at such times in Portuguese and French, and not just English. Never had official duty so suited an inquisitive temperament. And never had British inquisitiveness been better served by a talent for languages. He writes:

> The arrival of our expected illustrious refugees was long preceded by that of several Portuguese merchants and officers, who came to seek an asylum against assassination. But the Admiral desired me to explain to them that he and the ministers had agreed to remain perfectly neutral in any struggle that might ensue between the Lusitanian and Brazilian parties, and he requested them to leave the ship instantly. They went away amid much lamentations and loud requests to Heaven to protect them. I became affected by these painful transactions and advised the poor fellows to keep themselves quietly in their boats at a short distance from us; assuring them that they were secure for the moment lying under the guns of the British flagship...[4]

At daybreak on 7 April four boats approached the Warspite. It was the Bragança family.5 Officers and men were ready to receive the refugees.

[2] Koebel, *British Exploits in South America*, p. 342.

[3] Koebel did not directly credit the source of his quotations, but the account had in fact been published anonymously under the title 'Anecdotes of Dom Pedro and the Brazilian Mock-Revolution of 1831', in three parts, in *The United Service Journal and Naval and Military Magazine*, 1834, part III, pp. 465-473; and 1835, part I, pp. 42-49 and 205-216. Koebel made a few minor changes when quoting from the source, particularly by paraphrasing or omitting expressions in Portuguese (Translator).

[4] Koebel, p. 343. (Anon., 1835, I, p. 44 – Translator.)

[5] In a note written specially for this chapter, Octávio Tarqüínio de Sousa observes: 'In addition to Pedro II, who was then just five years old, his sisters the princesses Januária Maria, Paula Mariana and Francisca Carolina also stayed behind in Brazil. It is said that when Pedro I left the palace of Boa Vista after his abdication, he went to his children's rooms to say a final goodbye. The children were asleep, and after watching them for a long while, their father suddenly left without waking them. In view of his temperament and the fatherly feelings he had always shown for his children, legitimate or

According to the chronicler, Admiral Baker went down the ladder to help the empress[6] out of the boat and onto the ship. At that moment Dom Pedro I was heard to say in Portuguese, 'Recollect, my dear, you have no breeches on.' He then asked the captain who was with them for a chair on which the ex-empress could be hoisted on board. As the captain said that there was no such chair to be had, Dom Pedro insisted in French, 'Mais elle n'a point de pantalon.'[7] His sister, the Marchioness of Loulé told Dom Pedro that he was worrying about a trifle. She herself, the marchioness, had been up and down that ladder a few days previously 'sans caleçons'[8] without the least inconvenience. Thereupon the ex-empress took the admiral's arm and went up the Warspite's ladder.[9]

As she arrived on the quarter-deck, the ship's band struck up the Portuguese national anthem. The chronicler says the entire crew was moved to see the distress of the ex-empress of Brazil.

She was accompanied by the French admiral to the cabin reserved for her, as had been agreed with Admiral Baker. The Frenchman was in fact an old friend of the ex-empress. He had seen her and carried her in his arms when she was a child. Seeing her again in such tragic circumstances, he tried to cheer her with these words recorded by the attentive British chronicler: '*Courage, je vous en prie. Courage! Résignation!*' But in vain. Dona Amélia could not hold back her sobs and sat down on a sofa, weeping and hiding her face in a handkerchief.

The next to board the *Warspite* was the queen of Portugal, Dona Maria.[10] A girl of twelve. Because of her age, she seemed to be less moved than Dona Amélia at the drama that had overtaken the Braganças in Brazil. Some time later she was seen fishing.

The English chronicler writes that Dom Pedro I boarded the *Warspite* without showing any sign of being moved: as if he were going on a picnic. He was dressed like someone free of care, almost like a townsman on the morning of a sporting event: in a brown frock coat and a round hat. He did not look as if he had left a furiously hostile crowd near his palace in São Cristóvão. He was only concerned with bringing his vast amount of baggage on board. Everything considered, he looked calm and tranquil

not, one can well imagine what turmoil he must have felt at that moment.'

[6] Amélie de Leuchtenberg (1812-1876), a Franco-Bavarian princess, was Pedro I's second wife and only eighteen years old at the time of these events (Translator).

[7] 'But she has no breeches on.' The chronicler added the following footnote to the word 'pantalon': 'Meaning to say, "caleçons" (drawers); he being at that time not the best French scholar' (Anon., 1835, I, p. 45) (Translator).

[8] 'without drawers' (Translator).

[9] Koebel, p. 343. (Anon., 1835, I, pp. 44-45 – Translator.)

[10] Queen Maria II. See footnote 422 (Translator).

during the first few hours on board, with just some quixotic explosions of temper.

He had refused to come to the ship on an English barge – Admiral Baker's – which was armed with a small cannon. He did not want it said that he had left Brazil in fear of the Brazilians. An attitude that was highly characteristic of this brave, romantic son of Dona Carlota Joaquina, herself a characteristically Spanish woman.

But he was also the son of Dom João, and therefore always alert to the prosaically bourgeois side of life. And it was this Sancho Panza that the English 'naval spectator' saw carrying his boxes and packages himself and loudly quarrelling with his servants:

> He ran to and fro, quarreled with the chamberlains, scolded his domestics, hailed people alongside, and made a great noise.[11]

At about noon, gunfire was heard. It was from cannon on shore. The reason was that the future Dom Pedro II had just been presented to the crowd of patriots.

Moments later, Pedro I had to stop looking after the baggage to receive the farewells of ambassadors, ministers and high officials. The chronicler says that the deep bows made by these courtiers did not alter the dethroned emperor's indifference. He only made a respectful bow to the papal legate, the Archbishop of Tarsus,[12] when the latter paid him his respects.

After the ceremony, Pedro I was surrounded by a group of diplomats and other important people. With one hand in his breeches pocket and the other twisting his ample moustache, he then gave a kind of speech; but in conversational tone. The English chronicler, the *Warspite's* meticulous linguist, noted down some phrases from this speech that are of interest to the political historian of Brazil:

> I expect there will be a revolution in this country such as took place in France last year. I have been betrayed for a long while. The Brazilians do not like me: they look on me as a Portuguese. But I have never been afraid of them: I went down to the mines. I went into the streets the day before yesterday, when they were fighting on all sides. What on earth could I do, when the people assembled in the Campo de Santa Anna had the impudence to tell me to dismiss

[11] Koebel, p. 347. (Anon., 1835, I, p. 46. Quoted by Freyre in English – Translator.)

[12] Koebel miscopied this as 'Tarsis', in which he was followed by Freyre (Translator).

my ministers? I hadn't enough troops to disperse a mob like that. I was quite ready to put myself at the head of my guard, but – it had left me.[13]

At this point, he saw four imperial soldiers lying on the deck. He ran over to them, pulled them to their feet and tried to give them a martial appearance. And, as if they were not just four poor devils who had been left behind in São Cristóvão by their revolutionary comrades, who had not wanted to wake them from their deep sleep, he exclaimed with a theatrically quixotic gesture, 'All my troops have left me except brave garçons.' He then said to the men, 'João, Antonio, Manoel, Luiz, you indeed, have now reason for pride!' And to the spectators he continued, 'Here are the remains of my army. What could I do against the populace?' At the diplomats' discreet silence, he concluded, 'So I abdicated in favor of my son who was born in Brazil, and they have this morning proclaimed him emperor.'[14]

There was an enormous crowd of people on board: people accompanying or taking their leave of the ex-emperor and empress. About 150 people of all ranks and ages. Men and women. The imperial cabin[15] looked to English eyes like an oriental harem, so many were the Portuguese, Brazilian, German, French and black women squeezed into it as ladies-in-waiting, governesses, handmaids, dry-nurses, washerwomen, etc.

On the quayside was another crowd, in which the watchful chronicler caught sight of some people who viewed the approaching time for the imperial family to depart with real concern: merchants whose private debts had not been paid by certain members of that family. It seems that the Marchioness of Loulé was the one in greatest debt of all.[16] Even Empress Amélia was importuned by some of the most worried creditors, and she sometimes brought them to her husband's notice. In those circumstances, Pedro I's main concern was to collect money rather than disburse it. Very few creditors were satisfied; and almost only when the ex-empress appealed to her husband.

On the following day, the ex-emperor received a troop of money-

[13] Koebel, p. 348-349. (Anon., 1835, I, p. 47, gives the speech in French, as delivered by Dom Pedro. Freyre translated it into Portuguese from Koebel's slightly faulty English version, which is reproduced here – Translator.)

[14] Koebel, p. 349-350. (Anon., 1835, I, p. 48; languages in these quotations as in the previous note – Translator.)

[15] Koebel, based on Anon., in fact refers here to the ship's captain's cabin, not the emperor's (Translator).

[16] Koebel, p. 351. (Anon., 1835, I, p. 205 – Translator.)

brokers, Jews and slave-dealers. When he noticed a certain 'Mr. Buschental, a German Israelite', he exclaimed,

> 'Oho, Senhor Buschental, you are here too! I assure you if I had not been absent in Minas Geraës, you would never have succeeded in that job with the copper money of the bank.'[17]

That amused the bystanders greatly and made the Jew turn pale.

At that time, the future Pedro II was making his triumphal entry into the city of Rio de Janeiro, a festivity also attended by the English officer, chronicler – and sometimes official humorist – of the Warspite. The first group in the procession that attracted the attention of the sometimes over-critical humorist was of justices of the peace. They were carrying green flags and were mounted on spirited horses that were constantly threatening to throw their distinguished riders. The future emperor, a boy a little over five years old, came in a huge coach pulled by 'excited mulattoes'. The whole crowd was moved by the sight. And the triumphal chant sung by the choir accompanying the future emperor sometimes died away as the singers were overcome with emotion.[18]

Among the posters stuck on the walls on that feast day, the *Warspite's* humorist noticed one for a play to be performed that evening at the imperial theatre. Significantly, its title was *The Downfall of the Tyrant.* But that was not all. The actor who was to play the part of the tyrant had printed an advertisement also stuck to the walls or distributed in the streets in which he felt he had to explain to the people that the more perfectly he represented 'the monster', the more he disclaimed any similarity between himself (the actor José de Barros) and 'the despot'. For Heaven was his witness that there was nothing tyrannical about him, the actor, and that his heart had always beaten for liberty and the 'glorious Constitution'. He was going to assume attitudes on stage that were contrary to his real feelings. He wanted the audience to bear in mind that distinction between fiction and reality.[19]

When the chronicler returned on board, the English admiral took him to the cabin of the ex-emperor and empress. He introduced him to the empress: '*Voilà Monsieur X, qui a tout vu!*'[20] She asked the admiral if the officer spoke French. Then the chronicler told her, in French, all the

[17] Koebel, p. 352. (Anon., 1835, I, p. 206 – Translator.)

[18] Koebel, p. 353. (Anon., 1835, I, p. 208 – Translator.)

[19] Koebel, p. 354. (Anon., 1835, I, p. 207 – Translator.)

[20] 'This is Mr X, who has seen everything!' (Translator).

details of what he had seen in the streets of Rio de Janeiro. Dona Amélia interrupted him several times. She wanted to know how the future emperor, still so young, had conducted himself. The Englishman, considering from the heights of his Aryan or Nordic ancestry how a wave of black women had surrounded the imperial child to kiss his garments, replied, '*Comme un ange caressé par des demons.*'[21] When in fact the demons that would most torment the future emperor of Brazil would be less the good black women of the land than biblically red demons.[22]

The English officer was finishing his account to the ex-empress of the day's festivities in the streets of Rio de Janeiro when Dom Pedro I came in. He was carrying a boxful of silver spoons and forks under his arm. He immediately asked the English officer in Portuguese, 'What is the matter? What is the matter?' The officer told him that, by order of his admiral, he was relating to Dona Amélia the latest events. 'I know already! I know everything!' exclaimed the ex-emperor. And, turning to Dona Amélia, after placing the valuable silverware on the table, he said, '*N'importe, mon* [*sic*] *chère! Prenons garde à nos affaires ici!*'[23]

On his first Sunday on board, Dom Pedro I wished to see the English Royal Marines drilled. After watching that demonstration of British efficiency with great interest, he exclaimed, 'A sovereign who has such troops must be happy.'[24]

But he would not stop interfering with the ship's routine: at eleven o'clock one night he rushed around the whole *Warspite* blowing out all the sentries' lights. He later explained he had done so because there was such a large amount of gunpowder on board a man-of-war like that. So many naked lights were a danger. The English did not appreciate their guest's excess.

The *Warspite's* chronicler reports that when several friends came on board to pay their respects to Dom Pedro I, the ex-monarch embraced them emotionally; he even wept on the shoulders of some.[25] That was the impulsive Pedro I of Brazil. Inconstant. Sometimes exuberant, at other times cold. Sometimes generous, at other times mean. He dismissed and sent ashore the four Brazilian soldiers who had accompanied him to the *Warspite* and whom he had praised almost as if they were heroes, giving

[21] 'Like an angel caressed by demons' (Translator).

[22] A reference to the republican movement that would eventually overthrow the empire in 1889 (Translator).

[23] 'Never mind, my dear! Let's look after our things here!' The quotation shows Pedro I's imperfect command of French; his difficulties with English were remarked on in chapter 2 (Translator). Koebel, p. 355. (Anon., 1835, I, p. 209 – Translator.)

[24] Koebel, p. 356. (Anon., 1835, I, p. 209 – Translator.)

[25] Koebel, p. 356-357. (Anon., 1835, I, p. 209-210 – Translator.)

each of them a ridiculous gratuity which, according to the English ship's meticulous chronicler, was equivalent to just seven shillings and sixpence sterling.[26]

The whole time he was on board the *Warspite*, Pedro I was concerned with his cherished belongings. But less like a man absorbed by possessing valuable goods than like a boy excited at having rare playthings. Hence the childish delight with which he showed the English officers the old clock he had as a keepsake from his grandmother, the queen of Spain: he wound it up, made it strike and showed it off in every way possible.[27] And the English chronicler was there to record all these highs and lows of his temper and behaviour.

The *Warspite's* chronicler says that the ex-empress of Brazil, Dona Amélia, was much admired by the officers and crew of the English ship. She always remained well mannered, thereby charming the British.

A fact that did not escape the English chronicler's notice was that, at the very moment when he was leaving the *Warspite*, Dom Pedro I was still worrying about business and arguing with a Polish Jew, his 'chief commercial agent'. And the eavesdropping Englishman caught a few snippets of their conversation: matters of slaves, property and land. This was no longer the big boy excited at having rare playthings but a man absorbed by possessing people and goods.

The English officer saw the Jew give the emperor some leather bags filled with gold dust. And for twenty long minutes, while the officers ceremoniously awaited the refugee's departure, the men were standing at attention and the ex-empress was waiting for her husband in a boat at the foot of the ship's ladder, the ex-emperor and the Polish Jew were talking about slaves, property and lands. The chronicler writes that when he received the bags of gold dust from the Jew's hands, Pedro I smiled and said, '*Amicus certus in re incerta cernitur.*'[28] The *Warspite's* linguist knew his Latin too; as did the first emperor, or at least that proverb.

The captain of the *Warspite* felt obliged to interrupt the idyll between the ex-emperor and his commercial agent by officially informing His Majesty that 'the Queen was in the boat waiting'. On hearing this, Dom Pedro walked off arm in arm with the Jew, saying to him, 'Well then, come along with me on board the frigate!'[29]

At this point, it is worth noting that by a strange coincidence there

[26] Koebel, p. 358. (Anon., 1835, I, p. 212 – Translator.)
[27] Koebel, p. 359. (Anon., 1835, I, p. 212 – Translator.)
[28] 'A friend in need is a friend indeed' (Translator).
[29] Koebel, p. 362. (Anon., 1835, I, p. 215 – Translator.)

were lying together in the harbour of Rio de Janeiro the English frigate *Undaunted*, which had taken Napoleon Bonaparte to Elba, and the French brig *Inconstant*, on which he had escaped from that island.

Until the very last moments the eyes and ears of the Warspite's chronicler remained Britannically alert – does not every Englishman or Scotsman have a detective inside, and not just a mixture of sea-dog, businessman, humorist, missionary and poet? – to the gestures, attitudes and words of the dethroned emperor of Brazil. And it is in language more suited to a humorist in Punch than to a properly official chronicler of a British man-of-war that he records the final gestures and words of Pedro I of Brazil on board the Warspite:

> The last words which that legitimate Champion of the Constitutional Rights of Man – that Imperial Tom Paine of the age – was heard to utter in the gangway with emphasis were, 'To sell my slaves! – so very cheap – The paper money exceedingly low! – Eleven pence in copper.'[30]

Observing the faces of the many British spectators, the chronicler noticed that some were laughing at the scene; others were disgusted. Disgusted, it seems, at the excessive concern of an emperor who had appeared to be so romantic with such sordidly prosaic matters. A defect, however, which seems not to have been confined to the brave, exuberant and inconstant Dom Pedro I of Brazil but was shared by more illustrious European monarchs of the same and other periods. And not only monarchs who championed the Constitutional Rights of Man. Statesmen as well. And noblemen. And admirals. Including British admirals and noblemen like Cochrane, the future Earl of Dundonald and Marquess of Maranhão, who insisted so strongly on money in his dealings with Brazil, for whose independence he romantically fought against 'Portuguese despotism'.[31]

[30] Koebel, p. 363. (Anon., 1835, I, p. 215. Freyre mistakenly put '*seis pence*' – 'sixpence' – Translator.)
[31] In Maranhão, Cochrane came up against a Brazilian, Freire e Bruce – the province's first president after independence – who had been born there but was of Scottish origin. Knowing he was an intransigent man, Cochrane removed Bruce from government on the excuse that he was 'thinking of taking up arms' to resist the imperial marines commanded by the future Earl of Dundonald. Cochrane's real purpose in stripping Bruce of the provincial presidency seems to have been, 'once he was out of the way, to empty the coffers of all the revenue departments' (J. Ribeiro do Amaral, *Efemérides maranhenses*, Part 1, *Tempos coloniais*, Maranhão, 1923, p. 71). To do that he knew he could not count on the connivance of the near-Scottish, English-educated Miguel Ignacio dos Santos Freire e Bruce. The conflict between them reveals the clash between two constant British influences in Brazil: one represented by the pirate, the brave or clever but unscrupulous and money-grabbing adventurer; the other by the intransigently correct and conscientious man, steadfast in defending the dignity of his person and position.

Behind Cochrane's romantic actions, however, lay the incentive of making money out of the people whose freedom he was advancing.

The *Warspite's* chronicler reveals a certain bias when he sees in Pedro I's passion for land, slaves and money a scandalous sin of which the great lords of Great Britain, some of them champions of abolitionism and the Rights of Man, were incapable. But we have to acknowledge the value of his testimony, despite his overuse of anecdote and humour and, worse still, ethnocentrism, which sometimes mar it.

In the same facetious tone he also records that Dom Pedro I did not give the ship's company of the Warspite the slightest remuneration for all the hard work that the crew had had in hosting the imperial family.[32] The British commander-in-chief saved the situation to some extent by allowing them some extra grog and giving them some other treats. A surprising omission for the first emperor of Brazil, a man who was often generous. But he was a man of explosive temperament. And the highs and lows of his conduct were reported by the Warspite's chronicler with British precision. Precision that would make modern scientific scholars of human behaviour or personality envious.

[32] Here I have presented just a summary of the chronicle left by the observer of the *Warspite*, as presented by Koebel. The narrative contains other details. For example, the request made by Dona Maria da Glória to Admiral Grivel not to be saluted with the honours due to her as queen, as she did not wish to receive such demonstrations in the presence of her father, who could no longer be honoured as emperor. Her request was disregarded, apparently by mistake (Koebel, p. 361 [Anon., 1835, I, p. 214 – Translator]). The chronicler also reports the visit made to Dom Pedro by his field-marshal, the Count of Rio Pardo, who feared assassination on shore. Dom Pedro embraced the count for a long time, together with his 'intimate friend and valet-de-chambre' (Koebel, p. 356-357 [Anon., 1835, I, p. 210 – Translator]). The *Warspite's* chronicler also mentions the rumour that had begun to circulate in the city of Rio de Janeiro that Dom Pedro had repented of his abdication. This rumour caused unrest and even deaths, and led the English and French admirals to the conclusion that the Bragança family's departure should be hastened; it was decided that Dom Pedro and Dona Amélia would sail in the British frigate *Volage*, and Dona Maria da Glória and her aunt, the Marchioness of Loulé, on the French frigate *La Seine* (Koebel, p. 358 [Anon., 1835, I, p. 210 – Translator]).

# PREFACE:
# A SOCIAL HISTORY OF THE BRITISH PRESENCE IN BRAZIL

*Evaldo Cabral de Mello*[1]

*The English in Brazil*, first published in 1948, was to be the first volume in a trilogy that Gilberto Freyre planned to write on British influence on the life, landscape and culture of Brazil, a subject in which he had shown a long-standing and constant interest. His contacts with English culture had begun in his childhood as a pupil at the American Baptist School in Recife. They were deepened in the years he attended university in the United States and the months he subsequently spent in England, and were further developed after his return to Recife in 1923. In 1942 he collected together his newspaper articles on English topics, under the title *Ingleses*. Readers who wish to find out more about British influences on Gilberto Freyre should see the work by Maria Lúcia G. Pallares-Burke, in which she draws particular attention to an old essay by Walter Pater that played a decisive role in attracting Freyre to the relations between home and childhood. *The English in Brazil*, and *Um engenheiro francês no Brasil* as well, are in fact foreshadowed in his chapter 'Brazilians and Europeans' in *The Mansions and the Shanties*, which deals with the process of the re-Europeanization of Brazilian culture during the first half of the nineteenth century, after centuries of colonial segregation.

This re-Europeanization was the cultural face of the overthrow of the Portuguese monopoly on trade with Brazil. Because of that loss and her position on the sidelines of Western development, as well as her privileged relations with the Orient, Portugal was not in a position to take the lead when Brazil was opened up to the bourgeois Europe of the 1800s. It was England and France that spearheaded this process, each in her own way or, rather, each according to her relative cultural advantages. That means they treated Brazil as an economic and cultural condominium, the French

[1] Evaldo Cabral de Mello, an independent scholar and former diplomat, is one of the most respected and original historians of colonial Brazil. Among his acclaimed books are *Olinda restaurada: guerra e açúcar no Nordeste, 1630-1654* (1975), *O Norte agrário e o Império, 1871-1889* (1984), *Rubro Veio* (1986), *A Fronda dos Mazombos: nobres contra mascates, Pernambuco, 1666-1715* (1995), *O Negócio do Brasil* (2003), *A Outra Independência* (2004) and *Nassau: Governador do Brasil holandês* (2006). This article was originally written as a preface to the third Brazilian edition (2000).

specializing in the trade in luxury goods and fashion, while the English concentrated on the products of their industrial revolution. Perceptively, Gilberto Freyre even found this condominium expressed spatially in the location of the two nations' trading houses in Rio de Janeiro city centre, in streets that had very different appearances at that time, such as the Rua do Ouvidor on one hand and the Rua da Alfândega on the other. In another nineteenth-century Brazilian city, Recife, that difference affected whole areas, the old district of Recife proper with its famous ship-chandlers representing the domain of English trade *par excellence*, while Santo Antônio was home to the French. Moreover, in a misogynistic society like Brazil, such a distinction must also have involved an aspect of gender specialization, since access to the public street for women of some social status was necessarily confined to those thoroughfares where fashion shops were concentrated. Consequently, such streets could be described as properly feminine, as was still the case of the Rua Nova or Rua da Imperatriz in Recife when Gilberto Freyre himself was writing *The English in Brazil*, in comparison with the Rua do Imperador, for example, which was eminently masculine.

As a result of Great Britain's political and commercial dominance, which Portugal passed on to Brazil and reinforced following the royal family's move to Rio de Janeiro, it is only natural that anti-English resentment has been a constant in historical studies written in Portuguese. Portugal had an unresolved history of complaints against her old ally, from the treaty of 1661 until the crisis triggered by the British ultimatum in the 1890s, passing through the infamous Methuen treaties of the early eighteenth century. In Brazil the complaints centred on the disloyal terms of the 1812 treaty of commerce, renewed in 1825 as the price of independence, as well as the British government's opposition to the slave trade. The subject of the British presence in both Portugal and Brazil has therefore traditionally been limited to the areas of political, diplomatic and economic history, even when written by English-speaking historians, such as Alan K. Manchester and, more recently, Leslie Bethell or Richard Graham. The originality of *The English in Brazil* lies in the fact that Gilberto Freyre, disdainful as ever of a kind of analysis that to him seemed unforgivably superficial, as indeed it was when he began writing, chose to examine the social history of British influence in Brazil, giving us a book that is highly enjoyable to read in its casually essayistic style, far from the monographic stiffness of university theses.

The work comprises four chapters, each one an essay that could be read separately. The first ('Adventure, trade and technology') functions as an introduction to the subject of the English presence in Brazil, which is why, to use a baseball metaphor, the author had to 'touch all bases' by mentioning the countless aspects in which it made itself felt. To that end he even made use of the eminently literary technique – which should not be ruled out by historians just because of that – of what is termed chaotic enumeration, as on the pages where he lists the material and spiritual vestiges of British influence, from the *míster*, that is to say the Englishman in Brazilian popular lore, to the Brazilian taste for snooker. That word, spelt '*sinuca*', is in fact one of the countless Anglicisms that today form part of the Portuguese spoken in Brazil, which has always been much more accommodating in adopting English words than Portugal, where our *trem* ('train') and *bonde* ('tram', from the word 'bond') are still puristically and patriotically known as *comboio* and *eléctrico*. The second and third chapters of *The English in Brazil* examine British activity through newspaper advertisements, a technique which Gilberto Freyre is known to have pioneered within Brazil and, I suspect, outside it as well; and through the dispatches that His or Her Britannic Majesty's consuls sent to the Brazilian authorities.

In both respects, the author's preference for social history, and more specifically the history of private life, led him to uncover the importance and richness of sources that had been marginalized by political history: newspaper advertisements, in contrast to editorials or political articles; and consular correspondence, in contrast to strictly diplomatic correspondence, which had been thoroughly explored by his mentor Oliveira Lima. While newspaper advertisements have come to be used with some frequency in Brazilian historiography thanks to Gilberto Freyre, the same cannot be said for consular correspondence, which remains inexplicably neglected, perhaps for the reason Freyre himself points out. Indeed, while 'official correspondence' and 'consul' have dreary bureaucratic connotations, 'diplomatic papers' suggest the apparently glamorous world of international intrigue. As for the last chapter of *The English in Brazil*, it is a delightful gloss on the private aspects of an episode that by definition belongs to political history – the abdication of Dom Pedro I – based on the account left by an officer on the English warship *Warspite*, on which the emperor took refuge before sailing on to Portugal.

A late offshoot of Freyre's analysis of the re-Europeanization of Brazil, which he had begun in *The Mansions and the Shanties* – an analysis that included an examination of what might be considered the counterpart of the process, that is to say the resistance put up by the oriental influences with which Portugal had impregnated Portuguese America almost from the outset – *The English in Brazil* uses the same methods that the author had employed long before in *The Masters and the Slaves* to study the formation of the patriarchal Brazilian family. I have attempted to explain elsewhere what appears to be novel in Freyre's approach for the historian: the way he transposes to an historical type of society, Brazilian society, which until then had been examined exclusively by the diachronic methods of history, the synchronic view developed by English-speaking anthropologists to describe primitive societies. What was at the time a daring theoretical approach enabled the master from Apipucos to make one of the most original contributions to Western culture in the twentieth century. That is not mere preface writer's exaggeration. I will not go into the matter of the intellectual ostracism to which Gilberto Freyre was relegated in Brazil in the 1950s and 60s, precisely the years when the originality of his contribution began to be recognised in major European and North American centres. It is enough to remember that it was then that Roland Barthes pointed out that our author had performed the feat of presenting 'the historical man almost without detaching him from his living body, which for historians is almost like squaring the circle, the endpoint of historical investigation'.

That said, the limitations of Freyre's 'egg of Columbus' method deserve to be pointed out because they serve as a warning against the uncritical use of the anthropological approach in history, a recent phenomenon in Brazil which is not due to Gilberto Freyre but to reading French historians from Ariès onwards, who in the 1960s and 70s began to cultivate the history of private life. As Freyre's work itself shows, the shorter the timeframe adopted, the greater is the heuristic utility of treating a particular historical period synchronically. Because *The Masters and the Slaves* covers the three centuries of Brazil's colonial history, the description of Brazilian society that it contains seems to an historian less convincing and more vulnerable than that found in *The Mansions and the Shanties* or *The English in Brazil*, which are limited to the first fifty or sixty years of the nineteenth century. The danger in using synchronic methods over the long term lies not only in rendering the investigation liable to anachronism, but more especially in showing structural relations that would not stand up to diachronic examination. To be fair to anthropologists, however, I should point out that it is historians themselves who have taken the initiative in using and abusing the synchronic in history, dazzled by the success achieved by anthropology in the ambition shared by all human sciences of discovering the key to reconstructing social totalities.

The fact is that historiography in the nineteenth century had itself already discovered the value of the synchronic, thanks to German *Kulturgeschichte* and in particular Burckhardt in Switzerland and, later, Huizinga in the Netherlands. Croce blamed Burckhardt's *forma mentis*, which he accused of being essentially anti-historical, for the straightforward replacement of factual history with the history of culture and civilization, instead of trying to integrate them and to enrich the former with the contributions of the latter. Since it did not do so, Burckhardt's work seemed to him an 'entirely empirical and static history of culture', which annulled the drama and dialectics of human action, spending itself in the presentation of 'a fixed, solidified, immobilized reality'. Croce's remarks help to account for the unusual fact that *The Civilization of the Renaissance in Italy* remains a fascinating book even though almost all its specific analyses have been contested by historians who have dealt with the subject since that time. *The Renaissance in Italy* has clearly suffered the same fate that Dumézil mentioned in respect of his own work, when he predicted that, if people concluded that it was not scientific in nature it should not be thrown away but merely moved from the human sciences shelf to the literature shelf. When the scholarship of a great history book becomes outdated, the work survives for its historical imagination, a category different from other types of imagination, but just as valuable as they are. That is what is happening to *The Masters and the Slaves*.

Anthropology and history are the way they are because they cannot be otherwise, limited as they are by the shortcomings of the raw material that they process. If anthropology has set itself apart in synchrony, it is because anthropologists do not enjoy the variety and richness of sources for the study of primitive societies that historians have for the study of historical societies. If historians, for their part, have isolated themselves in diachrony, it is because they, unlike anthropologists, did not have the privilege of being eye-witnesses to Roman society at the end of the Republic or to the workings of the medieval manor. Anthropologists, of course, would like it if the Pataxó Indians had archives, but since that is not possible all they can do is get out their field notebooks and carefully observe what goes on in the tribe's daily existence, although if a miracle happened and primitive societies did suddenly acquire documentary archives, a good deal of anthropological knowledge would probably suffer the fate to which Dumézil alluded. On the other hand, it is undeniable that historians would love to be able to go back in time and watch Caesar's murder or spy on economic life in Florence under the Medici but, as that too is impossible, they are forced to reconstruct them laboriously by the analysis of their traces. It should be added, however, that given the fundamental differences between historical societies and primitive societies it is doubtful whether historians would be capable of benefiting more from what they could see with their own eyes than if they were to contemplate the society in which they themselves live. What happened to Fabrizio del Dongo at the Battle of Waterloo would be likely to happen to them as well. As a result, to use the distinction made by Montaigne, historians would probably choose to get to know Brutus through the words of Plutarch instead of going to visit him at home. After all, as Paul Veyne pointed out in an essential work of epistemological reflection, 'even if I were contemporary with and a witness to Waterloo, even if I were the main player and Napoleon in person, I would have only one perspective on what historians will call the event of Waterloo [...] Even if I were Bismarck, making the decision to release the Ems dispatch, my own interpretation of the event might not be the same as my friends', my confessor's, my official historian's or my psychoanalyst's, who might each have their own versions of my decision and think they knew better than I what I wanted.'

Historians need to use the synchronic dimension in a spirit of informed critique, which means subordinating it to the diachronic, which is their territory *par excellence*. If they do not do so, they will merely impoverish their ability to explain and understand the past. That impoverishment is in fact already beginning to show in historiographic production in general, thus repeating the same sterilizing reductionism with which the novelty of economism threatened it in the 1950s and 60s. Trends in the main economic variables, and even in some less important ones, thus became an 'open Sesame' for historians who were rightly tired of factual, positivist history. But at the end of the remarkable enrichment brought about by economic history from the 1930s onwards, it was realized in France, for example, that students no longer knew history and had never heard of the rivalry between Francis I and Charles V or the wars of religion, although they were well aware of the population growth in the 1500s and the century-long stagnation in the 1600s.

## NOTES ON THE TRANSLATION

*Christopher J. Tribe*

When considering the invitation to write about the issues involved in translating *The English in Brazil*, I felt initially that there would be little to say. After all, the 'issues' were essentially the same as those that have to be addressed in any translation. That reaction overlooked an important point, however: many readers, apart from those with a specific interest in the field, may not be aware of what those issues are. My view is that a good translation is one where readers may not notice the fact that it is a translation, but feel that they are reading the author's original text, albeit not in the original language. In other words, the translation itself should 'disappear'. Consequently, most readers are unlikely to give any thought to the challenges faced by the translator in crafting such an illusion.

Any act of translation renders the source material in a different medium. This generally means a different language, but it may also involve a shift in time and, almost inevitably, in cultural context, the aim being to produce a version that is both accessible and acceptable to a new audience. I would like to look briefly at some of the implications of this with specific reference to the translation of *The English in Brazil*.

Portuguese and English, of course, differ as languages in their vocabulary, syntax and phonology, and these factors, in turn, condition general stylistic preferences in the two languages. As an example, Freyre fully exploits the greater flexibility of Portuguese syntactic word order, often starting a sentence with the predicate and following it with an extensively developed grammatical subject. Direct translation into English does not work in such cases, and it is necessary to fall back on techniques such as reversing the order of elements, switching to the passive voice, supplying a different subject, resolving the various parts into two or more sentences, or, in the last resort, paraphrasing the sentence completely.

One of the most noticeable aspects of Freyre's style is his tendency to use long, complex, rambling sentences interspersed with shorter, verbless ones. Long, complex sentences are a common feature of Brazilian writing, to the extent that it almost feels as though simplicity of sentence structure is frowned upon. This is particularly true in literature and the humanities, though less so in scientific and technical writing. Freyre's style puts him squarely in the former camp, even though his subject matter is essentially concerned with the social sciences. Conversely, in English, highly convoluted sentences are generally less well received since greater value is placed on directness and concision, above all in scientific contexts.

If the same degree of sentence complexity were reproduced in the translation, English-speaking readers might well find it virtually impenetrable, whereas it may have been within acceptable limits for the original Portuguese-speaking audience. The challenge, therefore, is to produce a style in English that reflects the *relative* difference between Freyre's use of complex sentences and the average complexity found in Brazilian writing of this genre. The solution adopted has been to smooth out some of the complexity by rearranging the component elements – so as to require fewer commas, for example – and, in the longest and most involved cases, by splitting a single sentence in Portuguese into two or more in English. The result is a sentence style that is still more complex than is usual in twenty-first century English writing of this kind but not, I hope, to the extent that the reader loses track of the meaning.

The other feature of Freyre's style mentioned above is his use of short (or not so short) verbless sentences, which quite often repeat or expand on elements that have just been presented. Such secondary sentences – sometimes a whole string of them – usually depend syntactically on the preceding main sentence. This technique is in effect an extension of his use of complex, rambling sentence structures, but in this case he separates the elements with full stops rather than commas or semi-colons. By using this technique he can fill a whole page with just one such syntactically linked 'supersentence', which may contain only a single main clause. As this is such a distinctive feature of Freyre's writing it was essential to retain it in the translation, in most cases at least. I confess that sometimes I succumbed to the conditioning drilled into me since primary school – 'Every sentence needs a verb' – and supplied the word that was conspicuous by its absence, particularly in the second or third of a sequence of such orphan phrases, usually to clarify the syntactic and semantic relations involved.

Culturally specific concepts are a further source of difficulty in translation. Many ideas, allusions and references that would have been readily understood by Freyre's audience in Brazil in the late 1940s may well baffle a reader in Britain sixty years or more later, and so they need to be glossed within the translation or explained in footnotes. The word 'moleque', for instance, has no exact equivalent in English, so I have retained it in the text and added the following footnote: 'Derived from a Bantu word for 'boy', moleque originally referred to a slave child, but it has come to mean a mischievous youngster of any origin, or even a rogue, scoundrel or trickster.' Obviously, the extent to which such glossing is needed depends on the target readership. If the translation were aimed only at English-speaking historians with an interest in Brazil, for example, no explanation would be needed of the flight of the Portuguese court to Brazil during the Peninsular War, whereas the general public requires a certain amount of background information to understand such references. The challenge has been to strike a judicious balance between cluttering the text with too many footnotes and leaving things unexplained. As a general rule, I have given very brief biographical notes on Brazilian historical and literary figures when first mentioned, but not for personages from other countries. Of course, curious readers can now easily find additional information on nearly all these people on the Internet.

Other translation difficulties arise from the social and cultural changes that have taken place in the western world since the book was first published in 1948. Not only have tastes evolved, but also what is deemed acceptable in society. The fact that these processes are ongoing sometimes leaves me – and doubtless other writers and translators – unsure of what is currently permissible. In these days of racial sensitivity, for example, can one give a direct translation of '*uma pretalhona alegre*'? A safe option would be to describe her as 'a large, cheerful woman of African descent', but the spontaneity of the expression is lost. Sometimes it is impossible to avoid using 'black' and 'white' in the translation to refer to ethnicity. Guidelines as to whether or not these words should be capitalized in English vary; as it is difficult to tell in some cases whether they refer to an ethnic group or are merely descriptive of skin colour, I have chosen to use lower case throughout for the sake of consistency. It goes without saying that I mean no offence by that. Similarly, Freyre's use of racial and ethnic terms should be understood within the context in which he was writing, even if they are not acceptable today.

Gender equality is another area that was generally disregarded in Freyre's time. In addition to the translation issues arising from the differences between Portuguese and English in the treatment of grammatical gender, Freyre sometimes compounds the problem by explicitly using the word '*homem*' ('man'), as when he talks of his 'attempts to reconstruct and interpret the history and ethos of the *homem brasileiro*', the Brazilian man. As with traditional usage of the word 'man' in English, '*homem*' covers the concepts of both human being and male person (distinguished in German as 'Mensch' and 'Mann', respectively), but today it would seem inadvisable to use 'man' with the former meaning if it can be avoided. I have therefore sought alternatives in cases such as the example I have just mentioned.

Finally, a brief comment on the title of the book, *The English in Brazil*, which itself encapsulates several of the issues I have already outlined. First, there is a linguistic difficulty with the Portuguese word '*Ingleses*', the plural of '*inglês*': the equivalent word 'English' has no distinct plural form, unlike 'Greek/Greeks' or 'Italian/Italians', for example. Translating the title as '*English in Brazil*' would suggest the work was about the English language rather than English people. We cannot, of course, use the plural form '*Englishmen in Brazil*', as here we would fall into the gender trap. The solution adopted has been to add the definite article – '*The English in Brazil*'. Even this is not ideal, however: the title now refers to people, certainly, but it implies the English as a nation rather than a collection of English individuals. Freyre's title in Portuguese pointedly omits the article (it is not *Os Ingleses...*) to make it quite clear that he is dealing with individual English people and not the English nation as a whole.

Moreover, there is yet another cultural problem here: the conceptual (and geographical) space occupied by the word '*ingleses*', as used colloquially by Freyre and Brazilians in general, is broader than that of 'Englishmen and women' as understood in this country, as Freyre himself acknowledges in the first lines of his introduction, where he concedes: 'English in the sense of British, of course'. In the British Isles the distinction between the English, Welsh, Scots and Irish is now taken for granted, but that was not always the case, and many of the nineteenth-century English-language writers from whom Freyre draws his information use 'English' and 'England' as umbrella terms. Today as well, at a distance of 8,000 kilometres the distinction becomes a mere nicety, with the result that most Brazilians, like Freyre, use '*inglês*' to refer to people originating from anywhere in these islands. In the translation I have followed Freyre's usage, aware that some of those described in *The English in Brazil* may not in fact have been English at all.

# GILBERTO FREYRE – BIOGRAPHICAL NOTE

Gilberto Freyre (1900-1987) was born in Recife in the north-east of Brazil. He went to school in Recife but was sent to the USA by his parents for his university education, taking a Bachelor's degree at Baylor University in Waco, Texas and his Master's at Columbia, with a dissertation on 19th-century Brazilian history (1922). On his return to Brazil he was involved with the regionalist movement in Recife, worked for the local paper, the *Diário de Pernambuco*, and also as cabinet secretary to the governor of the state. When the governor went into exile following the revolution of 1930, in which Getúlio Vargas became President of Brazil, Freyre followed him abroad. While living in Lisbon he began working on what became his most famous book, *Casa Grande e Senzala* (1933), translated into English as *The Masters and the Slaves*. Freyre held a number of short-term academic positions at Stanford University, the University of the Federal District in Rio and elsewhere, and he served as a deputy in the Constituent Assembly (1946-50) that followed the Vargas regime. However, he was most active as a writer (essays, novels and poems), as an independent scholar and as a public intellectual, helping to redefine the identity of Brazil as a mixed society. His many books include *The Mansions and the Shanties* (1936) and *Order and Progress* (1959), continuing the history of Brazil (with special reference to the patriarchal family) that he had begun in *The Masters and the Slaves*. He also published many volumes of essays on history, literature and society, as well as a textbook on sociology and a pioneering study of environmental history, *Nordeste* ('North-East') (1937). Freyre has been famous in Brazil since the 1930s. After 1964, when he supported the new military regime, he fell out of favour with many intellectuals, but a revival of interest in his work has been visible since the late 1980s, linked to current debates on cultural hybridity, the black consciousness movement and multiculturalism.

# INDEX OF PERSONAL NAMES

H

L

S

Z